'Ideology is the centre of gravity of terrorism, extremism and exclusivism. Many in government and in the Muslim community do not understand the depth and dimensions of it. That is why the threat is elusive and has not been eliminated. Without understanding the belief system, no threat group can be fought efficiently and defeated effectively. *Fallacy of Militant Ideology* by Munir Masood Marath provides that comprehensive understanding for governments and partners to fight the current and emerging threat.'

Rohan Gunaratna, *Founder of the International Centre for Political Violence and Terrorism Research and Professor of Security Studies at Nanyang Technological University Singapore*

'Munir Masood Marath judiciously dissects the idea that Islamist militantism in Pakistan is a response to the ongoing impact of colonialism and postcolonialism, in particular in the Pakistani context. The abstraction of history causes Islamist extremists to act as pragmatists in the pursuit of ideological goals, not religionists in the pursuit of eschatology. Terrorism enacted in these ways is about politics, not religion. This book is a must-read for scholars, practitioners, and students exploring the framing of terrorism and radicalisation, and the misplaced roles played by those who seek to explain Islamist terrorism with allusions to the tenets of early Islam as the primary reason.'

Tahir Abbas, *Professor of Critical Terrorism Studies at the Institute of Security and Global Affairs at Leiden University in The Hague, Netherlands, and author of* Countering Violent Extremism *(2021)*

Fallacy of Militant Ideology

This book highlights the conflict between jihadist militants and the West as essentially ideological in character. It has serious implications internalized by Muslim societies, with the boundaries of faith changed by the interplay of socio-political variables.

Violence emerged in Muslim societies as a means of emancipation or identity when the state could not resolve the conflict situation. Although the militants were influenced by socio-political factors, they have always looked to religion to justify their acts of violence. This book, exposing the fallacy of the narrative evolved by the militants, offers a counter narrative. It reinterprets the primary sources, unravels the historical and socio-political constructs, unmasks the heroes and enemies, challenges the dichotomies between theory and practice, re-establishes the boundaries between heresy and faith, and attempts to transform the current ideological discourse.

This book will be of interest to students and scholars of the discourse between religion and security, political Islam, Islamic history, jihad, Middle Eastern studies, and South Asian studies.

Munir Masood Marath is a senior civil servant in Pakistan, currently serving as City Police Officer, Multan. Previously, he has served as Director General of the National Counter Terrorism Authority (NACTA), Pakistan. He has also served in the Counter Terrorism Department in Punjab, and in different districts of Punjab, including Multan, Chakwal and Layyah, as head of the district police. He holds a PhD in Political Islam from Government College University in Lahore, Pakistan.

Religion and International Security

Series Editor:
Lee Marsden
University of East Anglia, UK

In the 21st century, religion has become an increasingly important factor in international relations and international security. Religion is seen by policy makers and academics as being a major contributor in conflict and its successful resolution. The role of the Ashgate series in Religion and International Security is to provide such policy makers, practitioners, researchers and students with a first port of call in seeking to find the latest and most comprehensive research on religion and security. The series provides established and emerging authors with an opportunity to publish in a series with a reputation for high-quality and cutting-edge research in this field. The series produces analytical and scholarly works from around the world that demonstrate the relevance of religion in security and international relations. The intention is not to be prescriptive or reductionist in restricting the types of books that would be appropriate for the series and as such encourages a variety of theoretical and empirical approaches. International security is broadly defined to incorporate inter- and intra-state conflict, human security, terrorism, genocide, religious freedom, human rights, environmental security, the arms trade, securitisation, gender security, peace keeping, conflict resolution and humanitarian intervention. The distinguishing feature is the religious element in any security or conflict issue.
Recent books in the series include:

Race, Ethnicity and Religion in Conflict Across Asia
Kunal Mukherjee

Israel's Securitization Dilemma
BDS and the Battle for the Legitimacy of the Jewish State
Ronnie Olesker

Fallacy of Militant Ideology
Competing Ideologies and Conflict among Militants, the Muslim World and the West
Munir Masood Marath

For more information about this series, please visit: https://www.routledge.com/Religion-and-International-Security/book-series/RELSEC

Fallacy of Militant Ideology

Competing Ideologies and Conflict among Militants, the Muslim World and the West

Munir Masood Marath

Routledge
Taylor & Francis Group
LONDON AND NEW YORK

First published 2022
by Routledge
2 Park Square, Milton Park, Abingdon, Oxon OX14 4RN

and by Routledge
605 Third Avenue, New York, NY 10158

Routledge is an imprint of the Taylor & Francis Group, an informa business

British Library Cataloguing-in-Publication Data
A catalogue record for this book is available from the British Library

Library of Congress Cataloging-in-Publication Data
Names: Marath, Munir Masood, author.
Title: Fallacy of militant ideology : competing ideologies and conflict among militants, the Muslim world, and the West / Munir Masood Marath.
Description: Abingdon, Oxon [UK] ; New York, NY : Routledge, 2022. |
Series: Religion and international security | Includes bibliographical references and index.
Identifiers: LCCN 2021009960 (print) | LCCN 2021009961 (ebook) | ISBN 9780367759599 (hardback) | ISBN 9780367759629 (paperback) | ISBN 9781003164883 (ebook)
Subjects: LCSH: Violence--Religious aspects--Islam. | Jihad. | Ideology--Religious aspects--Islam. | Faith (Islam) | Heresy. | Religious militants. | Islam and politics. | Islam and social problems.
Classification: LCC BP190.5.V56 M37 2022 (print) | LCC BP190.5.V56 (ebook) | DDC 297.2/7--dc23
LC record available at https://lccn.loc.gov/2021009960
LC ebook record available at https://lccn.loc.gov/2021009961

ISBN: 978-0-367-75959-9 (hbk)
ISBN: 978-0-367-75962-9 (pbk)
ISBN: 978-1-003-16488-3 (ebk)

DOI: 10.4324/9781003164883

Typeset in Times New Roman
by MPS Limited, Dehradun

Dedicated to my parents

Contents

Preface and Acknowledgements x

Introduction 1

1 Nature of conflict 8

2 Heresy of ideas 39

3 Polemics revisited 52

4 Codification of violence 71

5 Codes of war 97

6 Killing fields 128

7 Fuel of faith: Pakistan – a case study 153

8 Counter narrative 168

Conclusion 209
Glossary 215
Bibliography 219
Index 238

Preface and acknowledgements

'Verily, God and His angels bless the Prophet: [hence,] O you who have attained to faith, bless him and give yourselves up [to his guidance] in utter self-surrender!' (Al-Ahzāb: 56). The Muslims believe that the Quran is the constitution of the universe and the greatest blessing of God bestowed upon humanity through the Prophet. They further believe that it aims to order human life according to divine design. It is also part of the Muslims' faith that the essentials of this design reached their culmination with the Prophet Muhammad, the seal of the prophets. Any deviation from these essentials would distract an individual from ordering his life according to the will of the Creator. As the divine design is the source of His blessings, to secure these blessings requires complete surrender to the divine design. It is also part of the belief system of the Muslims that the Prophet presented an ideal of practical conduct for human beings willing to secure the divine blessings through complete submission to His will. After the Prophet, his Companions, representing the sublime degree of submission, became reference points for posterity in the matters of faith. Theological principles developed in this way would be approved if linked with the conduct of these ideal personalities of faith. Any deviations would entail serious repercussions for the authenticity of practices associated with the belief itself. Any practice which came into the body of faith without linkage with the orthodox period would be labelled as heretic.

Nevertheless, links to tradition by no means diminish the dynamism of faith. The spirit is rooted in the nature of the divine plan of the universe itself. The spectrum of life changes gradually as the plan advances to its next phase. Every stage in the plan of the universe brings new challenges. These challenges warrant a space for the exercise of rational human faculties in finding solutions. Islam has given this space through delineating the broader principles in the Quran and Sunnah of the Prophet. Where issues are not categorically addressed in the primary religious scripture, believers have been authorized to explore solutions through rational endeavour, upholding the spirit of faith by all means. New ideas will emerge from this juristic exercise intrinsically linked with the past.

The limited, conditional and qualified human discretion may lead new practices to be labelled as heresies. Though all heresies do not amount to apostasies, they have the potential to redefine the boundaries of faith when juxtaposed with socio-political constructs. In Muslim history, the interplay of socio-political variables and heresy of ideas led to a codification of violence, which reached the level of the masses when the schisms were exploited by the external elements. This eventually led to an unbridgeable gulf between the Muslims on sectarian grounds. Militancy emerged from this gulf to challenge even the definition of faith itself. This happened when the linkage with the past eroded as a means of theological legitimacy. The militants evolved their ideology of violence by delinking themselves from the reference period of early Islam. However, they attempted to rely upon reactionary sentiments to claim public legitimacy. On the other hand, a class of modernists emerged who, too, fell victim to a legitimacy crisis, owing to weak linkage with early Islamic history. The militants wrongfully carved out a space for their ideology. Though they challenged Islamic theology evolved over centuries, they label only their brand of faith as authentic. They dismiss the modernist perspective for being devoid of evidence from early Muslim history. The modernists, on the other hand, unsuccessfully attempt to dismiss the militant narrative through rational interpretation of faith. The failure of narratives from both sides to uphold their theological veracity has led to unhindered violence. The undercurrents of violence are essentially ideological and are drawn from an array of sources. These include sectarian schisms, identity crises produced through colonial interventions, theatres of international aggression and above all, simmering wounds in the Muslim world like Gaza and Palestine.

The central idea of this book is that both the modernists and the militants are caught up in the same dilemma, leading to accusations and counter accusations of unbelief. Both evolved their narratives through delinking themselves from the early period of Islam. They failed to earn support for their narratives from the masses, who always identify early religious traditions with the ideals of faith. The erosion of linkage with the ideal traditions of faith led to the emergence of militancy. This squeezed the boundaries of faith on the trajectory of *takfīr,* though the fundamentals of faith have always remained constant. It is important to revisit the evidence from the ideal period of Islam and the works of Muslim scholarship in the medieval period of Islam, which still commands support from the Muslim masses for being strongly linked with the ideal period of Islam. The book exposes the fallacy of militant ideology through offering a counter narrative, exploring the accounts of Muslim history and theological discourse developed during the medieval period of Islam.

The book unveils various narratives as espoused by western and modern scholarship through a study of the historical evolution of terrorism labelled as 'Islamic', its transformation and its current state. The codification of violence has been studied and practices mapped and confirmed through empirical field research in Pakistan as a case study. This case study is important as it provides an insight into the undercurrents of militant ideology. Both qualitative and quantitative techniques were employed. The killing fields and the fuel of faith have also been investigated to link them with the boundaries of faith redrawn within the Muslim states and society to challenge the narrative of the militants. In order to pronounce the invalidity of the dominant discourse, evidence has been drawn from the earliest period of Islamic history.

The author is indebted to a close friend, Asim Gulzar, for his intellectual input during the course of research. The author is thankful to Emily Ross, Senior Editor, Routledge, Lee Marsden, Series Editor, *Religion and International Security,* and Hannah Rich for being always encouraging and welcoming during the course of publishing the book. The author is grateful to Jane Robson for carefully proofreading the manuscript and giving her invaluable input to make the text clear and concise. The author is indebted to his wife, Beelam, who has always been a source of encouragement for the completion of this book. The author also owes a heavy debt to other family members, Fatima, Mahnoor and Maleeha for being helpful and supportive during different phases of writing this book.

Munir Masood Marath

Introduction

Lenses of religion and politics have produced a different but sceptical view of jihad. The recent scholarship links it to terrorism. The asymmetrical warfare waged against the power centres of nation states and their ideology expressed through democracy is the forte of those who are showcased as militants or labelled as Islamic terrorists. In this war, the definition of a Muslim and Islam is challenged alongside the obliteration of Muslim and western states. Non-combatant Muslims as well as non-Muslims are wrapped into the fold of enemies, and the application of kinetic force is used as a strategy. One side employs beheadings and suicide bombings whereas the other utilizes drones and signature strikes. The conflict, however, transcends tactics and spawns into the ideological frontiers. 'Crusade' and 'Return of the Children of Ibn Taimmiyah' speak of the narratives that resonate from both sides. Heroes are resurrected, and battles are redrawn across the globe. Return to past and shameful violence is a conspicuous element of this clash. In this backdrop, the parties to the conflict have espoused three mutually divergent narratives.

The first narrative is based upon recasting multifarious local conflicts into a broader struggle between an 'authentic Islam' and the West, especially the United States. On this premise, Al-Qaida ascribes the notion of jihad as a mission and strategy to achieve their ultimate goal of building a universal Islamic caliphate. In Al-Qaida ranks, the views of Al-Zawahiri do not fully conform to any major school of Islamic scholasticism. His ideas have been defined by the political developments in the Middle East and *salāfī* traditions and have been contextualized to support the new ideology. For instance, Al-Qaida's ideology of *khurūj* (revolt) against Muslim rulers is inconsistent with the traditional theological Sunnite standpoint that does not approve of such actions except under specific conditions, which are not present in Al-Qaida's case. The militant narrative labels the Muslim rulers as 'agents of the West' and further alleges that 'apologists' have perverted the 'authentic Islam'. This narrative is based upon ideology, which has no space for dialogue with those taking an opposing view.

The narrative is rooted in the Egyptian fundamentalist traditions of the 20th century. It originates from Ikhwan and is shared by its franchises,

DOI: 10.4324/9781003164883-101

including Jama'a al-Islamīyah, Islamic jihad and Hamas. All vie for the establishment of Islamic political order through militaristic means, vouchsafed in the name of jihad waged against western forces, which Sayyed Qutb terms as 'forces of *jāhilliyah*'. However, this philosophy of resistance to the West underwent radical transformation under Al-Zawahiri. Jihad was hitherto a local phenomenon, seen in the resistance movements in Southeast Asia, the Middle East, South Asia and Africa. However, under Al-Qaida, it transformed into a global struggle against a common external enemy, which was standing between the liberation of the holy land of Palestine and powerless Muslims through its naked western support to Israel. On the fringes of this transformation, this narrative evolved strong ramifications for the Muslim societies as well. Through subscribing to Qutb's doctrine of 'nearer enemy' and Ibn Taimmiyah's decree against the Mongols, Al-Qaida brought violence to the domestic front to fight so-called elements of apostasy in Muslim states.

The second narrative revisits Islamic precepts through the western democratic context instead of redefining Islam in its exclusive framework. Those who follow this narrative are marked as 'apologists'. Some scholars like Maryam Jameelah term them as 'West-worshippers' and argue that these are mediocre end-products of their circumstances. This narrative finds its apologists in places ranging from India to Sudan. For instance, the early 20th century witnessed Sir Sayyed Ahmed Khan trying to remove ideological faultlines between the imperialist West and the Indian Muslims. He focused exclusively upon exploring common ground between the two. He wrote a bilingual commentary on the Bible titled *Tabyin-ul-Kalām* wherein he attempted to discover common ground between Christianity and Islam. He undertook to bring about reconciliation between the Christian British government and its Muslim subjects. Similarly, in Sudan, Mahmoud Muhammad Taha used this apologist approach. He advocated democracy and opposed implementation of a version of Shariah. He was convinced of gender parity and the equal status of Muslims and non-Muslims. He bifurcated between the Sunnah and Shariah and viewed the post-Hijra portion of the Quranic revelation in the context of that time-frame, whereas in his opinion it was only the Makkan portion of the Quranic revelations which provided guidelines for the modern age. This approach is in direct contrast to the majority opinion of Muslim ulema. This narrative ignores the basic tenets of the faith as agreed upon by the majority of ulema. It focused largely upon reconciling Muslim beliefs with the contemporary western values. It lost its credibility as it ignored the basic tenets of faith and did not highlight the differences between Islam and western ideology.

The third narrative refers to the dictatorial and westernized ruling elite in the Muslim lands. They are labelled as apostates for following an anti-Islamic and imperialist agenda in the Muslim heartlands. They focus upon the blatant use of force against the militant elements. They see this coercive approach as a panacea for this conflict situation. They attempt to give legitimacy to their violence through their ideological reliance upon the apologists' views. Nevertheless, this sole reliance upon the use of force has also failed to settle the conflict. It leads to an argument that both Al-Qaida and those whom they label as 'agents' employ the same strategy and the same levels of violence.

Against the background where all three available narratives have failed to end violence, this book aims to offer a counter narrative. The nature of narratives affirms that the conflict between them is essentially ideological, with strong internal implications for the Muslim societies. The ardent quest to expose these implications leads to a search to locate the trajectories of heresy, and this has changed the boundaries of faith. The fundamentals whereupon the boundaries of faith are ideally drawn have remained constant; therefore, this change in limits of faith is attributed to socio-political variables. These variables have transgressed into the theological discourse developed over centuries. Theologians championing the idealism of faith have not been able to insulate religious ideals against the pressures of these socio-political variables, which have led to the loose application of *takfīr* and *khurūj*. Classical theorists like Ibn Kathir and Ibn Taimmiyah did not approve of *khurūj* against rulers even if they do not fulfil the conditions ideally required for a Muslim ruler. They stressed the importance of *jama'at* and did not permit the believers to commit *khurūj* against the rulers unless they had abandoned the fundamentals of faith. Similarly, classical theorists believed that *takfīr* is invoked only in case of refutation of the fundamentals of the faith. Compared with the classical theorists, the boundaries of faith squeezed with Ibn Abdul Wahab, who developed his theology together with his contemporary socio-political variables. He did not identify those who happened to practise the faith different from his own brand as Muslims at all. He did not even recognize the Islamic character of his contemporary Arab society; rather, he identified the latter with pre-Islamic *jāhilliyah*. Ibn Abdul Wahab's narrative was supported by Sayyed Maududi and Sayyed Qutb but with differences between them. The former did not approve of armed struggle against the forces of *jāhilliyah* whereas the latter retained the option of armed resistance against these forces in final resort, to be launched through his 'vanguard' of committed volunteers. Subsequently, the militants adopted this narrative to internalize their violence towards the Muslim societies.

The ideas of heresy metamorphosed into polemics that provided a trajectory for permanent schisms within the Muslim societies. In historical context, these cleavages emerged largely on three questions regarding 'claim to prophetic inheritance', 'belief in imamate' and 'claim to the caliphate'. The answers to these questions defined the course of theological streams in Muslim history. Having found conflicting standpoints on these issues, the Sunnites and the Shiites plunged into physical and political conflict. This conflict was exacerbated when religious ideas were juxtaposed with socio-political variables. Sectarian empires like Fatimid Caliphate and Safavid dynasty emerged, which adopted sectarian violence as a tool of statehood.

The violent policies adopted by these sectarian empires led to historical prejudices and continued to serve as 'lessons of history' for Muslims in general during the periods to come.

Though the emergence of the Safavid Empire in the 16th century heightened the sectarian polarization in the Muslim world, it did not reach the masses until colonization took place in the Muslim lands. The colonial powers deliberately introduced such policies, which struck at the very roots of the national identity of the community whose political authority they usurped. The purpose was simply to strengthen their foothold in colonized societies. In areas where they seized political authority from the Muslims, the colonial initiatives led to identity crises for the Muslim masses. Through these well-thought-out policy interventions, the colonial powers eliminated any prospects of the future resurgence in the occupied areas, which could challenge their political and military supremacy. The identity crisis that continued to exist even in the post-colonial Muslim societies in terms of colonial hangover led to the codification of violence at the behest of religious ulema. The codification of violence in the colonial period continued to remain relevant even in the post-colonial context. Violence against the colonialists was contextualized as resistance against the colonial remnants in otherwise independent states. The Muslim caliphate in Turkey, which was at least a symbol of Muslim unity, was abolished. With its abolition, even the remote chances of Muslim unity on the model of Ummah were eliminated once and for all. The irrelevance of Ummah in bridging the sectarian divide in the Muslims paved the grounds for violence to be codified on the trajectory of sectarian schisms. In addition, as a means of emancipation from the colonial hangovers, nostalgia for the caliphate emerged as a factor behind the codification of violence.

Needless to say, even after the formal end of colonialism, the interests of the major powers did not recede in the areas previously under their control. However, in the post-colonial scenario, they pursued their interests through different modes. They managed to collaborate with the Muslim rulers to secure their interests. In this scenario, the triangular conflict involving the colonialists, the Islamists and the apologists had to accommodate a new target: labelled by militants as 'apostate rulers' in the Muslim lands such as Egypt, Somalia, Algeria, Saudi Arabia and Pakistan. This scenario provided a space to the militants in which they developed their codes of war. These codes sanctioned violence against the West and against those whom the militants term as the elements of apostasy in the Muslim societies. These include local supporters of the West labelled as 'nearer enemies' and the elements of heresy which also include the Shiites. Those who follow western democracy are also taken as supporters of the West. The codes of war sanction vengeance-based violence which observes hardly any distinction between the combatants and non-combatants. These codes of war reflect that conflict has been largely internalized in Muslim societies.

These codes of war draw strength from the space wrongfully carved out by the ideologues of militancy through misleading interpretations of the religious scripture. This space is not only exploited by the clergy in religious seminaries but also by the semi-literate local clergy who cut across every section of Muslim society. They have access to diverse sections of the society as compared to their colleagues in religious seminaries. They contribute indirect, secondary and informal indoctrination in otherwise secular segments of society. This indoctrination provides a shared ground for assimilation of militant ideology and leads to a common worldview across the militant fraternity. The common vision makes them a part of a loose network where organizational affiliation becomes subordinate to ideology. In the case of Pakistan, evidence suggests that having a common ideology and shared goals allows the militants to switch from one organization to another without hesitation. This makes the challenge of militancy even more fluid, formidable and hydra-headed. If one militant outfit is neutralized, its foot soldiers move to another outfit unhindered to achieve common goals.

The case of Pakistan reaffirms that the militants constitute a part of a broader militant fraternity. This is confirmed through corroborative evidence regarding uniformity in patterns of violence adopted by the field operators coming from various outfits. They also share common targets for their violent strikes. These commonalities in patterns of violence and selection of targets amongst the foot soldiers of different militant outfits reflect their shared beliefs and vision. This common worldview in the militant diaspora has resulted from the codification of violence in Muslim societies. The case study of Pakistan upholds the dynamic nature of the process leading to the codification of violence. Having emerged from a long, drawn-out freedom struggle, Pakistani society retained a non-violent religious character until socio-political variables carved out a space for the codification of violence. This happened in the context of the Afghan war against the Soviets and the Shiite revolution in Iran.

Beyond Pakistan, the killing fields of Al-Qaida and its affiliates reflect a similar picture where violence is committed on the pretext of liberating Islam. These flashpoints of violence emerged in the context of the sectarian split, state oppression by totalitarian regimes, simmering wounds in the Muslim world and, above all, theatres of international aggression. In the first instance, in Lebanon, Syria and Iraq, the militants did not surrender their sectarian identities despite sharing common anti-imperialist themes. In these states, they exploited the sectarian schisms to secure political and strategic gains. In the second instance, the flashpoints of violence were the result of state oppression by totalitarian regimes. This state oppression needs to be viewed in terms of a structural concept, which has multiple manifestations. It is commonly manifested in the form of economic exploitation, political marginalization and repression against a selective group. Three countries in the African continent – Somalia, Algeria and Egypt – are prime examples where state oppression drew these states into militants' killing fields. In the third instance, Gaza and Palestine are unhealed wounds in the Muslim world which provide legitimacy to the violence of the militants. In the last instance, theatres of international aggression like Iraq and Afghanistan provide space to the militants to assimilate their ideology of resistance to the west and their struggle for the liberation of Muslim Ummah.

The challenge of militancy is complex and intricate, with hardly any simple solution in sight. It wrongfully claims its origins in religion, which have to be dismissed. Nevertheless, literature has emerged in the last two decades, largely focused upon tracing the origins of militant ideology to the ideas of Muslim scholarship of the medieval ages like Ibn Taimmiyah or the 20th-century Egyptian fundamentalists like Sayyed Qutb. This literature has not been able to produce a high-value impact on the ground simply because modern scholarship could not delink militant ideology from classical Muslim theology. Muslims in general believe in the authenticity of theological discourse that developed in the early and medieval period of Islam. This failure on the part of contemporary scholarship could not prevent the militant outfits from drawing the fuel of faith from the Muslim world. Moreover, in the Muslim world, if any attempt was made to refute the militant ideology, it was made in the context of a modernist interpretation of Islam. This modernist interpretation could get recognition neither from the militants nor from traditional ulema who command the religious sentiments of Muslims in general. Both militants and traditional ulema claim to follow the medieval version of 'authentic Islam' instead of modernist interpretations. A few works claim to trace the genesis of jihad from the divine scripture and follow its transformation to the current streams of militancy. There are still others who examine the ideologies of militants but their overarching emphasis is upon the organizational structure of militant organizations and the strategies the militants adopt to achieve the goals of global jihad. Besides these works, a lot of literature exists which examines the ideology of militant outfits. Nevertheless, there exists hardly any exhaustive work to discredit the militant ideology through generating evidence from the primary texts of the early period of Islam, and theology that developed in the medieval period of Muslim history. This book aims to fill this vacuum.

The book exposes the fallacy of militant ideology by offering a counter narrative. It highlights the spaces in the theological discourse of medieval Islam which are wrongfully exploited by the militants to earn theological legitimacy for their violence. It explores the accounts of Muslim history and the theological sphere to invalidate the narrative of the militants. It aims to deny them a space to seek legitimacy to their acts of violence through a distorted interpretation of faith. It tests the militant ideological streams against the classical perspective of Islam. It further seeks to transform the contemporary ideological discourse by revisiting the primary sources and ultimately leads to the refutation of the militants' claim to follow an authentic Islam. The counter narrative, while examining two groups of sects in the course of Islamic history, redraws the boundaries of faith and develops an argument that only refutation of any fundamental of faith as such invokes *takfīr*. The first group includes Khawarij and the Shiites who were not excommunicated. Despite their multiple deviations from the path agreed upon by the majority of ulema, they did not refute any fundamental principle of faith as such. The second group includes Jahamiyyah and Qaramitah who came up with a categorical refutation of the basic tenets of faith and thus *takfīr* was invoked against them by the ulema. The counter narrative also invalidates the *khurūj* against the Muslim rulers even if they do not fulfil the ideal Islamic conditions required for the rulers. *Khurūj* is only permissible when the ruler foregoes any basic tenet of faith. Further, the counter narrative seeks to suggest that democratic principles like public consent, instruments of political division, candidature to the position of authority and territorial nationalism in terms of a means to revive the Ummah are theologically approved acts provided they uphold divine sovereignty. The counter narrative further revisits the primary sources and, by ascertaining the historical evidence, exposes the invalidity of grounds upon which polemics have been constructed. Furthermore, the counter narrative explores the ethics of war from the early period of Islamic history and challenges the militants' codes of war and their tactics.

1 Nature of conflict

The conflict between the West and the militants can be analysed by considering three parties within Muslim society: the militants, the apologists and the rulers in the Muslim world whom the militants accuse of following the agenda of the West against the fellow believers. Their ideas and respective positions with regard to socio-economic and political orders define their ideological vision in context of the Muslim world in general and Middle East and South Asia in particular. The narratives evolved by three actors makes the conflict among them as essentially ideological. As ideology is made up of religion, politics, economics and the social landscape, these areas are further investigated to develop a clear insight into their respective worldview.

Ideology

Definitions of ideology have always been controversial, but it refers to the set of ideas that orientate the thought process. It eventually leads to a normative vision essentially related to three spheres – religion, economics and sociology. The plurality of religious beliefs, social norms, cultural traits, and political and economic approaches are commonplace in societies. Given the diversity of intellectual undercurrents present in a society, this normative vision represents a worldview of the society as a whole regarding the collective spheres of human life. Instead of representing each intellectual stream, ideology as a thought process is a conglomeration of diverse intellectual streams which converge to form a worldview of the society as a whole. Nevertheless, this thought process that leads to form the ideological basis of a society is by all means a dynamic phenomenon. Intellectual courses in society keep on changing in terms of the degree of their influence vis-à-vis each other. With the advent of Islam, the Arabian Peninsula witnessed a radical shift in the social and cultural structure of society. The nature of societal faultlines changed – from tribal to ideological. History offers evidence of the transformation of political systems – from monarchies to democracies to military dictatorships. In the economic sphere, the evidence is not uncommon which shows the change in the economic systems.

DOI: 10.4324/9781003164883-1

Eastern Europe joined the Communist block after World War II. However, the Eastern bloc reverted to economic liberalism after the fall of the Soviet Union. However, despite being dynamic and diverse, the normative vision of society always relies upon the state order for its protection, promotion and projection. Where a supportive state order is the culmination stage of the ideological process, it is at the same time, an essential condition for the perpetuation of the ideological discourse as well.

Religion

Religion has plural spiritual manifestations, which include ritual-performance by the adherents and acknowledgement of faith to be the source of ultimate knowledge, which is channelled to human beings. The approach of religion towards metaphysical phenomena determines its character in terms of either 'divinity-based' or 'rationality-based'. Divinity-based religion presents practices and beliefs, which are informed through some sort of divine communication with human beings. This communication may be revealed or inspired to disseminate the divine providence to address the questions that fall in the domain of metaphysics. All Abrahamic religions believe that ultimate knowledge is divinely channelled to the prophets. Separate from theistic religions, which recognize the existence of God, man-made systems have emerged and eventually claimed many followers. Secularization of knowledge paved the way for renunciation of the link between metaphysics and knowledge. From these grounds, secular systems like communism, nationalism and democratic liberalism emerged almost as rationality-based religions. These systems do not affirm the sources of knowledge beyond the grasp of human reason and dismiss the realm of metaphysics in their quest of ultimate knowledge.

This taxonomy of 'divinity-based' and 'rationality-based' belief systems highlights the bifurcation between ideology and religion despite several similarities between the two. They both claim to order human conduct but there is a gap between the two in terms of scope. The scope of the ideology is usually limited to the temporal sphere, and the spiritual sphere is considered the exclusive domain of religion. However, the argument of mutual exclusivity between the two is not supported by historical evidence. The medieval history of Europe as well as Muslim historical discourse suggests that religion has played a part in statehood, especially in terms of defining its ideological character. Europe could not codify secularism until the period of Reformation. On the other hand, the Muslim societies have been classic examples of a mutually inclusive relationship between religion and ideology. Although secularism as an external factor could create ripples within Muslim society through generating debate on the inter-relationship of the two phenomena, in broader perspective, it could not overwhelm Islam as an 'ideology-producing force'.

Economics

An ideology also defines the socio-economic features of a society through evolving broader principles that determine the structure of economies. After World War II, two major economic ideologies, Marxian Communism and capitalism, emerged to define the international conflict scenario through projecting their ideological webs on their respective spheres of influence. The Communist ideology provided for the common ownership of the means of production, aiming at realization of a classless society, whereas capitalism sanctioned the private ownership of the means of production, and emerged as a global economic order through its projection by the transnational processes like globalization and imperialism.

Though both of these economic ideologies had their appeal across the Muslim world, they could not dislodge the ideological exclusivity of Islam even in the economic sphere. Islamic ideology that aims to construct a welfare state discredits the visions of welfare state systems of both the Communists and the capitalists. Communism developed on the basis of Marxian dialectical materialism which only recognized the material aspect of life. The exclusive focus on the material aspect earned the Communist ideology outright condemnation from Muslim ideologues because it could not achieve the sublime balance between the spirit and matter, which had always been a hallmark of Islamic ideology. Through their categorical condemnation of usury (*ribā*), which is a cardinal theme of the capitalist economies, the Islamists discredited capitalism as well. Their condemnation of capitalism and Communism further originates from the argument that, by going against the Islamic vision of creating a balance, Communism underestimates individualism and overestimates collectivism, and the reverse is the case with capitalism.

Sociology

Religious and sociological contexts are defined in terms of an approach to the supernatural.[1] The sociologists have been chiefly interested in examining the unifying effects of what they term 'civil religion'.[2] In this purview, functionalist theorists like Emile Durkheim identify religion as a tool of human socialization instead of human–God relations.[3] In the same stream, others like August Comte believed that religion in terms of an evolutionary stage became redundant with the advancement of historical process. They believe that if in the advancement of history religion survived, it survived only as a religion of humanity, entirely secular in nature.[4] As terminologies like 'sacred' and 'profane' occupy a central place in the sociological explanations of religion, the sociologists focus on defining these terms to find the universal values of all religions. They define the 'sacred' as something relating to supernatural phenomena, which can be achieved through some rituals whereas 'profane' is part of ordinary life.[5]

Notwithstanding the academic value of these sociological studies, Islam as a religion does not bifurcate life into spiritual and temporal spheres. Even 'civil religion' fell short of achieving its essence when tested in the Muslim lands. For instance, *dīn-e-elāhī* of Akbar, the Mughal emperor, which aimed at unifying heterogeneous Indian society, faced stiff resistance from ulema as well as the Muslim masses. Sheikh Ahmed of Sirhind, the revivalist of Islam in the 2nd millennium, publicly condemned this royal edict as heretical in character and did not let it secure public legitimacy. This encounter is taken to have marked the dawn of Islamism in the sub-continent.[6]

Orders and the state formation

The ideological spheres of religion, economics and sociology produce orders within which the state and ideology develop and define their dynamics.

Political orders

Political orders emerge from the respective ideological spheres. Ideologies define the principles of the political orders, which in their turn, determine the nature of political orders and keep their operation within the ideological framework. These principles include sovereign authority, the framework of conflict amongst the political orders and the role of the actors involved. It is on these trajectories that the following discussion will examine the dynamics of conflict in democratic and Islamic political orders.

Democracy as a political order has been selected for comparative analysis vis-à-vis Islamism. When put against each other, both political orders offer a dynamic framework for the conflict. Against democracy, Islamism is presented from the perspectives of the puritans and the apologists. The puritans draw inspiration from the orthodox period of Islam whereas the apologists seek to reconcile Islam with western democratic ideals. Three leading Muslim theorists, namely Ibn Taimmiyah, Sayyed Maududi and Sayyed Qutb, have been selected to unravel the puritanical narrative. The ideas of Muhammad Abduhu and Rashid Rida have been examined to explore the domain of the apologists. The selection of these theorists from the array of Muslim scholarship has been made because of the degree of their influence on Muslim intellectual discourse.

Sovereign authority

The nature of sovereign authority reflects the character of a political order. It determines the relationship between the rulers and the ruled and also state and society. The following discussion examines the nature of sovereign authority in western democracy vis-à-vis the Islamic political order chiefly in theoretical context and highlights the implications emerging from the nature of sovereign authority in both orders.

Western democracy

Democracy as a socio-political ideal denotes that the will of people shall govern the state institutions. As governance depends upon coercion to a certain degree, the theory of democratic governance itself is caught up in paradoxes. These paradoxes need to be resolved to explain the genesis of democracy in terms of a new universal religion.[7] These paradoxes have two aspects. First, as the state authority implies the 'right to rule' and the natural instinct of man is freedom or 'refusal to be ruled', the resolution of this apparently zero-sum game demands alternatives.[8] The first alternative finds its philosophical basis in the anarchists' presumption that as coercion, being the antithesis of human freedom, is inherently bad it must be avoided, even at the cost of the very existence of the political entity itself.[9] This elimination of coercion may not work, as society requires coercion even to control the unauthorized coercion of one member of society by another.[10] The second alternative, which appears more plausible, is to explore ways and means to regulate the exercise of coercion instead of eliminating it altogether. The regulation of coercion requires the state to be democratic so that coercion may be exercised in the collective interest of the community and not otherwise.[11]

The second paradox finds its roots in the very chemistry of a democratic state, which implies that all constituents share sovereignty of the state and so implies self-governance in terms of personal autonomy of the constituents.[12] Self-governance while living in a society demands that all constituents, while maintaining their personal autonomy, accept collective decisions. The problem comes up of who will make collective decisions (govern) and who will follow the decisions (governed) as all constituents have an equal and inalienable right to govern.[13] Rousseau in his *Social Contract* expressed this paradox thus: 'find a form of association that defends and protects the person and goods of each associate with all the common force, and by means of which each one, uniting with all, nevertheless obeys only himself and remains as free as before'.[14] This paradox remained unresolved even with Rousseau in the broader context of decision making in the democratic framework, as he suggested unanimity only to the extent of the original contract which provided for the creation of state, and left the subsequent decision making subordinate to the will of majority.[15]

However, the quest for alternatives to this paradox leads to the following key questions: can anyone guarantee equal consideration of interests than his own, and is there any better system other than democracy to make the decision making more representative? John Locke viewed 'equality' as the right to natural freedom without one being subject to another, and thus equality of rights and opportunities can be guaranteed if interests of each individual are given equal weight.[16] As each individual can better define his own interests, equal consideration of interests is possible if one has the authority to interpret one's own interests. This demands that each individual has access to the decision-making mechanism.[17] In a broader perspective, a majority cannot be a judge of a minority's rights. As democracy, as explained by Rousseau above, relies on majority decisions, what are the possibilities that any other system can make the decision making more representative? Evidence suggests that other systems rely on relatively smaller proportions of constituents than democracy for governance.[18]

To make democratic governance more reflective of public aspirations, two options may be suggested: structural and procedural. The former demands that democratic governance be devolved to the local level, which contributes to administrative efficiency as well as to the development of political faculties of the people. Though sometimes localities are dominated by a few who suppress others, and central government may protect against this suppression, local rule is superior as it provides a broader spectrum of political participation.[19] The procedural option, as suggested by Schumpeter, takes democracy as a procedure to make political decisions by means of electoral process.[20] The elections procedure is a mechanism to register public opinion. The democracy in terms of fair procedure provides for the most feasible course of decision making. By making the general public the ultimate authority to elect or reject any political party to assume power, the aim is to safeguard the interests of the minority against the possible tyrannical tendencies of the majority. Mill was concerned that majority rule may violate the individual rights indispensable for the working of democracy.[21] However, fairness of democracy as a procedure is conditional on the incorporation of the following elements: public trust in the procedure, access to information for making informed decisions, active public participation in decision making (people can better safeguard their interests from being abused by the government if, as J. S. Mill has suggested, they are themselves part of the decision-making process), equality in terms of the voting process to register their opinion and, finally, neutrality on the part of state in the process of public opinion formulation. This neutrality can be ensured if the role of the state in terms of service delivery reflects the democratic spirit.

This critique leads us to the following broad conclusions. First, democracy draws its genesis from the paradoxical relationship between the rulers and the ruled. There is inherent contradiction between use of coercive authority by the state and the inalienable right to freedom of an individual. Whether this contradiction could be removed by assigning the right to exercise the coercive authority through democratic political authority is a practical question that even John Locke could not address. He could not escape the puzzle of who would rule and who would be ruled as all had an equal and inalienable right to rule. This puzzle remained unresolved with Rousseau as well, who suggested agreement by consensus to the extent of the original contract that provided for the creation of the state and left further decision making to the will of the majority. Thus, democracy in the context of popular sovereignty could not transcend being the rule of the majority.

Second, no other system could be discovered which provides a governance model more representative than democracy. The structural and procedural measures to enhance the level of representation in democracy may not fit the purpose. Devolving democratic governance to the local level might merely add another tier that will again put minorities under the majority rule because the operational mechanism of the democracy will remain the same. Moreover, ensuring fair procedure in the process of registering public opinion will not help create a consensus government; rather, the majority will continue to rule the minority.

The above conclusions lead us to argue that the Lockean social contract whereupon democratic ideals flourished in Western Europe was itself a progeny of rationalism, which would not recognize any phenomenon but the one that could be experienced through human senses. Conversely speaking, as discussed earlier, rationalism discarded everything that would fall in the ambit of metaphysics.[22] Within the intellectual boundaries of rationalism, this social contract focused upon liberating individuals from the contemporary autocracies by transferring the sovereignty from a traditional monarch to the individuals themselves. By transferring the sovereign authority, Locke presumed that individuals had been granted their inalienable right to self-rule, but this transfer of sovereignty was nothing more than a redefinition of the context in which the autocracies were previously working. Monarchical autocracy converted into majoritarian autocracy. The new political order, democracy, was caught in a new paradox. Rousseau attempted to resolve this paradox by attributing the sovereign authority to General Will, which was claimed to represent consensus opinion of the individuals, but in actuality it happened to be an abstract rather than a real phenomenon. Recognition of every individual's inalienable right to rule and at the same time expecting the minority to be ruled by the majority created a fundamental paradox that could not be resolved by remaining within the framework of western democracy.

Islamic political order

Islamic political order claims to resolve the paradox between the individual's fundamental right to self-rule and the majority rule by repositioning the sovereignty. It claims that this paradox can be resolved if the individuals agree to assign sovereign authority to a higher metaphysical phenomenon to whom they render unqualified submission. In Islamic societies all believers render their unconditional submission to God. This unconditional submission to the sovereign authority of God is voluntary, and it is fundamental constituent of their faith. Every Muslim is supposed to be ruled by the word of God and acts of the Prophet. In Quranic terminology, human beings are not the repository of authority but have been declared as vicegerents of God.[23] In the decision-making process, no specific group of Muslims can claim ascendency over the other on any grounds whatsoever except piety (*taqwā*). In other words, Islamic political order does not acknowledge anyone's authority to rule but only in accordance with divine will. The Quran says, 'Whoso judgeth not by that which Allah hath revealed: such are disbelievers' (Al-Maidah: 44). Moreover, it affirms the finality of the arbitrative authority of God and His Messenger in case of dispute amongst the believers (Al-Maidah: 59). Furthermore, no individual can exercise legislative or executive authority in contravention of Quranic injunctions and Sunnah of the Prophet. It is evident from the following Quranic verse: 'And it becometh not a believing man or a believing woman, when Allah and His messenger have decided an affair (for them), that they should (after that) claim any say in their affair; and whoso is rebellious to Allah and His messenger, he verily goeth astray in error manifest' (Al-Ahzāb: 36). However, if the primary sources of Islamic law – divine scripture and traditions of the Prophet – are not categorically clear, human beings have the mandate to legislate and decide through ascertaining the real intent of the lawgiver regarding a particular issue (*ijtihād*). This process will exploit the collective wisdom of the believers through consultation (*shūrā*). Despite being the direct recipient of divine guidance, the Prophet was ordained to consult the believers on different issues. God has appreciated those who consult each other in settling their affairs. Allah says, 'Now whatever ye have been given is but a passing comfort for the life of the world, and that which Allah hath is better and more lasting for those who believe and put their trust in their Lord. And those who shun the worst of sins and indecencies and, when they are wroth, forgive. And those who answer the call of their Lord and establish worship, and whose affairs are a matter of counsel, and who spend of what We have bestowed on them'. (Ash-Shūrā: 36-38)

Divine injunctions do not permit a Muslim ruler to act arbitrarily. The Quran says, 'It was by the mercy of Allah that thou wast lenient with them (O Muhammad), for if thou hadst been stern and fierce of heart they would have dispersed from round about thee. So pardon them and ask forgiveness for them and consult with them upon the conduct of affairs. And when thou art resolved, then put thy trust in Allah. Lo! Allah loveth those who put their trust (in Him)'. (Al-Imrān: 159)

In compliance with these divine injunctions, the Prophet acceded to the opinion of the Companions even when it was against his own view.[24] Abu Hurayrah narrates that the Prophet himself always attributed importance to *shūrā* (consultation) more than anyone else. However, it is argued that this consultation will not lead to majoritarian autocracy, as is the problem with the western democratic process; rather, the decision making will be subordinate to overriding spirit of the faith. Islam does not permit any decision making that is repugnant to the spirit of Islam and is not authenticated by the Quran and Sunnah.[25]

Nevertheless, western scholarship dismisses Islamic *shūrā* for not being binding upon the rulers.[26] Sometimes, by labelling Islam as non-democratic, they draw a parallel between Islamism and western Fascism.[27] German, Italian and the Russian transnational political aspirations are compared with the Islamists' nostalgia to revive worldwide caliphate.[28] However, strict accountability during the early period of Islam refutes this notion. To quote one of many examples of accountability, during the caliphate of Umar, a woman raised an objection to the caliph's decision to fix the amount of dower (*mehr*).[29] She referred to the following Quranic verse, which does not limit the amount of dower (*mehr*): 'And if ye wish to exchange one wife for another and ye have given unto one of them a sum of money (however great), take nothing from it. Would ye take it by the way of calumny and open wrong?' (An-Nisā: 20). The caliph submitted to the divine verdict and instantly withdrew his decision. Muslims in general acknowledge the importance of consultation (*shūrā*) in terms of an essential check on the coercive authority of the rulers.[30] However, categorical verdicts of God and His apostle enjoy overriding status vis-à-vis *shūrā*. For instance, Abu Bakr, the first of the orthodox caliphs, declined the advice of leading Companions of the Prophet including Umar, not to dispatch expedition of Usama b. Zayd against the Romans. He turned down this advice because he could not cancel the expedition which was dispatched by the Prophet himself.[31] It was not his arbitrary decision but the Sunnah of the Prophet that prevailed over the advice of the Companions.

The puritans consider the caliphate on the prophetic pattern as the ideal Islamic form of government, which was a practical reality during the early period of Islam.[32] For Ibn Taimmiyah, political authority is religiously necessitated as enforcement of Quranic injunctions regarding enjoining good and forbidding evil (Al-Ara'af: 157) warrants coercive authority, which is neither an end in itself nor a means to achieve only temporal goals. The Prophet has been reported to have said, 'Whenever three of you are travelling, let one of you be the amir'.[33] Ibn Taimmiyah draws an inference that if the Muslims have been commanded to appoint an amir even when they are in such a little number and doing some trivial job, how could the whole Ummah ignore the need to appoint a political leader in managing their collective affairs?[34] He contends that, though politics is subservient to religion, both function in support of each other. Religion suffers in absence of power of the state required for the enforcement of religious tenets (*iqāmat ad-dīn*) whereas without a disciplined body of the laws, the state becomes a symbol of tyranny. As there is no bifurcation between the spiritual and temporal spheres of life, acquiring political authority should be taken as a means to secure the divine pleasure like other forms of worship (*ibādah*). In this sense, it is the individual obligation of the believers to strive to install a political authority that would promote the cause of Islam. However, he reiterates that quest for political authority must not be coupled with material avarice and that the political authority should be strictly employed in the service of religion.[35]

Ibn Taimmiyah further argues that, amongst religion and politics, the former has ascendency over the latter. This ascendency provides a common sphere for political authority to be exercised through an office that is guardian of the faith. This office is called caliphate, which demands religiously sanctioned submission from the believers. The Quran says, 'O ye who believe! Obey Allah, and obey the messenger and those of you who are in authority' (An-Nisā: 59). Abdullah b. Umar narrates that the Prophet said, 'Every Muslim should listen (to the authorities) and obey their commands whether he likes it or not except if he is asked to do something sinful, in which case he is not to listen and obey'.[36] Even in case of individual injustice, one is not absolved from obedience to those in authority. Abu Hurayrah reported that the Prophet said, 'You must listen and obey them in prosperity and in adversity, whether you like it or not, even when you are not given your due'.[37] In another tradition, the Prophet advised a man from *anṣār* (helpers of Madina) to have patience even in case of injustice on the part of those in authority.[38] Similarly, in another *hadith* the Prophet advised believers to be patient in case of injustice on the part of the rulers and pray to God to grant them what is their due.[39] Another *hadith* suggests that revolt (*khurūj*) against even sinful rulers is not permissible provided they establish prayers.[40] This evidence leads Ibn Taimmiyah to suggest that sanctity attached to obedience to those in authority is as overwhelming as observing the elements of the faith.[41]

Against Ibn Taimmiyah's ideal state on the pattern of early Islamic caliphate (*khilāfat-e-nabwiyyah*), the puritan perspective underwent radical revisions with Sayyed Maududi who labelled his polity a 'theo-democracy', which would be installed through a western-style electoral process. Nevertheless, the theo-democratic state, in a bid to secure divine blessings through reviving the absolute sovereignty of God, marks a conspicuous shift from secular statehood.[42] He agrees with Sayyed Qutb that it is only through acquiring the state authority that the usurpers of divine authority could be challenged.[43] The dogma of Islamic state anticipates resistance from the forces of *jāhilliyah,*[44] like the Prophet himself who encountered similar reaction from the pre-Islamic *jāhilliyah* order when he established Islamic political order after migrating (hijra) to Madina.[45]

In the case of the apologists, modernity provides a bridge between Islamic and western democratic ideals.[46] Muhammad Abduhu (1849–1905) through rationalist interpretation of Islam, pleaded for British representative democracy and further drew parallels between '*Shūrā* and western democracy' and '*ijma'a* and public opinion'.[47] Against the traditional Sunnite standpoint on *khurūj,* he, being moved by the Westminster parliamentary democratic traditions, does not hesitate to recognize the popular mandate to impeach the chief executive.[48] Under British influence, he became so liberal that he allowed a non-Muslim to rule in the Muslim lands provided it is in the public interest.[49] Similarly, his disciple Rashid Rida inherited an inclination towards Westminster traditions from his mentor, perhaps compelled by British imperialism.[50] He followed Abduhu in bringing about rationalization between the Islamic law and European civilization through an otherwise traditional instrument of *ijtihād.*[51] Despite being identified as a link to the modernists in theological discourse owing to his liberal ideas, he happened to view linkage between religion and politics from a fundamentalist position. This is evident from his reference to the 11th-century Shafi'ite jurist Al-Mawardi and his further reliance upon a tradition of the Prophet that whosoever dies without having a *baya'ā* dies the death of ignorance (*jāhil-liyah*).[52] Allegiance to the ruler is important for the believers. Moreover, delineating the purpose of political authority, Rida suggests that power is not to make one's will prevail over subjects; rather, its real objective is to develop Shariah and its enforcement without repulsion from within the Islamic state and without.[53]

The puritan Muslims tend not to validate the liberal version that Islam shares certain political norms like limited state authority, constitutionalism and separation of powers with western democracy.[54] They argue that the fundamental difference which overshadows the common features between the two lies in the position of state authority. Fundamentalists like Sayyed Maududi who avoid insisting upon the revival of caliphate on the model of early Islam yearn to defend the exclusivity of Islam. They argue that, though Islam does not document any specific form of state governance, it retains its dynamism through laying down macro-principles of statehood. The micro-level governance has been left to the believers' choice to adopt any form of political order which is otherwise not repugnant to the broader principles laid down by Quran and Sunnah.[55]

However, in the contemporary Muslim world, the ruling elite, being largely concerned to perpetuate their rule, follow western norms mainly to gain support of the western powers. They follow only those western traits that help them prolong their rule. Monarchies in the Middle East may not prefer to follow western democratic ideals, but they are accused of collaborating with the West against their fellow Muslims.

Conflict amongst political orders

In quantifying the progression of history in terms of securing optimum liberty for an individual on the trajectory of Hegel's dialectics, democratic liberalism is marked as the culminating phase of universal history. It is argued that democratic liberalism marks the final stage of historical evolution, as it is not anticipated that a system better than democratic liberalism can be found in guaranteeing human rights. This culminating stage is labelled the 'end of history'. A comparison has been drawn here between Islamism and democratic liberalism to develop the case that Islam, in terms of a political ideology, has hardly any appeal in the non-Muslim lands, whereas democratic liberalism enjoys tremendous appeal within the Muslim lands as well.[56]

Nevertheless, the Islamists take Islam not as a religion nor merely a culture but rather as a 'culture producing force' with universal appeal. Islamism also generates an appeal to Islamic fundamentalism.[57] They retain the right to declare something 'Islamic' or otherwise and therefore negate the exclusionary nature of the modernity thesis of the West that does not recognize modernity outside of liberal democratic ideals.[58] Islamists, reverting back to their past, explore their own parameters of modernity and suggest that Islamic fundamentalism constitutes a part of the reconstructed definition of modernity. This reconstruction needs to be viewed not in terms of negation but in the context of pluralistic redefinition of the term.[59] Moreover, Muslims in general follow a non-materialistic perspective coupled with a divine promise for better prospects for acquiring political sovereignty.[60] The modernity thesis developed on western secular grounds is considered alien to Muslim heritage.[61] There is a general understanding with the Islamists that, being a complete code of life, Islam provides guidance in every sphere of human life. It is not permissible for a Muslim to look towards political orders other than Islam for guidance in the political sphere.[62] The Islamists argue that if democracy is a gesture of public approval, it must honour other systems that enjoy public legitimacy.[63] The faultlines between Islamism and liberal democracy became harsher with the globalization of democratic liberalism. After the Cold War, 'democratic imperialism' sought to redesign the world order.

Conflict and its resolution

The Cold War era witnessed democratic liberalism pitched against Communism. However, with the end of the Cold War, the triumphant United States got a free chance to promote democratic ideals worldwide. Schumpeter argues that capitalist societies are not imperialistic societies as such because they do not promote their worldview through use of force.[64] However, this is contrary to the perception in the Muslim circles. Muslims believe that the West is bent upon imposing its political ideology upon countries, especially the Muslim block, without affording them an opportunity to discover a political system of their own choice. This is simply because the West considers Islamism as successor to the Communist threat.[65] Actually, the evidence that foreign aid to Germany and Japan after World War II helped promote democracies in these two countries have encouraged the West to follow the same policy vis-à-vis those countries which are not democratic or where democratic norms are weaker.[66] Muslims have been cautious about forcible democratization of the Muslim states, taking it as part of a revised imperialist policy of the West. Global capitalist theory provides a new perspective to examine revisions in the imperialistic patterns. This theory suggests that imperialism transformed from being a state-centred phenomenon into an instrument of a transnational capitalist class. It explains the US military interventions in terms of a support mechanism for this capitalist class vis-à-vis the counter imperialist forces. The United States undertook a policy to impose democratic liberal norms upon the rest of world not only through the power of ideas but through physical force as well. The ideological faultlines between Islamic and democratic political orders became physical conflict between the militants and the West. This conflict scenario is not limited to the external imperialist threat but rather it embraces elements internal to Muslim societies. In addition to the conflict with the West about imposing its democratic ideas in Muslim areas, even internally, this conflict has created rifts in Muslim societies leading to the emergence of the following three mutually divergent narratives.

In the first instance, liberals yearn to harmonize Islam with western democratic values. Though they constitute a marginalized section of the reformers in terms of their appeal to the Muslim masses vis-à-vis the puritan Muslims, the support from the West overcame their initial frustrations in not attracting the Muslim masses. Aided by the West, they got elevated to central positions to influence the ruling elite. This helped them redefine the state systems in their liberal mould. These redesigned state systems, when enforced by imperial authority, deprived the masses of being able to follow systems of their own choice. The compulsion to operate in a westernized state system and liberal interpretations of religious edicts allowed apologists to hold sway in otherwise traditional Muslim societies. These apologists provided theological concessions to the westernized state system. In the case of physical aggression by the imperialist powers into Muslim territories, it is, of course, not possible for any believer to refute the ultimate evidence associated with the philosophy of jihad. However, to avoid direct confrontation in this conflict scenario, the liberals instead of approving or disapproving of jihad in categorical terms prefer to look for alternatives by changing the perspective.[67] They attempt to make the point that, for the subdued Muslims, the way to survival lies not in confrontation but in reconciliation with the imperialist powers. In the wake of 1857 resistance against the British Raj, the voice of apology for the Indian Muslims was personified in Sir Sayyed Ahmed Khan, whose vision of western civilization was that of a subdued person (*maghlūb*). Being overwhelmed by the militarily dominant civilization, he could not develop an objective vision.[68] His fascination with the dominant western civilization led him to adopt the rationalism on which western civilization was philosophically based. He introduced philosophical revisions in Islamic ideology and negated any phenomenon that fell beyond human reasoning and could not be proved on the touchstone of the modern knowledge base.[69] As rationalism could not be assimilated by Islamic ideology that recognized metaphysical phenomena as the ultimate source of truth, structural reforms in education were introduced to serve the imperial interests, mollifying local resistance through neutralizing the faultlines between the two civilizations. On his return from England, Sir Sayyed Ahmed Khan reserved the post of the principal of his academic institutions exclusively for the British. Moreover, instead of promoting technical education aimed at industrial revolution on the model of the developed world, his reforms in curricula aimed at paving the grounds for the assimilation of the western value system by the Muslims.[70]

In Egypt, Mufti Muhammad Abduhu followed this liberal approach. Though Sir Sayyed Ahmed Khan and Abduhu belonged to different geographical environments, their apologies for the British imperialism had similar aspects. First, both of them preferred to explore grounds for reconciliation between the two civilizations through reforming the education system instead of direct confrontation; second, they accepted western rationalism as a source of ultimate knowledge. However, their religious approach could not earn recognition with the general Muslim masses as it was not supported by any major school of Islamic scholarship. Their conciliatory approach towards the imperialist challenge was taken to be violative of the divine scripture, prophetic traditions and acts of the *salaf*. One cannot find even an isolated instance where believers have been ordained to observe restraint against foreign aggression. It is an agreed view of all the recognized schools of Muslim jurisprudence that jihad, which is otherwise *fard-e-kafāyā*, becomes *fard-e-ayn* for the Muslims whose territory has been invaded by any foreign power.[71]

The Islamists have had the advantage in evoking the anti-imperialistic sentiment amongst the masses by highlighting various aspects of the imperialist challenge. These include territorial aggrandizement, threat to religious edifice, erosion of social values and, above all, economic exploitation of the Muslims. As against the apologists, the Islamists instead of undertaking an ecumenical approach take refuge in the basics of the faith in the face of the challenges emerging from western imperialism. The primary sources for the Islamists include the 'divine scripture', the prophetic traditions and the consensus opinion or acts (*ijma'a*) of the Companions of the Prophet. In fact, imperialism relies upon oppression of the marginalized sections of the society to thrive whereas the Quran condemns oppression in whichever form it may be. It enjoins upon the believers to wage jihad against every form of oppression. It says, 'How should ye not fight for the cause of Allah and of the feeble among men and of the women and the children who are crying: Our Lord! Bring us forth from out this town of which the people are oppressors! Oh, give us from thy presence some protecting friend! Oh, give us from Thy presence some defender! Those who believe do battle for the cause of Allah; and those who disbelieve do battle for the cause of idols. So fight the minions of the devil. Lo! the devil's strategy is ever weak'. (An-Nisā: 75, 76)

The Quran further says, 'And fight them until persecution is no more, and religion is all for Allah. But if they cease, then lo! Allah is Seer of what they do' (Al-'Anfāl: 39). If the non-Muslims fight against the believers it becomes the duty of the Muslims to pay them in the same coin. The Quran says, 'And wage war on all of the idolaters as they are waging war on all of you. And know that Allah is with those who keep their duty (unto Him)' (At-Tawbah: 36). The above quoted Quranic verses suggest that, if the non-believers attack the Muslim territories, the only legitimate option the believers are left with is to resist them. The Prophet himself participated in many battles against the forces of unbelief. Jihad differentiates between a hypocrite (*munāfiq*) and a believer. The Prophet said, 'Whoever dies neither having fought nor having made up his mind to do so, dies on a branch of hypocrisy'.[72] The Prophet further cautioned the believers that if they give up jihad, they would be punished and would be replaced by another people. The Companions of the Prophet followed him on the road to jihad. During the times of the first four pious caliphs, Muslim armies were dispatched to fight the Romans as well as the Persians. This evidence upholds the importance of jihad against the contemporary imperialism on one hand and legitimizes the Muslims' struggle to shield themselves behind their 'sacred past' to avert the identity crises on the other.[73]

For the Islamists, the ideological renaissance is measured against the corresponding level of the revival of political order based upon divine sovereignty. The struggle for ideological revival anticipates conflict with the competing forces of *jāhilliyah*. The forces include the imperialist powers who are bent upon exploitation of the Muslims' resources, the apologists who resolve to bring Islamic order in conformity with the western democratic norms and the Muslim rulers who collaborate with the imperialists against the fellow Muslims. This plurality of targets has invited diverse responses from the Islamists. In India, the religiously polarized society could not become politically diffused on the pattern of the European society, which could acquire egalitarian character through diluting the distinction between the church and the state. Owing to ideological biases in the religiously heterogeneous society, the liberal-cum-apologist approach could not prevent the Muslims from reverting to their pristine religious past to secure their distinct religious identity through the instrument of jihad. The seeds of resistance were sown by Sayyed Ahmed Bareili (1786–1831), who waged jihad against Sikh rule under the banner of the Mujahideen Movement. He is a role model for the current jihadi movements, who draw a parallel between English colonialism and the policies of the United States.[74] Similarly, Haji Shariatullah (1781–1840) initiated *Farāizī Tehrīk* in Bengal to eliminate heresies from the Muslim society. Muhammad b. Abdul Wahab was a common source of inspiration for both of them. Their theory of resistance remained relevant until 1857 when the Indian Muslims rose up against the British imperialism but were suppressed. Though in the 20th century the British did not have to face any organized resistance from the Islamists, they could not break linkage of the Islamists with their Islamic past. It is evident from *Tehrīk-e-hijrat* (Movement for Migration) of the Indian Muslims when the Ottoman caliphate was abolished in the 20th century. The Indian Muslims started this movement because India had become *dār-ul-harb* (land of war).

The ideological biases amongst different religious communities in Indian society continued to persist even during the post-independence period, as partition of British India happened to be a mere redefinition of the context in which the communal forces had been previously working. The ideological hostility between the Hindus and the Muslims in United India transformed into enmity between Hindu India and Muslim Pakistan. In this context, Sayyed Maududi emerged to occupy a central place in the Islamists' ranks who took Islam in terms of a counter-imperialism force. His anti-imperialistic ideas found exposition in his criticism of the United Nations and other great powers for encouraging India to use naked force in Kashmir.[75] Moreover, imperialist Indian designs were evident from the statements of Indian leaders, no less Mr Nehru himself. Maududi urged the Muslim community to support the jihadi elements in Kashmir fighting against India.[76] However, he ruled out armed conflict with the counter-revolutionary forces within the country and emerged more of a reformer than a revolutionary, at least within Pakistan.[77] In the war theatres outside Pakistan, he called for armed struggle against the imperialist forces and used the Quranic terminology of Hezbollah (Party of God).[78] Though Maududi was not a pluralist who believed in the coexistence of two or more belief systems dominating the power structure of a state, unlike Sayyed Qutb he ruled out the option of armed struggle at least within the Muslim states.

In Egypt, Islamism arose in a more virulent and organized form as compared to India. In 1928, Hassan Al-Banna (1906–49) established Ikhwan Al-Muslimeen (Muslim Brotherhood), which would become an umbrella organization for all Islamic revivalist movements in the times to come. He emphasized the need to wage jihad against imperialist forces. He shared views on jihad with Sayyed Maududi, who developed his anti-imperialist theory of jihad in the Indian context.[79] Another figure who has influenced the Islamists' ideology down to our days is Sayyed Qutb. In his book *Muālim fil tarīq* (Milestones), he laid down the road map of Islamic revolution against the imperialist forces, which he termed as forces of *jāhilliyah* (ignorance). His ardent opposition to the apologists is evident when he argues that offering an apology for the western imperialists is like following the traditions of *jāhilliyah* because Islam, being inconsistent with the western value system, possesses its distinct way of life.[80] Like Maududi, he uses the dogma of ideological renaissance to discover the Islamic political order based upon divine sovereignty vis-à-vis other political orders.[81] For him, revival of Islamic political order is imperative to revive public appeal of the faith, as people prefer to look towards living entities instead of mere abstractions. The practical revival of divine sovereignty is required to uproot existing ideologies which are bent upon exploitation of mankind. As these ideologies possess a tremendous material power base with which the Muslims cannot compete, the only choice left for Muslims is to rely upon the power of faith to stand in the face of these ideologies of oppression.[82] This conflict will naturally invite resistance to the Muslims, which can only be faced if jihad is taken in terms of a forceful tool to obliterate the oppressive political orders. A resourceful Islamic movement (vanguard) through a gradual process will launch this struggle. This process begins with an ideological struggle to expose the weakness of the system of *jāhilliyah,* and in the final stage, using physical force, the *jāhilliyah* order will be replaced with the Islamic system.[83] He distances himself from Maududi in sanction of the use of force against the political order of *jāhilliyah*. It is evident from history that Islamic movements would not succeed through peaceful struggle.[84] He categorically sanctions *khurūj* against the Muslim rulers who are found to be in collaboration with the western imperialists.[85]

Social orders

Democratic social order

A social order also reflects the nature of ideology that generates it. In democratic social order, 'individual good' occupies a central place vis-à-vis the state formation. 'Individual good' is an end in itself to be achieved through state formation. A diffused political authority was visualized through separation of church from the state, achieving this end by bringing discipline to the state's role in individuals' lives. Democratic liberalism approves of the state's interference in individuals' lives only if it aims to promote 'individual good'. Democratic liberalism generates social order that revolves around individualism and relegates the society as a whole to a subordinate position to serve the individual's interests. It is in this context that J.S. Mill argues that as an individual is sovereign over his body and mind, the state interference in his life may run counter to his individual sovereignty. The state should only discipline activities which are 'others-related' and avoid infringing upon an individual's liberty in activities that are 'self-related'. Mill's theory of 'human good' needs to be taken in terms of an extension of Jeremy Bentham's utilitarian approach to politics that legitimizes the state interference in human lives provided it secures 'the greatest happiness of the greatest number'. Though Mill did not subscribe to the utilitarians' quantitative happiness of an individual, he shared with them that it is individual good that provides space for the state interference in human lives. However, democratic liberalism that thrived upon the free-market economy could not cater for all classes in a society in uniform manner. The dawn of industrialization ushered in an era of unprecedented rate of production, but the system failed to ensure equitable distribution of the fruits of industrialization. This resulted in the emergence of a class of dispossessed on the one hand and failed to control the competitive search for new markets that caused imperialism to emerge as an inevitable result. Capitalism could neither avoid exploitation of the 'have nots' within the capitalist societies nor could the weaker nations escape its imperialistic designs.

Communist social order

Against democratic liberalism, Communism denotes a political theory that provides for transition from capitalism to socialism through transfer of power to the proletariat class. The transfer of power takes place through revolutionary means.[86] The proponents of Communism argue that the proletariats will emerge as a natural outcome of the class conflict between the 'haves' and 'have nots' within the capitalist society, in the way the capitalists supplanted the feudal class. Communists claim to realize the salvation of humanity through achieving a classless society based upon collective ownership of the means of production through a class-based revolutionary struggle.[87] However, in practical terms, the process of communism could not bring a classless society as the monopoly over sovereign authority passed on to the proletariats, empowering them to embark upon what Joad terms as 'expropriation of the exploiters'.[88] It proved counterproductive to the very *raison d'être* of the transition – from capitalism to Communism – as it, too, failed to eliminate the forces of class-based exploitation. It only resulted in a swap of actors of exploitation. Previous victims became the perpetrators of exploitation.

Both failed to create social cohesion as the society remained class-ridden. The exploitation in either case is linked with the problem of sovereign authority. Sovereign authority has been a resource for its bearer to exploit the one who does not bear the crown of sovereignty. The democratic framework does not provide any safeguard against the exploitation of political minority at the hands of political majority. On the other hand, though the socialists claim to have collective control of the means of production, in practical terms, the sovereign authority is exercised by the communist leadership, which creates a potential threat to those not subscribing to the communist ideology. Against both of these ideologies, Islam claims to ensure human salvation by refuting the human qualification to the sovereign authority. It seeks to ensure human salvation by bringing sovereignty into the metaphysical domain in terms of an attribute exclusive to God. This metaphysical attribution of sovereignty provides a solution to the extreme positions taken by democratic liberalism and Communism and helps create a sublime sort of balance between collectivism and individualism, though with a marginalized tilt towards collectivism. Islam sanctifies the fundamental rights of an individual but, at the same time, the inclination towards collectivism is reflected through the character of its rituals, its social-welfare-oriented economic program and, above all, through jihad, which is to be undertaken for the common good of the community.

The allocation of sovereignty to the transcendent metaphysical phenomenon broadens the ambit of the social order, transcending all territorial boundaries and aiming to create a global ideological brotherhood. It overshadows the elusive notion of national interest, which is central to modern secular statehood. Nevertheless, within the framework of Islam, the Islamists and the apologists differ upon the nature of the social order that Islam aims to establish.

Islamists like Sayyed Maududi and Sayyed Qutb, in response to western imperialism that had been striking at the very roots of Muslims' body politic in the last quarter of the 19th century, yearned to see Islam through the ideological lenses.[89] They took Islam as an ideology that aims to restructure the global social order according to its own principles through its committed volunteers.[90] Though both of them seek to revitalize the intellectual and moral spirit of the community to transform the social order, Sayyed Maududi opted for intellectual means like educational uplift through a countrywide network of schools whereas Sayyed Qutb preferred to bring about this transformation through armed struggle by a 'vanguard' of committed volunteers if required.[91] Both of them were exclusionists in terms of rejecting socio-political orders other than Islam. They asserted that these systems, being exploitative in spirit, must be replaced by the Islamic order to ensure human salvation.[92] They further argued that establishment of a universal state based upon divine sovereignty was the ultimate goal of Islam.[93] This goal would be achieved through jihad, which is an instrument of social transformation. This social transformation would secure the sanctity of human life on the pattern of the Prophet. The Prophet secured it through jihad against the forces of *jāhilliyah*, which had no reverence for human life.

The apologists' narrative of the social order is inclusionary vis-à-vis democratic social order. It aims to discover common ground between the western and Islamic social orders to bring about reconciliation between the two. In the Indian context, Sir Sayyed's attempts to bring social transformation in Indian society were aimed to bridge the social gap between the British and the local population.[94] He attempted to convince Muslims that there was no harm in following the eating patterns of the British.[95] One of his articles *Tarīqāh-i-Zindagī* (The Way of Life) serves as a window into his recommended life pattern for the Muslims.[96] In order to close the gap between the Christian British government and their Muslim subjects in India, Sir Sayyed wrote bilingual commentary on the Bible, *Tabyin-ul-Kalām,* wherein he attempted to discover common ground between Christianity and Islam.

This social transformation is secured through removing the religious barriers in the temporal sphere. The debate regarding the scope of religion has created sharp cleavages between the Islamists and the apologists. The former view life as a compact whole, indivisible in spiritual and temporal spheres, whereas the latter tend to limit the scope of religion in the temporal sphere of life. The apologists support the bifurcation of life into spiritual and temporal spheres, by taking religion as the antithesis to modernity,[97] whereas the fundamentalists subscribe to a restructured description of modernity that is based upon the linkage of the future with the past. They take religion to be a culture-producing force that disciplines every aspect of the believers' lives.[98]

Religious orders

The modernity thesis provides a paradigm to examine the approaches of the Islamists and the apologists. The apologists believe in an exclusionary relationship between religion and modernity whereas the Islamists subscribe to reconstructed definitions of modernity and approach religious dynamism not in terms of negation but in the context of a pluralistic redefinition of the term. The diversity of approaches between the Islamists and the apologists may be viewed in the context of two interrelated philosophical paradigms. These include 'status of human reason vis-à-vis revelation in the realm of knowledge' and 'inter-relationship between religion and politics'. The apologists like Abduhu and Rashid Rida exhausted their energies trying to reconcile Islam with the western intellectual and technological advancement as the symbol of western modernity. The Islamists like Qutb redefined their own parameters of modernity, which view the future strongly linked with the past.

Domain of knowledge

The channelling of divine knowledge to the prophets is called *Wahī* (revelation). It is part of the Muslims' belief system to acknowledge the authenticity of this channel of divine knowledge. However, Muslim theorists differ on the question whether revelation is the only channel to access the realm of ultimate knowledge. Can ultimate knowledge of universe be secured through rationalist interpretation of phenomena? The Islamists look solely towards revelation as a source of knowledge whereas the apologists identify rationalism as an important source of knowledge. The approaches to identify the source of knowledge determine the worldview of their followers through their respective education systems. Muhammad Abduhu and Sir Sayyed Ahmed Khan identified intellectual stagnation and internal strife in the body politic as the core causes of degeneration of the Muslim societies. To start with, both of them attempted to dispel the impression that western material advancement was alien to Islam.[99] They initiated the tradition of rationalist interpretation of divine scripture in their respective societies in the 19th century. Abduhu started this tradition through the pages of a newspaper *Urwāt-ul-Wuthqā* (the Strongest Bond).[100] It was originally brought out by Jamaul-ud-Din Afghani[101], his mentor in his mission of reformation of Muslim society.[102] In his endeavours to establish a harmonious relationship between the scientific knowledge and religious dogma, he emphasized the significance of human reason as a source of knowledge to explore the 'ultimate truths' of life. He further stressed to Muslims that the secret of civilization's progress lies in making scientific advancement through recognizing reason as an important source of human knowledge besides revelation.[103] Reason being an attribute exclusive to human beings elevates them to 'nobility' by helping them to discover, to quote M. H. Kerr, 'the principles of social morality' through discerning right from wrong.[104] Revelation being source of divine guidance addresses human queries in the domain of metaphysics. This domain falls beyond the limits of reason. The reason has access only to the extent of material phenomena. As human reason depends upon empirical knowledge to explore the vast horizons of knowledge, metaphysical phenomena, which cannot be grasped through empiricism, fall beyond its scope. In view of this, metaphysics becomes the exclusive sphere of faith to be explored through revelation.[105] Furthermore, revelation and reason both are creatures of one Creator; therefore, any inherent incompatibility between the two is unnatural. However, if any contradiction between the two surfaces, it may either be resolved through rational process or be referred to God on the presumption of human inability to discover the grounds of compatibility between the two.[106] Therefore, as Roxanne Euben remarks, 'the pursuit of unknowable is not only fruitless but transgressive of the precepts of faith as well'.[107] In other words, reason should be cautiously exercised in the spheres of religion to ensure the promotion of faith rather than its degeneration.[108] Similarly, in India, through his education reforms Sir Sayyed urged Muslims to follow the rationalist western civilization. He categorically repudiated the metaphysical phenomena that fall beyond human reasoning and could not be grasped through empirical knowledge.[109] His attempts at rational interpretation of religious miracles earned him hostility from the traditional ulema for whom the divine scripture instead of rationalism was a definitive proof of these miracles.

Leo Tolstoy's *Confession* is an important work to determine the scope of human reason to explore the ultimate truths of life. The author highlights the inadequacy of rational knowledge in revealing the meaning of life. Death is the ultimate truth, which exposes the emptiness of life itself. Rational knowledge explores the meanings of life through the experimental sciences and speculative philosophy. The experimental sciences seek to determine the causal sequence of material phenomena. They are concerned with positive knowledge and become irrelevant when the subject of inquiry is the ultimate cause. On the other hand, speculative philosophy addresses the questions relating only to the ultimate cause. Both streams of rational knowledge aim to bring perfectibility and progress in the world. However, perfectibility, progress or development become irrelevant in the realm of infinity. The philosophical insights into the meanings of life confront the same degree of rational inability. One gets closer to truth only to the extent that one moves away from life. If truth is not part of life, then life being reflection of untruth becomes an evil, and refuge from this evil as Schopenhauer suggests could be found only in nothingness. This nothingness, in the expression of Old Testament, is called 'vanity'. It renders everything in the world meaningless while death is the truth which proves that everything else is but a lie.[110] The failure of rational knowledge leads humanity towards escapism instead of confronting the questions regarding the meaning of life. This escapism has various possible manifestations. An individual may seek refuge in his ignorance of the emptiness of life. If he is aware of the meaningfulness of life, he may throw himself into the epicurean way of life to avoid confronting the bitter truths of life like old age, miseries, sufferings and eventually death. If he is convinced of the evil character of life as devoid of any meaning, he may commit suicide. If he does not commit suicide, despite being convinced of the 'necessity of suicide' on rational grounds, he keeps on living a meaningless life. Rational knowledge appears at a loss to comprehend the meaning of life.[111] If reason is the most transcendent way to uncover the truths of life, then reason will become the prerequisite of life. On the other side, if the rationale of life is beyond the grasp of reason, then reason is dependent on life. If there is no life, there would have been no reason. Life precedes reason in terms of causal sequence simply because reason is the product of life. Reason is an ungrateful creature which denies its very creator, life. Rational knowledge brings its bearers to a point where death appears more virtuous than life, whereas ignorance inspires its clients to live as if they have found the meaning of life. This inspiration of life emanates from irrational knowledge or faith. Faith ascribes meaning to life through linking the finite with infinite, which the rational knowledge could not. Through offering infinite meanings to the finite being, faith transforms life into a phenomenon which cannot be destroyed through miseries, sufferings and even death.

The Islamists like Sayyed Qutb (1906–66) redefined the contemporary Islamic ideology by challenging the apologists' view that human reason enjoys equal standing vis-à-vis divine revelation as a source of knowledge. Though Qutb recognizes human reason as a source of knowledge in the realm of physical and natural sciences, he was convinced of its inability to access the metaphysical spheres of the universe, which is the exclusive domain of revelation. This inability relegates human reason to a position subordinate to revelation.[112] It is empirical knowledge which determines the scope of rationalism. Empiricism can access only the phenomena, material and tangible, which may be experienced through human senses; any phenomena which are not tangible and material do not fall within the ambit of empirical rationalism. Conversely speaking, if rationalism is accepted as the source of knowledge, complete in itself, we will have to accept the negation of all intangible and metaphysical phenomena of the universe. It is in this context that Qutb argues that human reason unaided by divine guidance loses its direction and invites the forces of *jāhilliyah* to challenge divine authority – the highest metaphysical phenomenon. Consequently, rationalism, by repudiating all metaphysical truths which constitute the basis of human morality, exposes human nature to 'moral sickness'.[113] He further argues that as it is only Islam which addresses both the material and metaphysical aspects of the universe, it is in absolute harmony with human nature. As Islam stands for the salvation of mankind, the believers should make efforts to confront human misguidance created by this *jāhilliyah* order.[114] Similarly, Sayyed Maududi exposed the fallacy of western rationalism and argued that religious edicts could not be compromised on the grounds of rationalism.[115]

Scope of religion

As discussed earlier, the apologists in their attempts to limit the role of the religion to the spiritual sphere get confused, whereas the Islamists believe in the all-encompassing domain of the faith that does not bifurcate life into spiritual and temporal spheres. Abduhu's views reflect marked inconsistencies on the question of the linkage between politics and religion. On the one hand, he appears to be convinced of the inherent relationship between Islam and politics and, on the other, he switches over to be the champion of secularism. He recognizes the Quranic laws as the constitutive force behind the social order but at the same time he hesitates to grant a legislative role to the scripture.[116] It is, perhaps, due to this inconsistency in approach that he is placed in the ranks of the secularists.[117] On the other hand, Abduhu regards religion and politics as body and soul.[118] In 1886, in a letter to Sheikh-ul-Islam in Constantinople, he argued that fidelity to the Ottoman caliphate constituted the third pillar of the faith.[119] He denied the claim that Christianity affirms secularism by pointing out that Christian theology places ordinary things under subordination to the clergy.[120] He further argued that western claim of championing the cause of secularism did not answer the counter argument that, if the Queen of England and political leadership of France could claim to be the custodians of their respective churches, then why could the Ottoman Caliph not claim to be the spiritual head of the Muslims.[121] Moreover, for Abduhu, human beings are responsible for the creation of the Islamic civilization in the capacity of vicegerents of God on earth.[122] He does not relegate religion to a subordinate position to reason, and he acknowledges the divine role in every sphere of human life.[123] In view of the foregoing, we find ourselves in agreement with M. H. Kerr when he argues that Abduhu 'hedged his espousal of secular notions and avoided a clear-cut rejection of orthodox conceptions with ambiguous results'.[124]

Being against Abduhu, Sayyed Qutb, like Sayyed Maududi, representing the Islamists' perspective, followed the traditional view of Muslim theologians who affirm the relationship between religion and politics. He regarded sovereignty to be an exclusive privilege of God, which is expressed through divine communication to the Prophet. The laws revealed through this communication are so comprehensive and all-encompassing that they do not leave any sphere of human life unaddressed. As the modern world approaches the phenomenon of the universe through empirical rationalism, it denies divine sovereignty because it cannot be grasped through empirical experience. It recognizes popular sovereignty, which amounts to usurpation of the sovereignty of God. The restoration of sovereignty to its real Owner is the basis of his theory of revolution against the modern secular world.[125] Likewise, Sayyed Maududi's anti-secular approach is explicit from his idea of the theo-democratic state that provides that under divine sovereignty people will exercise limited popular sovereignty not as the repository of power but as viceroys of God on earth.[126] Some critics argue that, as in Maududi's theo-democratic state, authority to interpret the political ideology of Islam vests with the clergy; therefore, this theo-democracy would turn into 'modern theocracy'.[127] This criticism does not hold ground for long. The Constitution of Pakistan was promulgated in 1973 through consensus by all political parties, including Jama'at-e-Islami under the leadership of Sayyed Maududi himself. This constitution recognizes the sovereignty of God but does not provide for theocracy in Pakistan.

Apart from what has been said above, the scope of faith has always been the core area of differences between the Islamists and the apologists. It is in this area that both sides have developed their arguments and counter arguments. The apologists do not consider it imperative to revive the caliphate on the pattern of pious caliphs (*khilāfat-e-rāshidā*) in modern times. The Islamists make it obligatory upon every Muslim to make efforts to create a 'nucleus for Muslims' in the form of the caliphate.[128] Moreover, the apologists argue that, though Islam was able to mitigate the differences between the politically fragmented Arabs,[129] these differences did not vanish completely. They further argue that Arabs united under the Prophet not in the political but in the religious sphere. They also argue that the Prophet never interfered in the mechanics of governance of the society.[130] The Islamists explore historical evidence contrary to this argument. They argue that the Prophet was not just a spiritual leader; rather, he was the ultimate leader in all aspects of the believers' lives. His unqualified submission is the prerequisite to enter into the fold of Islam.[131] He exhibited in his life pattern a practical model for a true believer.[132] In his personal conduct, he set examples for the believers as a trader, commander of armies and person in charge of foreign affairs of the state. Prophethood was not limited to the spiritual sphere of life alone; rather, the Prophet controlled the forces of history through establishing an ideal Islamic state in Madina.[133] The Islamists further argue that Islam literally means submission to the will of God, and as the will of God is all-encompassing, life is taken as a compact whole. In the terminology of the Quran, human beings are viceroys of God on this earth (Al-Baqarah: 30) and they have been entrusted to translate the will of God into practice. Moreover, the Quran urges the believers to enter into the fold of Islam completely, meaning that a believer is required to submit to the will of God in every sphere of his life (Al-Baqarah: 208). Furthermore, emphasizing the mutually inclusive relationship between politics and Islam, the Prophet declared the whole earth a mosque.

Having explained the competing strands of all three actors to the conflict, it becomes clear that each of them aspires to create a state system that corresponds to their vision. The apologists aim to evolve a state system which conforms to the western model of state governance. They draw support from the secular ruling elite to project their vision in Muslim societies. The ruling elite also draw upon the apologists and the West for support to perpetuate their rule. Against them, the Islamists aim to revive the state system on the pattern of the orthodox caliphate. They explore venues of support from the masses through highlighting religious authenticity of their narrative. As the vision of the apologists and the ruling elite stands in sharp confrontation with worldview of the Islamists, they are bound to engage in a hostile relationship. Since the contested narratives originate from an ideological space, the question is to define the character of both the faith and the state. All three parties adopt whatsoever means to achieve their ends. The rulers with the support of the apologists take repressive measures against those who do not share their vision. On the other hand, the Islamists accused them of collaboration with the West against the fellow believers. They also charge the apologists of committing heresies by following the democratic norms of the West.

Notes

1 Ronald Johnstone, *Religion and Society in Interaction: The Sociology of Religion* (Eaglewood Cliffs: Prentice-Hall Inc.,1975), 20; also see, Paul B. Horton and Chester L. Hunt, *Sociology* (Singapore: McGraw-Hill, 1984), 265; also see, Ian Robertson, *Sociology* (New York: Worth Publishers Inc, 1987), 398.
2 Robert N. Bellah, 'American Civil Religion in 1970s', in *American Civil Religion*, ed. R. E. Richev and D. G. Lones (New York: Harper & Row Publishers, 1974), 255–272.
3 Emile Durkheim, *The Elementary Forms of Religious Life*, trans. Carol Cosman, (Oxford: Oxford University Press, 2001); also see, Horton and Hunt, *Sociology*, 267.
4 Ibid., 266, 267.
5 Durkheim, *Elementary Forms of Religious Life*.
6 Husain Haqqani. 'The Ideologies of South Asian Jihadi Groups', in *Current Trends in Islamist Ideology*, vol.1, eds. Hillel Fradkin et. al., (Washington, D.C.: Hudson Institute, 2005), 12–26. For details see, S. M. Ikram, *History of Muslim Civilizations in India and Pakistan* (Lahore: Institute of Islamic Culture, 1989), 269–286.
7 P. Corcoran, 'The Limits of Democratic Theory', in *Democratic Theory and Practice*, ed. G. Duncan (Cambridge: Cambridge University Press, 1983).
8 Robert A. Dahl, *Democracy and Its Critics* (New Haven and London: Yale University Press, 1989), 43–45.
9 Ibid., 37–42.
10 Ibid.
11 Ibid.
12 John Stuart Mill, *Considerations on Representative Government*, ed. C. V. Shields (Indianapolis: Bobbs-Merril, [1861] 1958), 93.
13 John Locke, *Two Treatises of Government*, 2nd ed. (Cambridge: Cambridge University Press, [1689–90] 1970), 322.
14 Jean-Jacques Rousseau, *On the Social Contract with Geneva Manuscript and Political Economy*, ed. Roger D. Masters and Judith R. Masters (New York: St. Martin's Press, [1762] (1978), 53.
15 Ibid., 110.
16 Stanley I. Benn, 'Egalitarianism and Equal Consideration of Interests', in *Equality*, eds. R. Pennock and J.W. Chapman (New York: Atherton Press, 1967), 61–78.

17 Dahl, *Democracy and Its Critics*, 112.
18 Ibid., 90.
19 Trevor Jones, Tim Newburn and David J. Smith, *Democracy and Policing* (London: Policy Studies Institute, 1994), 41.
20 J. A. Schumpeter, *Capitalism, Socialism and Democracy* (London: Allen and Unwin, 1961), 269.
21 John S. Dryzek and Patrick Dunleavy, *Theories of Democratic State* (Hampshire: Plagrave Macmillan, 2009).
22 For Ruhullah Khomeini's views on the subject, see, Shahrough Akhavi, 'Islam, Politics and Society in the Thought of Ayatullah Khomeini, Ayatullah Taliqani and Ali Shariati', *Middle Eastern Studies* 24, no. 4 (1988): 404–431.
23 The Quran reads, 'And when thy Lord said unto the angels: Lo! I am about to place a viceroy in the earth, they said: Wilt thou place therein one who will do harm therein and will shed blood, while we, we hymn Thy praise and sanctify Thee? He said: Surely I know that which ye know not' (Al- Baqarah: 30). For Abduhu, the responsibility of an individual in the capacity of 'viceroy of God on earth' is to present Islam in terms of 'culture-producing force'. See, Yvonne Haddad, 'Muhammad Abduh: Pioneer of Islamic Reform', in *Pioneers of Islamic Revival*, ed. Ali Rahnema (London: Zed Books Ltd, 1994), 46.
24 In the battle of Uhud (3AH.), the Prophet consulted his Companions regarding the place where to confront the enemy. The Companions' opinion was in favour of facing the enemy in open fields outside the city of Madina whereas the Prophet's personal opinion was to face the enemy while remaining within the city. Despite the difference of opinion, he acceded to the opinion of the Companions. For details see, Ibn Ishaq and Ibn Hasham, *Seerat An-Nabi* vol.2, trans. Sayyed Yasin Ali Hasni Nizami Dehlvi (Lahore: Idara Islamiyyat, 1991), 82, 83.
25 Abdul-Haqq Ansari, *Ibn Taymiyyah Expounds on Islam: Selected Writings of Ibn Taimmiyah on Islamic Faith, Life and Society* (Fatawa 28:386–7) (comp. and trans.) (Independently Published, 2000), 508–510. http://theauthenticbase.files.wordpress.com/2010/09/expounds-on-islam.pdf. accessed on August 13, 2013.
26 Malcolm H. Kerr, *Islamic Reform: The Political and Legal Theories of Muhammad Abduh and* Rashid Rida, (California: University of California Press, 1966), 134.
27 Francis Fukuyama, *The End of History and the Last Man* (New York: Free Press, 2006).
28 Richard Schifter, 'The Clash of Ideologies', *Mediterranean Quarterly* 15, no. 3 (2004): 12–23.
29 *Mehr* is the amount to be paid by the husband to the wife at the time of marriage. However, the payment may be delayed through agreement between both of them.
30 Ibn Taimmiyah and Muhammad Abduhu both appreciated the concept of *Shūrā* as an instrument to restrain arbitrary exercise of political authority by the rulers. For Abduhu's views, see Kerr, *Islamic Reform*, 133, 134; also see Haddad, *Muhammad Abduh*, 54. Though Rashid Rida being disciple of Abduhu was part of liberal scholarship, his approach seems to be confused regarding the powers of the caliph. On one hand like Abduhu, he argues in favour of granting constitutional status to the caliph whose powers are restrained by Quran, Sunnah and acts of the Companions of the Prophet, but on the other hand, he extends unlimited authority to the caliph by authorizing him to interpret the Shariah and enforce his model of Shariah. See Mahmoud Haddad, 'Arab Religious Nationalism in Colonial Era: Re-reading Rashid Rida's Ideas on the Caliphate', *Journal of American Oriental Society* 117, no. 2 (1997): 253–277.

31 Abi Ja'afar Muhammad Bin Jarir Al-Tabri, *Tarīkh al-Umam wal Mulūk*, Vol. 2, Part II (Karachi: Nafees Academy, 2004), 37, 38. The Prophet had dispatched this expedition under the command of Usama b. Zayd in his last days. When the sad news of the passing away of the Prophet reached Usama, he instantly returned to Madina.
32 Islamic Caliphate is not a utopia; rather, it is a concrete reality. See Nilufer Gole, 'Snapshots of Islamic Modernities', *Daedalus* 129, no. 1 (2000): 91–117.
33 Abu Dawood, *Sunan Abu Dawood, Kitāb al- jihad*, 2602.
34 Ansari, *Ibn Taymiyyah Expounds on Islam*, 502.
35 Ibid., 364, 504–508.
36 Imam Bukhari, *Sahih Bukhari, Jihad*, 2955, *Kitāb al-Ahkām*, 7144; Imam Muslim, *Sahih Muslim, Kitāb al-Imārah*, 4533, 4534. This tradition has also been quoted in other books of *ahādīth,* including Sunan Abu Dawood, Sunan Al-Tirmidhi, Sunan An-Nasai, Sunan Ibn Maja and Musnad Ahmed.
37 Imam Bukhari, *Sahih Bukhari, Kitāb al-Ahkām*, 7212.
38 Ibid. Manāqib Al-Ansar, 3792, 3793, 3794; Muslim, *Sahih Muslim*, 4524; also see Ansari, *Ibn Taymiyyah Expounds on Islam*, 510–514.
39 Imam Bukhari, *Sahih Bukhari, Kitāb al-fitan*, 7052, *Kitāb al-Jizyah*: 3163; Imam Muslim, *Sahih Muslim, Kitāb al-Zakah*: 2303. In another *hadith*, Ubadah b. Samit stated that they submitted to the Prophet that they would obey him in every condition, good or bad, even when they were not given their due. See Imam Bukhari, *Sahih Bukhari, Kitāb al-Ahkām*, 7199, 7200; Ansari, *Ibn Taymiyyah Expounds on Islam*, 510.
40 Muslim, *Sahih Muslim*, 4569–4575.
41 Ansari, *Ibn Taymiyyah Expounds on Islam*, 511.
42 Abul al'a Maududi, *Tafheem-ul-Quran* vol. 1 (New Delhi: Markazi Maktaba Islami Publishers, 1998); also see Charles, J. Smith, 'The Ideology of Mawlana Mawdudi', in *South Asian Politics and Religion*, ed. Donald E. Smith (Princeton: NJ, 1966), 371–397.
43 Abul al'a Maududi, *Let Us Be Muslims*, trans. Khurram Jan Murad (Leicester: Islamic Foundation, 1985).
44 Noor Muhammad, 'The Doctrine of Jihad: An Introduction', *Journal of Law and Religion* 3, no. 2 (1985): 381–397.
45 Ibid.
46 Kurzman argues that Islamic teachings are unbiased towards democratic liberalism and if there is any dichotomy between the two, it can be removed by developing mutual understandings through dialogue. See Charles Kurzman, 'Liberal Islam: Prospects and Challenges', *MERIA* 3, no. 3 (1999), 11–19.
47 Roxanne L. Euben, 'Premodern, Anti-modern or Post-modern? Islamic and Western Critique of Modernity', *The Review of Politics* 59, no. 3 (1997), 429–459.
48 'Islam wa'n-Nasraniyya', 65 quoted in, Kerr, *Islamic Reform*, 148, 149.
49 Charles D. Smith, *Islam and the Search for Social Order in Modern Egypt: A Biography of Muhammd Husayn Haykal* (Al-bany: University of New York Press, 1983), 21.
50 'Islam wa'n-Nasraniyya', 65 quoted in, Kerr, *Islamic Reforms*, 148, 149.
51 Haddad, 'Arab Religious Nationalism in Colonial Era', 253–277.
52 Abu Al-Hassan Al-Mawardi, *Ahkām al- Sultāniyyāh* (London: Ta-Ha Publishers); for *hadith* reference, Imam Bukhari, *Sahih Bukhari, Kitāb al-Imārah*, 4555–4557, accessed on April 29, 2021, https://www.kalamullah.com/Books/Al-Ahkam%20as-Sultaniyyah.pdf?__cf_chl_jschl_tk__=7cb21bee01d5d6f33cf8e4d3199111c4ec32a7cd-1619726675-0-AWtQRUDpPMuW9-stgM8H5CF-6eEJ5xk1eUBES8loaUGmHkv2_WvQ7AknW9_U1RPgsat70GribWa73B8GctB-9GUTUyZIZXiQ-tyw0qbF6ilFp1250Rski9mjK

8ZLIpn5S_tbFuESqfMuySu7ilJUJnF-DpkaO2IDcuBSBoMkuuZmGphZnZpm3p6HRG2qHYLFTs-od54l9kGBbZx1UuPyKG2gXPT3-ObttQIaIddR8efMrWmpaKvr-DshIPlKhgm1rlmZUfWnSUJC78X7vs9Y4CA2Y1T3XYKeCm0r09kDZjmnIrcx3rfLaMlzMZGSytU_Beyd-EyVEPYdwF3JByKd7C0itl5fg9v_wG8u0YOxa9BX2IVsOz1iTidmLrtQyitp9TS-jRdGRA3QwF1kqH4mI0uLyIcipr-E370jJW3Ua1U-SvoA3QO1C_nf_ORKONJxag

53 Haddad, 'Arab Religious Nationalism in Colonial Era', 253–277.

54 Abdel Wahab El-Affendi, 'What Is Liberal Islam? The Elusive Reformation', *Journal of Democracy* 14, no. 2 (2003): 34–39.

55 For detailed analysis of the principles of state governance as laid down by Islam, see Abul a'la Maududi, 'The Political Theory of Islam', in *Contemporary Debates in Islam: An Anthology of Modernist and Fundamentalist Thought*, eds. Mansoor Moaddel and Kamran Talattof (New York: St. Martin Press, 2006), 270, 271.

56 Fukuyama, *The End of History*, 40–50.

57 Ibid. 45,46; also see W. Dietl, Holy War 13–47 (1984) quoted in Muhammad, 'The Doctrine of Jihad', 381–397.

58 Abdel Salem Sidahmed and Anoushiravan Ehteshami, eds. *Islamic Fundamentalism* (Oxford: West View Press, 1996), 14.

59 For debates on Secularism, modernity and rationalism from western and Islamic perspectives, see Tamara Sonn, 'Modernity, Islam and the West', in *Muslims and the West: Encounter and Dialogue*, eds. Zafar Ishaq Ansari and John L. Esposito (Islamabad: Islamic Research Institute, 2002), 216–231.

60 Yvonne Yazbeck Haddad, 'Islamism: A Designer Ideology for Resistance', in *Muslims and the West: Encounter and Dialogue,* eds. Zafar Ishaq Ansari and John L. Esposito (Islamic Research Institute, 2002), 274–295.

61 Laith Kubba, 'What Is Liberal Islam? Faith and Democracy', *Journal of Democracy* 14, no. 2 (2003): 45–49.

62 Al-Muhajiroun, *Khilāfat: Aik Mukhtāsar Guide.*

63 P. Hirst, 'Representative Democracy and Its Limits', *The Political Quarterly* 59, no. 2 (1988): 190–205.

64 Fukuyama, *End of History*, 260; also see Schifter, 'The Clash of Ideologies', 12–23.

65 Radwan A. Masmoudi, 'What Is Liberal Islam? The Silenced Majority', *Journal of Democracy* 14, no. 2 (2003): 40–44.

66 S. W. R. de A. Samarasinghe, *Democracy and Democratization in Developing Countries* (Boston: Harvard School of Public Health, 1994); also see Stephen Brown, 'Foreign Aid and Democracy Promotion: Lessons from Africa', *The European Journal of Development Research* 17, no. 2 (2005): 179–198.

67 Sir Sayyed Ahmed Khan, *Jihad Ka Qurani Falsafa*, in *Mazāmeen-e-Sir Sayyed* (comp.) Muhammad Akram Chughtai (Lahore: Sang-e-Meel Publications, 2008), 113. For Sir Sayyed, Jihad is a tool of resistance to defend the faith against the non-believers. He permits to wage jihad to defend the territorial boundaries of a Muslim state. This defensive view of Jihad stands in direct conflict with the views of the majority of ulema who do not limit the scope of Jihad to the extent of defence of Muslim areas.

68 Syed Abu Al-Hassan Ali Nadvi, *Muslim Mamalak me Islamiyyat aur Maghrabiyyat ki Kashmakash* (Karachi: Majlis Nashriāt-e-Islam), 96.

69 Ibid., 95.

70 Ibid. 101–103.

71 Jihad in terms of *fard-e-kafāyā* connotes that it is a collective responsibility which if performed by a group of believers compensates all others, and if no one

performs it, the believers' community as a whole would be held responsible for this omission. However, in terms of *fard-e-* Ayn, it becomes an individual obligation like other elements of faith.

72 Imam Nasai, *Sunan An-Nasai, Kitāb al-jihad:* 3099.

73 Martin E. Marty and Scott R. Appleby, *Fundamentalism Observed* (Chicago: University of Chicago, 1991).

74 Haqqani, 'The Ideologies of South Asian Jihadi Groups', 12–26.

75 Abul a'la Maududi, *Kashmir: A Call to the Conscience of Humanity* (Lahore: Jamat-e-Islami Pakistan, 1966).

76 Ibid.

77 Unlike reformers, the revolutionaries believe that change in society can be brought only through uprooting the existing socio-economic order. For details, see Horton and Hunt, *Sociology*, 502–503.

78 Abul a'la Maududi, *Jihad fī Sabeel Allah* (trans.) Khurshid Ahmed (Birmingham: UK Islamic Mission Dawah Centre, 1995).

79 Hassan Al-Banna, *Jihad.*

80 Sidahmed and Ehteshami, *Islamic Fundamentalism*, 10; Sayyed Qutb, *Muālim fil tarīq* (New York: Globosz Publishing).

81 Ibrahim M. Abu- Rabi, *Intellectual Resurgence in the Modern Arab World* (Albanay: State University of New York Press, 1966), 129.

82 Qutb, *Muālim fil tarīq*. Sayyed Qutb discredited the defensive view of Jihad through raising a basic question from the course of Islamic history. Had the pious caliphs been satisfied that the Roman and the Persian empires were not going to attack the Arabian Peninsula, would they not have waged Jihad to spread the message of Islam?

83 Ibid.

84 Ibid; also see, Sayyed Qutb, 'Jihad in the Cause of Allah', in *Contemporary Debates in Islam: An Anthology of Modernist and Fundamentalist Thought* eds. Mansoor Moaddel and Kamran Talattof (New York: St. Martin Press, 2006), 225–226.

85 Bonney, *Jihad*, 215, 216.

86 C. E. M. Joad, *Introduction to Modern Political Theory* (London: Oxford University, 1964), 88.

87 Ibid., 90.

88 Ibid.

89 Smith, *Islam and the Search for Social Order*, 12; in recognition of Sayyed Maududi's efforts to revive the ideological spirit of Islam, the ideological version of Islam is taken in terms of brain-child of Sayyed Maududi; see, for instance, S. V. R. Nasr, 'Democracy and Islamic Revivalism', *Political Science Quarterly* 110, no. 2 (Summer, 1995): 261–285.

90 Abul a'la Maududi, *Jihad fī Sabeel Allah.*

91 Qutb, *Muālim.*

92 C. J. Adams, 'Mawdudi on the Necessity of Divine Government for the Elimination of Oppression and Injustice', in *Muslim Self-Statement in India and Pakistan, 1857–1968*, eds. A. Ahmed, and G. E. Grunebaum (Wiesbaden: 1970).

93 Abul a'la Maududi, 'Nationalism and India' (Pathankot, 1947), 10 quoted in ibid., 92; also see Qutb, *Muālim.*

94 Sayyed Ahmed Khan, 'Mazhab-o-Muāshrat', in *Mazāmeen-e-Sir Sayyed*, 154–157.

95 Sayyed Ahmed Khan, '*Tariqah-i- Tanawul-i- Ta'am*', (trans.) Kamran Talattof, in *Contemporary Debates in Islam: An Anthology of Modernist and Fundamentalist Thought*, eds. Mansoor Moaddel and Kamran Talattof (New York: St. Martin Press,2006), 187, 188.

96 Ibid.
97 Kubba, 'What Is Liberal Islam?' 45–49.
98 Dietal, 'Holy War', 13–47 quoted in Muhammad, 'The Doctrine of Jihad', 381–397.
99 The idea that Islamic and western societies are inherently different from each other is the product of the 18th century. See Albert Hourani, 'Islam and Philosophers of History', *Middle Eastern Studies* 3, no. 3 (1967), 206–268.
100 Sarfraz Khan, *Muslim Reformist Political Thought: Revivalists, Modernists and Free Will* (London: Routledge Curzon, 2003), 163.
101 Jamal-ud-Din Afghani (1838–1897) was an advocate of Pan-Islamism in the face of western imperialism.
102 Yvonne Haddad, 'Muhammad Abduh: Pioneer of Islamic Reform', in *Pioneers of Islamic Revival*, ed. Ali Rahnema (London: Zed Books Ltd, 1994), 32.
103 Roxanne L. Euben, 'Premodern, Anti-modern or Post-modern? Islamic and Western Critique of Modernity', *The Review of Politics* 59, no. 3 (1997): 429–459.
104 Kerr, *Islamic Reform*, 107.
105 Euben, 'Premodern, Anti-modern or Post-modern?', 429–459.
106 Ibid.
107 Ibid.
108 Ibid.
109 Nadvi, *Muslim Mumalik me Islamiyyat*, 95, 102.
110 Leo Tolstoy, *Confession*, trans. David Patterson (New York: W. W. Norton & Company, 1983), 35–48.
111 Ibid., 49, 50.
112 Qutb, *Muālim*.
113 Euben, 'Premodern, Anti-modern or Post-modern?' 429–459.
114 Sidhamed and Ehteshami, 'Islamic Fundamentalism', 10.
115 Abul al'a Maududi, 'Fallacy of Western Rationalism', in *Contemporary Debates in Islam: An Anthology of Modernist and Fundamentalist Thought*, eds. Mansoor Moaddel and Kamran Talattof (New York: St. Martin Press, 2006), 207–222.
116 Kerr, *Islamic Reform*, 143.
117 Moaddel and Talattof, (eds.) *Contemporary Debates in Islam*, 3.
118 Kerr, *Islamic Reform*, 150.
119 Ibid., 148.
120 Originally, Abduhu made this point in response to the argument of Farah Antun, the publisher of journal *Al-Jamia,* that an inclusive relationship between Islam and politics has been a catalyst in bringing decline to Islamic civilization. See Haddad, 'Muhammad Abduh: Pioneer of Islamic Reform', 52, 53.
121 Ibid., 55.
122 Ibid., 46.
123 Kerr, *Islamic Reform,* 150.
124 Ibid., 143.
125 Gilles Kepel, *Muslim Extremism in Egypt: The Prophet and Pharaoh* (Berkeley: University of California Press, 1986), 45.
126 B. P. Baura, *Eminent Thinkers in India and Pakistan* (New Delhi: Lancer Books, 1991), 95.
127 Ishtiaq Ahmed, *The Concept of an Islamic State: An Analysis of the Ideological Controversy in Pakistan* (London: Printer, 1987), 118.
128 Muhammad Abd al-Salam Faraj, *Al-Faridah al-Gha'iba*, http://www.juergensmeyer.com/files/Faraj_The_Neglected_Duty.pdf. (accessed September 1, 2013); also see Qutb, *Muālim*.

129 'And hold fast, all of you together, to the cable of Allah, and do not separate. And remember Allah's favour unto you: How ye were enemies and He made friendship between your hearts so that ye became as brothers by His grace; and (how) ye were upon the brink of an abyss of fire, and He did save you from it. Thus Allah maketh clear His revelations unto you, that haply ye may be guided' (Al-Imrān: 103).

130 Al-Raziq, "The Problem of Caliphate," in *Contemporary Debates in Islam: An Anthology of Modernist and Fundamentalist Thought* eds. Mansoor Moaddel and Kamran Talattof (New York: St. Martin Press, 2006), 95–110.

131 'Whoso obeyeth the messenger hath obeyed Allah, and whoso turneth away: We have not sent thee as a warder over them' (An-Nisā: 80).

132 'Verily in the messenger of Allah ye have a good example for him who looketh unto Allah and the Last Day, and remembereth Allah much' (Al-Ahzāb: 21).

133 Dr. Muhammad Iqbal, *Reconstruction of Religious Thought in Islam* (Lahore: Ilqa Publications, [1934]2019), 137–160.

2 Heresy of ideas

The manifestations of the conflict originating from competing ideological visions in Muslim society are horrific. The fundamentals of faith which have remained constant since the dawn of Islam have been challenged. Militants have introduced socio-political variables, seeking to redefine the limits of faith. Through this process they aim to secure a theological space to fight the Muslim rulers and their local supporters, whom they accuse of collaborating with the West. They have evolved the ideas of heresy, ultimately culminating in the emergence of *takfīr* (excommunication).

The Abrahamic religions provide for a point of complete submission to God, usually though not always via a theological path. The Arabs prior to the advent of Islam had no theological discourse to follow to render their submission to God. Nevertheless, they entered the fold of Islam. Theology emerged as an external process that would define the issues and provide for the methodologies to address them. Moreover, theology as an instrument of acquiring a belief depends upon a validation process for authenticity. However, as a finite being a theologian cannot reach the infinite and thus cannot draw conclusions about God who is infinite in nature (*al-Awwal, al-Ākhir*). Theology, therefore, is subservient to revelation as a source of divine knowledge. In other words, a belief (*aqīdah*) may not necessarily be derived from theology but it may have developed directly on the basis of knowledge received through revelation.[1]

Orthodoxy and heresy (*bida'ā*)

In literal sense, *bida'ā* (heresy) means innovations. It includes ideas or acts that are not originally part of the body of a religion as informed by primary religious scriptures and the early followers whose spirit of faith was ideal. In the classical perspective, heresy was not identified with apostasy, but a fine line always existed between formal and material forms of heresy: the former being the outcome of deliberate insistence on error and the latter being the product of unintended mistakes.[2] However, labelling any act in terms of *bida'ā* requires a great deal of intellectual ordeal. Whether a theological framework is a pre-requisite for this process is a question that requires further inquiry.

DOI: 10.4324/9781003164883-2

In Christianity a formal authority could determine some acts to be orthodox or heretical. Though the unity of believers was ordained by the primary teachings of the Christian faith, theological interventions fragmented this. The faith divided into religious denominations – Orthodox, Catholics and Protestants. Each of them claimed exclusive righteousness and labelled each other as heretics. Their mutual intolerance originated from historical presuppositions linked with socio-political constructs. It transformed religiously sanctioned love into animosity amongst the believers of the same faith.[3] Given the subordinate status of theology vis-à-vis revelation as a source of knowledge, it was hampered in its attempts to prescribe orthodoxy in Islam. There was no such formal authority, except a few schools of Muslim jurisprudence which had their respective positions on different questions.[4]

However, some argue that an informal authority did exist in the Islamic context that could determine the veracity of some acts. This informal authority would be informed by the collective opinion of some schools of thought within the Muslim clergy.[5] However, biases associated with this informal authority could not help but inform interpretations of different acts. I am not suggesting that a formal authority to determine orthodoxy can close the doors on heresy. Formally authorizing someone to categorize different acts as orthodox or heretical will limit the scope for diverse interpretations because difference with such formal authority's opinion will attract the label of heresy by default.

Apostasy (*irti'dād*), excommunication (*takfīr*) and revolt (*khurūj*)

Apostasy may be defined in terms as a Muslim reverting to unbelief. It has been defined by the Quran in the following words: 'And whoso opposeth the messenger after the guidance (of Allah) hath been manifested unto him, and followeth other than the believer's way, We appoint for him that unto which he himself hath turned, and expose him unto hell – a hapless journey's end' (An-Nisā: 115). Nevertheless, what constitutes apostasy and what it implies needs detailed analysis.

Takfīr labels someone a non-believer who is otherwise a believer, for committing an act or holding a belief. It has strong implications both for the person upon whom it is exercised and the one who exercises it. If exercised justifiably it renders the person whom it is exercised liable to the punishment specified for an apostate. Its unjustified exercise places the one who exercises it outside the pale of Islam. Abdullah Ibn Umar narrated that the Prophet said, 'If a man declares his brother to be a non-believer, it will apply to one of them'.[6]

Khurūj means to rise in revolt against rulers who have foregone the right to command the obedience of the believers.

Perspectives on *khurūj*, *irti'dād* and *takfīr*

These principles can be approached from classical, modernist and militant perspectives. In the classical domain, Ibn Taimmiyah and Ibn Kathir have been chosen to explore the genesis of these principles. First, because their theological authenticity and their intellectual contribution to theological knowledge in the period of medieval Islam is undisputedly acknowledged. Islamic legal structure owes much of its evolution to Ibn Taimmiyah, a 13th-century Hanbalite theologian who challenged the finality of all four schools of Sunnite Muslim jurisprudence and claimed the authority of interpreting the Islamic law (mujtahid) for himself. He revolted against the idea of blindly following (*taqleed*) the recognized schools of jurisprudence. The degenerate conditions of the Muslims at the end of the Abbasid caliphate gave legitimacy to his ideas. His opposition to *taqleed* left a permanent impression on subsequent Muslim scholarship and opened the doors of dynamism for Muslim thought through *ijtihād*. Similarly, Ibn Kathir, a historian and commentator on the Quran, is credited with tracing the origins of the sects in Islamic history and determining their religious standing.[7] Secondly, the militants refer to these theorists to give theological legitimacy to their acts of violence.[8] They frequently refer to Ibn Taimmiyah's decree that permitted revolt (*khurūj*) against the Mongol rulers to justify their *khurūj* against contemporary Muslim rulers.

To explore the modernist perspective, Muhammad Ibn Abdul Wahab (1703–1792), Sayyed Qutb and Sayyed Maududi have been preferred owing to their influential contributions to Muslim thought during their respective timeframes and contexts.[9] Their contributions have been acknowledged across the spectrum and are still relevant. Subsequent generations of Islamists still draw inspiration from them. Ibn Abdul Wahab was the intellectual spirit behind the revolution in Arabia during the 18th century that brought the house of Saud to power. He sought to eliminate the signs of pre-Islamic *jāhilliyah* (ignorance) from the contemporary Arab society. He identified *taqleed* (blind following) as the root cause of degeneration of the Arabian society. His efforts culminated in a political revolution that awarded political authority to the house of Saud, and his so-called Wahabi ideology came to dominate the religious sphere.[10] He is a thread linking the classical and the modernist perspectives on the fundamentalist version of Islam.

Likewise, Sayyed Qutb, being the pioneer of *takfīr* in the 20th century, has a central place in the fundamentalist fraternity.[11] Through juxtaposing Ibn Taimmiyah's allowance for *khurūj* against invalid Muslim rulers and Ibn Abdul Wahab's *jāhilliyah* thesis, he potently provided new direction to Islamist ideology. He retained the option of military jihad against the Muslim rulers for siding with the forces of *jāhilliyah*, which are bent upon obliterating Islamic ideology and Muslim identity.

As for Sayyed Maududi, his influence is reflected in Muslim resistance movements across the globe. Though he did not subscribe to the option of military jihad, the Ikhwan leadership in Egypt (including Hassan Al-Banna and Sayyed Qutb) shared his ideology in seeking to uproot what they claim are 'invalid Muslim rulers'. Instead of opting for military jihad, Sayyed Maududi preferred to join the political process in Pakistan to bring about change in the system.[12]

The militant perspective has been examined through inquiring into the worldview of Al-Qaida's ideologues. The militants use violence against those accused of undermining the purity of faith by introducing *bida'ā*. These ideologues include Azzam, Bin Laden, Al-Zawahiri, Al-Maqdisi and Al-Zarqawi. Azzam was the first to use the term *Al-Qaida al-Sulbah,* denoting a precept or a base for a vanguard of the committed volunteers to continue their jihad even after the withdrawal of Soviets from Afghanistan. He focused chiefly on jihad against the external enemy, whereas Bin Laden, Al-Zawahiri and Al-Zarqawi unleashed violence within Muslim societies to purge them of elements of apostasy. Currently, the militant diaspora follows the same ideology to spread their violence in the Muslim world.

Revolt against rulers (*khurūj*)

Classical perspective

Like a star in the galaxy or a drop in the ocean, every believer is part of *jama'at*, a religiously sanctioned community of believers. In order to protect the integrity of *jama'at*, Ibn Kathir emphasized the importance attached to obedience to rulers. Following the way of the *salaf*, he opposed the Kharijites for their *khurūj* against Ali. He strongly disapproved of their sheer disregard for the sanctity of human life. He did not permit *khurūj* against the rulers even if they were imperfect and did not fulfil the criteria of an ideal Muslim ruler. In the same vein, Ibn Taimmiyah quoted many prophetic traditions that subordinate individual interests to the collective interests of the believers' community. For him, a believer was religiously obliged to render obedience to the rulers even in case of individual injustice on the part of the rulers. He declared that obedience to those in authority was equal in importance to the elements of faith. Given the paramount importance associated with obedience to *ulil amr* (those in authority), he argued that even an invalid ruler has the right to command obedience from the believers provided he does not forego any basic principle of the faith. In precise terms, the believers are not permitted to commit *khurūj* against the rulers, even if they are less legitimate. Ibn Taimmiyah and Ibn Kathir, even though reluctantly, accepted the transition of caliphate into monarchy. Revolt is sanctioned if rulers forego the basic elements of faith.

Modernist perspective

Ibn Abdul Wahab was the ideological spirit behind the Saudi revolution, which extended political and religious authority to Muhammad b. Saud and

Ibn Abdul Wahab, respectively.[13] Initially, this power-sharing arrangement between Ibn Abdul Wahab and the house of Saud related to the state of Diriyah, where Muhammad bin Saud already had some political influence on a tribal basis. However, Ibn Abdul Wahab's puritanical beliefs paved the way for rapid expansion of Saud's political authority in conjunction with his own religious ideas. At the outset, he distanced himself from Ibn Taimmiyah's theory of right to rebel against the rulers not following shariah, but later on Wahabi activists drew on his philosophy to overthrow their rulers, labelling them as non-believers.[14] Ibn Taimmiyah restricted the right to rebel to rulers who violate the fundamental principles of Islam whereas Ibn Abdul Wahab expanded the scope of *khurūj* beyond the rulers, including different segments of society in its ambit. He placed Muslims practising Islam in any way different from his brand of the faith in a distinct category, declining to acknowledge them as Muslims in the first place, and identifying them as followers of pre-Islamic *jāhilliyah* against whom jihad was waged.

After Ibn Abdul Wahab, Ibn Taimmiyah's narrative of jihad against the Muslim rulers got intellectual backing from a new generation of Islamists. Sayyed Abul Hassan Ali Nadvi and Sayyed Maududi in India and Sayyed Qutb in Egypt subscribed the *jāhilliyah* thesis. Sayyed Maududi argued that Muslims were still living in the state of *jāhilliyah.*[15] In the Egyptian context, Sayyed Qutb shared this view, labelling the western civilization as *jāhilliyah* and further drawing a parallel between the pre-Islamic *jāhilliyah* and the modern civilization. However, Sayyed Maududi preferred to participate in the political process to change the system instead of uprooting the existing political order through military jihad. He ruled out the option of armed struggle at least within the Muslim states on the basis of six major arguments:

First, in the case of an armed struggle, the anti-revolutionary forces may get control of the armed forces, and in this case an armed clash would have a catastrophic effect on the revolutionary movement.

Second, even if the revolutionary forces get hold of the state machinery, they would hardly be able to Islamize the society. The institutions of society would not be yet prepared for moral transformation that Islam demands, and if un-Islamic legacy continues to persist under the Islamic power structure, it may disillusion the masses from Islam itself.

Third, an armed revolution would open the doors to a series of revolutions and counter-revolutions and destabilize society.

Fourth, to undertake an armed revolutionary struggle one has to organize the movement in the style of secret organizations. As the type of work necessitates, those who operate such organizations turn out to be intolerant, and by the time such a struggle succeeds, they become even greater tyrants than the existing ones.

Fifth, these organizations resort to violence and other immoral means to achieve their ends, which Islam does not permit. It becomes virtually impossible for one to imagine that after assuming power they can run the state according to the principles of Islam.

Finally, revolution brought about by physical force requires perpetual use of force for its stability. As a result, one type of despotism is replaced by another.[16]

He sought to revitalize the intellectual and moral spirit of the community to transform the society according to the Islamic principles.

Sayyed Maududi's ideas on jihad found partial reflection in the approach of Sayyed Qutb. He despised modern civilization as what Maududi labelled as the state of *jāhilliyah*. On this premise, Qutb evolved his two-pronged theory of jihad. He localized the conflict at the centre of the Muslim society by developing the concept of 'near' and 'far' enemy. Ibn Abdul Wahab created space through relegating a segment of society to the times of pre-Islamic ignorance. Sayyed Qutb filled these spaces through prioritizing jihad against the Muslim rulers over jihad against western imperialism.[17] For him, jihad was a gradual process, which initially targets the elements of *jāhilliyah* through peaceful means. If peaceful means fail to achieve the objectives, an armed struggle is be launched to uproot the system of *jāhilliyah*.[18]

The impact of the surrounding political milieu might be a defining factor for their difference of approach to jihad. Maududi developed his ideas in the context of United India, where the Muslims constituted the largest minority in the world, whereas Sayyed Qutb assimilated the jihadist struggle in an otherwise Muslim country. Maududi focused his jihad largely on the external front against the imperialist challenges whereas Qutb, in addition to the external enemy, pronounced *takfīr* on what he termed the 'apostate rulers' in the Muslim world. He pronounced *takfīr* on these rulers by accusing them of following the western agenda and supporting the infidels against the fellow believers. His narrative of applying *takfīr* to the local Muslim rulers brought jihad to the home front and provided future direction to the evolution of militants' codes of war.

To summarize the modernist perspective, all three theorists adopted the *jāhilliyah* thesis in seeking to change the existing political orders in their respective contexts. Ibn Abdul Wahab and Qutb aimed to uproot the *jāhilliyah* order through use of force whereas Maududi preferred peaceful struggle. Ibn Abdul Wahab extended the scope of *khurūj* to the societal level against those not following his brand of Islam. Sayyed Qutb was a key figure who directed jihad against the Muslim rulers whom he termed as 'near enemies'.

Militant perspective

Sayyed Qutb's narrative on *khurūj* being deviant from the Sunnite standpoint could not find a way with the jihadi fraternity while Abdullah Azzam was their ideologue. He was a link in the chain of traditional Sunnite scholarship, which would not sanction *khurūj* against the Muslim rulers even if they do not meet high standards. Once Bin Laden and Al-Zawahiri became the chief ideologues of Al-Qaida, they relied on Sayyed Qutb to develop their codes of war. A radical shift in the theory of jihad became obvious when Al-Qaida brought the violence to the home front against the 'nearer enemy'.

To reiterate in brief terms, Al-Qaida's ideology of jihad aims to revive the caliphate. Its ideologues believe every system except caliphate to be heretical and thus deserves to be uprooted. They further believe that Muslim rulers' collaboration with the West gives legitimacy to *khurūj* (revolt) against them.[19] It is to be noted that for Al-Zawahiri, enforcement of Shariah by the rulers does not insulate them against *khurūj* as long as they continue to pursue the western agenda. The militants proclaim *takfīr* against the Saudi rulers simply on the charges of being part of the US scheme in the Middle East, commitment to the Crusaders as reflected through their putting the sanctuaries of Islam under their occupation and also for supporting communists against the believers in Southern Yemen.[20] Al-Qaida believes that supporting the infidels against the believers constitutes unbelief and makes the believers religiously obliged to commit *khurūj*.[21] Al-Zawahiri views the Arab spring in terms of *khurūj* against the rulers who had virtually joined the infidels' ranks.[22] In the same vein, Al-Maqdisi justifies *khurūj* against Muslim rulers who become tools of non-believers to exploit the Muslims' resources. Moreover, though Bin Laden believed in religious obligation of revolt against the 'nearer enemy', he directed Al-Qaida's field formations to target the 'distant enemy' in the first place. Al-Zawahiri, Al-Maqdisi and Al-Zarqawi believed in violence against the 'nearer enemy' was the priority. Though the militants claim to follow Ibn Taimmiyah's narrative of *khurūj*, they appear closer to Ibn Abdul Wahab because they do not limit *khurūj* against the Muslim rulers but extend it to the level of society.

Grounds to invoke *irti'dād* and *takfīr*

Whether the commission of *bida'ā* invokes *takfīr* is a crucial question which has been addressed by Muslim scholarship from classical times to the modernists. The issue has colossal implications for the collective identity of the believers. It developed a divide within the Hanfites when the followers of the Deoband school of thought started accusing Barelvis, a co-Hanfite sect, of contaminating the purity of faith through introducing innovations into its practice. In return, the Barelvi ulema condemn their accusers for being violent and label them as *takfīrī*.[23] In addition to intra-sect divisions, the question of introducing *bida'ā* into the faith has led to schisms between sects as well. *Ahl-e-hadith* sect, which claims to believe in the purity of faith, charges the Barelvis of polytheism (*shirk*) for introducing practices which had never been part of the original body of faith. The Barelvis charge them of undermining the benevolent spirit of faith through following an approach based upon *takfīr*. As the question of *bida'ā* provides a space for evolving *takfīr*, it can be exploited to unleash inter-sect violence in Muslim societies.

Classical perspective

The classical theorists including Ibn Taimmiyah, Ibn Kathir and Al-Ghazali decline to accept that every sort of heresy invokes *takfīr*.[24] It is refutation of the fundamentals of faith alone that leads to unbelief. This limited scope of *takfīr* is evident in Muslim history where certain sects like Jahamiyyah and Qaramitah were condemned as non-believers whereas sects like Khawarij and the Shiites were not. Despite fighting against the Khawarij, the companions of the Prophet showed restraint in pronouncing *takfīr* on them. Similarly, in the case of the Shiites, despite conspicuous differences with the Sunnites, classical Sunnite scholarship, in a large part, has avoided excommunicating them as a whole. Despite introducing radical innovations into the practice of faith, the Khawarij and the Shiites were not excommunicated. Jahamiyyah and Qaramitah were excommunicated simply for foregoing the fundamentals of the faith. Jahamiyyah questioned the attributes of Allah whereas the Qaramitah recognized the prophethood of Zoroaster and preferred to follow the Persian philosophers instead of Islam. Even in the case of refutation of the fundamental principles of faith, the mitigating criteria exempt those whose refutation flows from ignorance or mistake.[25]

Modernist perspective

The boundaries of faith were squeezed by modernists like Ibn Abdul Wahab, who developed their theology in juxtaposition with contemporary socio-political constructs. Theology now appeared to be serving politics and vice versa. To nurture his ideas, Ibn Abdul Wahab adopted a paradigm that contemporary Arabian society reflected the traits of pre-Islamic ignorance which needed to be purified from all the innovations that had become part of it. He stressed reversion to the *salaf* to rejuvenate the orthodox spirit of Islam. He had the understanding that this objective could only be achieved if politics and religion could work in a mutually supportive framework. While delineating different aspects of *jāhilliyah*, which had become part of the Arabian society, he developed his theory of *takfīr* and aimed to change the politico-religious dynamics of the Arabian society. He based his theory of *takfīr* on the following aspects of the Arabian society.

First, he argued that the contemporary Arabian society had lost the spirit of faith which was infused by the Prophet. The decline of religious spirit is reflected through involvement of the people in polytheism (*shirk*). Second, the Arabs reverting to pre-Islamic *jāhilliyah* had again started believing in intercession between themselves and Allah to secure divine closeness, which was strictly forbidden by Allah in these words, 'And those who take associates apart from Him, (say): "Surely pure religion is for Allah only." And those who choose protecting friends beside Him (say): "We worship them only that they may bring us near unto Allah." Lo! Allah will judge between them concerning that wherein they differ. Lo! Allah guideth not him who is a liar, an ingrate' (Az-Zumar: 3). For the elimination of the distinction between belief and unbelief, the polytheist Arabs became a legitimate target of military jihad. The Quran says, 'And fight them until persecution is no more, and religion is all for Allah. But if they cease, then lo! Allah is Seer of what they do' (Al-'Anfāl: 39). Third, sectarian fragmentation in the Arab society was also a reflection of *jāhilliyah,* which the Quran did not approve of (Ar-Rum: 32; As-Shūrā: 13; Al-Ana'am: 159; Al-Imrān: 103, 105). Fourth, in spite of categorical prophetic transmissions, they did not render obedience to those in authority. Fifth, like those in pre-Islamic *jāhilliyah,* they believed in blind following (*taqleed*), which is strongly disapproved by Islam (Az-Zukhruf: 23; Luqman: 21; As-Saba: 46). Sixth, they consider the opinion of the majority and of the powerful segments of society as proof of being right. Seventh, they followed blindly their wicked scholars, which was against the spirit of Islam (At-Tawbah: 34; Al-Maidah: 77). Eighth, they preferred speculation to revelation. Ninth, they resorted to magic, which was prohibited in Islam (Al-Baqarah: 101, 102). Tenth, they immersed themselves in materialism and perceived Allah's blessings in terms of material advancement (As-Saba: 35). Ibn Abdul Wahab based his ten nullifiers of faith on these aspects of the days of ignorance.[26]

These nullifiers include the following: (1) to commit *shirk*; (2) to believe that someone has the right to intercede with God; (3) to have doubts in the unbelief of the polytheists; (4) to have conviction that a source of guidance other than what the Prophet brought is more complete; (5) to hate something brought by the Prophet; (6) to make a mockery of some beliefs of the faith; (7) to get involved in magic spells; (8) to support the non-believers against the believers; (9) to believe that someone is exempted from following the Shariah of the Prophet and (10) neither to learn what constitutes the divine faith nor to make endeavours to implement it in one's life.[27] Ibn Abdul Wahab is a link in the chain of puritanical theologians starting from Ibn Taimmiyah.[28] Though the Wahabi movement of the 18th century owes a lot to Ibn Taimmiyah, Ibn Abdul Wahab was distinctive in extending *takfīr* to the societal level.[29] His *jāhilliyah* thesis allowed subsequent generations of Islamists, including Sayyed Qutb and Sayyed Maududi, to draw parallels between modern civilization and pre-Islamic *jāhilliyah.* Moreover, the militants' narrative of the 'nearer enemy' finds its origin in Ibn Abdul Wahab, who pronounced *takfīr* on those who support non-believers against the believers.

Ibn Abdul Wahab's *jāhilliyah* thesis remained relevant with Sayyed Qutb, who aimed to eliminate the modern form of polytheism through jihad. An Islamic society will be established on the ruins of modern exploitative civilization. The society thus established would be based upon recognition of divine sovereignty and would lead to liberation of mankind. He realized that deification of human legislation was a modern form of polytheism, which needed to be eradicated in the new society. In this society, authority of lawgiving would rest with God, as obedience to man-made laws was tantamount to worshipping the architects of those laws who represented the forces of modern *jāhilliyah*. The modern *jāhilliyah* was bent upon exploitation of mankind under the umbrella of either Capitalism or Socialism. It was but natural that when Muslims embarked upon revolt against these oppressive ideologies, which were backed by such a powerful material base, they would face stiff resistance. In the opinion of Qutb, jihad would not be taken as defensive but as a forceful tool to obliterate the oppressive political orders that represented modern *jāhilliyah*. This struggle aimed at the liberation of humanity would be undertaken by an organized and resourceful Islamic movement (vanguard) through a gradual process. The process will begin with an ideological struggle to expose the weaknesses of the system of *jāhilliyah* and will culminate in replacement of the *jāhilliyah* order with the Islamic system using physical force.[30] This approach translated into a practical struggle when *takfīr* was invoked against the so-called Muslim rulers of Egypt and violence was directed against them and their western imperialist masters.[31] He joined Ibn Abdul Wahab in rejection of Muslim theology that had developed over centuries, which would not approve of *khurūj* against the Muslim rulers, even if they were invalid.

Militant perspective

Proclamation of *takfīr* against the Muslim rulers and their Muslim supporters is the core of militant ideology. Bin Laden's initial stress to his fellow militants to fight the 'distant enemy' was merely to avoid distortion of the organization's image in the Muslim societies; otherwise, he sanctioned *takfīr* even against secular political parties in Muslim countries. He took democracy as *bida'ā* because it acknowledges popular sovereignty instead of divine sovereignty. He pronounced *takfīr* on those who follow the democratic process.[32] Similarly, Al-Zawahiri condemns the majority-worship under democracy and excommunicates the Muslims who follow a system which supports the West.[33] For Al-Maqdisi, too, participation in the democratic process, *mawālāt* (support) to the infidels[34] and rendering voluntary submission to non-believers are acts which attract *takfīr*.[35] Likewise, besides sharing the grounds of *takfīr* with the fellow militant ideologues, Al-Maqdisi's theory of *takfīr* reflects deviation from the classical narrative in the case of the Shiites. The classical theorists, despite their strong disapproval of the *bida'ā* committed by the Shiites, avoided proclaiming *takfīr* against them, at least in collective terms, whereas Al-Maqdisi's *takfīr* in their case is categorical. Al-Zarqawi follows the same line in this regard.[36]

It is evident that the militant narrative regarding the boundaries of faith has evolved. No evidence is available to suggest that Azzam pronounced *takfīr* to the Muslim rulers. It began with the transfer of ideological leadership of Al-Qaida to Al-Zawahiri. Being part of Egyptian traditions of jihad pioneered by Sayyed Qutb, he made *takfīr* a defining feature of the subsequent course of transnational militancy. However, Al-Qaida leadership that otherwise believes in *takfīr* is not unanimous on the question of primacy associated with the label. For instance, Al-Maqdisi, Al-Zawahiri and Al-Zarqawi are unanimous in fighting against the so-called elements of apostasy within the Muslims as a means to muster strength to resist the forces of unbelief whereas Bin Laden, moved by pragmatism, appears to have advised the fellow militants to focus on the distant enemy. Moreover, evidence is also available that the lower formations of Al-Qaida are in favour of observing restraint in violence within the Muslim societies.[37] Furthermore, Al-Qaida leadership and their offshoots like Al-Qaida in Arabian Peninsula (AQAP), Tehrīk-e-Taliban Pakistan (TTP) and Al-Qaida affiliates in the Far East and Africa redefine the boundaries of faith by broadening the scope of *takfīr* to those who support the non-believers against the believers, follow democratic ideals, the Shiites and, above all, those who follow western cultural traits. Last but not the least, though Al-Qaida theorists claim not to follow Khawarij in identifying commission of sin with apostasy, in practical terms they excommunicate those who commit sins like involvement in *ribā*-based banking and follow the cultural traits of the West.

In view of the foregoing, it is argued that theological marking of the boundaries of faith is not independent of the socio-political constructs. The evolution of theology is linked with the historical process. The definition of the boundaries of faith is far from objective. Historical presuppositions made concessions to extremism in theological discourse. In some cases, it resulted in dissipation of the distinction between theology and religion. Difference of opinion in the humanly driven theological domain has been taken as refutation of the injunctions of faith. Such theology left hardly any space for divergent views, even on the questions of secondary religious importance. Militants generally exploit this space to invoke *takfīr* against those who do not follow their brand of Islam. They accuse the people of committing heresies and subsequently excommunicate them for heretical ideas.

Notes

1 Sherman A. Jackson's introductory note to Abu Hamid Al-Ghazali, *Faysal al-Tafriqā Baynā al-Islam wa al-Zandaqā* (On the Boundaries of Theological Tolerance in Islam), trans. Sherman A. Jackson (Oxford: Oxford University Press, 2005), 3–32.

2 Ibid.

3 Tolstoy, *Confession*, 85–87.

4 W. M. Watt, *Islamic Philosophy and Theology* (Edinburgh: University Press, 1985), 19.

5 Jackson's introductory note to Al-Ghazali, *Faysal*, 3–32.

6 Imam Bukhari, *Sahih Bukhari, Kitāb Al-Adāb*, 6103, 6045; Imam Muslim, *Sahih Muslim, Kitāb Al-Eemān*, 116.

7 His luminous works include among others *Al-Bidāyah wal Nihāyah* (History of Ibn Kathir), *Tafsīr Ibn Kathir* (exegesis of the Quran) and *Ghazwāt-ur-Rasul* (Battles of the Prophet). Being an important addition to the knowledge base,

these works are justifiably considered authentic sources for research into Muslim history.

8 During 2003, Bin Laden quoted Ibn Taimmiyah more than once to legitimize their conflict with the West.

9 Militant Ideology Atlas suggests that by 2006, the Al-Qaida leadership had quoted Ibn Abdul Wahab nine times, Sayyed Qutb ten times and Sayyed Maududi four times. See William McCants and Jarret Brachman, *Militant Ideology Atlas: Executive Report 2006* (West Point, New York: Combating Terrorism Centre, 2006), 13–15.

10 His works include 'Ten Nullifiers of Islam', 'Aspects of the Days of Ignorance' and *Kitāb al-Tawhid* (Book of Tawhid). These works are relevant to our study because these highlight his views regarding the boundaries of faith.

11 His book *Muālim fil tarīq* (Milestones) highlights the dynamics of modern jihadi ideology. He also wrote commentary on the Quran titled *Fi Dhalal al-Quran* (In the Shadow of Quran).

12 His important works include among others *Khilāfat-o-Malūkiyyat,* (Caliphate and Hereditary Kingship), his commentary of Quran in Urdu language titled *Tafheem al-Quran* (Towards Understanding of Quran), *Islamic Law and Constitution* (Lahore: Islamic Publications, 1990) and *Islami Riyāsat* (Islamic State) (Lahore: Islamic Publications Ltd, 1988).

13 Though originally belonging to the Hanbalite School of Islamic scholasticism, he eschewed the *taqleed* (following) of major schools of Muslim jurisprudence and developed his own *salāfī* approach in theology. This shift in approach owes a lot to Muhammad Hayya Al-Sindi, one of the teachers of Ibn Abd al Wahab, whose profound influence resulted in his denunciation of the commentaries of the four Sunni Imams. See John Voll, "Muhammad Hayya Al-Sindi and Muhammad Ibn Abd al Wahab: An Analysis of an Intellectual Group in Eighteenth-Century Madina," *Bulletin of the School of Oriental and African Studies* 38, no. 1 (1975): 32–39.

14 Natana DeLong Bas, "Wahabi Islam: From Revival and Reform to Global jihad," (New York: 2004), 256 quoted in Richard Bonney, *Jihad*, 121.

15 Muhammad, "The Doctrine of Jihad," 381–397.

16 Interview with Abul a'la Maududi, *The Muslim*, February, 1967.

17 Rohan Gunaratna, "Al Qaeda's Ideology," in Fradkin et al., eds. *Current Trends in Islamist Ideology*, Vol. 1 (Washington D.C.: Hudson Institute, 2005), 56–67.

18 Qutb, *Muālim.*

19 Osama Bin Laden's second letter to the Muslims of Iraq, October 18, 2003, in *Al Qaida in Its Own Words*, trans. Pascale Ghazaleh, eds. Gilles Kepel and Jean-Pierre Milelli (Cambridge: The Belknap Press of Harvard University Press, 2009), 68; also see Osama Bin Laden, Interview by Hamid Mir, *Daily Pakistan*, March 18, 1997.

20 Osama Bin Laden, Interview by Peter Arnett and Peter Bergen, *CNN*, May 12, 1997; also see Osama Bin Laden, Interview by Robert Fisk, *The Independent*, July 10, 1996.

21 Anwar al-Awlaki, "The New Mardin Declaration: An Attempt at Justifying the New World Order," *Inspire* Fall, 2010.

22 Don Rassler, et al., *Letters from Abbottabad: Bin Laden Sidelined* No. SOCOM-2012-0000013 (Combating Terrorism Centre, May 03, 2012).

23 Ahmed Yar Khan Naeemi, *Ja'a-ul-Haq* (Lahore: Naeemi Kutb Khana, 2011), 7–13.

24 Ansari, *Ibn Taymiyyah Expounds on Islam*, 556; also see Sherman A. Jackson's introductory note to Al-Ghazali, *Faysal*, 3–32. He argues that labelling of *takfīr* depends upon the scope of criteria that determines orthodoxy.

25 Ansari, *Ibn Taymiyyah Expounds on Islam*, 565, 566.

26 Muhammad Ibn Abdul Wahab, *Masā'ail Al-Jāhilliyah*, trans. Isma'eel Alarcon (Al-Ibaana Publishers). Published Online July 2004. Available at https://abdurrahmanorg.files.wordpress.com/2014/08/aspects-of-days-of-ignorance-shaykh-bin-abdul-wahaab-al-ibaanah-com.pdf, accessed April 30, 2021

27 Muhammad Ibn Abdul Wahab, *Sharah Nawāqidh Al-Islam* (Al-Ibaana Book Publishing, 2003), Muhammad Ibn Abdul Wahab, Sharah Nawāqidh Al-Islam, accessed May 5, 2021, http://www.kalamullah.com/Books/Explanation%20of%20the%20Nullifiers%20of%20Islam.pdf?__cf_chl_jschl_tk__=81953142b49c8f7f05faf0f0647db1749e2a90bc-1620240683-0-AXSonj5LKXolAX952zEVM2tF-fjf4PoAhwZiOscvkQZt449b7NkLdg8lvQbBo78ecOTp3KA2goDBYKsbW4Knp-VxnGcrd2GmlIdA3dRABDDtOMdX1sDOj4IsS6MOKYNNYqGV1Uys9EdSy-AYEkcIjeHFWG8-Jtdn5vnWBF70Kd3fZmi03pOO9b0ledMqw27D-dxeQGwbA-rt7CVE8ZC6_vRdg8nE6zPdtPkwhdPqyehP3ewIxEdUHqoomXXi_w6t7bwKSL JICRQYRT3CbB310Ohj3T86Rq_tuxyQWZRMEJniGZM3PBevwjQ77bfvZ7qfS Qwr1d3MN3rIuKuPRISJX745zaqp-siU0EnsqxXagzE19A2Ysb1qwRAA2dYfk-u4NAWTA9FxB9TLRiHA-Ys3AU_sVmTqTWhdPfXib5bhSeZHjkpioR4fr0_k07ePhOuEhd4h062cOIfcET8dhk-k_f1U6cjPgxvND9m9Sx8AYpk_Gllpo.

28 Ibn Taimmiyah, *Letters from Prison*, (comp.) Shaykul Muhammad Sulaiman al-Abdah (London: Message of Islam), accessed April 3, 2020, http://shaykhulislaam.wordpress.com/2012/11/07/ibn-taymeeyahs-letters-from-prison-download-pdf/

29 Voll, "Muhammad Hayya Al-Sindi and Muhammad Ibn Abd al Wahab," 32–39.

30 Qutb, *Muālim*.

31 Bonney, *Jihad*, 215, 216.

32 Osama Bin Laden, "Second letter to the Muslims of Iraq October 18, 2003," in *Al Qaida in Its Own Words*, 67, 68.

33 Al-Zawahiri, "Shifa Sudur al-Momineen," quoted in Maha Azzam, *Al-Qaida: The Misunderstood Wahabi Connection and the Ideology of Violence* Briefing Paper No. 1 (Royal Institute of International Affairs, Middle East Programme, 2003).

34 Abu Muhammad al-Maqdisi, *This Is Our Aqeedah*, 2nd ed. (At-Tibyan Publications), accessed July 16, 2013, http://www.kalamullah.com/Books/This%20is%20our%20Aqeedah.pdf.

35 Ibid., 65.

36 Fradkin et al., *Current Trends in Islamist Ideology*.

37 Rassler et al., *Letters from Abbottabad*, No. SOCOM-2012-0000018.

3 Polemics revisited

The ideas of heresy evolved into polemics, which created faultlines in Muslim societies. The sectarian schisms find their genesis chiefly in three political issues rooted in Muslim history: 'claim to prophetic inheritance', 'belief in imamate' and 'claim to the caliphate'. The difference of perspectives on these issues led to the bifurcation of theological streams in the Muslim world. The theological perspectives which emerged sharply divided the Muslim Ummah. The Sunnites and the Shiites sat on opposite sides of the fence to each other. As the divergent theological narratives germinated in political spaces, these have always been part of political discourse in the Muslim world. Where the sectarian schisms provided a rationale to sectarian empires in Muslim history, the ruling elite promoted polemics to claim legitimacy for their statehood. From the combination of sectarian theology and state emerged presuppositions, leading to unending mistrust amongst Muslims.

Genesis of the polemics

The sectarian schisms sneaked into the body politic of Islam not long after the Prophet passed away. The Prophet himself anticipated the sectarian split, which would become a permanent feature of the Muslim societies. He said, 'The Jews divided into seventy-one sects, all of which will go to hell except one; the Christians will divide into seventy-two sects, all of which will go to hell except one; this Ummah will divide into seventy-three sects, all of which will go to hell except one'.[1] The sectarian rift primarily emerged in the Muslim society between those who held Ali to be the legitimate religious and political heir of the Prophet and those who believed that the first three caliphs, being equally eligible, were rightfully elected to the office of caliphate through *ijma'a-e-Ummah* (consensus amongst the Companions of the Prophet).

Right to prophetic inheritance

On the question of inheritance, the Sunnites believe that none has the right to claim to inherit whatever the Prophet left behind. On the contrary, the Shiites argue that Ali, having a close blood relationship and being the son-

DOI: 10.4324/9781003164883-3

in-law of the Prophet, was his heir. They refute the Sunnite view through drawing inference from the following Quranic verses: 'And Solomon was David's heir' (An-Naml: 16).

The Sunnite argument, in this regard, originates from a *hadith* (tradition of the Prophet) which has been quoted by Ibn Kathir that none has the right to claim to inherit what the Prophet left as whatever he left comes within the definition of *māl-e-Sadaqāt* (property for freewill offerings).[2] Ibn Kathir argues that the Shiites' inferences drawn from the Quranic verses regarding the succession of prophet Suleman to prophet Dawud are without sound reasoning. Suleman was the successor to Dawud not in the matters of the property but in the matters of prophethood, in political authority and, further, in adjudication amongst the Children of Israel.[3] Similarly, prophet Zakariya's prayer for his successor-prophet Yahya was not aimed to have a successor for the material property as, being a prophet, he was not concerned about material belongings. He prayed for a son who would succeed him in prophethood and in reforming the Children of Israel.[4] This is explicitly clear from the following Quranic verses: 'Kaf. Ha. Ya. A'in. Sad. A mention of the mercy of thy Lord unto His servant Zachariah. When he cried unto his Lord a cry in secret, Saying: My Lord! Lo! the bones of me wax feeble and my head is shining with grey hair, and I have never been unblest in prayer to Thee, my Lord. Lo! I fear my kinsfolk after me, since my wife is barren. Oh, give me from Thy presence a successor Who shall inherit of me and inherit (also) of the house of Jacob. And make him, my Lord, acceptable (unto Thee)' (Maryam: 1–6).

Belief in imamate

Imamate is the core of the Shiite model of state governance.[5] It guarantees human salvation through collective action in terms of enforcement of imam's justice.[6] The Shiites believe that lofty ideals of socio-economic justice, political order and Muslim unity cannot be achieved without this institution. They subscribe to the following statement of Fatima al-Zahara: 'the imamate exists for the sake of preserving order among the Muslims and replacing their disunity with unity'.[7] The institution is needed to protect the fundamentals of faith and revive its glory.[8] The paramount importance associated with the institution of imamate leads Ibn Mutahir to recognize it in terms of an element of faith.[9] He draws this inference from a *hadith* (tradition) of the Prophet, which reads: 'He who dies without recognizing imam of his times dies the death of *jāhilliyah*'.[10] On the other hand, the Sunnites argue that since the religion has been completed in all respects and the divine guidance has reached its culmination through the Prophet, the believers have no need of further guidance through the institution of imamate.[11] The believers are required only to follow whatever has been handed down through the Prophet. Ibn Taimmiyah does not recognize the authenticity of the above-quoted *hadith* because of weakness in narration-linkage. He argues that the actual wording of authentic *hadith* is as follows: 'he who dies in such a condition that he is without *baya'ā* (allegiance to the ruler), he dies the death of *jāhilliyah*'.[12]

Right to caliphate

As far as the question of the right to caliphate is concerned, the Shiites believe that as he had a close blood relationship with the Prophet, Ali's right to caliphate was foremost. They further draw inference from two traditions of the Prophet. First, in a famous *hadith* of *ghadīr khumm*, the prophet said, 'Ali is the lord of those whose lord I am'.[13] Secondly, in another narration while proceeding to Tabuk expedition, the prophet appointed Ali as his deputy in Madina, stating, 'You are to me as Harun was to Musa'.[14] The Shiites infer from these traditions that the Prophet intended Ali to be caliph after him. They further infer that primacy of Ali's right to caliphate was confirmed by none other than the Prophet himself.

However, with regard to these traditions, the Sunnites hold a different standpoint. The *hadith* of *ghadir khumm* has been noted by many distinguished Sunnite scholars but they have interpreted the Arabic term *ma'wlā* (lord) which was used in the original text differently. They argue that the term refers to a person with whom closeness exists and does not invoke the sense of imam.[15] With regard to the appointment of Ali as deputy by the Prophet when leaving for Tabuk, Ibn Taimmiyah does not find any plausible evidence to support the Shiite viewpoint.[16] Sunnite scholars argue that the case of prophets Harun and Musa does not provide a context to address the question of succession because prophet Harun passed away prior to prophet Musa.[17] Besides this, Abi Ja'afar Muhammad b. Jarir Al-Tabri[18] has recorded the Friday sermon delivered by Ali after the martyrdom of Uthman, the third pious caliph, wherein he recognized the popular prerogative for the election of the caliph. He declined to become caliph without popular consent.[19] On this account, the Sunnite scholarship nullifies the Shiite claim that, instead of a popular prerogative to be exercised through consensus, the caliphate was the exclusive right of Ali on the basis of close blood relationship with the Prophet.

Nevertheless, the Sunnite standpoint on the question of prophetic nomination of the successor is divided.[20] One argument takes the appointment of Abu Bakr as leader of the prayer by the Prophet during his illness in terms of prophetic intent to nominate him as his successor. In support of this argument, Ibn Sa'ad has quoted Ali as having said that as the Prophet chose Abu Bakr leader of the spiritual domain by appointing him leader of the prayers during his illness, the companions agreed to his being head of the temporal sphere as well.[21] Some argue that appointment of Abu Bakr as imam of the prayers is a confirmatory reference to his high standing amongst the Companions but does not reflect the Prophet's intent to nominate him as his successor. Another view in Sunnite scholarship on the question of succession is that, though the Prophet did not appoint anyone his successor, he expressed his intentions in favour of Abu Bakr through different means. The Prophet has been reported to have advised a woman to seek guidance, if required, from Abu Bakr in his absence.[22] However, the dominant view in Sunnite scholarship is that the Prophet deliberately did not appoint anyone his successor.[23] This view is supported by the historical evidence that, following the Sunnah (conduct) of the Prophet, none of the pious caliphs nominated the successor. Abu Bakr's recommendation of Umar cannot be taken as a nomination because it was subject to the approval of the believers at large. Umar said that if he did not appoint his successor it would be on the model of the Prophet who had also not appointed his successor and left the decision to the collective will of those who loose and bind (*ahl al- hall wa'l-aqd)*. He conveyed his will to Ibn Abbas that, following the Prophet, he had not appointed his successor.[24] Moreover, according to Ayesha Siddiqa, had the Prophet intended to nominate anyone as caliph, he would have been Abu Bakr.[25] Similarly, Ibn Taimmiyah does not subscribe to the argument that the Muslims used to call Abu Bakr by the title of *Khalifāt-ur-Rasūl* (Deputy of the Prophet), which reflects his nomination because deputy is a position which is always filled through appointment by some authority. He argues that the title does not connote the nomination as such; rather, caliph can be appointed by some authority or even can be self-appointed. The title *Khalifāt-ur-Rasūl* does not suggest that the Prophet necessarily nominated Abu Bakr.[26]

As said earlier, the debate on the right to caliphate proved to be overwhelmingly prejudicial to the unity of the Muslim Ummah. However, the debate was generated by the elements who were external to the claim of caliphate. Ali never disputed the legitimacy of the first three caliphs. He recognized Uthman the most deserving one to be elected to the office of caliphate.[27] He continued to perform important judicial and executive functions during the tenure of the first three caliphs. It confirms that Ali, who was undisputedly a court of final appeal on all the issues, would never have discharged these state functions had he not believed in the legitimacy of the caliphs.

However, these differences could not divide devout Muslims, who drew their religious spirit directly from the Prophet. Only the hypocrites who were otherwise bitter enemies of Islam exploited these schisms. They aimed to promote their personal agenda at the expense of Islam. Abdullah b. Saba was one of them. He was successful in misleading simple Egyptians through his propaganda. As part of his scheme to damage the faith, he attempted to make the case that Ali was the only rightful claimant to the caliphate, which was unjustly taken over by others.[28]

These hypocrites amassed enough strength to challenge the authority of the caliphate in Madina. The chaos (*fitnah*) ultimately ended up in the martyrdom of Uthman, the third pious caliph, and split Muslim unity. The battle of *Camel* (36 AH), fought between Ali and Ayesha Siddiqa, took place amid such undercurrents. Ayesha demanded Ali as caliph take *Qisās* (retribution) of Uthman from the rebels. Ali's position was that he would ensure *Qisās* once he had sufficient military strength to fight the rebels. Nevertheless, political history witnessed the subsequent battle of Siffin fought between Ali and Mu'awiyah. This battle took place when Mu'awiyah claimed autonomy in Damascus from the caliphate of Ali at Madina. The misgivings were strong enough to turn unity into disunity; trust into mistrust; strengths into weaknesses; cohesion into chaos and idealism into realism. The Ummah divided into two camps: *Shi'ān-e-Ali* (Camp of Ali) and *Shi'ān-e-Mu'awiyah* (Camp of Mu'awiyah). The tragedy of Karbala[29] (61 AH) is also a link in the chain of events. The pre-Islamic tribal rivalries of the Makkan society, which had been overcome by the Islamic revolution, resurfaced and were exploited.

Theological labelling

The sectarian schisms divided the theological discourse into two opposite streams: the Sunnites and the Shiites. The Sunnites labelled the Shiites as Rawāfidh (rejectionists) for refuting the legitimacy of the claim of the first three caliphs to the caliphate. The Shiites branded the Sunnites as Nawāsib (hostile to Ali). However, despite sharp mutual dissensions reflected in this labelling, both sides avoided invalidating the faith of each other. Nevertheless, the theological labelling highlights that theological discourse was now fraught with dichotomies and conflicts. The conflict became so glaring and irreconcilable that, in most of the cases, both sects based their theological edifices on different sources. Moreover, the criteria followed for historical inquiry was also not uniform. This diminished the prospects of mutual convergence between the two sects.

Classical Sunnite scholarship questions the authenticity of the traditions of the Prophet transmitted by the Shiites on the grounds that, instead of ascribing importance to the strength of character of the narrator, they believe in the narrator's commitment to the Shiite doctrine. The Sunnite ulema do not follow this standard of authentication of *hadith*. They hesitate to believe in the veracity of a Shiite narration unless it meets their own standards of authentication. In this context, when confronted by a Spaniard who ventured to question the veracity of the Quran on the basis of the Shiite narrations, Ibn Hazam dismissed the Shiite narration for not originating in valid sources.[30] Similarly, Ibn Khaldun, a 14th-century historian-cum-sociologist, was reluctant to recognize the authenticity of the historical evidence produced by the Shiites because it was not acknowledged by the majority of the Muslim scholarship.[31] Imam Malik and Imam Sha'afi, too, do not accept the credibility of the *ahadith* narrated on the authority of the Shiites.[32]

In addition to this, classical Sunnite jurists question the legitimacy of the Shiite doctrine as a whole. Ibn Kathir does not affirm the legitimacy of the Shiite doctrine of twelve Imams.[33] He further argues that shallow theological bases incapacitate the Shiites from discerning right from wrong and expose them to propaganda aimed at promoting unfounded beliefs.[34] Carried away by this, they introduce heresies even in the observance of rituals. Their timings and pattern of prayers vary from the rest of the Muslim community. The Sunnite ulema also object to their slandering of the Companions of the Prophet.

Ibn Taimmiyah charges them with leaving the collective community of Muslims (*Jama'at*). He bases his argument on the grounds that the primary objective of the caliphate lies in the assumption and exercise of political authority. This objective is legitimately fulfilled when someone occupies the office through consensus of the people of authority.[35] As obedience to those in authority is obligatory (*wājib*) upon the believers,[36] the Shiites who do not acknowledge the legitimacy of the first three caliphs are considered to have committed *khurūj* (revolt) against the caliphate. Nevertheless, despite all these theological dichotomies in both sects, classical Sunnite theorists do not excommunicate Shiites en masse.

Socio-political constructs in the sectarian domain

The doctrinal differences between the two sects, when juxtaposed with political and historical constructs, ignited physical and political conflict in the Muslim world. In certain patches of Muslim political history, there emerged political orders, which were essentially sectarian in nature. The case of these political orders confirms that the interplay of politics and sectarian theology produced fertile grounds for violence.

Fatimid caliphate

The Fatimid caliphate (909–1171 AD) was an Ismailite-Shiite caliphate that flourished in North Africa. The Fatimid rulers claimed their lineage from Fatima al-Zahra, the exalted daughter of the Prophet. Egypt was the ultimate centre of the Fatimids. They took over de facto political authority from the Sunnite rulers of North Africa who, despite claiming political autonomy, did not reject the symbolic religious suzerainty of the Abbasids. Al-Mahdi, the leader of the Shiite movement, broke completely with the Abbasids and aspired to take over the politico-religious authority himself. It was in the 9th century that the Ismailite missionaries launched propagation against the Abbasids from Yemen and eventually succeeded in installing their caliphate in North Africa under Ubayd Allah al-Mahdi. This nascent political order had to withstand tough ordeals from within the Ismailite sect and without. Internally, Al-Mahdi had to face opposition from those very Ismailites who brought him to power and, externally, he had to face the Malik'ite Sunnite majority and the hostile Khawarij, who would not acknowledge religious legitimacy of their religious identity. On the political front, he had to encounter troublesome Berber tribes and aggressive Byzantines as well.

However, these challenges did not stop the Fatimids from unleashing the forces of sectarian frenzy to challenge the political configurations largely dominated by the Abbasids. The conquest of Egypt (969 AD) was the first important step towards translating their dream of establishing a universal Ismailite imamate into reality. Fatimids held sway over vast lands, including Hejaz, the land of two holy sanctuaries. They had strong military expansionist and revolutionary ambitions to be pursued under their caliph. The Ismailite caliph, being the imam, had an extended authority in spiritual as well as temporal affairs. Against the Abbasids, they aimed to increase their strength by winning over converts to the Ismailite doctrine. They managed to propagate their religious teachings through a clandestine missionary network. This network subsequently turned into an instrument to subvert the political authority of the Abbasids wherever possible. The Chief Missionary based in Cairo was in charge of this network. The disciplined politico-religious authority of the Chief Missionary was novel in the medieval history of Islam. It was identical to an institutionalized state church. This office provided a platform to launch intellectual efforts for the promulgation of fundamental Ismailite doctrines. They used their ideology to refute the religious sanction behind the claim of the Abbasids to the caliphate and further to validate their own claim to the caliphate.

Apart from these missionary activities, the Fatimids aimed to establish a worldwide Ismailite imamate to achieve both political as well as religious objectives. They pursued tremendous commercial activities through an alternate trade route passing through the Red Sea between Asia and the Near East. This economic policy sought to counterbalance the monopolistic control of the Abbasids over the traditional economic route passing through the Persian Gulf. This economic strategy enabled the Ismailites to gain trade independence from the Sunnite-dominated routes of the Red Sea and Yemen and to export their doctrines to Eastern Arabia, Central Asia and India. The Ismaili'te caliphate reached its zenith in 1057–1059 AD.

However, the caliphate had a setback when the Turks drove them out of Baghdad. Several causes contributed to the ultimate fall of the Ismailites. Owing to its sectarian character, the Ismailite caliphate was victim of legitimacy crises from the beginning. Its legitimacy base was restricted in scope to the Ismailites alone. It was always threatened by a powerful Sunnite majority, which was harshly averse to their sectarian ideology. The Sunnites did not trust their faithfulness in Islam and projected them as enemies of ulema. They further saw them as desirous of the downfall of the Muslim Ummah.[37] A major factor contributing to the legitimacy crises of the dynasty emerged from its creation from within the Abbasid caliphate. A common view in medieval Muslim scholarship was that Islam does not permit plurality of the caliphs. This view persisted in the Sunnite theological discourse until the 14th century when Ibn Khaldun redefined it.[38] The

Sunnite scholarship was sceptical of the legitimacy of their faith even. Jalaluddin Sayyuti in his luminous work on the historical accounts of the Muslim caliphs titled *Tarīkh Al-Khulāfā* (History of Caliphs) did not even discuss the Fatimids simply because he did not consider them believers.[39] He quoted Qadi Iyad, saying that someone asked Abu Muhammad Al-Qairwani, a notable Maliki scholar, if Ubaydis[40] force someone to convert to their faith, what should one do? He replied that one must prefer death to accepting their belief. Likewise, it was declared obligatory upon the believers to migrate from the lands under the Ubaydis' control.[41]

The Ismailite caliphate was beset by identity crises from the start. Sunnite scholarship refuted the Fatimids' claim of being from the lineage of Fatima. The legitimacy of their claim to the caliphate, based exclusively upon their ancestral link with the Quraysh, got eroded.[42] Sayyuti prefers to call them Ubaydis after Ubayd Allah Al-Mahdi, the founder of the dynasty, instead of Fatimids. He traces the ancestors of Ubayd Allah al-Mahdi and links them either to the Jews as argued by Qadi Abdul Jabbar Basri or to the Zoroastrians after the opinion of Ibn Khalqan.[43] The identity question exacerbated the legitimacy crises for the Fatimids. These crises put the dynasty in decline.

Moreover, the Crusades that ushered in an era of physical conflict between the Christians and the Muslims created a sense of integration amongst the Muslims at large. They realized that they could not afford any schism in the body politic of Islam during the physical clash with Christian Crusaders. This ultimately diminished the prospects of the Fatimid caliphate flourishing in the land, which was dominantly Sunnite. The Muslim majority did not trust them to fight against the Christian Crusaders.

Safavid empire

With the degeneration of Tamerlane's political authority in Persia, the Safavids got an opportunity to rise to political power. Shah Ismail exploited this opportunity and established his empire. The Safavid Empire (1501–1722 AD) was a Shiite theocracy that flourished in predominantly Sunnite Iran. Its territorial limits extended beyond Persia to the areas falling within modern Turkey and Georgia. The ruling elite followed an aggressive policy of forced conversion of the Sunnite population to Shiism. The ideological origin of the Safavids dates back to the 13th-century Sufi order started by one Safi Al-Din (1252–1334), who had converted to the Shiite version of Islam. This Sufi order mustered enough political strength to transform the future course of politics. This politico-religious fraternity declared formal independence from the Ottomans under Shah Ismail in 1501. They claimed autonomy from the Ottomans, mainly in reaction to the Ottomans' plans to proscribe Shiism. Shah Ismail I successfully brought the whole of Iran under his political suzerainty within a decade.

The Ottomans, being the chief rivals of the Safavids, believed that recruitment of the Shiites from Anatolia by the Safavids would be a challenge to the Sunnite beliefs as well as their political interests. The Ottoman emperor Sultan Bayezid II shifted many Shiites from Anatolia to other parts of his empire so that they would not join the Safavid cause. The Ottomans also defeated Shah Ismail I and captured his capital. Though the Safavid Empire survived this defeat, it exposed the claim of the Safavid king to be invincible for having divinely ordained status. The hostilities between the two Empires became even more intense, with long-lasting effects on the future policies of the Safavid Empire. The sectarian hostility between the two Empires prompted the Safavids to resort to stringent policies against their Sunnite subjects.

Though there were large concentrations of the Shiites in certain localities like Qom and Sabzevar from the 8th century, the majority in Persia were still the Sunnites. Shah Ismail I proclaimed the *athnā ʿashariyya* Shiite doctrine as state religion to confront the political power of Sunnite Ottomans. The Safavids imported Shiite brains to develop a powerful religious aristocracy under state supervision. This aristocracy worked as a powerful tool to suppress the rival Sunnite belief intellectually as well as using brute force. The subsequent course of history witnessed ruthless state persecution of the Sunnite clergy and forced conversion of the Sunnite population to Shiism. Under the Safavids, state persecution was not limited to Sunnites; rather, the Shiites, following a brand of Shiism different from the ruling elite, were also persecuted with the same vigour. The policy of shiitization of the Sunnite Muslims aimed to cultivate a religious and cultural identity of the Persians radically distinct from the rival Ottomans. This distinct identity was a powerful military tool to counter the Ottomans. The Safavids presumed that complete shiitization of the population would strengthen their political control through creating a loyal popular base. Moreover, in newly conquered lands like Azerbaijan and Iraq, where the dominant majority of the Muslim population was Sunnite, the conversion policy aimed to eliminate the support base of the Ottomans through breaking the strength of the Sunnites. Sectarian violence was adopted in what Leo Tolstoy terms 'rule of state necessity'.[44]

The Safavids built their empire through creating a nexus between sectarian theocracy and state authority under the supreme authority of the king. The theocracy provided strong foundations to the state. The state further enhanced its power through successfully exploiting its geographical location at the heart of trade routes. Moreover, the ruling elite successfully developed the distinct cultural identity of Safavid Persia through patronizing art and literature. In this milieu of state-sponsored sectarian conflict, it was the persistent threat from the rival Sunnite Ottomans that kept the Safavids politically united and militarily robust. However, with the receding of the Ottoman threat, the forces that were initially a source of power for the Empire turned into catalysts of disintegration. There were squabbles over political authority. The king was no longer the ultimate source of politico-religious and military strength. The de facto authority passed to the powerful religious clergy. The religious aristocracy, once created to serve the interests of the king, now claimed political authority itself on the pretext that the right to rule rests only with *mujtahids* (the learned men of the community). However, the clergy could not safeguard their unimpeachable political authority for long. They were forced to surrender this authority through a power-sharing scheme with the Afghans. The clergy were now restricted to the religious sphere, and the temporal authority passed on to the Afghans.

To summarize, the Safavid Empire marked a sharp break from the past when the Twelver Shiites coexisted with the Sunnites. The policies of the Safavids brought the hostilities between the two sects to such an extreme that coexistence between the two became virtually impossible. The Sunnites in the empire got concentrated within certain geographical pockets close to the borders with the Sunnite states. Moreover, being partners in the exercise of political authority, the clergy institutionalized themselves. The adoption of polemics by the Safavids resulted in redrawing the state boundaries on sectarian trajectory. The geographical limits of Turkey, Afghanistan and Iran resulted from this sectarian divide. Most important of all, the forced conversion by Shah Ismail I continued to serve as a 'lesson of history' for the Sunnites, whereby the Sunnites would draw legitimacy to violently resist the Shiites and their ideology.

Iranian Revolution 1979

During the 20th century, the sectarian conflict had a pattern different from the period of the Fatimids and the Safavids. These sectarian dynasties had to carve out space to pursue their shiitization policies within the powerful Sunnite caliphate. In a hostile Sunnite-dominated scenario, these Shiite dynasties adopted violent means to achieve their goals. In 20th-century Iran, the population was already following Shiism. On the peripheries, there was hardly any Sunnite power that could challenge them. The fulcrum of economic and military power had already tilted to the western world. The challenge was no longer from the Sunnite world but from the western front with entirely new policy designs. Naturally, this changed situation required new trajectories of conflict to revive Shiism in Iran. The new tracks of conflict emerged as 'anti-imperialism', 'uprooting the existing state system through reviving the dogma of Islamic state' and 'desire to eliminate the socio-economic exploitation in the society'. However, despite all other factors having changed – international conflict scenario, internal situation and approach to revive Shiism – one factor, deeply embedded in history, remained constant. These were the 'lessons of history' which the Sunnite world had learnt from the Fatimids and the Safavids.

Khomeini revived political activism in the Shiites, which ultimately culminated into revolution in Iran in 1979. The success of revolution made the clergy more assertive, which increased sectarian tensions. The *athnā-e-ashriyyā* (Twelver Imam) school of Shiite theology does not provide for political activism during the period of occultation. Owing to his personal belief in mysticism and theosophy (*erfān*), Khomeini attached surpassing importance to human intuition and cognition in terms of sources of knowledge vis-à-vis rationalism.[45] Despite eschewing rationality in favour of intuition, he introduced political activism during the period of occultation through his superb juristic rationality.[46] He successfully eliminated the dichotomy between traditional Shiite non-activism and the dynamic spirit of the faith. He argued that during the imam's occultation, no one was appointed to run the affairs of the state. This does not imply that the principles of Islam have lost their practical utility. It is the duty of believers to establish an Islamic government to protect the fundamentals of faith till the time the imam returns to rejuvenate the glory of Islam himself.[47] As ulema (living mujtahids) are the symbol of authority in the absence of imam, they are bound not to let religion degenerate and the oppressed be exploited.[48] This redefinition of the clergy's political role provided them with an opportunity to become active political actors in the drama of power politics in Iran. His *ijtihād* in the realm of politics turned the clergy into sole guardians of Islamic law (*vilayet-e-faqih*).[49]

Khomeini argued that revolution is a tool to resist the imperialist powers bent upon destroying the political power of the Muslims through undermining their unity.[50] He criticized the imperialist powers for disintegrating the Ottoman caliphate, the symbol of the believers' unity. The imperialists installed their cronies on the ruins of the Ottoman caliphate. These rulers created class conflicts in Muslim societies through their exploitative policies.[51] His acknowledgement of the Ottoman caliphate as a symbol of Muslim unity appears to be a strategic move to win the support of the Sunnites against the imperialist powers. He argued that the believers were duty bound to get rid of these rulers in order to revive the unity and discipline amongst the believers' ranks. He referred to a statement of Ali who entrusted to his exalted sons, 'Be an enemy of the oppressor and helper to the oppressed'.[52] Moreover, his opposition to the Shah's government became more intense when, in 1963, the Shah of Iran granted capitulatory rights to Americans and contracted a $200 million loan from the United States to purchase military equipment. He further urged upon the leaders of prayers to use the pulpit to address issues other than those of purely theological nature, including the imperialist designs in the Muslim world.[53]

He aimed to revive the dogma of the Islamic state through exploring the evidence from the early Islamic era. He sought to discover rational grounds for the establishment of an Islamic government but indeed on the Shiite model with the imamate at its pivot. He idealized the state governance on the model of the Prophet. This Shariah-based state would provide a regulatory framework for not only the religious but also the socio-economic and political affairs of the society.[54] He took the Islamic government as a necessity to preserve the Islamic order and to defend territorial integrity and the independence of Muslim Ummah.[55] He labelled this model of state governance as 'government of law'. On this narrative, he claimed legitimacy to uproot the Shah of Iran's monarchy. The critics of Iranian revolution justifiably argue that historically the clergy did not challenge the institution of monarchy on ideological grounds. Their protest remained limited only to the policies of the state, which were either damaging to their local interests or supportive to imperialist powers.[56] It is further argued that even in the 19th century, the ulema's approach to social and economic problems of the Iranian society was secular. It was evident from the living conditions of the peasantry on the lands possessed by the ulema, which were no better than of those working on the lands possessed by the landed aristocrats.[57] As clergy in 19th-century Iran had the monopoly over education and the court system, they were not in favour of reshaping the political order. Their opposition to the state began only when the government expressed its resolve to secularize education and to mitigate the influence of the religious courts.[58] It was the reform package of the Shah of Iran which triggered the opposition of the clergy, whose head was Khomeini. He criticized the Bill on Women Franchise published by the government on September 8, 1962, as being repugnant to Islam.[59] However, despite his criticism, Khomeini did not start active opposition until he was personally targeted by the regime as an agent of Iraq and Great Britain.[60]

Khomeini used the dogma of Islamic government to support his revolutionary struggle. He argued that *tāghūt* (oppression) had re-emerged in the form of the existing socio-economic and political order. Under this exploitative system, Islamic laws cannot be enforced, and the Islamic way of life cannot be observed.[61] With *tāghūt*, a believer has no other option but to either become part of it or revolt against it. He argued that the believers were obliged to uproot the rule of corruption simply because perpetrators of corruption represented the Pharaohs of Egypt about whom the Quran says, 'Lo! Pharaoh exalted himself in the earth and made its people castes. A tribe among them he oppressed, killing their sons and sparing their women. Lo! he was of those who work corruption' (Al-Qasas: 4).[62] On these grounds, he urged Muslims to rise against the existing order and replace it with an Islamic system through revolutionary means. The revolutionary struggle should be launched in terms of the Shiite doctrine of 'collective action' through enforcement of imam's justice.[63] It is only through this pattern of struggle that human salvation is guaranteed. He pledged to follow the way of Ali of accepting political authority to eliminate the economic exploitation of the masses.[64] In order to give an emotional character to revolutionary struggle against the Shah's regime, he used religious rhetoric and symbolism representing the Shiite historical traditions. He urged the Iranian people to revive the spirit of sacrifice after the traditions of Imam Hussain to get rid of present-day Yazid.[65] He avoided limiting the dynamism of Islam to mere rituals; rather, he discovered within Islam a powerful spiritual force, that, in the words of a western scholar of Islam, 'governs the life of Muslims from cradle to grave'.[66]

Sectarian rapprochement

Though political channels have been used in history to promote sectarian intolerance, they have also been used to foster efforts for sectarian rapprochement in the post-Safavid period. In terms of a political compromise, as early as 1743, Nadir Shah effected a formal agreement between the two sects whereby the Shiites agreed not to slander the Companions of the Prophet and the Sunnites agreed to extend recognition to 'Twelver Shiism' as an authentic school of Muslim scholarship.[67] Similarly, in the early 20th century, this spirit was evident from the correspondence between Abd al-Husayn Sharaf al-Din, a Lebanese Shiite scholar and Salim al-Bishri, the rector of Al-Azhar. In this period, Rashid Rida, a prominent Sunnite revivalist, appeared to be expressing his support for such rapprochement in his dialogue with Iraqi Shiite jurist Muhammad al-Husayn Al Kashif al-Ghita.[68] The cause of sectarian rapprochement continued to characterize the historical discourse by the second half of the 20th century. In 1959, Iranian Shiite scholar Muhammad Taqi Qummi who was heading a group called *Jama'āt al-taqrīb* again got Twelver Shiism recognized as an authentic school of Muslim jurisprudence by Mahmoud Shaltut, the then head of Al-Azhar.[69]

Nevertheless, during the last quarter of the 20th century, the 'lessons of history' learnt during the period of the Fatimids and the Safavids overshadowed enthusiasm for rapprochement between the two sects. The sectarian violence was strengthened by the Sunnites' apprehensions that Khomeini would spearhead the drive to export the Shiite ideology to the Sunnite-dominated areas through a network of cultural centres and consulates.[70] In this scenario, the Sunnite ruling elite in Muslim lands revived the sectarian schisms as a tool to contain the possible inflow of Shiism into the Sunnite lands. In this changed scenario, a few sections of the Sunnite clergy unleashed a campaign to challenge the ideological character of the Iranian revolution. They argued that Shiite revolution in Iran had revived the pre-Islamic Zoroastrianism.[71] The Sunnite clergy argued that Iranian hostility towards the Arabs dates back to the conquest of Persia, when Arabs destroyed pre-Islamic Persian glory, which was a source of pride for the Iranians. Out of this hostility, they took part in every move, whether it was from the Qaramitah, the Buwayhids or the Fatimids, that aimed to weaken the foundations of Islam.[72] It was in this backdrop that the Iranian revolution served to revive the violent extremism on sectarian lines. The unpleasant memories of the Safavids stirred up apprehensions in the Sunnites that a Shiite clergy-led Iran could promote its hegemonic designs in the region through shiitization policy on the Safavid model.[73] It was further apprehended that the projection of success of the clergy-led Shiite revolution might attract Sunnites to convert to Shiism as well.[74]

Moreover, the post-revolution era witnessed the rise of enthusiasm in the Shiite community to safeguard their interests. The Shiites in Pakistan who constituted the second largest community beyond Iranian soil, established Tehrīk Nifāz Fiqah Ja'afria (TNFJ, Movement for Enforcement of Ja'afria Jurisprudence) in the revolution year (1979) under the leadership of Arif Hussain al-Hussaini, a student of Khomeini himself. Though the major objective of the organization was declared to protect the rights of the Shiites, the timing of its foundation and the intellectual relationship that the founder of this organization had with Khomeini were enough to raise suspicions within the Sunnite clergy regarding the possible export of Shiite ideology to Pakistan. It was against this backdrop that in 1985 Anjuman Sipah-e-Sahābah (Organization for the Defence of the Companions), a Deobandi-dominated organization, was launched to counterbalance sectarian conflict in Pakistan. The conflict between the two organizations was not confined to the political sphere as they engaged in physical conflict as well. Both organizations developed militant wings in the early 1990s. Lashkar-e-Jhangvi[75] and Sipah-e-Muhammad emerged as militant affiliates of Sipah-e-Sahābah and TNFJ, respectively. The Shiite clergy's political ascendancy in Iran was a source of tremendous inspiration for the Shiite militant outfit in Pakistan, and the Afghan jihad was a channel for inflow of sophisticated weapons and trained manpower to the Sunnite militant outfit in Pakistan.[76] In the following years, the Sunnite militant outfits resorted to physical violence to justify their existence, in terms of stopping the spread of Shiite ideology, whereas the Shiite militants exploited the notion of protection of the fellow Shiites against the numerically strong Sunnite militants.

Even after the lapse of more than four decades since the Iranian revolution, there continue to be apprehensions across the Muslim world regarding the export of Shiite doctrines, and these codify the violence on sectarian lines. Even moderate clergy in Sunnite states have expressed concerns about Iran's efforts to export Shiite ideology to the Sunnite lands, such as Egyptian cleric Yusuf Qaradawi, who is noted for his use of soft vocabulary for the Shiites. Speaking at a Doha conference in 2007, he categorically refuted the claim of Iranian Ayatullah Taskhiri that the shiitization campaign just came from some individuals.[77] Similarly, other moderate voices like Nasr Farid Wasel, the former Mufti, have also joined Qaradawi in protesting against the shiitization of the Sunnite lands.[78] In Morocco, there are reports regarding the spread of Shiite ideology by Moroccans who work in Europe, where they are being indoctrinated by the institutions connected to Iran.[79] In 2007, the Algerian Religious Affairs Ministry also highlighted shiitization activities.[80] In Sudan, too, the increase in popularity of Hezbollah leadership, evident through the proliferation of Hezbollah's flags, suggests that Shiite ideology has managed to secure popular appeal.[81] Similar trends have been reported in Jordan as well.[82] In the absence of empirical data, no concrete observation regarding the veracity of such shiitization trends can be made; yet, the perception that shiitization does exist has increased sectarian tension and also the potential for physical violence.

Viewed from this context of mistrust and mutual suspicions, the US attack on Iraq was a trigger for sectarian violence in the Muslim lands. The fall of the Baath regime turned Iraq into a theatre of sectarian conflict between the Sunnites and the Shiites. The Shiites found an opportunity to marginalize the political ascendancy of the Sunnites, which they had long held with the support of the invading forces. This approach alarmed the Sunnites, who were already struggling to withstand the blow to their position in a changed political context.[83] This sectarian cleavage strengthened the already predominant tone of mutual hostility deriving from historic accusations of treason, heresy and support to the enemies of faith.[84] The attempt on the part of the Shiites to assume political authority in Iraq with the collaboration of the invading US forces has been viewed by the Sunnite militants in terms of treachery and debauchery.

The discussion in this chapter leads us to draw the following conclusions. First, the theological differences between the two sects could create historical prejudice when juxtaposed with political constructs. Sectarian Empires like the Fatimid caliphate and the Safavid dynasty emerged on the basis of these divisions. Second, these theological differences on sectarian lines that emerged in the early period of Islam got aggravated on the axis of politics during the subsequent centuries. Historical evidence further highlights the pragmatic use of the polemics to secure the political advantage by the respective camps. Third, sectarian empires have attempted to export Shiite ideology to the Sunnite lands. This passion of the sectarian empires has generated apprehensions that still reverberate into the minds of the rival Sunnites. Fourth, the response of the Sunnites vis-à-vis the Fatimids and the Safavids has always been of mistrust and lack of confidence. The Sunnites have suspected the loyalties of the Shiites towards the fellow Muslims vis-à-vis the infidels. Traditionally the Shiites have been admonished by the Sunnite scholarship for collaborating with non-believers to uproot the Sunnite governments. Last but not the least, though the doctrinal differences between the two sects have been there since the early phase of Islamic history, these differences did not translate into violent extremism, which renders coexistence of the two sects unthinkable. This could only happen when forced conversion under the sectarian empires served as 'lessons of history' for the Sunnites.

Notes

1 Abu Dawood, *Sunan Abu Dawood, Kitāb al-Sunnah*, 4579.
2 Imam Bukhari, *Sahih Bukhari, Kitāb Farā'ed al-Khums*, 3093; *Kitāb Fadhāil As-Sahāb al-Nabi*, 3712.
3 Ibn Kathir, *Al-Bidāyah wal Nihāyah*, Story of Prophet Sulaiman, (trans.) Abu Talha Muhammad Asghar Mughal, Vol. 2 (Karachi: Dar-ul-Asha'at, 2008), 470.
4 Ibid., 51, 52.
5 Sub-sects in the Shiite theology differ in details of *Imamate*. The Twelver Shiites (*athnā-e-ashriyyā*) believe in twelve imams whereas the Ismailites believe in a living imam.

6 Akhavi, 'Islam, Politics and Society', 404–431.
7 Imam Ruhullah Khomeini, 'The Necessity of Islamic Government', in *Contemporary Debates in Islam: An Anthology of Modernist and Fundamentalist Thought*, eds. Mansoor Moaddel and Kamran Talattof (New York: St. Martin Press, 2006), 257.
8 Imam Ruhullah Khomeini, 'The Pillars of an Islamic State', in *Contemporary Debates in Islam: An Anthology of Modernist and Fundamentalist Thought*, eds. Mansoor Moaddel and Kamran Talattof (New York: St. Martin Press, 2006), 247–250.
9 Ibn Mutahir was a distinguished student of Nizam-ul-Mulk Tusi and a recognized scholar of Shiite Islam.
10 Imam Muslim, *Sahih Muslim, Kitāb al-Imārah*, 4555–4557.
11 Ghulam Ahmed Hariri's introductory note in Ibn Taimmiyah, *Al-Muntqā min Minhāj al-Sunnah al-Nabawiyyah* (Aqeedah Library, 2010), 25, 26.
12 Imam Muslim, *Sahih Muslim, Kitāb al-Imārah*, 4555–4557, quoted in Ibn Taimmiyah, *Al-Muntqā min Minhāj al-Sunnah*, 45.
13 Imam Muslim, *Sahih Muslim, Kitāb al-Manāqab Ali*, 6225, 6226. *Hadith* of *ghadīr* refers to the address of the Prophet on the pond of *Khumm* in 632 AD. The Shiites commemorate this event on the 18th day of the last month of the Islamic calendar.
14 Imam Bukhari, *Sahih Bukhari, Kitāb al-Manāqab Ali*, 3706; *Kitab Fadhāil As-Sahāb al-Nabi*, 3706; also see Muhammad Bin Sa'ad, *Tabqāt Ibn Sa'ad*, Urdu trans. Abdullah Al-Amadi (Karachi: Nafees Academy) 2, 154.
15 Bonney, *Jihad*, 493.
16 Ibn Taimmiyah, *Al-Muntqā min Minhāj al-Sunnah*, 82, 88.
17 Quoted in Bonney, *Jihad*, 494.
18 He (839–923) is a famous historian of the early period of Islam. His luminous work titled *Tarīkh al-Umam wal Mulūk* is considered an authentic source of Islamic history. He is also an exegete of the Quran.
19 Al-Tabri, *Tarīkh al-Umam wal Mulūk*, Vol. 3, Part II, 18.
20 Quoted in Ibn Taimmiyah, *Al-Muntqā min Minhāj al-Sunnah*, 79–85.
21 Quoted in Hafiz Jalaluddin Abdur Rehman Bin Abu Bakr Al- Sayyuti, *Tarīkh Al-Khulāfā*, trans. Iqbal-ud-Din Ahmed (Karachi: Nafees Academy, 1983), 24.
22 Imam Bukhari, *Sahih Bukhari, Kitāb al-Ahkām*, 7220; Imam Muslim, *Sahih Muslim, Kitāb Fadhāil As-Sahāb al-Nabi*, 5878.
23 Bazaz has quoted in his Musnad a *hadith* on the authority of Abu Yaqzan, which reads as follow: 'Once people asked the Prophet the reason for not appointing an amir after him. The Prophet replied that if he had appointed an amir, the people would have disobeyed him and anger of God would engulf them'. However, Sayyuti quotes Hakim that authority of Abu Yakzan is weak. See Al-Sayyuti, *Tarīkh Al-Khulāfā*, 23.
24 Muhammad Bin Sa'ad, *Tabqāt Ibn Sa'ad*, Vol. 2, 114, 115.
25 Imam Muslim, *Sahih Muslim, Kitāb Fadhāil As-Sahāb al-Nabi*: 5877.
26 There are certain sections who argue that the Sunnite theology extends allowance to a caliph to nominate his successor provided he is satisfied regarding his successor's qualifications and further that public, too, will accept him as caliph. The Sunnite theology also gives the caliph an option to refer the matter of election of caliph to *ahl al-hall wa'l-aqd* (those who lose and bind). See Maulana Muhammad Manzoor Naumani, *Ma'arif Al-Hadith,* (Urdu) Vol. vii (Karachi: Dar Al-Asha't, 2007), 573.
27 Al-Tabri, *Tarīkh al-Umam wal Mulūk*, Vol. 3, Part I, 259.
28 Maulana Muhammad Manzoor Naumani, *Irani Inqilab,* Imam *Khomeini aur Shi'yyat*, (Lahore: Maktaba Madniyyah, 1984), 103–110.

29 Yazid b. Mu'awiyah did not have qualities to become a legitimate caliph of the Muslims after Amir Mu'awiyah. Imam Hussain b. Ali, the grandson of the Prophet, the most exalted personality of Islam at that time, refused to acknowledge the legitimacy of his rule. Consequently, the Battle of Karbala took place in 61 AH, resulting in the martyrdom of Imam Hussain and his family.
30 Ghulam Ahmed Hariri's introductory note of Ibn Taimmiyah, *Al-Muntqā min Minhāj al-Sunnah*, 19; Ibn Hazam (994–1064 AD) was a Sunnite Spanish Clergy.
31 Al-Raziq, 'The Problem of Caliphate', 2006, 95–100.
32 Ibn Taimmiyah, *Al-Muntqā min Minhāj al-Sunnah*, 34.
33 Ibn Kathir, *Al-Bidāyah wal Nihāyah* Vol. 8, Part II, 576–577.
34 Ibid., Vol.11, 259.
35 Ibn Taimmiyah, *Al-Muntqā min Minhāj al-Sunnah*, 89. The people in authority are called *ahl al-hall wa'l-aqd* (those who loose and bind).
36 Imam Bukhari, *Sahih Bukhari*, *Kitāb al Fitan*: 2; *Kitāb al-Ahkām*: 4; Imam Muslim, *Sahih Muslim*, *Kitāb al-Imārah*: 53–56, 58.
37 Qadi Abu Bakr Baqilani quoted in al-Sayyuti, *Tarīkh Al-Khulāfā,* 21, 22.
38 Ibn Khaldun was the first distinguished Muslim historian who created space for the plurality of caliphs. He argued that Islam is not convinced of spiritual headship devoid of political authority. As caliphate has expanded to remote areas rendering it impossible for the caliph to exercise his political authority from the central seat of caliphate, a rationale for the plurality of caliphs can be drawn from these conditions.
39 Al-Sayyuti, *Tarīkh Al-Khulāfā*, 20.
40 Fatimids are called Ubaidis after Ubayd Allah al-Mahdi, the founder of the Fatimid caliphate.
41 Ibid., 20–22.
42 Imam Muslim, *Sahih Muslim*, *Kitāb al-Imārah*, 447–448; Imam Bukhari, *Sahih Bukhari*, *Kitāb Al-Hadūd*: 6830, *Kitāb Al-Ahkām*: 7222, 7223. According to these *ahadith,* the Prophet has been reported to have said that the caliphs would be of the Qurayshite descent. The traditional Sunnite scholars like Al-Mawardi and others consider the condition of the Quraysh descent essential for the selection of the caliph. See, for example, Al-Mawardi, *Ahkām al- Sultāniyāh*, 12.
43 Al-Sayyuti, *Tarīkh Al-Khulāfā*, 20.
44 Though violence is contrary to the teachings of the Christ, the church sanctioned its use to serve the interests of the state. He further argues that true Christian teachings occupied space in human consciousness not through violent means but through love and peace. He has referred to the contributions of proponents of 'non-resistance' to evil. They argue that the modern Christian world has adopted false Christianity, which has no connection with the original teachings of the Christ. The theological distortions crept into original Christian teachings in the period of Constantine the Great, when theology was employed to serve the interests of the political elite. See Tolstoy, *The Kingdom of God Is within You*, 4–15.
45 Roxanne L. Euben, *Enemy in the Mirror: Islamic Fundamentalism and the Limits of Modern Rationalism: A Work of Comparative Political Theory* (Princeton: Princeton University Press, 1999).
46 Akhavi, 'Islam, Politics and Society', 404–431.
47 Khomeini, 'The Pillars of an Islamic State', 247–250.
48 Khomeini, 'The Necessity of Islamic Government', 251–262.
49 Nikki R. Keddi, 'Iran: Change in Islam; Islam and Change', *International Journal of Middle Eastern Studies* 11., no. 4 (1980): 527–542.
50 Even in 19th century Iran, opposition to state was defined by ulema's concern to promote territorial integrity of the Muslim lands against the designs of imperialist

forces; for details see William M. Floor, 'Revolutionary Character of the Iranian Ulama: Wishful Thinking or Reality?' *International Journal of Middle East Studies* 12, no. 4 (1980): 501–524.

51 Khomeini, 'The Necessity of Islamic Government', 257, 258.

52 Ibid.

53 Kazem Ghazi Zadeh, 'General Principles of Imam Khumayni's Political Thought', trans. A. N. Baqir Shahi, *Message of Thaqalayn: A Quarterly journal of Islamic studies* 2, no. 2 & 3, accessed December 13, 2020, https://www.al-islam.org/printpdf/book/export/html/21747.

54 Khomeini, 'Necessity of Islamic Government.'

55 Ibid.

56 Shahrough Akhavi, 'The Ideology and Praxis of Shi'ism in Iranian Revolution', *Comparative Studies in Society and History* 25, no. 2 (1983): 195–221; also see Floor, 'Revolutionary Character of the Iranian Ulama', 501–524.

57 Ibid.

58 Ibid.

59 Ibid.

60 C. M. Lake, 'Problems Encountered in Establishing an Islamic Republic in Iran 1979–1981', *Bulletin (British Society for Middle Eastern Studies)* 9, no. 2 (1982): 141–170.

61 Ibid.

62 Khomeini, 'The Necessity of Islamic Government', 256.

63 Akhavi, 'Islam, Politics and Society', 404–431.

64 Khomeini quoted the following statement of Ali, the fourth pious caliph from Nehj al-Balagha: 'I have accepted the task of Government because God, exalted and Almighty, has exacted from the scholars of Islam a pledge not to sit silent and idle in the face of gluttony and plundering of the oppressors, on the one hand and hunger and deprivation of the oppressed on the other – were it not for all this, then I would abandon the reins of the Government and in no way seek it. You would see that this world of yours with all of its position and rank, is less in my eyes than the moisture that comes from the sneeze of a goat.' Khomeini, 'The Necessity of Islamic Government', 258.

65 The reference is to Shah of Iran. See Floor, 'Revolutionary Character of the Iranian Ulama', 501–524.

66 Quoted in Noor Muhammad, 'The Doctrine of Jihad: An Introduction', 381–397.

67 Martin Kramer, *Islam Assembled: The Advent of the Muslim Congresses* (New York: Columbia University Press, 1986).

68 Shmuel Bar, 'Sunnis and Shiites—Between Rapprochement and Conflict', in *Current Trends in Islamist Ideology*, Vol. 2, eds. Hillel Fradkin et al., (Washington, D.C.: Hudson Institute, 2005), 87–96. For primary sources, see Kramer, *Islam Assembled*, 1986.

69 Mohamad Jawad Chirri, *Inquiries about Islam* (Detroit: The Islamic Centre of America, 1986), accessed August 2, 2013, http://www.al-islam.org/inquiries/.

70 Nibras Kazimi, 'Zarqawi's Anti-Shi'a Legacy: Original or Borrowed?' in *Current Trends in Islamist Ideology*, Vol. 4, 53–72.

71 Abdullah Muhammad al-Gharib, *Wa ja'a dawr al-Majūs: al ebād al-tarikhiyaat wal aqa'aidiat was Siyasiyyat le thurat ul-Iraniyyat* (Then Came the Turn of the Majūs), 1406 AH.

72 Ibid.

73 Israel Elad-altman, 'The Sunni-Shi'a Conversion Controversy', in *Current Trends in Islamist Ideology*, Vol. 5, 1–10.

74 Ibid.

75 This militant outfit took its name from an extremist Sunni cleric Haq Nawaz Jhangvi, who hailed from a district Jhang in Pakistan.
76 Husain Haqqani, 'Weeding out the Heretics: Sectarianism in Pakistan', in *Current Trends in Islamist Ideology,* Vol. 4, 77–88.
77 Shaykh Yusuf al-Qaradawi's address in Doha Conference for Dialogue of Islamic Schools of Thought: The Role of Reconciliation in the Ummas's Real Unity, Doha, Qatar, 20–22 January 2007.
78 Ahmed el-Beheiri, Ayman Hamza, and Hisham Abdel Halim, 'Al-Azhar Scholars Warn of a Dangerous Shiite Tide', *Al-masry Al-youm* no. 1587, October 17, 2008.
79 Ahmad Majidyar, 'Morrocon Officials Accuse Iran of Spreading Shiism in the Sunni Kingdom', Middle East Institute, March 30, 2017.
80 Boualem Ghomrassa, 'Al-Sulutat al-Jaza'iriyyah Tuhaqqiq fi Nashat Majmu'at Shi'iyyah', *Al-Sharq al-Awsat*, January 6, 2007.
81 Uthman Isa, '*Hatta la Yuqal: Kana al-Sudan Baladan Sunniyyan*', *Albainah*, no. 166.
82 Elad-altman, 'The Sunni-Shi'a Conversion Controversy', 1–10.
83 Bar, 'Sunnis and Shiites- Between Rapprochement and Conflict', 87–96.
84 Ibid.

4 Codification of violence

The ideological nature of the conflict between the Islamists and the West was a catalyst not only in remodelling the international security context but also in transforming the internal dynamics of the Muslim societies. When juxtaposed with the realpolitik, the ideological character of the conflict germinated militancy as a response to repressive policies of the West. The militancy appeared to be a tool to resist the imperialist West, but it also affected the socio-religious fabric of Muslim societies. Increased ex-communication emerged in theological discourse as a broader theological base got contaminated with extremism. This changed the boundaries of faith on one hand, and the militants got an opportunity to exploit the old schisms between the Sunnites and the Shiites to legitimize their violence on the other.

It is evident that the Islamic society was not polarized across sectarian lines until the emergence of the Safavid Empire in the 16th century. Popular and syncretic culture remained one of the main targets of the elite class of the clergy. This turned into wide-scale persecution when championed by the political objectives of the ruling elite. At times, this deviance cut across socio-political dynamics and was fiercely contested. The case of the Roshinya movement is one glaring example where force was used to quell deviant ideas, which were simultaneously supported through codification of the use of violence. The same trend is also discernible in the broader spectrum of the Muslim history, especially in terms of Ayubid's role in the takeover of Egypt. In this case, the *raison d'être* for violence against the fellow Muslims was treason-cum-collaboration with the Crusaders. In both instances, the violence was resorted to as a political settlement achieved through religious injunctions. The case of Ibn Taimmiyah against the Mongols reflects another trend of negotiating political stability through the use of violence against fellow Muslims. These events demonstrate an inherent imbalance that was always a dominant aspect for elite clergy as well as political rulers. However, it never reached the level of the masses. This became possible only when colonization took place in the Muslim lands. Colonization as a phenomenon codified public and private Islamic law, which was later replaced by European codes at least in the public sphere. However, with the advent of the printing press and the downfall of the

DOI: 10.4324/9781003164883-4

Muslim elite, the tendencies to violence were further developed, codified and transmitted against the general masses in the 18th and 19th centuries.

The search for religious identity has unmasked the trends of the 19th century, when religion was coupled with state patronage of the use of violence to attain political objectives. This cyclic outburst has been the product of the codification of violence, which was undertaken at the behest of the ulema – from Shah Abdul Aziz to Maulana Manzoor Ahmed Naumani. The current chapter discovers the trajectories upon which violence emerging from identity crises was codified. These trajectories include 'linkage between violence and collaboration with the colonialists', 'sectarian violence due to irrelevance of Ummah' and 'correlation between violence and ideological nostalgia produced by the abolition of Muslim caliphate'. Violence has been adopted at the individual or group level as a means of emancipation and identity when the state structure was incapacitated to resolve the conflict situation and when the society failed to bridge the sectarian cleavage. This led to the codification of violence at individual or group levels or at times between the states within the fold of Islam.

Violence and identity crisis

National identity is an expression of the beliefs of a group of people that attributes them a character distinct from others. The urge to assume a national identity may be available in different groups but the elements that provide food to this urge may vary.[1] These elements may include psychology, culture, common history, political orientations and territorial considerations. National identity stems from the confluence of these factors but they may not all have equal impact. One element may overshadow the other in a particular case. For instance, religion is a major factor that provides nationhood to Jews. History has also witnessed racial discrimination in the quest for nationhood. These challenges inspired leaders like Nelson Mandela in South Africa to devote their whole lives to preserving and protecting their nationhood through resisting racial apartheid.

However, the relevance of a particular pattern of national identity recedes into the background when an alternative replaces it during the course of history. Nationalism as a source of national identity reverted to a subordinate position when during the Cold War era ideology divided the world into two blocks – one block of nations sought to draw their national identity from Communism and the other preferred to draw it from capitalism. Even states with distinct ideological affiliations like the Muslim states could feel the appeal of these ideologies. Nasser in Egypt introduced Arab socialism whereas in Pakistan in the early 1970s popular sentiments were stirred up by the political leadership who introduced socialist elements into the political sphere.

In pre-Islamic Arab society, tribal affiliations were more relevant than anything else in the constitution of nationhood. A review of pre-Islamic

Arab literature suggests that the Arabs used to take pride in their tribal affiliations, which they considered their source of physical strength.[2] These tribal affiliations, being deeply rooted in history, were part of the Arab culture. The proclamation of faith by the Prophet Muhammad changed this political configuration altogether and introduced the Arabs to a new concept of nationhood which they were hitherto unaware of. In a short span of time, nationhood developed on the basis of the belief system. Badr (2 AH) was the first battlefield to test the strength of this new configuration. Previously, battles had been fought between parties who drew their strength from tribal pride and affiliations, but in the case of Badr, the dynamics of conflict changed – from tribal rivalries to ideological faultlines. Those who professed the new faith constituted a nation vis-à-vis those who refuted and resisted the new faith. The strength of faith overshadowed even blood relationships. For instance, Abu Bakr fought against his son Abdur Rehman, who was still in the ranks of pagans. Similarly, Umar killed his uncle Aas b. Hasham.[3] Ibn Jozi narrates that, while at Makkah, Aas b. Hasham had defended Umar against the pagans of Makkah when he declared his profession of faith.[4]

The evidence affirms the correlation between identity and violence where the state as an actor was involved. For instance, the ideological conflict between Communism and capitalism had state apparatus behind it. Even in the early period of Islam, Muslims fought to preserve and protect their distinct identity after the establishment of the city-state of Madina. Tamils in northern Sri Lanka started a campaign to secure their separate national identity and formed Liberation Tigers of Tamil Elam (LTTE) in 1976. This was a separatist militant organization that aimed at establishing a separate state for the Tamils. Similarly, the rise of the Khalistan movement in the 1970s in Indian Punjab constituted another example of the interrelationship between identity crises and violence at the societal level. Besides this, the intifada that started in 1987 in Palestine was also associated with the national identity question against the occupation of Israel.

The following discussion will outline the codification of violence emerging from identity crises on three trajectories.

Linkage between violence and collaboration with the colonialists

In recent history, the Europeans used ideology to justify their exploitation of the resources of the colonized lands. They portrayed themselves not as invaders or agents of exploitation but rather as instruments of civilization for the otherwise 'uncivilized' people of the third world. However, the subject population could not be overwhelmed by this ideology, and attempts to legitimize colonialism were soon confronted by the aspirations of the local population articulated in terms of nationalism. It resulted in the eventual collapse of the entire edifice of colonialism.[5] The conflict between local aspirations and colonial ideals affirmed the linkage between violence and colonialism. The phenomenon of the emergence of violence can be analysed in three strands: 'threat to traditional cultural values', 'emergence of class conflict' and 'economic exploitation'.

Threat to cultural values

The colonization process resulted in the erosion of traditional cultural values, which commanded the emotional attachment of the population. For instance, in Africa, the traditional system of conflict resolution got eroded, and weaker democratic institutions were replaced by colonial authoritarianism.[6] The importation of westernization in the garb of modernization to the African lands was seen as an attempt to impose a foreign culture upon the traditional values.[7] In the African political context, some may adopt the thesis of the positive effects of colonialism as a way to understand the process of democratization and westernization of African society.[8] However, this thesis is rejected for being devoid of historical evidence as the society had already developed solid state structures on democratic foundations even before the dawn of colonial rule. Colonialism was a catalyst in the erosion of social fabric and state structures instead of bringing any positive effects.[9] On the social side, colonialism posed a challenge to the strong family structure by sowing the seeds of individualism. With the weakening of social structures, the pace of urbanization also accelerated. Moreover, with the westernization of the African society, affiliation with the native language also declined, and the tendency to speak a foreign language developed.

The case of colonial India also confirms a strong correlation between violence and identity crises. The Muslims' national identity emerged more distinctively after the fall of the Mughals. It originated from the exploitative measures taken by both the Hindus and the British. The fall of the Mughals followed by the advent of the British resulted in the dismantling of well-established Muslim cultural identities. Traditional Muslim institutions like Islamic laws, Islamic seminaries and the Persian language were arbitrarily replaced with British laws, Christian missionary schools and the English language, respectively.[10] Besides the British government's initiatives to westernize the Indian society, two unofficial agencies – the English press and missionaries – played an important role in helping western values find a foothold in Indian society. As far as the English press is concerned, *Statesman* and *Times of India* played a vital role in transforming the opinion of Indians in favour of the British. With the growth of an Anglophone class in India, the impact of these newspapers on the cultural transformation of the society increased manifold.[11] Cultural transformation in Indian society also owes a lot to the Christian missions in India. The British government aided the missionary elements' work in India, in support of popularizing the western outlook in Indian society. Christian missionaries were encouraged to extend their sphere of work from preaching to teaching. Presbyterian Alexander Duff's Foundation was established in 1830 in Calcutta and claimed to have appeal for the Indians ranging from the common man to the intellectual elite. Subsequently, a network of mission education institutes like Madras Christian College was established. Besides education activities, the missionary elements were also encouraged to participate in philanthropic activities to promote pro-western sentiment in Indian society.[12]

This cultural onslaught by the British, widely supporting Hindu interests, had a two-way impact on the regional socio-economic and political environment. In the first instance, it humiliated the Muslim community, causing them utmost frustration and a sense of deprivation. The same cultural onslaught encouraged the opportunist Hindus to make strides in the environment, which was enormously discriminatory against the Muslims. The British-Hindu nexus became further evident when the orthodox Hindu common man, mostly under the influence of the politico-religious Hindu elite, did not resist the anti-Muslim overtures of the British.[13] These policies produced widespread frustration in the Muslim community, which led to a Muslim resistance movement as a natural course of action against the threats to Muslim identities.

Nonetheless, discontentment against colonial rule was not experienced just by Indian Muslims. The Hindus took the advent of the British as an opportunity to secure political gains vis-à-vis the Muslims from whom the colonialists had usurped the political authority. However, they were averse to the colonial domination of India. In this contextual framework, though the ruling elite in United India surrendered political authority to the British, the Hindu and Muslim communities did not surrender to the cultural onslaught of the West. Though complete alienation of both the Hindus and the Muslims from the colonial culture was not possible, their policy of aloofness and opposition to technological innovations successfully avoided the cultural fusion of all three – Hindus, Muslims and the British. Nevertheless, Indian society did feature this cultural surrender but in a partial manner. The westernization of society was more evident around Calcutta, where secular rationalism triumphed over the conservatism peculiar to the Indian society. This triumph, however, produced a reaction that culminated in the emergence of religious rhetoric that called for violence against the alien threats. With the Hindus, this codification of violence emerged through Brahmo Samaj in 1928, which may aptly be termed an intellectual response to the western threat, whereas with the Muslims, this codification of violence emerged through testing the Wahabi ideology against the colonial challenge by Sayyed Ahmed of Bareilly in the early 19th century.[14] He declared India to be *dār-ul-harb* (land of war) because it had fallen to foreign occupation.[15]

Emergence of class conflict

The colonial powers created social stratification in colonized societies to perpetuate their control. With the backings of powerful military machines, this divisive policy stopped the locals from rising up against the foreign rulers.[16]

This policy aimed to achieve its goals by targeting the existing traditional education system. In Kano City of Nigeria, the British introduced a curriculum for ulema which was a semblance of secular and Islamic education and replaced the traditional education system that was in conflict with colonial objectives. Traditional centres of learning which had been producing traditional clergy got a blow when the British established Kano Law School to provide a new scheme of education.[17] This school distracted the students from following the traditional Maliki code. Similarly, in Sudan, the British attempted to bring religious ideals in conformity with the social ideals of British society. Likewise, in India, after the fall of the Mughals, the British took over the reins of government and introduced the British secular approach into the functioning process of the government. Islamic laws were replaced with British laws, Muslim seminaries with missionary schools and the Persian language with English, not just for official proceedings but even as the medium of education as well. This made it virtually impossible for Indians to enter government jobs without acquiring proficiency in the English language.[18] The Islamic cultural heritage was, thus, either demolished or relegated to the background, making room for alien secular traits in all walks of life. In reaction, the clergy made endeavours to preserve and protect the religious and cultural fabric of society through establishing religious seminaries like Dar-ul-Uloom Deoband (1866) and Dar-ul-Uloom Nadwatul Ulema Lakhnow (1894). On the other side of the fence, Sir Sayyed Ahmed Khan aimed to reconcile Islam with western democratic ideals through establishing Muhammadan Anglo-Oriental College (1877). Later on, this college was upgraded to Aligarh University with the collaboration of the British. Moreover, Sir Charles Wood's educational policy of 1854 led to the foundation of three universities at Madras, Bombay and Calcutta. In the post-1857 scenario, this policy was a success in establishing a network of public schools and British government-funded private schools across India.[19]

Though the impact of the colonial approach to create social stratification may not be quantifiable, evidence suggests that the British were successful in creating complex faultlines in colonial societies on the trajectories of two mutually divergent phenomena: rationalism and traditionalism. British-supported rationalism found its advocates in otherwise traditional societies where traditionalism could draw strength from historically deep-rooted traditions. In the African context, Kano provides a case study where the British attempted to bring the ulema in line with colonial objectives through a rational interpretation of religious precepts. However, these efforts could not yield the desired results because traditional ulema remained committed to their traditional religious standpoint.[20]

In a larger perspective, the socio-religious divisions further strengthened when a class of apologists emerged who exhausted their energies in exploring similarities between Islamic values and western democratic ideals. Their narrative, which found common ground with the apologists ranging from India to Sudan, revisited Islamic precepts through western democratic lenses instead of redefining Islam in its own framework. As already noted, the early 20th century witnessed Sir Sayyed Ahmed Khan making endeavours to remove ideological faultlines between the imperialist West and the Indian Muslims. He focused upon exploring the common ground between the two. Similarly, in Sudan, Mahmoud Muhammad Taha was an advocate of democratic norms, which earned him the opposition of the majority of ulema in society. These Muslim rationalists were accused of changing the spirit of the faith and were labelled as apologists. Nevertheless, the conflict between the rationalists and traditionalists became a permanent feature of Muslim societies, which led to the codification of violence.

Economic exploitation

In economic terms, colonialism can be defined as a design by powerful nations to exploit the resources of the weaker nations. During the colonial era, the Europeans treated the colonized lands as the nurseries of cheap labour, markets of raw material and grounds to strengthen their respective economies and military muscle.[21] In Africa, colonialism redesigned the patterns of agricultural production to support the economies of the colonial powers instead of fulfilling the demands of the local farmers. This policy helped the colonialists to prosper but hunger, starvation and deprivation became the destiny of the local population.[22] Similarly, India was taken as a market for British commodities where the investors could enjoy a monopoly over the means of production as well as sources of raw material for the British industry. Colonialism transferred the purchasing power of the local middle class either to the foreigners or to those locals who through their social proximity with the foreigners had tastes for foreign goods. Imports increased, which caused huge damage to the local industry. Local savings drained out of India.

After World War II, colonialism did not surrender its relevance to power politics but the colonial patterns, of course, changed. Instead of physically invading, the two major powers – the United States and the USSR – both sought to bring different states under their hegemony through extending their respective ideological webs and bifurcating the world into two ideological camps. The phenomenon underwent further transformations during the post-Cold War period. These changes might be examined from the perspective of global capitalist theory. The theory explains shifts in the tactical patterns of imperialism from being a state-centred phenomenon to an instrument of the transnational capitalist class.[23] It explains the US military interventions as a support mechanism for the capitalist class. Iraq was the testing ground for the new imperialist tactics as part of the transnational capitalist design. International oil companies that represent the international capitalist elite have a leading role in the larger design.[24] Reportedly, the capitalist elite have the potential to manoeuvre the United States' decision making to secure their interests worldwide. A report suggests that President George Bush did not sign the Kyoto Global Warming

Treaty partly due to resistance from the powerful oil company ExxonMobil.[25] These international oil companies have the capacity to resist US energy policy if it does not suit their interests.[26]

Notwithstanding the changing tactical patterns of colonialism, the phenomenon has always earned resentment from Muslims in general and resistance from the Islamists. As said earlier, colonialism triggered armed resistance in the subcontinent and further codified violence on the trajectory of Wahabi ideology that drew its spirit from Ibn Taimmiyah. Though in the aftermath of World War II traditional colonialism gave way to so-called sovereign statehood, the major world powers continued to exploit the economic resources of Muslim states through changed tactics. The hostility of Muslims against the colonial powers continued with the new dynamics. During the classical colonial period, their animosity was solely directed to the foreign colonial powers. Now it found in Muslim rulers a new target in addition to the previous one. These Muslim rulers are charged with pursuing the western agenda. The changed international scenario revised theological discourse regarding the nature of the relationship between believers and non-believers. Collaboration with infidels emerged as a factor to invoke *takfīr* in the Muslim world.

Ibn Taimmiyah, being a resource for the Islamists, occupies the central stage in redrawing the boundaries of faith on the premise of *mawālāt* (collaborating with non-believers). He discussed the question of *mawālāt* at length and argued for its clear refutation as a natural requirement of the faith. To put it another way, non-rejection of friendship with non-believers constitutes a characteristic feature of hypocrisy, which is condemned by the Quran: 'Bear unto the hypocrites the tidings that for them there is a painful doom. Those who chose disbelievers for their friends instead of believers! Do they look for power at their hands? Lo! all power appertaineth to Allah' (An-Nisā: 138, 139).[27] However, he further argues that obedience to the non-believers' infidelity under compulsion does not amount to approving of unbelief. The Quran says, 'Let not the believers take disbelievers for their friends in preference to believers. Whoso doeth that hath no connection with Allah unless (it be) that ye but guard yourselves against them, taking (as it were) security. Allah biddeth you beware (only) of Himself. Unto Allah is the journeying' (Al-Imrān: 28). Ibn Taimmiyah considers the act of helping the non-believers and avoidance of categorical rejection of their faith equal to the approval of unbelief as such.[28] He makes it clear that friendship with the non-believers falls in conflict with the following Quranic injunctions, 'O ye who believe! Take not the Jews and the Christians for friends. They are friends one to another. He among you who taketh them for friends is (one) of them. Lo! Allah guideth not wrongdoing folk. O ye who believe! Take not the Jews and the Christians for friends. They are friends one to another. He among you who taketh them for friends is (one) of them. Lo! Allah guideth not wrongdoing folk' (Al-Maidah: 51, 52).[29]

The Quran further says: 'Thou wilt not find folk who believe in Allah and the Last Day loving those who oppose Allah and His messenger, even though they be their fathers or their sons or their brethren or their clan. As for such, He hath written faith upon their hearts and hath strengthened them with a Spirit from Him, and He will bring them into Gardens underneath which rivers flow, wherein they will abide. Allah is well pleased with them, and they are well pleased with Him. They are Allah's party. Lo! is it not Allah's party who are the successful?' (Al-Mujaadilah: 22).

This narrative was borrowed by Muhammad b. Abdul Wahab as one of his ten nullifiers of Islam.[30] This narrative codifies the anatomy of violence in Muslim societies.

Sectarian violence due to irrelevance of Ummah

As discussed earlier, with the advent of Islam, the secular divisions in the Arab society were replaced with ideological ones by supplanting the tribal pride with religious *assābiyah* (group feelings) as a resource to nationhood. The old social stratification was based upon traditional patterns of tribal status, racial considerations, martial capacity and financial position. This social structure was done away with in the new Arabian society. The new faith identified piety (*taqwā*) as the only criterion of social ascendancy. The Prophet in his farewell sermon categorically abolished the traditional model of social stratifications peculiar in the Arab society and replaced it with a universal brotherhood of the believers. He declared, 'All mankind is from Adam and Eve, an Arab has no superiority over a non-Arab nor a non-Arab has any superiority over an Arab; also a white has no superiority over black nor a black has any superiority over white except by *taqwā* (piety) and good action'. He further said, 'Learn that every Muslim is a brother to every Muslim and that the Muslims constitute one brotherhood. Nothing shall be legitimate to a Muslim, which belongs to a fellow Muslim unless it was given freely and willingly. Do not, therefore, do injustice to yourselves'.[31]

The ideological community was established with the proclamation of faith by the Prophet in Makkah. The believers were identified as a community distinct from the non-believers. The subsequent armed conflict between the believers and non-believers confirmed this new ideological divide. *Mawākhāt-e-Medina* (Brotherhood at Madina) is a classic example of this ideological brotherhood. The Prophet established the ideological brotherhood amongst *ansār* (helpers at Madina) and the emigrants from Makkah. The believers internalized fellowship with unprecedented vehemence.[32] The brotherhood imbued with the unprecedented spirit of sacrifice defined the pattern of the social life of the Muslims in Madina and naturally was a role model for Muslims during the subsequent ages. This spirit of sacrifice on the part of the believers earned divine commendation in the following words: 'And (as for the believers) hath attuned their hearts. If thou hadst spent all that is in the earth thou couldst not have attuned their hearts, but

Allah hath attuned them. Lo! He is Mighty, Wise' (Al-'Anfāl: 63). Another verse reads as follow: 'Lo! those who believed and left their homes and strove with their wealth and their lives for the cause of Allah, and those who took them in and helped them: these are protecting friends one of another. And those who believed but did not leave their homes, ye have no duty to protect them till they leave their homes; but if they seek help from you in the matter of religion then it is your duty to help (them) except against a folk between whom and you there is a treaty. Allah is Seer of what ye do' (Al-'Anfāl: 72).

This brotherhood was ordained by Allah in these words: 'And hold fast by the covenant of Allah all together and be not disunited, and remember the favour of Allah on you when you were enemies, then He united your hearts so by His favour you became brethren; and you were on the brink of a pit of fire, then He saved you from it, thus does Allah make clear to you His communications that you may follow the right way' (Al-Imrān: 103) (Al-Hujurat: 10, Al-Tawbah: 71).

The Quran disapproves of those who stir up division amongst the community of the faithful. It says, 'Lo! As for those who sunder their religion and become schismatics, no concern at all hast thou with them. Their case will go to Allah, Who then will tell them what they used to do' (Al-'An`ām: 159). The Prophet declared this spirit of brotherhood to be a prerequisite for the faithful and essential for eternal success in the hereafter.[33]

The divine Will to create such an integrated community of believers not only aimed to create a socially harmonious society but also a community that could be entrusted with the coercive authority to enforce discipline in the world. The Quran reads as follows: 'Ye are the best community that hath been raised up for mankind. Ye enjoin right conduct and forbid indecency; and ye believe in Allah. And if the People of the Scripture had believed it had been better for them. Some of them are believers; but most of them are evil-livers' (Al-Imrān: 110). This authority is exercised through the caliphate, which commands not the will of the majority, as is the case with western democracy, but rather the will of the entire community of believers. During the period of *rāshidūn* (the pious caliphs), the authority to choose the caliph vested with *ahl al-hall wa'l-aqd* (those who loose and bind).[34] It was a selective committee from the close Companions of the Prophet whose commitment to the faith was undisputedly recognized. The nature of the caliphate was essentially ideological. As the caliph was to represent and exercise the coercive authority of the Islamic state, he was chosen from the people, most creditable in religious terms. Given his uncontested religious credibility, the caliph could legitimately command the will of the entire Muslim Ummah. Moreover, as the majority of the close Companions of the Prophet, whose juristic (*ijtihādī*) qualifications were undisputedly acknowledged, were residing in Madina, their *baya'ā* to the caliph was enough to earn him legitimacy across the Muslim society. Moreover, caliphate was not considered as a prize but rather a responsibility to the people as well as to

Allah. The *rāshidūn* were undoubtedly ideal disciples of the Prophet, but none of them ever desired to hold the political office and instead always accepted it with disinclination. The Prophet refused to entrust political authority to the one who asked for it.[35] Umar even forbade anyone from his tribe Banu Adī from assuming this office after him.[36]

Even with the radical shift in political order from *shūrā*-based caliphate to hereditary rule (*malūkiyyat*), the legitimacy arising out of *baya'ā* (allegiance) of the exalted personalities of the faith did not recede. Yazid's insistence on securing *baya'ā* from Hussain was actually aimed to earn legitimacy for his rule which, given the unparalleled religious authenticity associated with the personality of Hussain, was otherwise not possible. However, his refusal to recognize the invalid rule of Yazid affirmed the mutually inclusive relationship between legitimacy crises and violence in the Muslim historical discourse. The question of legitimacy produced schisms in the body politic of the Muslims. When juxtaposed with politics, these schisms led to the emergence of sectarian empires. The Shiite Fatimid and Safavid Empires emerged out of the Sunnite Abbasid and Ottoman caliphates, respectively. The emergence of sectarian empires resulted in the plurality of the power centres as well as multiple centres for legitimacy. The Sunnite power centres could draw legitimacy from their Sunnite subjects whereas the Shiite could explore legitimacy amongst the Shiite population. After the pious caliphate, the spirit of the political order changed radically; yet, the ruling elite continued to draw legitimacy from the nomenclature of caliphate even though symbolically. Even after the evaporation of the political authority of the caliph, his name continued to be mentioned in the Friday sermons in recognition of his spiritual headship. The symbolic value of the caliphate did not diminish altogether until the early years of the 20th century when a class of apologists emerged as a by-product of western colonialism that had strong likings for western democratic values. Though Rashid Rida, a 19th-century Egyptian reformer, subscribed to western constitutionalism against the absolutism prevalent in contemporary Muslim societies, he could never delink himself from the classical approach to the caliphate.[37]

Nevertheless, with the abolition of the caliphate in the early 20th century, the Ummah became irrelevant to exercise coercive authority through the caliphate. As the nation-state system that replaced the caliphate had hardly any theological approval, it could not earn legitimacy to exercise this authority. This legitimacy crisis strengthened the historically embedded interrelationship between legitimacy crises and violence. Different groups of Islamists emerged who claimed legitimacy to exercise the coercive authority which was hitherto the sphere of the caliphate. They claimed legitimacy to use violence to resist the imperialists who had been hostile to the caliphate, which was the symbol of Muslim unity. They urged that resistance against the imperialists was the foremost religious duty of Muslims. The Islamists argued that, as the collective body of the Muslims to exercise the Quranic laws that govern the Islamic state had already become irrelevant, it had become the individual responsibility of Muslims to perform this duty. This changed scenario helped a new generation of Islamists to assume the authority to exercise violence by themselves. Unlike the apologists, instead of adopting an accommodative approach, they directed their resistance against the imperialists to avenge the termination of the caliphate and exploitation of the resources of the Muslims.[38] The most iconic figures amongst the Islamists were Hassan Al-Banna, Sayyed Qutb, Sayyed Ahmed Shaheed and Sayyed Maududi.

Though the codification of violence on sectarian lines started with the emergence of sectarian empires, it could not reach its culmination as long as the mandate of exercising coercive authority remained with the Ummah as a whole. With the erosion of the legitimate coercive authority of the Ummah exercised through the caliphate, the sectarian power centres were free to exercise the authority in pursuance of their sectarian designs. As the colonialists developed the nation-state system on the ruins of the Sunnite caliphate, the Sunnite resistance groups charged the Shiites with collaborating with the colonialists to undermine their political influence. The Sunnite scholarship, besides contesting the theological narrative of the Shiites, labelled the Shiite belief system an outcome of hypocritical political ambitions. Both the classical and the modern Sunnite theorists own and project this narrative.

Amongst the classical theorists, Ibn Taimmiyah seeks to refute the theological veracity of Rawāfidh and Nawāsib, both being astray from the truth as the former rejects the right to the caliphate of the first three caliphs and the latter disapproves of Ali being the part of the chain of the rightly guided caliphs. He argues that the views of both groups stand in contravention to the prophetic tradition that the caliphate of the *rāshidūn* will last for 30 years.[39] He argues that, by not subscribing to the traditions of the Prophet wherein he has been reported to have declared *khurūj* against even an invalid Muslim ruler as external to the faith itself, the Shiites leave the *jama'at* as they decline to render their allegiance to the caliphs who command complete recognition from the Muslims.[40] The Shiites' preference to follow the path deviant from the majority of the Muslims leads Ibn Taimmiyah to undertake a strict approach against them. He shares the conviction held by Sunnite scholars, including Imam Malik and Imam Shāfʾī, that the Shiite narrations are devoid of any religious credibility.[41] He also supports Ibn Hazam, who declined to rely on Shiite traditions to prove the veracity and integrity of the Quran while arguing with a Spanish clergyman.[42] Nevertheless, he claims to follow the Companions of the Prophet and the Hanbalite traditions that observe restraints in excommunicating the Shiites.[43] He avoids proclaiming *takfīr* of the Shiite *mufādilah* simply for believing in the primacy of the right of Ali to the caliphate.[44]

However, socio-political and religious constructs of his time need to be examined in conjunction with his ideas to discern his response to the question of polemics. He was the primary figure to offer a cogent response to the Shiite approach to polemics as contained in Ibn Al-Mutahir's *Minhaj al-Karama,* through his seminal work *Minhaj al-Sunnah.* He traced the origin of *bida'ā* in Muslim societies from the Shiites, the Jews, the Christians, the Mongols and the new converts who happened to confront the politico-religious authority of the Sunnite clergy. He argued that mystical practices carried forward through new converts were external to the faith and these caused innovations to flourish in Muslim societies. For instance, the transmission of Coptic Christian practices to Muslim life is attributed to Christian converts.[45] He argued that the Shiite claim that the proclamation of jihad was an exclusive domain of the imam was not based on Islamic principles. He physically participated twice in the military campaigns of the Mamlūks against the Shiites in Kasrawan in the early 14th century when the latter entered into an alliance with the forces of Unbelief – Franks and Mongols. He also issued a religious decree against these Shiites to legitimize fighting against them. In this context, Ibn Taimmiyah's support to the Sunnite Mamlūks, through military campaigns as well as through issuing religious decrees, may be interpreted as an attempt to contain the influence of the Shiites.[46]

Moreover, theological interpretations, which squeezed the definitional scope of heresy, were primarily produced through historical prejudices which could codify orthodoxy into the Islamic discourse through hostile rhetoric and criticism by the formal sectarian leadership. Informal criticism had the potential to be abused as well. The polemics of Abu al-Mutahir al-Hilli and Ibn Tammiyah defined the distinction between the Sunnites and the Shiites. This distinction paved the way for further sectarian refutations and counter-refutations.[47]

In the 18th-century subcontinent, the anti-Shiite narrative became more prominent when the puritanical views of Ibn Abdul Wahab got a stricter exposition with Shah Abdul Aziz (1745–1823).[48] He traced the origin of the Shiites to Abdullah Ibn Saba, who attempted to introduce unfounded and wrong traditions into the teachings of Islam.[49] Ali strongly reproved these attempts to contaminate the purity of faith. Nevertheless, Ibn Saba succeeded in splitting the supporters of Ali into four groups. These included *Shi'ān-e-Mukhliseen*, who were sincere supporters of Ali as well as the cause of Islam; *mufādilah*, who believed in Ali's primacy to the caliphate; those who slandered the Companions of the Prophet; and finally, *ghāli Shiā,* who exaggerated the status of Ali.[50] The slanderers exploited the controversies surrounding issues like the battle of *Camel* and the Garden of Fidak.[51]

Shah Abdul Aziz joined the medieval Sunnite scholarship in questioning the authenticity of the Shiite narrations.[52] Relying upon the sources of the Shiites like *Usūl-e-Kāfi* and the views of even then extinct Shiite sub-sects, he made the point that the Shiites extended controversies to the fundamentals of the faith. He challenged the Shiite notion of the exclusivity of reason to unravel the ultimate truth. He upheld the Sunnite view that the conjunction of reason and revelation was a conduit to explore the ultimate truth. The

Sunnites build their argument on the fundamental question that, if knowledge is the sole domain of reason, what is the purpose of prophethood in terms of human salvation? He discredited Imam Kalaini's[53] view that it was obligatory upon the believers to acknowledge the divine attributes through rationalism because such a sublime theosophical capability (*erfān*) could be developed only through divine Will reflected through the prophethood.[54] He reprimanded the Ismailite Shiites for not believing even in the divine attributes like oneness, omnipresence, omnipotence, all-hearing, all-knowing and exclusive divine eternity. These views stand in categorical contradiction of the Quran, *ahadith* and the narrations even in *Nahj-ul-Balagha*. He further argued that the Shiites doubted the authenticity of the Quran, which was a clear negation of divine proclamation that its protection would rest with Allah Himself.[55] Shah Abdul Aziz further argued that such contradictions continued to persist in details of the revelation of the prophethood. He refuted the Shiite belief that revealing the Prophet to mankind was obligatory upon God. On the contrary, he upheld the Sunnite view that God being omnipotent was free from any obligation and the prophethood was a divine blessing for humanity. The Quran says, 'Allah verily hath shown grace to the believers by sending unto them a messenger of their own who reciteth unto them His revelations, and causeth them to grow, and teacheth them the Scripture and wisdom; although before (he came to them) they were in flagrant error' (Al-Imrān: 164). He argued that the Shiites tended to elevate Ali to a position higher even than the prophets except Prophet Muhammad on the day of resurrection. He questioned the Shiites' belief in the finality of the prophethood for their wrong interpretation of a tradition wherein the Prophet was reported to have stated that Ali was to him what Harun was to Musa. The Shiites draw this analogy in a manner that amounted to co-sharing of the prophethood and negation of the finality of the prophethood of Prophet Muhammad as Ali continued to live after the Prophet. He further identified certain sub-sects of the Shiites which claimed that the Quranic commandments regarding the rituals did not need to be taken in the literal sense; rather, they had implied meanings, which were known only to the imams.[56]

This hard-line sectarian narrative got further codification with Maulana Manzoor Naumani who, by examining Khomeini's codification of the Shiite belief system as contained in his three important works *Al-Hakūmat al-Islamiyyah*, *Kashf-ul-Isrār* and *Tahrīr Al-Waseelā,* sought to identify the essentially Shiite character of the Iranian revolution in 1979 and dismissed its ideological character.[57] He joined the ranks of the Sunnite scholarship to back the Sunnite version of Islamic history. It is also argued that Khomeini realized that the occultation of the imam posed a dilemma of political authority that led to inaction during the period of occultation.[58] He resolved to end this inaction by associating political infallibility with the Shiite clergy by acknowledging them as mujtahids (the living jurists), the role held by the imams after the Prophet. These living jurists were to act as guardians of the faith until the imam reappears.[59] Maulana Naumani drew the inference that the infallible status assigned to the architects of the Shiite revolution affirmed the mutually inclusive relationship between unqualified belief in the concept of imamate and *vilayet-e-faqih* during the period of occultation and the right to assume political authority. Though Khomeini believed in the infallible status of the twelve imams and further that their teachings being eternal enjoyed the highest level of *wajūbiyyat* (the status of being mandatory[60]), Maulana Naumani identified political pragmatism in his polemical narrations in *Al-Hakūmat al-Islamiyyah.* He followed the traditional Shiite claim regarding the primacy of Ali's right to caliphate as reflected by the incident of *ghadīr-e-khūm*. However, out of political pragmatism, he distanced himself from *athnā-e-ashriyyā* traditions of criticizing the first three caliphs even when he discussed the discourse of Islamic history. His political pragmatism became more conspicuous when he avoided questioning the authenticity of the Quran but at the same time, he showed reverence to Nuri Tabrasi, who questioned the authenticity of the Quran in his book *Faisal al-Khattāb fī Ithbāt Tehreef-e-Kitāb Rab-ul-Arbāb.*[61] Nevertheless, as Maulana Naumani argues, his political pragmatism dissipated in his book *Kashf-ul-Isrār,* where he challenged the pious caliphs. Questioning the integrity of the Companions of the Prophet, who were witness to the divine revelation, amounts to contesting the authenticity of the divine scripture. He further claims that the veracity of the traditions of the Prophet, which have been transmitted to Ummah through diffused congruence (*ahadith-e-mutawātrā*)[62], was also challenged. Moreover, questioning the integrity of the Companions implied as a natural consequence that the prophetic companionship and training fell short of producing developed personalities.[63] Apart from this, Maulana Naumani traced the juridical faultlines between the two sects from Khomeini's *Tahrīr Al-Wasēlah.*[64] He drew parallels between Christianity and the Shiite belief in terms of exaggerated love and hostility on the part of certain people towards both Jesus and Ali and elevation of such exaggerations to the level of beliefs.[65] He corroborated the views of Shah Abdul Aziz regarding the genesis of Shiite belief and, relying upon *Usul-e-Kafi,* identified such views that stood in direct conflict with the Sunnite belief system. These include the authority of the imams to discern lawful from unlawful, obedience to imams as part of divine ordainment, the ultimate salvation through belief in the infallibility of imams, the ascendency of imams to the prophets other than the Prophet Muhammad and, last but not the least, imams to be the bearers of supernatural powers like the prophets.[66]

The hard-core sectarian approach led to the codification of polemics. In these codifications, militancy found room to operate. The efforts for sectarian rapprochement could not withstand the anti-shiitization narrative across the Muslim world. The sectarian divide so created is still relevant in international politics and breeds violence in Muslim societies. The case of the Middle East suggests that the nation-state system could not replace polemics in producing national identity.

Violence and ideological nostalgia

The linkage between violence and ideological nostalgia produced by the abolition of the Muslim caliphate is well established. The nation-state system, not being rooted in Muslim history, could not claim public legitimacy. It has always been taken to be a foreign idea. Moreover, in certain states like Turkey, this system was transplanted at the expense of the religiously approved political order that was symbolically important to the Muslims across the globe. The abolition of the caliphate and its replacement with a nation-state system created a vacuum. Nostalgia for the caliphate flourished in this vacuum. The new political orders were devoid of public legitimacy. A legitimacy crisis emerged on the faultlines between the modernists and the traditionalists. The modernists extended a supporting hand to the idea of the nation-state whereas the traditionalists remained discontented with it. The conflict of ideas gave birth to violence within Muslim societies and without. Within the Muslim societies, the violence could be witnessed between the militants and the modernists, whereas externally it can be seen in terms of a violent struggle between the militants and the West.

The nation-state system that emerged through Peace of Westphalia (1648) shifted the nucleus of political authority from feudalism and the Catholic Church to a secular political set-up in Europe. It not only secularized the future political discourse in Europe but also provided a new basis for national identity. While subscribing to the doctrine of the absolute sovereignty of Hobbes, it provided an insulating cover against external interference. Europeans were alienated from the tradition that the road to heaven went through Rome. This radical shift in political order was necessarily an outcome of the Protestant Reformation, along with the erosion of feudalism. The authority of the church was eroded by decades of religious wars and the shattered religious identity of Europe, while the emergence of a relatively strong middle class and the rise of a commercial society were serious blows to the feudal power structure in Europe. However, the nation-state system that brought about radical transformations in the socio-economic and political configuration of European society did not get caught up in legitimacy crises. The shift of power from the Catholic Church and feudalism to the nation-state did not stir public disapproval whereas transplanting the same system to the colonized Muslim world invited public resentment. When the new system failed to win public legitimacy, the public resentment translated into physical violence in the Muslim lands. The new order had the support of the apologists who had become clients of western values during the colonial era. Nevertheless, the majority being inimical to the new order confronted both the apologists and the colonial West.

The factors which contributed to public disapproval of the nation-state system may be enumerated as follows:

First, the idea of the nation-state system was introduced by the colonial powers whose very presence in the Muslim lands was itself devoid of any legitimate grounds. Legitimacy can be achieved when people recognize the 'right to rule' of the authority even though they may differ in specific matters, whereas in the case of the colonized Muslim lands, the authority was vested with the European colonial powers, which had no legitimate grounds to rule these lands. In this scenario, the introduction of the nation-state system by the foreign powers was taken as an instrument to perpetuate their rule. The phenomenon could not earn itself public legitimacy in the colonized Muslim lands because of the inability of the political authority to command voluntary public compliance, culminating in its failure to find a foothold in the social system.[67]

Second, in the context of the Middle East, the introduction of the nation-state system was not part of any philosophical renaissance aimed at securing the welfare of the individuals, as contained in the social contract theory. Rather, it was a colonial scheme of power-sharing. It aimed to exploit economic resources through establishing hegemony on the colonized lands. After World War I, the British and French were all set to materialize their scheme to finish 'the eastern question' by dismembering the Ottoman Empire. This scheme was materialized through the Sykes-Picot Agreement (1916).[68] The nation-state system developed in the Middle East as a by-product of the efforts of the British and the French to divide their areas of influence in the region.

Third, the process of installing the nation-state system itself could not escape public condemnation.[69] As a part of the process to divide the Middle East, the French and the British introduced the Mandate system under the League of Nations. Under this system, the French took over the control of Syria and Lebanon whereas Iraq and Palestine went to the British. Though this system provided for the eventual self-rule of the nation-states, it was not acceptable to Muslims in general. As discussed earlier, Islam – being ideologically non-receptive and non-accommodative to imperialism – fuelled the resistance against colonial rule. In the Indian context, different resistance movements like Farāizi Tehrīk of Haji Shariatullah and more significantly Tehrīk-e-Jihad of Sayyed Ahmed Shaheed arose to drive out the imperialists. Islamism in South and Central Asia owes a lot to Sayyed Ahmed Shaheed, who introduced the puritanical ideas of Muhammad b. Abdul Wahab in these regions.[70] The reproduction of his writings in contemporary militant literature affirms that his ideas are subscribed by contemporary militants, especially in South Asia.[71] Similarly, in Egypt, Ikhwan rose for jihad against the imperialist forces. This resistance narrative has never lost its popularity with the militants in their struggle against the West. For instance, one of the major irritants in the Muslim world upon which the violent struggle of Al-Qaida is based is the imperialistic approach being followed by the United States in the Middle East. In 1996, Bin Laden issued a decree titled 'Declaration of war against Americans occupying the lands of two Holy places' whereby he called upon every Muslim to launch jihad against the infidels who had violated the sanctity of the two holy cities in

Hejaz by deploying their troops therein.[72] Moreover, in the wake of the US invasion of Iraq in 2003, the militants' use of titles like 'Muhammad's Army', 'Saladin Brigades' and '*Ansār* as-Sunnah' etc. and their resolve to continue with jihad till the liberation of Palestine and Spain indicates their disdain for the forces of imperialism. They claim to inherit this resistance narrative from their heroes in Muslim history.[73]

Fourth, as Muslims claim to draw their identity from ideology instead of territorial limits, they took territorial nationalism as a prelude to identity crises. In the West, the nation-state system, when pitched against waning theological and feudal structure, could successfully secularize the national identity parameters. However, in Muslim societies, it was translated as an instrument to shatter the ideological unity and identity of the Muslims expressed (even though symbolically) through the Ottoman caliphate. The plan to dismember Turkey, which was the seat of the Muslim caliphate subsequent to the Treaty of Sevres (1920), ignited religious rhetoric across the Muslim world.[74] Moved by religious sentiments, the religious leadership in British India started the Khilāfat Movement to support the caliphate in Turkey against the imminent threat from the colonial powers. As a part of the Muslims' struggle to defend the integrity of the Ottoman Empire, the Muslims launched a large-scale hijra (migration) from India on the grounds that, as the British were posing a serious threat to the Muslims' symbolic unity, British India had become *dār-ul-harb*. This situation left the Indian Muslims with only two alternatives: either to leave the land or to launch jihad. Apart from India, almost all the colonized Muslim lands were gripped by similar identity crises. An attempt to introduce secular state institutions, such as the secular constitution of Tunisia in 1861 and the introduction of democratic norms in Egyptian society, bifurcated the Muslims into modernists and traditionalists. The modernists supported the new socio-political set-up, and the traditional segment preferred to look back to the early period of Islam to explore the religiously approved system of governance. This change in socio-political fabric encouraged the religious segments to organize to resist the emerging threat to religion itself. In the case of Egypt, even the modernists like Abduhu and Rashid Rida upheld the traditional theological position that religion and caliphate were mutually inclusive to each other. In 1886, in a letter to Sheikh-al-Islam in Constantinople, Abduhu argued that fidelity to the Ottoman caliphate constituted the third pillar of the faith.[75] Likewise, Rashid Rida regarded the Islamic caliphate as a prerequisite to enforcing Shariah, which is the primary objective of the Islamic state.[76] Ikhwan was founded in 1928, and subsequently became a torchbearer for Muslim fundamentalists across the world. In India, in 1941, Jama'at-e-Islami, an institutional manifestation of the ideas of Sayyed Maududi, was founded as a revivalist party for the establishment of an ideological state.[77] The ideological state would embody the spirit of Islamic law and be distinguishable from secular statehood.[78] The purpose of this political party was to pursue the case of Islamism as a political ideology.[79]

It aimed to restructure the social order of the world according to Islamic principles.[80] Similarly, in Sudan, Muhammad Ahmed, a cleric from the Samaniyya order, being influenced by puritanical thought in the Muslim world proclaimed himself Al-Mehdi in 1881 in reaction to the western influence on the Muslim ruling elite headed by Khedive, the viceroy of Egypt.[81] In Algeria, Abdul Hamid b. Badis founded the Association of Algerian Muslim Ulema in 1931 to protect the cultural identity of the Algerian Muslims against French imperialism and to purify Islamic life from deviant practices.

It is pertinent to refer to a radical shift in Muslim political thought as espoused by Ibn Khaldun (1332–1406), a Tunisian Muslim historian and sociologist who acknowledged the plurality of caliphs in the Muslim world. Prior to this, Muslim ulema like Al-Mawardi (972–1058) were almost unanimous in support of the unity of political authority represented by a global caliphate. As this shift in the dynamics of political Islam was not external to Islam, it did not affront the Islamists in general. However, the westerners' attempt to change the mode of governance in the Muslim lands could not avoid resistance from the Muslims. A few Muslim scholars from the ranks of the fundamentalist fraternity like Sayyed Maududi in Pakistan preferred to Islamize the existing political system by becoming part of it whereas others like Sayyed Qutb resorted to physical violence to uproot the existing order.[82] Though the contributions of Sayyed Maududi in the realm of political Islam are acknowledged worldwide, militants are more inclined to the violent struggle of Sayyed Qutb instead of Maududi's peaceful struggle.[83] They prefer to revive the caliphate of the early period of Islam instead of what Maududi terms as theo-democracy. The revival of the caliphate is the nucleus of contemporary global jihad.[84] Bin Laden in his correspondence declared the restoration of the caliphate the main objective of jihad.[85] He clearly outlined the differences between western democracy and the Islamic caliphate. In the former, even an invalid and a non-virtuous person could become ruler, and the government could make laws that were against the Will of the Creator, whereas in the latter, it was neither possible for a person who did not fulfil certain qualifications to become caliph nor could legislation be made against the spirit of the faith.[86] Al-Qaida categorically refutes the validity of the instruments through which the nation-state system was created and believes in the validity of the caliphate alone.[87] The militants also understand that their narrative will trigger violence between those who resolve to restore the caliphate and the West, which has the tenacity to withstand its revival through military means. The western opposition to the realization of Islamic ideals was exposed through their opposition to the Moroccan caliphate established by Sheikh Abdul Karim Al-Khatabi (1882–1963).[88] The militants seek to draw popular rationale for their struggle to weaken the West in general and the United States in particular, to ensure the sustainability of the Islamic caliphate. Al-Qaida's strikes in the United States may be taken in this contextual framework.[89]

Abolition of the caliphate triggered a surge of violence amongst those Muslims who rejected the apologists' attempts to reconcile Islam with western democratic ideals. They yearned to revive this institution through forceful means. Naturally, their strategy of force was directed against those who removed the Muslim caliphate and installed the nation-state system in its place. Apart from mainstream Al-Qaida, the revival of the caliphate is foremost on the agenda of the militants across the spectrum. For instance, the approach of ISIS is instantaneous as compared to Al-Qaida in terms of reviving the caliphate. Al-Qaida had the vision that militant struggle would end up in the revival of the caliphate whereas Abu Bakr Al-Baghdadi proclaimed his caliphate in Iraq and Syria at the outset, with the vision to extend its boundaries across the globe through militant struggle from its platform.

Furthermore, under the Mandate system, Palestine went to the British, and the British were in favour of creating a Jewish state. The creation of Israel in the heart of the Arab world sowed the seeds of perpetual violence in the Middle East, which continues to the present day. The Palestine conflict has always had violence-triggering effects not only for the region but also for the entire Muslim world. This irritant has provided the Islamists with grounds to seek legitimacy for their violence against the West. Hamas (Ḥarakat al-Muqawamat al-Islamiyyah) emerged as a Palestine chapter of Ikhwan.[90] Even today, Palestinians' struggle is inspired by three important figures of Ikhwan, namely Al-Banna, Qutb and Izz al-Din al-Qassam.[91] The Charter of Hamas suggests that it is dedicated to raise the banner of Islam across the Palestinian land (Article 6). Hamas believes that the land of Palestine is a sacred trust to all Muslims, and no one has the right to forgo even a single inch of this sacred land. Resisting the state of Israel and liberating the Palestinian land through the instrument of jihad becomes the ideological responsibility of the believers on one hand and refers to the ideology of the organization on the other. This ideology is based upon religious nationalism (Article 11).

Apart from Hamas that aims to liberate Palestine, militant organizations like Al-Qaida pursue a more uncompromising approach to the issue and rule out the scope of any international arrangement that permits the existence of a Zionist entity on the Palestinian land.[92] Bin Laden, in his message to the American people in 2004, argued that Al-Qaida pursues a violent struggle against the United States for its alliance with Israel to inflict atrocities on the Palestinians.[93] He further criticized the West for branding those Muslims as terrorists who are defending themselves against oppression on the part of Israel and the United States.[94] He urged the United States to liberate Palestine as a key to ending violence.[95] Moreover, for Al-Zawahiri, the Palestine issue surpasses even the implementation of Shariah in importance.[96] Though militant violence is not solely associated with the Palestine conflict, as Muslim states which are not directly linked with the Palestine issue are also faced with violence, the militants justify the use of violence from conflicts like Palestine.[97]

The discussion on the codification of violence leads to the following conclusions. First, historical evidence affirms a positive relationship between national identity crises and violence. In the case of Muslim societies, national identity was largely challenged through the instrument of colonialism. This resulted in violence either with state involvement or at the societal level. Second, lessons from colonialism suggest that it has been a catalyst in generating violence within Muslim societies directed on two fronts – against the respective colonial power and against those elements who view reconciliation with the colonialists as a key to survival and thus are labelled as 'the apologists'. Third, even in the post-colonial context, this discord continued to persist. The post-colonial period was a mere redefinition of the context in which these conflicting streams were flowing during the colonial period. Islamists' resistance against the colonial rulers translated into their defiance against those Muslim rulers who were accused of being in collaboration with the West and thus were labelled as 'agents of the West' or 'apostates'. Moreover, the Islamists continue to disapprove of the so-called moderates who prefer to support these apostate Muslim rulers instead of subscribing to the militant brand of Islam. Fourth, the schisms that crept into the early political history of Islam could only polarize the Muslim society as a whole when the violence was codified consequent upon the rise of sectarian empires like the Safavids in the 16th century who resorted to violence on a sectarian trajectory to secure their political gains against the rival Sunnite Ottomans. This codification of violence on the polemical lines kept prejudices alive. The Sunnite apprehensions regarding the 1979 Iranian Revolution were an outcome of these historical prejudices. Fifth, the 'Ummah' used to reflect the aspirations of the believers through the caliphate whose legitimacy to exercise coercion was acknowledged across the Muslim world. The rise of sectarian empires and the abolition of the Ottoman caliphate culminated in the irrelevance of Ummah. The erosion of legitimate coercive authority resulted in the relegation of violence to the group or individual level. Sixth, the irrelevance of Ummah created a vacuum that has been filled by the militants' nostalgia, calling for the revival of the caliphate. It provided militants with the grounds to evolve their codes of war against the West. Last but not least, the conditions of the 18th and the 19th century pitted Muslims against each other, transformed the relationship between state and society and sharpened the sectarian differences to new heights where violence was codified not only at the level of society but at the level of the state formation as well. This process culminated in the formation of new states, which derived their ideological formation from sectarian acrimony against another Muslim sect chiefly in the Middle East. Colonialists served as catalysts in crystallizing these ideological differences into states. Iran and the Gulf States are an outcome of such a transformation produced through indirect colonial interventions based on new imperialistic designs. The post-Cold War era saw a new trend of further extension of these influences in the Muslim hinterlands and at its frontiers that ushered in a new level of violence relegated from state to society within the Muslim countries.

Notes

1 Montserrat Guibernau, *The identity of Nations* (Cambridge: Polity Press, 2007), 11; also see Anthony D. Smith, *National Identity* (London: Penguin Books, 1991), vii.
2 Maulana Safi-ur-Rehman Mubarakpuri, *Al-Rahīq al-Makhtūm* (Lahore: Al-Maktabah al-Salafiyyah, 1998), 56.
3 Ibid., 302–306.
4 Abdul Rehman Ibn Jozi, *Manāqib Umar b. al-Khattab*, trans. Muhammad Tariq Qadri (Lahore: Shakir Publications, 2014), 25, 26.
5 Robertson, *Sociology*, 264.
6 N.O. Mimiko, 'Tradition, Governance, Challenges and the Prospects of Change in Africa', in *Toyin Falola: The Man, the Mask, the Muse,* ed. Niyi Afolabi, (North Carolina: Carolina Academic Press, 2010), 641–642.
7 K. Kasongo, 'Impact of Globalization on Traditional African Religion and Cultural Conflict', *Journal of Alternative Perspectives in the Social Sciences* 2, no. 1 (2010): 309.
8 D. Arowolo, 'The effects of western civilization on Africa', *Afro Asian Journal of Social Sciences* 1, no.1 (2010): 7.
9 Mimiko, 'Tradition, Governance, Challenges and the Prospects of Change in Africa', 640.
10 Choudhury Mohammad Ali, *The Emergence of Pakistan* (New York: Columbia University Press, 1967), 7.
11 Vincent A. Smith, *The Oxford History of India* (Karachi: Oxford University Press, 1988), 723, 724.
12 Ibid., 723–725.
13 Richard Symonds, *The Making of Pakistan* (London: Faber and Faber, 1950), 26; Henry Frank Goodnow, *The Civil Service of Pakistan: Bureaucracy in a New Nation* (New Heaven: Yale University Press, 1964), 26.
14 Smith, *The Oxford History of India*, 729–739.
15 Ibid., 802.
16 Robertson, *Sociology*, 292.
17 The British established Shahuci Judicial School in 1928 to impart this new course of education. In addition to the traditional subjects like Islamic Jurisprudence and Quranic studies, new subjects like arithmetic were also incorporated in the curriculum. See Tijjani Muhammad Naniya, 'The Dilemma of the Ulema in a Colonial Society: The Case Study of Kano Emirate', *Journal of Islamic Studies* 4, no. 2 (1993): 151–160.
18 Smith, *The Oxford History of India*, 719.
19 Ibid.
20 Naniya, 'The Dilemma of the Ulema in a Colonial Society', 151–160.
21 Robertson, *Sociology*, 292.
22 R. A. Alkali, *International Relations and Nigeria's Foreign Policy* (Kaduna: North Point Publishers, 2003). For the effects of economic policies during the colonial rule in Africa, see Howard Stein, *Economic Development and the Anatomy of Crisis in Africa: From Colonialism through Structural Adjustment*, Centre of African Studies, University of Copenhagen, March 5, 2001.

23 Leslie Sklair, 'Democracy and the Transnational Capitalist Class', The *ANNALS* 581 (May, 2002): 144–157.
24 In 2006 ranking, XXEON, SHELL and BP were amongst the 10 top-ranking oil companies of the world. 'The Energy Intelligence Top 100: Ranking the World's Oil Companies', 2007 and 2001 editions, quoted in Robert Pirog, 'The Role of National Oil Companies in the International Oil Market', *CRS Report for Congress*, August 21, 2007.
25 John Vidal, 'White House sought advice from Exxon on Kyoto Stance', *The Guardian,* June 8, 2005.
26 Vlado Vivoda, 'International oil companies, US Government and energy security policy: an interest-based analysis', *International Journal of Global energy Issues* 33, no. ½ (2010): 73–88.
27 Ibn Taimmiyah, *The Book of Eemān: The Basis, Reality and Invalidation of Eemān,* trans. Muhammad Naeem Yasin (London: Al-Firdous Ltd), 206–209, accessed August 31, 2013, http://www.kalamullah.com/ibn-taymiyyah.html.
28 Ibid., 204–206.
29 Ibid., 207.
30 Ibn Abdul Wahab, *Sharah Nawāqidh Al-Islam.*
31 See Last Sermon of the Holy Prophet.
32 Mubarakpuri, *Al-Rahīq al-Makhtūm*, 257.
33 The Prophet has been reported to have said: 'Do not have malice against a Muslim; do not be envious of other Muslims; do not go against a Muslim and forsake him. O the slave of Allah! Be like brothers with each other. It is not allowed for a Muslim to desert his brother for over three days.' Imam Muslim, *Sahih Muslim, Kitāb Al-Birr was-Salat-i-wa'l Adab*, 6205.
34 These were the qualified individuals who had the authority to select or depose the caliph.
35 Narrated Abu Musa: 'Two men from my tribe and I entered upon the prophet. One of the two men said to the prophet, 'O Allah's Apostle! Appoint me as a governor', and so did the second. The prophet said, 'We do not assign the authority of ruling to those who ask for it, nor to those who are keen to have it', Imam Muslim, *Sahih Muslim, Kitāb al-Imārah*, 4489.
36 Al-Tabri, *Tarīkh al-Umam wal Mulūk*, Vol. 3, Part I, 253.
37 He borrows a traditional approach to caliphate from Al-Mawardi and relies on a tradition of the Prophet that a Muslim who dies without extending allegiance to a caliph dies the death of *jāhilliyah*. Imam Bukhari, *Sahih Bukhari, Kitāb al-Imārah*: 4555–4557.
38 Gole, 'Snapshots of Islamic Modernities', 91–117.
39 Abu Dawood, *Sunan Abu Dawood, Kitāb al-Sunnah*: 4629; Ansari, *Ibn Taimmiyah Expounds on Islam*, 495.
40 Imam Muslim, *Shaih Muslim, Kitāb al-Imārah*: 4551; Imam Bukhari, *Shaih Bukhari, Kitāb al-Fitan*: 7052–7057; also see Ansari, *Ibn Taimmiyah Expounds on Islam*, 495; Ibn Taimmiyah, *Al-Muntqā min Minhāj al-Sunnah*, 45.
41 Ibid., 34.
42 Ibid., 19.
43 Ansari, *Ibn Taimmiyah Expounds on Islam*, 556.
44 Ibid., 553.
45 Subhi Labib, 'The Problem of Bida' in the Light of an Arabic Manuscript of the 14th Century', quoted in Tariq Al-Jamil, 'Ibn Taymiyya and Ibn al-Mutahhar al-Hillī: Shi'i Polemics and the Struggle for Religious Authority in Medieval Islam', in *Ibn Taimmiyah and His Times*, eds. Yossef Rapoport and Shahab Ahmed (Karachi: Oxford University Press, 2010), 233.
46 Ibid.

47 Ibid.

48 He was the son of Shah Waliullah. He emphasized the rational interpretation of the religion and preferred to denounce the following (*taqlid*) of any major school of Muslim jurisprudence like Ibn Abdul Wahab; see, for instance, Aziz Ahmed, *Studies in Islamic Culture and Indian Environment* (Oxford: Clarendon Press,1964), 201. However, it still requires further inquiry whether it was the influence of Ibn Taimmiyyah working behind this religious approach or it was a common tree of teachers in Madina which was behind the common thinking of both afore-mentioned scholars of the 18th century. There is no denying the fact that Muhammad Hayya Al-Sindi, one of the teachers of Ibn Abd al Wahab, had a profound influence on this student to denounce the commentaries of the four Sunni Imams. Since Shah Waliullah was the student of Abul Tahir Al-Kurani, a teacher of Al-Sindi, it may lead us to presume that similarities between Ibn Abdul Wahab and Shah Waliullah had their roots in a common source of learning. See John Voll, 'Muhammad Hayya Al-Sindi and Muhammad Ibn Abd al Wahab: An Analysis of an Intellectual Group in Eighteenth-Century Madina', *Bulletin of the School of Oriental and African Studies* 38, no. 1 (1975): 32–39.

49 Shah Abdul Aziz, *Tohfā Athnā-e-Ashriyyā*, trans. Maulana Khalil-ur-Rehman Naumani (Karachi: Dar-ul-Ashaat), 200.

50 The belief system of the *ghālīs* is subject to intra-sect criticism as well. The Shiites refer to a tradition of Imam Ja'afar Sadiq wherein he has been reported to have directed the Muslims to keep their youth at a distance from the *ghālīs*. Also see Naumani, *Irani Inqilab,* Imam *Khomeini aur Shi'yyat.*

51 Aziz, *Tohfā,* 26–29.

52 Ibid., 230–247.

53 For details, see Sheikh Muhammad Yaqoob Kalaini, *Usul-e-Kafi*, trans. Sayyed Zafar Hassan (Karachi: Zafar Shamim Publications Trust, 2003).

54 Aziz, *Tohfā,* 269–309.

55 Ibid.

56 Ibid., 310–343.

57 Against those who criticize Imam Khomeini and the Iranian revolution of 1979, Kalim Siddiqui claims that Imam Khomeini stands for all Muslims of the world irrespective of their sectarian affiliations. Quoted in Richard Bonney, *Jihad*, 244.

58 Akhavi, 'Islam, Politics and Society', 404–431.

59 Khomeini, 'The Pillars of an Islamic State'; also see Ruhullah Khomeini, *Al-Hakūmat al-Islamiyyah* (Karachi: Kitab Markaz), 37.

60 Naumani, *Irani Inqilab,* Imam *Khomeini aur Shi'yyat*, 30–40.

61 Quoted in ibid., 38–49.

62 A *hadith* is called *mutawātrā*, which has several chains of reporting (*Kathīr-ul-Asāneed*). See Ibn Hajar al-Asqalani, *Nuqbat-ul-Fikr,* accessed December 8, 2020, www.maktabah.net. The rationale for the condition of several chains of reporting is that several narrators cannot unite on a tradition which is untrue. It is further emphasized that the narrators must be from every generation of the chain. Moreover, it is important that the chain of narration must end up with a narrator who himself is the listener of the tradition or have directly watched something reported in *hadith* (*amr-e-hissī*). Another condition of *hadith-e-mutawātrā* is that the listener must secure the benefit of *ilm al-yaqeen* (sure knowledge) from the *hadith*. However, some argue that the benefit of *ilm-ul-yaqeen* is not the condition but the result of *hadith-e-mutawātrā*.

63 Naumani, *Irani Inqilab,* Imam *Khomeini aur Shi'yyat*, 50–85; also see Nawab Mohsin-ul-Mulk Sayyed Muhammad Mehdi Ali Khan, *Aayāt-e-Bayyanāt* (Karachi: Dar-ul-Asha'at, 1975).

64 Imam Rouhullah Khomeini, *Tahrīr Al-Wasēlah,* trans. Sayyid Ali Reza Naqvi (Institute for Compilation and Publication of Imam Khomeini's Works, 2001).
65 Naumani, *Irani Inqilab*, Imam *Khomeini aur Shi'yyat*, 94.
66 Ibid., 96–166.
67 Legitimacy may be defined in terms of an attribute by which an authority commands voluntary public compliance. It is an 'appraisal of action in terms of shared or common values in the context of the involvement of the action in the social system'. See T. Parsons, *Structure and Process in Modern Societies* (New York: Free Press, 1960); also see M. Weber, *Economy and Society* (New York: Bedminster, 1968).
68 Mike Shuster, 'The Middle East and the West: WWI and Beyond', interview by Robert Siegel. *NPR News*, August 20, 2004.
69 The French and British colonialism emerged on the ruins of Muslim caliphate. See, for instance, William McCants, 'Al Qaida's Challenge', *Foreign Affairs* 90, no. 5 (2011): 20–32.
70 Haqqani, 'The Ideologies of South Asian Jihadi Groups', 12–26.
71 'Maktūbat Amir al-Mumineen Sayyed Ahmed Shaheed', *Hittin*, issue 8, 1433 AH. Idara Hittin.
72 Osama Bin Laden, 'Declaration of Jihad against the Americans Occupying the Land of the Two Holy Sanctuaries issued on March 23, 1996', in *Al Qaida in Its Own Words,* eds. Gilles Kepel & Jean-Pierre Milelli, trans. Pascale Ghazaleh (Massachusetts: The Belknap Press of Harvard University Press, 2009), 47–50. One of the prime objectives of Al-Qaida's organization is to defend the holy places of Islam against the infidels; see, for instance, Shaykh Adil al-Abbab, 'Targeting non-Muslims Civilians and Yemeni Soldiers', interview by Al-Malahem Media. *Inspire*, issue 4, 2010; also see Don D. Chipman, 'Osama Bin Laden and Guerrilla War', *Studies in Conflict and Terrorism* 26, no. 3 (2003): 163–170.
73 Jeffrey Haynes, 'Al Qaida: Ideology and Action', *Conflict Review of International Social and Political Philosophy* 8, no. 2 (2005): 177–191.
74 Under this treaty, Turkey was to lose those lands, which were not originally part of Turkey.
75 Kerr, *Islamic Reform,* 148.
76 Haddad, 'Arab Religious Nationalism in Colonial Era', 253–277.
77 Bonney, *Jihad*, 199.
78 Smith, 'The Ideology of Mawlana Mawdudi', 371–397.
79 In recognition of Sayyed Maududi's efforts to revive the ideological spirit of Islam, some regard the ideological version of Islam as the brain-child of Sayyed Maududi; see, for instance, Nasr, 'Democracy and Islamic Revivalism', 261–285.
80 Maududi, *Jihad fī Sabeel Allah.*
81 For detailed analysis, see John Voll, 'The Sudanese Mahdi: Frontier Fundamentalist', *International Journal of Middle East Studies* 10, no. 2 (1979): 145–166.
82 Sayyed Maududi appears to be more of a reformer than of a revolutionary. The revolutionaries believe that change is possible only through uprooting the existing socio-political order.
83 Maududi, interview by *The Muslim*, 1967.
84 Schifter, 'The Clash of Ideologies', 12–23.
85 Rassler et al., *Letters from Abbottabad,* SOCOM-2012-0000003; also see Shaykh Adil al-Abbab, interview by Al-Malahem Media. *Inspire*, issue 4, 2010; also see Haynes, 'Al Qaida: Ideology and Action', 177–191.
86 Osama bin Laden, interview by Hamid Mir published in *Daily Pakistan,* March 18, 1997.

87 Al-Awlaki, 'The New Mardin Declaration', *Inspire*, issue 2.
88 Rassler et al., *Letters from Abbottabad*, SOCOM-2012-0000016.
89 Quoted in Don D. Chipman, 'Osama Bin Laden and Guerrilla War', 163–170.
90 See Article 2 of Hamas Charter, Muhammad Maqdisi, 'Charter of the Islamic Resistance Movement (Hamas) of Palestine', *Journal of Palestine Studies* 22, no. 4 (1993): 122–134.
91 Hamas military unit Al-Qassam Brigade is named after Izz Al-Din al-Qassam.
92 Osama Bin Laden, 'Until We Taste What Hamza Bin Abd Al-Muttalib Tasted', *Inspire*, issue 2 (2010).
93 Osama Bin Laden, 'Message to the American People October 20, 2004', in *Al-Qaida in its Own Words*, 71–77.
94 Osama Bin Laden, interview by Al-Quds Al-Arabi March 9, 1994, in *FBIS Report – Compilation of Usama Bin Laden Statement 1994–January 2004*, 2.
95 Osama Bin Laden, interview by Al-Jazeera, December, 1998, in *Al-Qaida in Its Own Words*, 57–59.
96 Maha Azzam, 'Al-Qaida: the misunderstood Wahabi connection', 2003.
97 Schifter, 'The Clash of Ideologies', 12–23.

5 Codes of war

The ideological conflict between the Islamists and the West provided a sphere for the militancy to flourish when introduced to political realism within the Muslim societies. Though violence crept into the body politic of Islam at an early stage, its codification resulted from the adoption of the sectarian violence at the state level and ultimately documentation of public and private Islamic law during the colonialism, which was later on replaced with the secular European codes. In the post-colonial context, when the imperialists revised their tactics of exploitation in terms of achieving their goals through collaboration of the Muslim rulers, the triangular conflict involving the colonialists, the Islamists and the apologists got redesigned to accommodate a new target whom the militants term as western agents or apostate rulers. This phenomenon has led to serious internal as well as external ramifications, which include the desire for ideological renaissance by galvanizing the denunciation of the West, renewed anti-imperialism notions, passion to liberate the sanctuaries of Islam and desire to neutralize the forces of unbelief for their oppression against the Muslims. In this backdrop, the militants evolved codes of war in their resistance against the West and the elements of apostasy within the Muslim societies. These codes of war include targeting those who follow democracy, fighting against the imperialists, non-observance of distinction between combatants and non-combatants and, above all, cleansing the elements of apostasy within Muslim societies.

Militants' codes of war

Targeting those who follow democracy

Given the irrelevance of Ummah to exercise the coercive authority through caliphate and the resulting legitimacy crises, violence was adopted at the societal level to secure national identity through the ideological renaissance. Secular democratic ideals were discredited as foreign ideas, and the western attempts at their promotion in the Muslim societies were taken as a part of the scheme to marginalize the Islamists who resolved to revive the early political order of Islam through the instrument of jihad.[1] The United States'

DOI: 10.4324/9781003164883-5

efforts to democratize the Muslim societies on the model of post-World War II Germany and Japan by promoting democratic elements through foreign aid ended up prompting the militants' nostalgia to revert to the early Islamic system. This nostalgia provided a well-defined separate framework vis-à-vis the apologists and the Muslim rulers who are accused of promoting the western agenda in the Muslim countries.

At the outset, Bin Laden highlighted the incompatibilities between democracy and the Islamic system in terms of the selection process of the rulers and the allocation of sovereignty that defines the nature of legislative procedures.[2] He gave clarity and precision to the militants' vision to eradicate democracy through reviving the caliphate. He argued that sovereignty, which is an exclusive divine attribute, if allocated to individuals, as is the case with democracy, leads to autocratic tendencies with the ruling class.[3] Al-Zawahiri argues that following a system that claims to share a divine attribute amounts to committing apostasy by converting to a new faith of 'majority worshipping'. On these grounds, he condemns the democratic constitutions in Muslim countries as the instruments of Unbelief. He further argues that the installation of Jewish control on the Palestinian land was inspired by this majority mood in the West that seeks to protect and promote imperial interests in the Muslim lands through cultivating a class of apologists as their support base.[4] The militant fraternity, as a whole, disregards the streams followed by Hamas and Ikhwan by denouncing their participation in the democratic process to bring change in the Muslim countries.[5]

This narrative was furthered by Al-Zarqawi and Al-Maqdisi who, labelling democracy as heretic in spirit, emphasized the need to eliminate it through global jihad.[6] Al-Zarqawi argued that law-giving is the domain exclusive for God, and the democratic system, through recognizing a human role in this domain, leads to polytheism.[7] Regarding the question of secularism, which provides for the separate domain for politics and religion and at the same time provides the basis for democracy to flourish, Al-Zarqawi insisted that separation of politics and religion amounts to advising God 'what is and what is not His prerogative'.[8] In furtherance of this narrative, Al-Maqdisi pronounced *takfīr* on those who prefer man-made laws to the divine laws. Democracy constitutes an innovation (*bida'ā*) for seeking a religion other than Islam, and this innovation may lead to apostasy.[9] However, his views on those who take part in the democratic process are shrouded in confusion. He proclaimed *takfīr* for the elected representatives whereas the common men who elect them were not excommunicated simply because they elected them as a routine matter and were not seeking democracy in terms of religion.[10] This narrative earned Al-Maqdisi an important place in the array of militants and further strengthened the association between him and Al-Zarqawi, who would subsequently rely on the same narrative to discredit those who took part in the 2005 elections in Iraq.[11] Al-Zarqawi followed Al-Maqdisi in declaring democracy a separate religion, which was based upon seven principles which were contradictory to the basic spirit of Islam. These principles included popular sovereignty, freedom of faith, freedom of expression, a popular mandate to resolve the conflicts, secularism, freedom to form political parties and predominance of the majority opinion.[12]

This narrative is also shared by Al-Qaida affiliates worldwide, including Al-Qaida in the Arabian Peninsula (AQAP), Harkat al-Shabbāb al-Mujahideen in Somalia – commonly known as Al-Shabbāb – and Tehrīk-e-Taliban Pakistan (TTP). AQAP resolved to fight those Muslims who converted to what they term the 'religion of democracy'. Al-Shabab's 2014 attack on the Somali parliament and Boko Haram's offensives during the presidential election campaign need to be viewed as part of a larger militant perspective based on this narrative.[13] Iraq experienced a similar reaction against the democratic process in the 2014 elections when the militants stormed the polling stations.[14] In Pakistan, TTP claims to follow the same narrative.[15]

Apart from Al-Qaida and its affiliates, ISIS follows the same rhetoric to revive the Islamic caliphate, through a somewhat different roadmap. For Al-Qaida, reviving the caliphate requires extensive homework in terms of developing a means to withstand anticipated resistance from the United States, as happened in the case of Al-Khatabi's emirate in Morocco.[16] ISIS, however, has already declared a caliphate in Syria and Iraq as a launching pad for the revival of Islamic order across the globe. Nevertheless, ISIS follows the same extremist ideology that views the democratic process as infringing upon the divine domain and condemns those who participate in the process as apostates.[17]

As nation-states provide a sphere for democracy to function and both operate in terms of 'mutually dependent logics', the militants' hostility is equally directed against nationalism as well.[18] They label the constitutions of the Muslim nation-states as 'Shariah of nationalism' and condemn their followers as apostates and clients of *tāghūt* (Unbelief). The militants claim to draw this narrative from historical accounts of different prophets who surrendered their national affiliations and preferred to migrate from their respective homelands when their fellow nationals refused to submit to their faith and attempted to intimidate them by the tool of nationalism (Al-Ibrahim: 13). They intimidated prophet Shoaib by threatening to expel him from his homeland (Al-Ara'af: 88). Prophet Lūṭ also faced similar threats (Al-Ara'af: 82). Prophet Muhammad had to face threats of expulsion from Makkah (Al-'Anfāl: 30). The militants argue that the Prophet's preference to migrate to Madina for the sake of faith suggests that his Shariah does not recognize any virtue in nationalism and, further, that it is faith that warrants the believers' submission instead of the nation-state as such. The militants label the national institutions as organs of apostasy, which are liable to be fought against.[19] This approach towards nationalism is shared by the militant landscape as a whole that does not acknowledge any sort of theological legitimacy of democratic institutions.

Fighting the imperialists

The militants' codes of war in terms of fighting against the imperialists have gradually evolved from Abdullah Azzam to the contemporary militant ideologues. Azzam followed Imam Qurtubi's viewpoint that jihad (resistance) against imperialist forces, bent upon destroying the believers' assets, is obligatory upon the believers.[20] It is evident from the Holy Quran, 'Go forth, light-armed and heavy-armed, and strive with your wealth and your lives in the way of Allah! That is best for you if ye but knew' (At-Tawbah: 41).[21] Moreover, Quranic injunctions categorically denounce the avoidance of jihad in these words: 'If ye go not forth He will afflict you with a painful doom, and will choose instead of you a folk other than you. Ye cannot harm Him at all. Allah is Able to do all things' (At-Tawbah: 39). Given the all-encompassing nature of these divine injunctions, the believers' discretion with regard to resistance against the infidel imperialists becomes virtually non-existent. The Prophet did not exempt even a blind Companion Ibn Umm-e-Makhtum until the divine verdict regarding exemption, in this case, was revealed.[22] The significance associated with jihad is evident from the conduct of the Prophet and his Companions. The Prophet himself participated in 27 battles, fighting in 9 of them. Azzam argued that jihad would be launched from a base called *Al-Qaida al-sulbah* by a vanguard of committed volunteers. He further argued that jihad, being a touchstone to discern hypocrisy from sincerity, would provide space to test the commitment of these volunteers and would also help them experience the practical realization of divine unity (*tawhid al-Uluhiyyah*) as distinct from its theoretical aspect (*tawhid al-Rabubiyyah*). The practical aspect of tawhid could be better understood through military jihad instead of mere intellectual ordeals (Al-Ankabut: 69).[23] This military jihad as an instrument of protection of the oppressed against the oppressors was essential for the eternal salvation of the believers.[24] In this context, Azzam termed *ribāt* (guard duty) as the most exalted form of worship, which was equally essential for avoiding disgrace to Ummah.[25] Given the importance attached with the subject of military jihad, he corroborated the viewpoint of Ibn Rushd and Imam Hajar Asqalani, who inclined to interpret jihad, when used in its generalized sense, in terms of armed struggle.[26] His theory is the basis from which subsequent generations of militants developed their codes of global jihad on the following lines.

First, Azzam argues that on the offensive side, jihad will continue to be *fard-e-kafāyā* (voluntary duty) until all submit to the call of Islam whereas it will convert into *fard-e-ayn* (individual obligation) in the case of non-believers' aggression into a Muslim territory or if they capture a group of believers. His approach reflects the strong influence of all four major schools of Islamic scholasticism. With Shafi'ites, jihad becomes *fard-e-ayn* when the distance between the invading enemy and the believers becomes shorter than the distance that permits the believers to offer a shortened prayer. Similarly, the Hanfites believe that jihad becomes an individual obligation when any Muslim territory is exposed to foreign invasion. Malikites believe that, if the invading enemy makes a surprise attack on Muslim territory, jihad becomes *fard-e-ayn*. Ibn Qadamah, a Hanbalite theorist in his *al-Mughni,* identifies three situations that convert the nature of jihad from voluntary duty to individual obligation. First, when the forces of unbelief confront the believers on the battlefield; second, when the non-believers aggress into a Muslim territory; and third, when the imam calls the believers to march forth. Nevertheless, Ibn Taimmiyah's views regarding the transformation of jihad from *fard-e-kafāyā* to *fard-e-ayn* provided grounds for revisions whereupon Azzam based his theory of global jihad. Ibn Taimmiyah takes the Muslim lands as a whole and argues that foreign aggression on any part of the Muslim lands invokes individual obligation of jihad on the trajectory of 'nearer enemy doctrine'. This individual obligation of jihad is next in importance only to faith itself.[27] In practical terms, it implies that if the local believers upon whom aggression has been made are incapacitated, the individual obligation will shift to the next circle of the believers nearer to the theatre of aggression and so on. In this way, the individual obligation may encompass the whole Muslim Ummah.

Second, for Azzam, though jihad is *fard-e-kafāyā* in its offensive mode, its obligatory status changes into *fard-e-ayn* in the face of an enemy's aggression, as Islam attaches utmost significance to the protection of five fundamental elements including faith, life, honour, mind and property, even if the aggressor happens to be a Muslim. He argued that the emphasis upon resisting the invading enemy is reflected in the fact that Islam enjoins upon a woman to fight to avoid her surrender if her honour is under threat.[28] The genesis of 'nearer enemy doctrine' finds its roots in the early period of Islam which, for example, is evident from the dialogue between Rabia'ah b. Amir, the commander of the Muslim army in Syria, with Sergius, his Roman counterpart. Rabia'ah held that jihad against the Romans was preferred in the first instance as they were nearer than the Persians.[29] However, if an imminent threat originates from a distant enemy, he will be fought prior to the nearer enemy as the Prophet preferred to fight against Harith Abi Dirar and, on another occasion, against Khalid b. Abi Sufiyan, who posed a threat more imminent than the nearer enemies.[30]

Third, apart from linking Ibn Taimmiyah's 'nearer enemy' doctrine to contemporary global jihad, his interpretation of 'individual obligation' (*fard-e-Ayn*) grants theological sanction to wage jihad by the believers in their personal capacities without permission of those in authority. He argues that when jihad becomes *fard-e-ayn*, permission is not required even from parents as no permission is required to observe other fundamentals of the faith. It entails the same level of religious obligation as is associated with other basic elements of the faith.[31] As *fard-e-ayn* surpasses all other religious obligations, if there is a likelihood that the caliph has already suspended jihad or will not allow jihad to be waged or if waiting for permission will harm the cause of jihad, it is not obligatory upon the believers to get permission from the caliph.[32]

Though Azzam's resolve to fight the imperialist infidels persisted with Bin Laden and other contemporary militants, his 'nearer enemy' doctrine underwent radical revisions. It no longer remained limited to the invading infidels, but those who happened to collaborate with infidels were also defined as 'nearer enemies'. This perspective got reinforced in the context of the US invasion of Iraq and their military presence in Hejaz. The militants charge the United States with pursuing a scheme to control and exploit the Muslims' resources largely through the transnational companies backed by military power. These companies could take the opportunity to exploit the oil resources in this part of the Muslim world.[33]

In this perspective, Bin Laden decreed that Muslims' humiliation vis-à-vis Israel and exploitation of their resources invoked individual obligation of jihad upon the believers.[34] He subscribed to the fatwa issued by the Afghan Union of Ulema, which approved of the views of Imam Malik, Ibn-al-Mundhir, al-Jawzajani, Sheikh Salman al-Awdah and Sheikh Safar al-Hawali regarding the non-permissibility of seeking the help of the infidels.[35] He dismissed the theological legitimacy of the Saudis' claim to seek help from the United States for the defence of Hejaz.[36] In his fatwa titled 'Declaration of Jihad Against the Americans Occupying the Land of the Two Holy Sanctuaries', he stressed that believers should fight against the forces of Unbelief headed by the United States and their local allies to force them to liberate Jerusalem as well as to ensure their exit from the holy sanctuaries of Islam in Hejaz.[37] The land of Hejaz, being the direction of prayers and the seat of prophecy, is out of bounds for non-believers. He excommunicated the Saudi regime for being loyal to the United States.[38] He further accused them of violating the will of the Prophet by inviting the US army into the land of Hejaz because the Prophet had directed the believers to expel non-believers from this land.[39]

However, at times he used the premise of secular history to reject the western portrayal of the Muslims as terrorists if they defend themselves.[40] If the Europeans had the right to defend themselves against the Nazis, how could Muslims be deprived of the exercise of this right against the Jewish–Christian alliance that has killed the children of the Muslims?[41] Bin Laden urged the militants to target specifically the interests of only those states which perpetrate violence against the Muslims.[42] He offered a premise to evolve 9/11 and subsequent violence in terms of reactionary and preemptive strikes of oppressed Muslims to counter the oppressor West, especially the United States, through economic boycott and military jihad.[43] Nevertheless, he sought to evoke religious frenzy amongst the Muslims by putting the US presence on Arabian soil in the context of Crusades.[44] The Crusades-thesis calls for resistance on the part of the believers as decreed by a Saudi cleric Sheikh Bin Uthaymin.[45] In this Crusade context, jihad will be directed against the imperialist forces and their local allies. The local allies include the pro-west rulers, Arab nationalists, socialist political parties and the apologist intelligentsia.[46] Owing to his unflinching devotion to driving Crusaders from the Islamic sanctuaries, he disapproved of his militant peers like Ikhwan and Hamas for their relatively mild standpoints about the international charter that recognized the Zionist entity on the Palestinian land.[47] However, despite ruling out options of a peaceful solution to the conflict, strategic pragmatism was evident in his theory. He explored the evidence of making strategic peace with the infidels from the early history of Islam, like the Prophet's offer of one-third of the agriculture produce to Ghatfan to neutralize them during the Battle of Ahzāb (5 AH) and, later on, his conduct at Hudaybiah (6 AH). He shared this strategic pragmatism with Ibn Taimmiyah when he explored room to defer jihad during conditions that may result in a loss (*mufāsidah*) instead of benefit (*maslāhā*) to the Muslims.[48]

Notwithstanding certain ideological differences[49] between Bin Laden and Al-Zawahiri regarding the formal fusion of certain localized militant outfits like Harkat al-Shabbāb al-Mujahideen with mainstream Al-Qaida, which the former did not sanction in his lifetime, the proclamation of global jihad on the trajectory of 'distant' as well as 'nearer' enemies confirms the predominant influence of Al-Zawahiri on Bin Laden.[50] This lends credence to the argument that, in the post-Afghan War scenario, Bin Laden provided a front and finances to Al-Qaida whereas Al-Zawahiri provided the intellectual spirit of the organization. He argued that, given the military superiority of the United States, it would not be possible for believers to secure a local power base. The military superiority of the United States could be neutralized only through transnational jihad, which would simultaneously be directed not only against the external enemy but also against their local support base.

The militants share the idea of jihad as an anti-imperialistic tool but in a variety of ways. For Al-Maqdisi and Al-Zarqawi, resistance to the imperialist forces in order to preserve the Muslims' resources constituted a part of the faith.[51] In converse terms, to surrender the Muslims' resources to the non-believers was to forego one's faith.[52] On this premise, they declared the Muslim rulers who surrender their resources to the imperialists as apostates. AQAP undertook a similar approach that jihad against the imperialists and their local collaborators will remain *fard-e-ayn* until the expulsion of the Americans and their allies from the Arabian Peninsula.[53] The case of Mali suggests that Tanẓīm al-Qā'idah fī Bilād al-Maghrib al-Islāmī, also called Al-Qaida in the Islamic Maghreb (AQIM), follows an anti-imperialist approach largely against the French militaristic imperial designs alongside the Mauritanian army since 2010 with utter disregard of Malian political leadership.[54] Similarly, in 2012, Jama' at at-tawḥīd wal-jihād fī gharb afrīqqīyā, also called Monotheism and Jihad Movement in West Africa (MOJWA), which is a branch of AQIM, threatened to fight the states following imperialist policies in Mali.[55] Apart from the formal worldwide affiliates of Al-Qaida, this perspective is followed by the militant fraternity as a whole including ISIS, one of whose proclaimed objectives is driving out the invading Americans from Iraq and uprooting the existing autocracies through self-proclaimed caliphate.[56] In Thailand, a document in Yawi script titled *Berjihad di Patani* seized from the militants calls for jihad against the colonialists.[57]

The militant front against western imperialism is not limited to military resistance; rather, it encompasses economic and cultural areas as well. Bin Laden urged believers to fight American imperialism through economic boycott in addition to military struggle. A document titled 'Mujahideen's Roadmap' signed by the Abu-Hafs al-Masri Brigades, an Al-Qaida affiliate in Iraq, emphasized undermining the trust of investors in the US economy.[58] Furthermore, the Bali bombing orchestrated by Jama'a al-Islamiya in 2002 was linked to the militants' reaction against the cultural onslaught of the West. Jama'a al-Islamiya, in its quest for the revival of Dar-ul-Islam, constituted a strong nexus between Islamism in Southeast Asia and transnational militancy.[59]

Nevertheless, in the whole diaspora of the militants belonging to different geographical and cultural landscapes, the Afghan Taliban appear closest to Azzam's classical approach to jihad. They are an isolated example where resistance against western imperialism is not mostly directed to what the militants label as 'nearer enemies'.[60] Notwithstanding the inherent difference of approaches and the question of theological legitimacy, the fact remains that contemporary Islamists use the anti-imperialistic nature of Islam to mobilize the jihadi support to counter the West.

Eradicating apostasy in Muslim societies

The rhetoric of eliminating the elements of apostasy in the Muslim societies has led to the evolution of the codes of war on following three basic trajectories: purging the Muslim societies of heresies, fighting the Shiites and violence against the local support base of the West. The militant perspective sees all these elements as constituents of a broad spectrum of apostasy within Muslim societies.

Purging the Muslim societies of Heresies

The militants' perspective on what they term as 'heresy of ideas' is essentially an outcome of Al-Zawahiri's approach to cast the puritanical views of Ibn Abdul Wahab and Sayyed Qutb into a militant ideological frame.[61] He has been strongly influenced by the *jāhilliyah* thesis of Ibn Abdul Wahab and Sayyed Qutb. Ibn Abdul Wahab identified his contemporary Arabian society with pre-Islamic *jāhilliyah*. As already discussed, he claimed that the faith got contaminated by heresies (*bida'ā*) soon after the Prophet and the Islamic society reverted to pre-Islamic *jāhilliyah*. He sought to discredit the theology developed over almost 1,000 years. The same discourse got a new shape with Sayyed Qutb, who sought to draw parallels between the western civilization and the *jāhilliyah* order that had to be confronted through military jihad and further denounced the Muslim leadership as 'apostates' for being loyal to the imperialist West. He took jihad not only as an instrument to defend the faith in the face of imperialism but also to fight all un-Islamic practices within Muslim societies.[62] With this contextual background, the militants seek to revive the purity of faith by fighting heretics in Muslim societies. Like Ibn Abdul Wahab and Sayyed Qutb, they identify modern societies with the pre-Islamic *jāhilliyah* order for being engrossed in polytheistic practices.[63] They put those who do not follow a 'pure brand of faith' outside the pale of Islam. They unanimously label the political transformation from the caliphate to democracy as heretical. They argue that adapting to democracy amounts to converting to a new faith and invoke the question of apostasy. Likewise, the militants view secularism as an instrument to limit the scope of faith in the temporal sphere. They declare it heretical as it amounts to defining the scope of divinity as such and calls for submission to man-made laws.[64] Bin Laden excommunicates secular political parties working in the Muslim countries and argues that participation in a democratic process that culminates into submission to man-made laws amounts to negation of the Lordship of God.[65]

The militant diaspora, as a whole, shares this narrative. Harkat-al-Shabbāb al-Mujahideen in Somalia aims to rejuvenate the Ummah through purifying the faith of all innovations (*bida'ā*).[66] Likewise, Ansār Din Group, an Al-Qaida affiliate in Northern Mali, destroyed many Sufi shrines in Timbuktu as they consider these shrines to engender idolatrous practices.[67] In Nigeria, Boko Haram considers participation in any social activity associated with western civilization as forbidden in Islam and aims to fight against those who take part in any such activity.[68] AQAP aims to fight against the forces of *jāhilliyah* through abolishing man-made systems.[69] In Syria, Al-Nusra Front killed the administrator of Khalid b. Walīd's shrine. In Pakistan, TTP and its local chapters also resolve to eliminate innovations and elements of *shirk* (polytheism) through the instrument of jihad.[70] It seeks to eradicate Sufism for contaminating the purity of faith by introducing innovations into it. It has been involved in plotting to kill prominent Muslim scholars belonging to the Barelvi sect in the country. It claimed responsibility for targeting the shrines of Sufis across Pakistan and has claimed to target Eid Milad-un-Nabi (Celebration of the Prophet's birthday) processions.

Besides Al-Qaida, ISIS also appreciates Al-Zarqawi for his pronouncing of *takfīr* and subsequent killings of Kurdish secularists Barzani and Talabani and further those who follow democracy because it amounts to *shirk*.[71] Moreover, ISIS militants like the Wahabi movement are prompt in erasing anything they believe to be pagan accretions introduced through heresies. They claim to erase the remnants of pre-Islamic civilizations on the pattern of Prophet Muhammad and the prophet Ibrahim who broke idols to establish the unity of God. Besides targeting pre-Islamic remnants like

Assyrian antiquities, they are keen to level different shrines to the ground, not unlike the Wahabi originators of the 18th century. ISIS has even targeted the tomb of the prophet Younous in Mosul.[72]

Violence against the Shiites

The shrinking of the boundaries of faith on the premise of reverting to its purity led to a proliferation of decrees pronouncing *takfīr* on sectarian grounds. There is hardly any sect in Muslim societies that could escape such sort of labelling. The Shiites, owing to their distance from the Sunnite majority, suffered unhindered violence unleashed by the Sunnite militants. The militants' approach towards polemics is informed largely by two key figures: Al-Maqdisi and Al-Zarqawi. Initially, Al-Maqdisi was categorical in pronouncing unqualified *takfīr* for the Shiites. He declared his disavowal (*bara'at*) from both Rawāfidh[73] and Nawāsib because of the former's derogatory attitude towards the exalted Companions of the Prophet and the latter's hostility towards the family of the Prophet.[74] However, he developed moderation on the question of sectarianism after his arrest by the Jordanians. Ecumenism is evident in his agreement with Ibn Taimmiyah that the Rawāfidh may not be identified with the Christians and the Jews. He became critical of the violent campaigns against them for having the potential to create chaos in Muslim societies. He criticized Al-Zarqawi for his blind violence against the Shiites in Iraq. He argued that medieval Muslim scholars like Ibn Taimmiyah accorded sanction to the killings of only the Shiite elite. The violence has not been sanctioned against the Shiite laity, who have hardly any rudimentary knowledge of their belief system. He further argued that the sanction accorded to violence against the Shiites by the Sunnite scholarship during the Iran–Iraq War had a pragmatic basis instead of any theological sanction.

Al-Maqdisi failed to inculcate this moderation in Al-Zarqawi, who continued with his unabated violence against the Shiites. He declined to observe discrimination between the Shiite laity and the elite class on the grounds that the democratic framework dilutes this distinction since the authority to elect the rulers rests with the common man.[75] In the context of Iraq, he did not incline to Al-Maqdisi's renewed narrative borrowed from Ibn Taimmiyah to limit violence only against the Shiite elite. Al-Zarqawi argued that contemporary realities were altogether different from the 13th-century context in which Ibn Taimmiyah drew a line of distinction between these classes of Shiites. He undertook to explore evidence from historical accounts of political Islam to legitimize his killings of the Shiites who could not be outright declared as apostates because of the conflicting opinions of the jurists. He identified the contemporary Shiites in Iraq with the 13th-century Abbasid vizier Al-Alqemi for their hypocritical conduct in supporting the infidels against fellow Muslims.[76] Al-Alqemi is accused of supporting the Mongols against the Muslims. Al-Zarqawi developed a thesis that eliminating the Shiites was a prerequisite to securing victories against the external enemy, as happened in the case of the pious caliphs who could bring vast lands into the fold of Islam only when they eliminated apostasy from Hejaz. Moreover, he viewed the sectarian violence as a factor to unite the Sunnites for jihad and further as a 'final solution' to the Shiite problem through their complete elimination.[77]

Bin Laden also owned Al-Zarqawi's violent approach in defining the militants' response against the Shiites across the globe. He agreed with Al-Zarqawi that sectarian violence in Iraq was linked with the Shiites' collaboration with the US invading forces. On the premise of collaboration with the US forces, violence against the Shiites became a major feature of the militant ideology across the globe. AQAP target the Shiites for being partners in what they term the 'triangle of the enemies of Muslim Ummah' along with the Zionist–Crusaders alliance and apostate regimes.[78] Al-Qaida does not hesitate to excommunicate the Shiites on the grounds of protecting the honour of the Prophet. AQIM shares the standpoint of AQAP in placing the Shiites in the ranks of Zionists and Crusaders.[79] Al-Nusra Front supports the anti-Shiite narrative of Al-Qaida that views Shiites as traitors for their alleged collaboration with the enemies of Islam. Similarly, TTP declares Shiites to be elements of apostasy within Muslim societies. TTP's war manual (*Nisāb-e-Harb*) does not recognize the Shiites to be part of the faith owing to their innovations in the fundamentals of the faith.[80] The Taliban argue that corruption in faith is due to the misleading ideas of the Shiites. They further argue that history is replete with instances of their treason against the Muslims in collusion with the non-believers, whether they were Mongols in the 13th century, the Crusaders against Salahuddin Ayubi, the British imperialists in Bengal in the 18th century, the Indian Hindus on the issue of Ayyodiah Mosque and more recently, the American invaders in Iraq in 2008. The militants drawing upon this historical evidence sum up that the Shiites do not believe in the sanctity (*hurmat*) of the blood and the property of the Sunnites.[81]

On the question of polemics, ISIS subscribes to a narrative of unremitting violence against the Shiites.[82] It is evident from their high tributes to Al-Zarqawi and the projection of the Sunnites killed by the Shiites as heroes. In the case of ISIS, the Sunnites' political marginalization in post-Saddam Iraq at the hands of the Shiites, allegedly through engineered elections with the collaboration of the West, has earned popularity for ISIS's rhetoric with the Sunnites. The bid by former premier Nur al-Maliki to transform Iraq into a Shiite state through repressive means has also been a conduit to channel the Sunnite volunteers to join the ranks of ISIS. This context led to Al-Zarqawi's frequent and widespread appreciation in the ranks of ISIS. It was evident from their reference to his speech titled 'And Thus the Way of the Criminals Becomes Evident' (*Wa li Tastābinā Sabīl-ul-Mujrimīn*). Abu Muhammad al-Adnani ash-Shami, an official spokesperson for ISIS, also praised the ISIS fighters for killing Shiites.[83] He declared fighting the Shiites even after the withdrawal of the US forces from Iraq as one of their prime objectives.[84]

Fighting the 'Nearer Enemy'

Even within the ideological frontiers of the militants, one can fairly identify figures like Abdullah Azzam, who always avoided directing their war against fellow Muslims. Though he did not excommunicate Muslim rulers in general, he laid down such strict criteria for the Muslim rulers to make peace with the non-believers that even a benign distraction therefrom would render them liable to be labelled as apostates by the subsequent generations of militants. He developed these limits largely on three grounds. First, he validated the militant perspective that foregoing a piece of Muslim land fell beyond the legitimate authority of the Muslim rulers. Second, permitting the non-believers to reside in the two holy sanctuaries of Islam was in conflict with the established Islamic practices sanctified through a prophetic tradition that calls for the expulsion of the non-believers from the territorial limits of these holy places. Third, the question of seeking help from non-believers would warrant careful rationalization of two apparently conflicting traditions of the Prophet. One tradition refers to the Prophet's refusal to accept help from a polytheist at Badr, but the second tradition suggests that the Prophet accepted the assistance of Safawan b. Ummayah at Hunayn.[85] The rationalization of these two traditions led Azzam to argue that acceptance of assistance from the non-believers must be a cautious exercise that should be performed only in extremely hard situations.[86] It is evident that, though he avoided the loose application of *takfir,* his affirmation of hijra from *dār-ul-harb* confirmed his partial subscription to *takfīr* of Qutb and further affirmed his linkage with the classical theorists like Qurtubi.[87]

After Azzam, the militants ushered in an era of loose application of *takfīr*. For instance, Bin Laden exhorted the believers across the globe to review their loyalties towards their respective rulers who happened to support the heretics.[88] His conviction of the 'nearer enemy' doctrine was informed through the following points. First, he defined the Muslim rulers who became part of the western plan to fight the militants in Somalia and Yemen as 'apostates'. Second, he desired to create revolutionary ripples in Arabia to uproot what he labelled as the 'apostate' Saudi regime that had lost its legitimacy for inviting the US forces to the land of Hejaz. Third, the Saudis supported the Communists vis-à-vis the believers in Southern Yemen.[89] The 'nearer enemy' doctrine also embraces the apologist clergy who support western clients.[90] He welcomed the recent Arab Spring for having provided a chance for the collapse of the Middle Eastern autocracies that had become agents of the western powers.[91] However, the evidence suggests that he agreed with the advice of Al-Qaida's lower formations to eschew violence in Muslim countries through directing resistance solely against infidel forces – and that too preferably inside the war theatres. His advice to TTP leadership to shift their focus of war to the external fronts reflects his pragmatic approach to the issue, aimed at maintaining the public image of the organization.[92] He further resolved to take the battle to the US soil through enlisting the Muslim emigrants in the United States having US citizenship as long as they had not pledged not to damage the American interests.[93] He further urged his field formations to identify the killing fields, keeping in view the low security alert, optimum impact potential and marginalized chances of collateral damage to Muslims.[94]

Not unlike Bin Laden, Al-Zawahiri legitimized violence against the Muslim rulers who were alleged to be in collaboration with the Crusaders. He, too, appreciated the current Arab Spring in Tunisia, Egypt, Jordan and Yemen against the rulers whom he called the 'Zionist Arabs' for their collaboration with the Crusaders against the believers by joining the United States in its war against the believers and further for extending brutal treatment to the Muslim fighters on their arrest. He condemned the secular Egyptian rulers for their corruption and for being loyal to the Zionists. This loyalty was reflected through providing Nile water and gas to Israel, denying medical treatment to the people of Gaza and permitting the Israelis to enter Sinai without visas.[95] Jihad, which was previously directed against the forces of Unbelief, was re-invented into a global struggle encompassing even Muslim rulers.[96] Al-Zawahiri subjected Abdullah Saleh, the former President of Yemen, to severe criticism and called for an uprising against him for his fighting against the militants alongside the Americans.[97] Though Bin Laden and Al-Zawahiri both called for violence against the 'apostate rulers' of the Muslim states, the strategic restraint to avoid collateral damage which was evident with Bin Laden was absent from Al-Zawahiri.[98] The labelling of Muslim rulers as apostates was generalized with Bin Laden whereas it became more precise with Al-Zawahiri as reflected in his doctrine of 'individual responsibility'. Moreover, Bin Laden had always been concerned about the positive image of Al-Qaida, at least in media presentation, which naturally warranted at least neutral relations with media, whereas Al-Zawahiri did not hesitate to ex-communicate the media as well for being state-friendly. Al-Zawahiri emphasized Palestine more than the enforcement of Shariah. It was evident from his condemnation of the Saudi regime for their slackness regarding the Palestine issue despite that they enforced Shariah.[99]

Al-Maqdisi claimed to follow a middle road between the Khawarij, who excommunicated the believers for the commission of major sins, and the Murji'ah, who unduly avoided pronouncing *takfīr* when it was duly warranted.[100] Though he is considered the pioneer of radical Islamist ideology, his theory is caught up with multiple contradictions. He claimed to follow the traditional Sunnite school, but he permitted *khurūj* against the Muslim rulers. He is acknowledged as a reference person for Al-Qaida militants; yet, his approach to jihad is somewhat different from other ideologues of Al-Qaida. Bin Laden declared violence against the Muslim rulers who collaborate with the infidels as the priority. He followed the traditional approach of resisting the enemy, which was the nearest one.[101] Al-Maqdisi did away with distinctions between distant and nearer enemy. The primacy to fight the apostate rulers in the Muslim world vis-à-vis the actual infidels was an outcome of his conviction that unbelief arising out of apostasy was more severe than actual unbelief. He identified the prayer leaders appointed by the invalid rulers (*tāghūt*) with the soldiers who defended the policies of *tāghūt;* yet, he avoided invalidating the prayers behind them. He was the first to declare the house of Saud as non-believers.[102] Following Ibn Abdul Wahab and Sayyed Qutb, he drew a parallel between the pre-Islamic *jāhilliyah* and modern society. He argued that modern society reflects the traits of pre-Islamic *jāhilliyah.* He differed from those who defined 'unbelief' as an outcome of negation of faith by heart alone. He argued that verbal statements and acts lead to unbelief. He further argued that those who did not believe that their actions or verbal statements led to unbelief support the forces of modern *jāhilliyah.* While relying upon the incident of Hatib from the early accounts of Islamic history, he argued that supporting (*mawālāt*) the non-believers would entail the label of *takfīr* whether it was affirmed by heart or otherwise.[103] Following this narrative, he excommunicated the Saudi monarchy for supporting the United States against fellow Muslims.[104]

Militant outfits worldwide share the narrative of fighting the 'nearer enemy'. It was under the influence of Al-Zawahiri that AQAP developed the narrative of *khurūj* against the rulers on the following grounds. First, the believers are permitted to rise against the rulers, as is evident from early Muslim history, which has the examples of revolts of Hussain b. Ali against Yazid b. Mu'awiyah, the rising of Abdullah b. Zubair against Marwan and Muhammad Al-Nafs Al-Zakiyyah and Zaid b. Ali against the Abbasids. Second, as agreed by the majority of classical ulema, the believers are not permitted to rise against the rulers even if they are oppressors and invalid. Al-Qaida's branch in Arabia believes that, if the rulers commit unbelief, the believers come under an obligation to uproot them through force.[105] Nevertheless, the interpretation of 'unbelief' is also subject to Al-Zawahiri's influence, as he holds that helping the forces of unbelief against the believers necessarily constitutes 'unbelief'. He labelled the Egyptian and Arab rulers as apostates for supporting the Crusaders. He supported the Arab Spring in an attempt to uproot them.[106] In this pursuit, AQAP takes *khurūj* as *fard-e-ayn* for the believers.[107]

Tehrīk-e-Taliban Pakistan (TTP) shares this narrative of individual obligation. It argues that in its religious spirit, this obligation is as important as the five elements of faith. This religious obligation will continue to exist upon the believers as long as the rule of these 'apostate rulers' exists.[108] Al-Qaida in Islamic Maghreb (AQIM) aims to uproot the 'apostate rulers' as well.[109] They resolved to support the efforts to overthrow the regimes in Tunisia and Algeria through military means. They also approved of the efforts of Al-Jama'a al-Islamiyyah al-Muqātilah bi-Libya commonly known as The Fighting Islamic Group (FIG) to uproot Gaddafi's regime in Libya. FIG's armed resistance aimed to uproot Gaddafi's regime, which was subjecting fellow Muslims to inhuman repression and exploiting the economic resources of the country.[110] FIG sought to identify Gaddafi with the Pharaohs for his treatment of the Libyan Muslims on an Israeli pattern.[111] In

Nigeria, Jama'at Ahl as-Sunnah lid-Da'wah-wal-jihad, commonly known as Boko Haram, also aims to replace the existing rulers whom they consider as apostate with the Islamic caliphate.[112] Their allegiance to ISIS also confirms their rejection of the existing political order in religious terms. Likewise, Al-Shabbāb in Somalia has been fighting against President Sharif Ahmed who was head of the Transitional Federal Government. ISIS has proclaimed its caliphate, which runs counter to the existing political orders and, in practical terms, demands their elimination through violent means.

In view of the foregoing, it may be argued that the militant perspective on the right to rebel against the Muslim rulers lacks coherence and uniformity. Abdullah Azzam never supported the revolt against the rulers in the Muslim lands. Al-Zawahiri, Al-Maqdisi and Al-Zarqawi supported targeting the 'nearer enemy' first to mobilize the believers to fight the 'distant enemy'. In the case of Bin Laden, he categorically pronounced *takfīr* on those Muslim rulers who followed the western agenda but the evidence is available that, being moved by pragmatism, he directed the Al-Qaida apparatus to focus on resistance to the western enemy to avoid distortion of the organization's public image and erode their support base. The ascendancy of Egyptian elements in Al-Qaida leadership has transformed the ideological orientations of the organization from pursuing the traditional Sunnite approach of Azzam to Al-Zawahiri's reactionary approach, which is aligned more with Qutb and Al-Faraj[113]. Azzam was moderate in terms of extending the label of *takfīr* within the Muslim society and directed his philosophy towards the defence of the Muslim lands in face of foreign aggression rather than fighting Muslim governments.[114] He did not label the contemporary Muslim rulers as apostates and followed the traditional Sunnite standpoint that did not permit revolt even against the imperfect Muslim rulers. As long as his philosophy configured the resistance model of the Islamists, the codes of war remained predominantly on a traditional Sunnite pattern. For instance, the phenomenon of suicide terrorism remained external to the jihadi tactics in the war against the Soviets.

Fighting the local support base of the 'nearer enemy'

The militants seek to fight against the local support base of the Muslim rulers whom they accused of collaborating with the West. This suppor base includes the apologists, the government functionaries and, above all, the media.

THE APOLOGISTS

As said earlier, the militants' definition of 'the nearer enemy' covers the apologists who extend their support to 'the apostate regimes' in the Muslim world and do not follow the militants' brand of Islam.[115] They further believe that western ideologies can be transplanted into Muslim lands.[116] Bin Laden condemns the Muslims as the apologists who call for compromise with the 'apostate regimes' and their western masters instead of waging jihad against them.[117] In more precise terms Al-Zawahiri, while referring to certain works of a leading American think tank, recognizes the apologists as their allies committed to promoting American interests in the Muslim world.[118] In the militant landscape, though a few like Al-Maqdisi claim that difference of opinion does not entail violence, they condemn the clergy who support the non-believers against the Muslims and give their fatwa according to the whims and wishes of their apostate regimes.[119] In the same perspective, in Pattani, Thailand, the militants share the Al-Qaida narrative regarding *takfīr*. *Berjihad di Patani* excommunicates those who support the non-Muslims, declaring them as hypocrites (*munāfiqūn*).[120]

In addition to those who support 'the nearer enemy', the militants as a whole unleash violence against those who make allowance for western cultural values in Muslim societies. Al-Maqdisi argues that physical identification with non-believers does not attract excommunication; yet, the militants' attacks against the music outlets, obscenity and prostitution should be viewed in this context. In 2005, Hamas banned music and dance in some areas under their control including the Gaza Strip. In Pakistan's Khyber Pakhtunkhwa province, the militants have been acting to thwart this cultural fusion through violent means. Further, Al-Maqdisi asserts that acquiring education in public schools run by the non-believers, though undesirable, does not make one subject to *takfīr*. However, militant outfits like Boko Haram promote a version of Islam which renders it forbidden (haram) for Muslims to take part in political or social activities associated with western society, including voting in elections, wearing shirts and trousers or receiving a secular education.[121] In Nigeria, Boko Haram categorically declares acquiring western secular education not only non-permissible (haram) but also reprehensible. Abu Bakr b. Muhammad Shekau, the chief of Boko Haram, while affirming linkage between their jihad in Nigeria and global militancy, resolved to target 'the outposts of the western culture'.[122] Besides this, AQIM's association with Boko Haram affirms their approval of the latter's objectives, including resistance to the western culture in Muslim societies. Moreover, Jama'a al-Islamia orchestrated the Bali bombing in 2002 on the pretext of confronting the onslaught of the western culture in Indonesia.[123] Al-Shabbāb in Somalia claims to revive the purity of the Islamic way of life by wiping out western cultural influences from Somali society. In the area under their control, it forced radio stations not to play music. In the same vein, the ISIS affiliate in Libya burnt musical instruments to express their puritanical ideology.[124] Worldwide militancy has led to distinctions between radical militants and modernists in Muslim societies.[125] Interestingly, both sections have failed to earn public legitimacy as a whole. The former failed because they undertake violent means to achieve their goals and the latter could not succeed because of their overemphasis on the westernization of Muslim societies. The majority has been moderate but has never delinked itself from the basics of the faith.[126]

GOVERNMENT FUNCTIONARIES

The militant narrative of violence against government functionaries in Muslim states lacks uniformity. Al-Maqdisi did not proclaim *takfīr* on those doing jobs within the system of unbelief.[127] However, Al-Zawahiri's concept of 'individual responsibility' broadens the scope of *takfīr* to the government functionaries as well. He argues that no one can claim exemption from being subject to *takfīr* merely because he is following the orders of the government. He drags members of the security mechanism into the ambit of *takfīr* for becoming a party to the commission of crimes by extending compliance and support to their governments.[128] Similarly, AQAP legitimizes the killings of Muslim soldiers in Yemen by charging them of committing apostasy through joining the Americans in fighting the Muslims, guarding institutions including the parliament, *ribā*-based banks, embassies and cultural centres, extending protection to the Ismailite sect and, above all, hindering the establishment of the caliphate.[129] The militant outfits follow the narrative based on 'individual responsibility' worldwide. Besides the law enforcement agencies (LEAs), the militants target the polio vaccination teams and those pursuing the western agenda to control population growth in the third world.[130] In Thailand, *Berjihad di Patani* calls for launching suicide attacks against the LEAs to defend Pattani Dar-ul-Islam. ISIS claimed responsibility for a suicide attack in Jalalabad on government functionaries in April 2014.[131] Thailand sanctions the killings of the civilian

MEDIA

As already noted, Bin Laden was concerned about the positive media image of Al-Qaida whereas Al-Zawahiri did not hesitate to target state-friendly media.[132] TTP categorically threatened to attack the media if they did not stop denigrating their public image.[133] In Nigeria, Boko Haram threatened to target media outlets for distorting their image and for their offences against the faith. A few media reports suggest that they have waged war against the media in Nigeria.[134] The Somali-based Al-Shabbāb follows the same anti-media approach.[135] ISIS also declares the media as apostate for tarnishing the image of the militants.[136] In December 2013, they claimed responsibility for attacking Salaheddin TV in Tikrit[137] because the media outlet was distorting the image of the Sunnite Iraqis.[138] The militants also attack media companies for importing western cultural values into Muslim societies.

No distinction between the military and civilian targets

Violence against non-believers

The reactionary tone of the militants that has led to erosion of the distinction between the military and the civilian targets results from three major irritants that include the US military presence in Hejaz, Israeli occupation of Al-Aqsa and the threat of western aggression into the Muslim world. This reactionary tone has been quite loud in the conflict between the militants and the West. Bin Laden exhorted the militants to direct violence against both civilian and military targets. He decreed the targeting of US civilians alongside the military targets on the following grounds. First, the United States itself did not observe any distinction between civilian and military targets for nuclear strikes during World War II. Second, US civilians cannot be absolved from responsibility for the sins of their governments which come into existence through their will and, further, they support their governments through their taxes.[139] Third, even having a religion other than Islam is ground enough to target the non-believers.

This narrative is followed universally by the Al-Qaida-affiliates. AQAP fully supported the suicide operation on the US plane in 2009, which was launched to avenge the killings of the Muslim civilians belonging to Yemenite tribes in Abyan province.[140] AQAP further reinterprets evidence from Islamic history to justify the killings of the non-believers merely for not following Islam. Al-Awlaki argues that, during the early period of Islam, Arabian pagans, the Persian Zoroastrians and the Roman Christians were killed simply because they continued to follow their respective belief-systems.[141] Al-Abbab further argues the classification between the civilians and the military targets has hardly any grounds in Shariah.[142] He refers to a tradition of the Prophet wherein the Prophet was reported to have enjoined upon the believers to fight against those who do not believe in Allah. He further refers to Ibn Hajar who infers from the Prophet's dispatching of his Companions to kill one Ibn Abi al-Haqiq without offering him warning that, if one does not embrace Islam after receiving the divine message, one becomes liable to be killed.[143] In this regard, he quotes a tradition of the Prophet wherein he has been reported to have said, 'I was instructed to fight the people until they say: "There is no one worthy of worship but Allah." Whoever says "There is no one worthy of worship but Allah", has protected his life and wealth from me except with its right and to Allah is his accountability'.

Other militant outfits follow the same suit. To quote a few examples, in Pakistan TTP resorted to the massacre of religious minorities, mainly Christians. Al-Shabbāb targeted the non-believers in Garissa University Campus in Kenya in April 2015 and, earlier, the Christians in Northern Kenya.[144] They also singled out non-Muslims for killing at Westgate Mall in 2013.[145] Similarly, Boko Haram offered the Nigerian Christians the only choice – either convert to Islam or be killed.[146] ISIS follows the same approach, which is evident from their treatment of the non-believers. It claimed responsibility for beheading more than 20 Coptic Christians in Libya in February 2015.[147] The indiscriminate killings of the Yazidis in northern Iraq at the hands of ISIS evidently confirm it shares the militant narrative of killing civilian non-believers merely because they follow their own faith.[148]

Violence against the believers

The narrative based upon disregarding the distinction between the combatants and the non-combatants is not limited to the non-believers. It also embraces within its ambit those who either do not come up to the militants' image of a true Muslim or as a tactic to pressurize governments. They have been killing the Muslims largely on the following pretexts: (1) they do not fulfil the criteria of being a true Muslim; (2) their killings may be sanctioned as part of collateral damage because necessity makes a thing legal which is otherwise illegal;[149] and (3) they support the non-believers against the fellow Muslims. *Berjihad di Patani* in Thailand sanctions the killings of the civilian Muslims for their support to the non-believers.[150] In Pakistan, though there is no scarcity of evidence that proves TTP's frequent involvement in the killings of innocent civilians, the Peshawar school incident in 2014 is the worst case, which left more than 100 innocent students killed.[151] Similarly, Boko Haram targeted the students in the Yobe state of Nigeria in 2013.[152] They also claimed responsibility for killing dozens of Muslims in a mosque attack in Nigeria in 2014.[153] ISIS, too, has reportedly killed scores of the Sunnite Muslims in Syria and Iraq.

Though there have been certain voices from the mainstream Al-Qaida leadership against the indiscriminate killings of the Muslims by certain militant outfits, the dominant factor behind these voices has been strategic instead of ideological.[154] They learnt from the Iraqi experience that killing Muslims by the militants resulted in their alienation in Muslim societies. They had to face social alienation following their attack on the children of Al-Anbār tribe in Iraq.[155] Nevertheless, there are ideological reservations against the killings of civilians on the part of the Afghan Taliban, as is evident from their Urdu website. They condemned the Peshawar school incident as being un-Islamic.[156]

No space for peace agreements with non-believers

The militant perspective has hardly any space for peace agreements with non-believers. Azzam argued that the provision of peace agreements as reflected through Hudaybiah Pact was withdrawn through the Verse of Sword when the Muslims were no longer militarily weak. He argued that when jihad became *fard-e-ayn*, it nullified the previous peace treaties with the non-believers. He further argued that peace treaties were permitted only if they would promote the Muslims' interests. As the Muslim lands were *waqf* lands for the entire Muslim Ummah so any compromise on them would fall beyond the purview of any peace agreement with the non-believers. Moreover, if any agreement entails compromise on the approved practices of the faith, it will lose its legitimacy. For instance, if any agreement provides for the polytheists to reside in Arabian Peninsula or to return a Muslim woman to the infidels, it will lose its legitimacy because it will amount to negation of categorical injunctions of the Quran and Sunnah (*nasūs-e-qatt'iyā*).[157] Moreover, it is also not permitted to enter into such agreements with the non-believers that result in the projection of the values and socio-religious norms of unbelief into Muslim societies.[158]

As far as the sanctity of peace agreements with the non-believers is concerned, the militant perspective lacks coherence. Interestingly, in this case, a piece of Bin Laden's correspondence suggests that Al-Qaida field formations were more extremist than himself.[159] The militants, in general, have no reverence for international treaties with states at war with the believers on the following grounds. First, Adel al-Abbab argues that Islam extends guarantees of protection only to either the dhimmis (non-Muslims who are guaranteed protection by the Islamic state in lieu of tax) or to those with whom the believers enter into a covenant (*Ahl al-ahad*).[160] As the United States in particular and the West in general are at war with the believers, they cannot be included in these categories.[161] Second, most of the Muslim governments are not entitled to enter into covenants with the non-believers on behalf of the believers because they are governed through man-made laws, ally with the non-believers and, above all, as Anwar al-Awlaki argues, the nations that are fighting the Muslims constitute *dār-ul-harb* with which no peace treaty is permitted in Islam.[162]

Commission of major sins warrants takfīr

The militants' narrative on the religious status of those found to have committed major sins is also caught up in categorical contradictions. Though they claim not to follow Khawarij for proclaiming *takfīr* on those charged with the commission of major sins, at the same time, they do not refrain from labelling them 'apostates'. Al-Maqdisi claims to differ from Khawarij with regard to invoking *takfīr* against those who commit major sins. He further observes restraints in excommunicating the people of *irja'ā* (those who defer the judgement) unless their *irja'ā* does not lead them to the negation of tawhid (oneness of Allah).[163] Similarly, Al-Awlaki argues that Al-Qaida cannot be identified with Khawarij for not following their extreme position on *takfīr* on the grounds of the commission of major sins.[164] On the other hand, they direct violence against those involved in the acts of moral turpitude and commit major sins. They base their perspective of violence on the pretext that Islam ordains the killing of those who commit offences like robberies even if they are otherwise believers.[165]

Vengeance-based violence

Almost the whole body of the militant literature is replete with references to the religious scripture. The purpose of these references is to earn theological approval for their violence. However, it is also commonplace for militants to take vengeance either directly or indirectly and leave the question of theological legitimacy in the background. In theory, the militants identify themselves with the local civilian Muslims; yet, in practice, there is no scarcity of evidence to prove their frequent involvement in the killings of innocent civilians, mostly in revenge for the killings of their fellow militants. The Peshawar school incident in 2014 has already been cited.[166] Moreover, TTP claimed responsibility for twin attacks in Karachi in November 2013 and said they were committed in reaction against Ashura violence in Rawalpindi on November 25, 2013, in which Shiites killed many Sunnites. It appeared from the statement issued by TTP that it attacked the civilians to pressure the government to meet their demands regarding the arrest of those involved in Ashura violence.[167]

Contradictions and gaps

The militants' narrative lacks coherence and uniformity. It is caught up with multiple contradictions between theory and practice, which reveals their theological immaturity.

First, certain militant outfits who champion unremitting violence on the question of polemics claim not to believe in physical violence on a sectarian basis. TTP's Mohmand Chapter claims not to believe in physical violence on sectarian grounds.[168]

Second, in theoretical terms, the militants claim not to adopt violent means against those who have a difference of opinion with them, but in practice, they do not tolerate those who do not subscribe to their version of faith.[169] TTP condemns the Muslim scholars in Pakistan as apologists who do not subscribe to their version of Islam and condemn TTP's anti-state activities.[170] In June 2009, TTP claimed responsibility for killing Maulana Sarfraz Ahmed Naeemi, a Barelvi Muslim scholar, for issuing a decree labelling suicide bombing as non-permissible (haram) in Islam. In the same pursuit, ISIS executed six Muslim clerics for their condemnation of burning a Jordanian pilot alive by the ISIS militants as disgusting and alien to Islam.[171] (ISIS had burnt the pilot Mu'ath Kasasbeh alive after he was taken hostage by ISIS after the issuance of a fatwa.)

Third, the proponents of *Nisāb-e-Harb* – the War Manual of TTP – argue that for non-believers the sources from where the morals of war originate are international conventions. They violate these morals repeatedly as they find hardly any binding force behind them. On the other hand, Islamic Shariah lays down the morals of war (*Ada'āb al-Qitāl*) or grounds of war (*Illat al-Qitāl*). The proponents of *Nisāb-e-Harb* argue that Muslims cannot violate these morals because these have divine sanctions behind them even if the enemy crosses all limits in violation of war morals as enunciated by international conventions. They claim that there is no evidence available in Muslim military history where they have molested the honour of a woman or where they have killed innocent children.[172] There is no denying the fact that Islam has laid down morals of war with divine sanctity behind them in terms of binding force. These morals were enforced with full vigour during the prophetic era and afterwards during the period of the early caliphate. However, the evidence suggests that, in the case of TTP, there exists a huge gap between theory and practice with regard to the observance of the morals of war as laid down by Shariah. Their massacre at the Peshawar school in December 2014 and many other examples of civilian massacre reduce their claims of observance of the morals of war to ashes.

Fourth, according to TTP's *Nisāb-e-Harb* political warfare aims to uproot what the militants term as 'apostate rulers in the Muslim lands' largely through political tools. These tools include political means to increase public support and reduce opposition from society.[173] The evidence highlights a huge gap between theory and practice. The militants use military means against the state and the ruling elite to achieve what they term as political objectives. They express the objectives only for theoretical purposes, but for all practical purposes, they rely upon military means. Non-violent means like preaching material and websites are used as the support base for physical violence. Attacks on the ruling elite and politicians are examples of the use of military means to achieve political objectives. In Egypt, military means instead of economic means were adopted to damage the tourist industry, which was a major part of the Egyptian economy. Tourists were attacked to discourage them from visiting Egypt. Likewise, the Bali bombing was an example of military means being adopted to curtail the onslaught of western culture into Muslim societies.

In brief, the following conclusions may be drawn.

First, the militants proclaim *takfīr* on those who follow democracy. Participation in the democratic process amounts to infringing upon the divine domain of law giving. In other words, following democracy implies conversion to a new faith and warrants the killings of its followers as a legal requirement (*hukm-e-shar'i*). As democracy functions in the sphere of the nation-state system, by rejecting nationalism, the militants condemn those who follow the constitutions of the nation-states as apostates and clients of unbelief. Second, jihad in terms of individual obligation does not require permission from the rulers. Abdullah Azzam followed the traditional Sunnite version of jihad, focusing solely on the aggressor enemy. Subsequently, the militants challenged the theological discourse developed over centuries by introducing radical revisions in the theory of jihad. In addition to the aggressor enemy, they redirected jihad to the home front against those who collaborate with infidels against fellow believers. Third, the militant narrative of jihad is predominantly under the influence of Wahabi ideology. Fourth, the militants' narrative on the sectarian issue is more hard-core and stricter than even the classical theorists. Fifth, besides approving of violence against the 'nearer enemy', they also sanction violence against the 'apologists'. These apologists include the local supporters of the 'nearer enemy' and further those who believe in the assimilation of western socio-political and cultural values. Based on Al-Zawahiri's account of 'individual responsibility', the militant perspective embraces within itself *takfīr* for those who follow the system which they are a part of, including government functionaries and the media. Sixth, the militants' ethics of war do not recognize any distinction between the military and civilian targets. Seventh, Western aggression into the Muslim states which invokes the individual obligation of jihad leads not only to the nullification of previous peace agreements between the two nations but also eliminates the prospects of peace until the liberation of the occupied lands. Last but not least, the militant narrative is caught up with multiple gaps between theory and practice. Their urge to secure strategic and political gains, and that too under theological cover, leads to these gaps. Their narrative is caught up with multiple contradictions and incoherence when, despite glaring inconsistencies between the commandments of faith and their violent actions, they insist on seeking theological legitimacy to their violence.

Notes

1 Statements of Al-Zawahiri released in response to Arab Spring; see Rassler et al., *Letters from Abbottabad,* no. SOCOM-2012-0000013.
2 Osama bin Laden, Interview by Hamid Mir, *Daily Pakistan*, March 18, 1997.
3 Osama Bin Laden, 'Second Letter to the Muslims of Iraq, October 18, 2003', and 'Message to the American People, October 30, 2004', in *Al Qaida in Its Own Words*, 67–77.
4 Al-Zawahiri's statement in the aftermath of the Arab spring, Rassler et al., *Letters from Abbottabad*, no. SOCOM-2012-0000013.
5 For TTP narrative on the issue, see *Geo News*, February 21, 2014 – 1350 PKT; also see *Dawn News*, February 7, 2014, 1728 PKT.
6 Al-Maqdisi's ideas have influenced scores of contemporary militants, including Abu Musa'ab Al-Zarqawi. He is known to be the most influential jihadi theorist and is acknowledged as a reference person in the circles of Al-Qaida. See Samir Khan, 'The Central Issue', *Inspire*, Issue 2.
7 Hillel Fradkin, 'Recent Statements of Islamist Ideology: Bin Laden and Zarqawi Speak', in *Current Trends in Islamist Ideology*, Vol. 1, 5–11.
8 Ibid.
9 Abu Muhammad al-Maqdisi, *Al-Deemoqratiyya Deen*; also see Al-Maqdisi, *This is Our Aqeedah*, 55, 56.
10 Ibid.
11 Nibras Kazimi, 'A Virulent Ideology in Mutation: Zarqawi Upstages Maqdisi', in *Current Trends in Islamist Ideology*, Vol. 2, 59–73.
12 Abu Musa'ab al-Zarqawi, 'Jamhuriyyat, Aik Mustakkil Madhab', *Hittin*, 8, 131–144. For discussion on the militant perspective vis-à-vis democracy, see Joas Wagemakers, 'The *Kāfir* Religion of the West: *Takfīr* of Democracy and Democrats by Radical Islamists', in *Accusations of Unbelief in Islam: A Diachronic Perspective on Takfīr*, eds. Camilla Adang et al. (Leiden: Brill, 2016), 327–353.
13 Shaykh Abu Basir, Interview by Al-Malahem Media, *Inspire,* issue 1; also see al-Abbab, Interview by Al-Malahem Media, *Inspire*, issue 4; 'Qaideen-e-jihad ke Aqwāl' (Statements of Jihadi Leadership), *Hittin* issue 8; for Tehrīk-e-Taliban, Pakistan (TTP) narrative, see *Ahyā-e-Khilāfat*, 2013; for analysis of violence on

the part of Al-Shabbāb and Boko Haram, see Mark Doyle, 'Al-Shabab can hit almost at will', BBC Report on Somalia Parliament Attacked by al-Shabab in Mogadishu, May 24, 2014; also see Aryn Baker, 'Boko Haram Militants Are Back on the Attack in Nigeria as a Presidential Election Looms', *Times*, January 9, 2015.

14 'Iraq militants kill 21 in polling station attacks ahead of elections', *The Guardian*, April 28, 2014; also see 'Iraq militants in military uniforms attack balloting centre in predominantly Sunni area', *CBS News*, April 22, 2014, 0839 PKT.

15 'Qaideen-e-jihad ke Aqwāl', 8. The militants' websites unequivocally term democracy as system of Unbelief and besides humiliating the politicians in general, label even certain heads of Politico-religious parties as apostates. See for instance, *Jihad blog*, accessed January 21, 2015, http://jihadepakistan.blogspot.com/search/label/.

16 Rassler et al., *Letters from Abbottabad*, nos. SOCOM-2012-0000016, SOCOM-2012-0000017; also see Don D. Chipman, 2003.

17 'The Return of Khilafa', *Dabiq*, issue 1, 1435 AH.

18 Marc Helbling, *Nationalism and Democracy: Competing or Complimentary Logics?* Living Reviews in Democracy, November, 2009, Centre for Comparative and International Studies (Zurich: University of Zurich), 1–14.

19 Maulana Asim Umar, 'Watniyyat Ka Global Butt', (Nationalism: A Global Deity) *Hittin*, issue 8

20 Abdullah Azzam, *Ad-Difa'a un a'aradi al-Muslimeen a'aham farud al-a'yan* (Defence of the Muslim Lands – the First Obligation after Eemān), accessed June 17, 2013, http://www.kalamullah.com/Books/defence.pdf.

21 As quoted in Abdullah Azzam, *Join the Caravan* (Religio-Scope Archives, 2002).

22 Ibid., also see Imam Muslim, *Sahih Muslim*, *Kitāb Al-Imārah*: 4677; Imam Bukhari, S*ahih Bukhari*, *Kitāb al-Jihad*, 2831.

23 Abdullah Azzam, *Tawhid Al-Amali, Al-Awal min Silsala-tul-Maqalat, Reha' min jannat al-Firdous* (The First of the Series of Treatises: Breezes, From the Gardens of Firdaws) (At-Tibyan Publications), accessed June 17, 2013, http://www.kalamullah.com/Books/tawheed_action.pdf.

24 'How should ye not fight for the cause of Allah and of the feeble among men and of the women and the children who are crying: Our Lord! Bring us forth from out this town of which the people are oppressors! Oh, give us from thy presence some protecting friend! Oh, give us from Thy presence some defender! Those who believe do battle for the cause of Allah; and those who disbelieve do battle for the cause of idols. So fight the minions of the devil. Lo! the devil's strategy is ever weak' (An-Nisā: 75,76).

25 Azzam, *Join the Caravan.*

26 Ibid.

27 Azzam, *Ad-Difa'a un a'aradi*. Jihad during the era of the Prophet was of varying types. For instance, Badr was desired (*Mustahabb*) whereas The Trench and Tabuk were declared as *fard-e-ayn* and Khyber happened to be *fard-e-kafāyā* where only the witnesses of Hudaybiah (6 AH) were permitted to participate. See Azzam, *Join the Caravan.*

28 Azzam, *Ad-Difa'a un a'aradi.*

29 Imam al-Waqidi, *Fūtuh as-Sham* (The Islamic Conquest of Syria), trans. Maulana Sulayman Al-Kindi (Ta-Ha Publishers Ltd.), 16–18, accessed September 2, 2013, http://www.kalamullah.com/conquest-of-syria.html.

30 Azzam, *Ad-Difa'a un a'aradi.*

31 Three Imams-Abu Hanifa, Al-Shaaf'i and Malik identify jihad (*fard-e-ayan*) with *Salat* and *Zakat* in religious obligation. However, Ahmed b. Hanbal gives preference to *Salat*. Azzam argues that abandoning jihad without any valid excuse is like eating during day of *Ramadan* without any excuse. Moreover, jihad like other fundamentals of faith is permanent in their obligation. See Azzam, *Join the Caravan*.

32 Abdullah Azzam, *Extracts from the Wasīyyat*, trans. Ahmed Farooq (Muslim World Data Processing Pakistan, April 12, 1986), accessed September 2, 2013. http://sirat-e-mustaqeem.com/wasiat-shaikh-abdullah-azzaam_book-4461.html, accessed June 27, 2013.

33 Abdel-Muhsin al-Rafi, 'The Rafidhi-Crusader Alliance in Iraq 'Al-tahaluf al-rafidhi al-salibi fil Iraq', quoted in Kazimi, 'Zarqawi's Anti-Shi'a Legacy'. Even after the withdrawal of the US troops from Iraqi soil, the oil companies would be staying behind to inflate their profits from huge investment made by them. See Dahr Jamail, 'Western Oil Firms Remain as US Exits Iraq', *Al-Jazeera*, January 7, 2012. The oil-producing capacity of these companies increased from 55 wells in 2009 to 313 by 2013. This capacity increase of these companies resulted in a corresponding rise in the value of petroleum exports from $39,307m to $89,402m during the same timeframe. As a result, the net income of these transnational companies also increased exponentially. For instance, the net income of BP rose 72%, from $13,740m in 2009 to $23,681m in 2013. Similarly, ExxonMobil increased its income by 132% in 2012 from $19,280m in 2009 to $44,880m in 2012. Likewise, Shell also increased its income by 113% in the three years to 2012. See OPEC. Annual Statistical Bulletin, 2014, accessed September 17, 2014, http://www.opec.org/opec_web/static_files_project/media/downloads/publications/ASB2014.pdf.

34 Osama Bin Laden, 'World Islamic Front Statement Urging Jihad Against Jews and Crusaders 1998', in *Al-Qaida in Its Own Words*, 53–56.

35 *FBIS Report* January 2004, 63, 64.

36 'Osama Bin Laden Declares Jihad on Americans', *FBIS Report* January 2004, 22.

37 Osama Bin Laden, Rassler et al., *Letters from Abbottabad*, no. SOCOM-2012-0000019; Osama Bin Laden, 'World Islamic Front Statement Urging Jihad'; also see Bin Laden, 'Declaration of Jihad against the Americans Occupying the Land of the Two Holy Sanctuaries issued on March 23, 1996'; Umar, the second caliph of Islam expelled the Jews from Hejāz, see Imam Bukhari, *Sahih Bukhari, Kitāb al-Hara'th wal Mazra't*: 2338, *Kitāb al-Fazāil al-Madina*: 1881, *Kitāb al-Jihad*: 3053; Imam Muslim, *Sahih Muslim, Kitāb al-Jihad*, 4363, 4366, 4367.

38 Bin Laden, 'Interview with Peter Arnett and Peter Bergen.'

39 Bin Laden, 'Declaration of Jihad against the Americans Occupying the Land of the Two Holy Sanctuaries issued on March 23, 1996'; also see Abdel Bari Atwan, *The Secret History of Al-Qaida* (London: Abacus, 2006), 38.

40 Bin Laden, 'Interview by al-Quds al-Arabi', in *FBIS Report*, January, 2004.

41 Bin Laden, 'Interview by Robert Fisk', July 10, 1996.

42 Rassler et al., *Letters from Abbottabad*, no. SOCOM-2012-0000016.

43 Bin Laden, 'Message to the American People, October 30, 2004'; also see Bin Laden, 'Declaration of Jihad against the Americans Occupying the Land of the Two Holy Sanctuaries issued on March 23, 1996'. This declaration is also quoted jihadi literature; see *Nawa-i-Afghan Jihad*, June, 2012; also see Rassler et al., *Letters from Abbottabad*, no. SOCOM-2012-0000016.

44 Osama Bin Laden, Interview by Gwyen Robert, Channel 4, 2100 GMT February 20, 1997, *FBIS Report*, January, 2004, 38. According to the US

Secretary of Defence, William J. Perry, the US presence on Saudi soil was aimed at securing the vital American interests. See *Defence* 11, no.8 (1996).

45 Atwan, *The Secret History of Al-Qaida*, 38

46 Bin Laden, 'Second Letter to the Muslims of Iraq, October 18, 2003; Bin Laden, Interview by Robert Fisk; also see Atwan, *The Secret History of Al-Qaida*, 38.

47 Bin Laden, 'Until We Taste What Hamza Bin Abd Al-Muttalib Tasted', *Inspire*, Issue 2.

48 Rassler et al., *Letters from Abbottabad,* no. SOCOM-2012-0000017; Ibn Taimmiyah has quoted the following Quranic verse to make the point that adverse effects should not outweigh the positive ones during enjoining of good and forbidding of evil: 'O ye who believe! Ye have charge of your own souls. He who erreth cannot injure you if ye are rightly guided. Unto Allah ye will all return; and then He will inform you of what ye used to do' (Al-Maidah: 105); see Ibn Taimmiyah, *Enjoining Good and Forbidding Evil*, trans. Salim Abdallah ibn Morgan, accessed April 5, 2020, https://d1.islamhouse.com/data/en/ih_books/single/en_Enjoining_Right_and_forbidding_wrong.pdf.

49 Rassler et al., *Letters from Abbottabad,* no. SOCOM-2012-0000014

50 Ibid., no. SOCOM-2012-0000006; Bin Laden, 'Until We Taste What Hamza Bin Abd Al-Muttalib Tasted', *Inspire*, Issue 2.; also see, Bin Laden, 'Second Letter to the Muslims of Iraq, October 18, 2003.'

51 Al-Maqdisi, *This Is Our Aqeedah*; Al-Zarqawi, too, followed this narrative in his resistance during the US invasion in Iraq.

52 Ibid., 65.

53 Khan, *The Central Issue*; Abu Basir, Interview by Al-Malahem Media, *Inspire*, issue 1.

54 Siv O'Neall, 'Chronicle of a Programmed Collapse in Mali', in *Axis of Logic*, trans. Jean-François Bayart, January 27, 2013, accessed December 14, 2020, http://axisoflogic.com/artman/publish/printer_65350.shtml.

55 'Al Qaeda in Islamic Maghreb issues Mali warning', *Hindustan Times*, July 1, 2012.

56 'Qaideen-e-jihad ke Aqwāl,' *Hittin* 8.

57 Wattana Sugunnasil, 'Islam, Radicalism, and Violence in Southern Thailand: *Berjihad di Patani* and the 28 April 2004 Attacks', *Critical Asian Studies* 38, no.1 (2006): 119–144.

58 *Mujahideen Roadmap*, 2004.

59 Abdullah Sungkar and Abu Bakar Ba'asyir founded Jama'a al-Islamiya in the 1990s in Malaysia; see Angel M. Rabasa, 'Radical Islamist Ideologies in Southeast Asia', in *Current Trends in Islamist Ideology*, Vol. 1, 27–38; for further details regarding the ideology of Jama'a al-Islamiya, see Rohan Gunaratna, 'The Ideology of Al-Jama'ah Al-Islamiya', in *Current Trends in Islamist Ideology*, vol.1, 68.

60 Ayman Al-Zawahiri, 'Message to the People of Yemen', *Inspire*, issue 1.

61 Gilles Kepel, 'The Brotherhood in the Salafist Universe', in *Current Trends in Islamist Ideology,* vol. 6, eds. Hillel Fradkin et al. (Washington, D.C.: Hudson Institute, 2008), 20–28.

62 Rohan Gunaratna, 'The Ideology of Al-Jama'ah Al-Islamiya.'

63 For the war tactics of Tehrīk-e-Taliban Pakistan, see *Nisāb-e-Harb* (Manual of War), Vols. 1 & 2, 1st ed., September 2012.

64 Hillel Fradkin, 'Recent Statements of Islamist Ideology: Bin Laden and Zarqawi Speak', in *Current Trends in Islamist Ideology*, Vol. 1, 5–11.

65 Bin Laden, 'Second Letter to the Muslims of Iraq, October 18, 2003'.

66 '*Qaideen-e-jihad ke Aqwāl.*'

67 'Timbuktu shrine destruction 'a war crime', *The Telegraph*, March 20, 2015; also see 'Ansar Dine fighters destroy Timbuktu shrines,' *Al-Jazeera*, July 1, 2012.
68 Farouk Chothia, 'Who are Nigeria's Boko Haram Islamists?' *BBC News*, January 21, 2015.
69 Al-Abbab, Interview by Al-Malahem Media, *Inspire*, issue 4; also see 'Qaideen-e-jihad ke Aqwāl', 8.
70 *Nisāb-e-Harb*, 22; also see *Ahyā-e-Khilāfat*.
71 'The Return of Khilafa', *Dabiq*, issue 1.
72 Kareem Shaheen, 'ISIS Attacks on Ancient Sites Erasing History of Humanity', *The Guardian*, March 9, 2015.
73 Those who reject the right of the first three caliphs to the office of Caliphate.
74 Al-Maqdisi, *This is Our Aqeedah*, 38.
75 Nibras Kazmi, 'A Virulent Ideology in Mutation: Zarqawi Upstages Maqdisi', Vol. 2, in *Current Trends in Islamist Ideology*, by Hillel Fradkin, Husain Haqqani and Eric Brown, 59–73. Washington D.C.: Hudson Institue.
76 Al-Zarqawi's statement on May 19, 2004, quoted in Bar, 'Sunnis and Shiites – Between Rapprochement and Conflict.'
77 The narrative that the Shiites have been supporting to the forces of unbelief against the Sunnite Muslims is commonplace amongst the Militants. See Nibras Kazimi, 'Zarqawi's Anti-Shi'a Legacy.'
78 Haynes, *Al Qaida: Ideology and Action*; also see Al-Abbab, Interview by Al-Malahem Media, *Inspire*, issue 4.
79 Thomas Joscelyn, 'Al Qaida Branches Urge Jihadist Unity against US', *The Long War Journal*, September 16, 2014.
80 *Nisāb-e-Harb*, 24, 25.
81 '*Ahl-e-Sunnat ke Seenay par Rafidhi Riāsat kā Khawāb*', (Dream to establish Shiite State at the heart of *Ahl al-Sunnah*), *Hittin* 8.
82 'The Return of Khilafa', *Dabiq*, issue 1.
83 'Excerpts from 'Indeed Your Lord Is Ever Watchful'', *Dabiq*, issue 4.
84 'Qaideen-e-jihad ke Aqwāl', 148–154.
85 Imam Muslim, *Sahih Muslim*, *Kitāb al-Jihad*: 4472; Ibn Kathir, *Al-Bidāyah wal Nihāyah*, Ghazwā Hawāzan Youm-e-Hūnayn, vol. 2, Part-IV, 736.
86 Abdullah Azzam, *Ad-Difa'a un a'aradi*.
87 Azzam has taken a reference from *Tafsīr-e-Qurtubi* regarding the significance of *hijra* and has quoted a narration on the authority of Ikrimah that Durmah b. Ays in the wake of divine permission of *hijra*, despite being seriously sick, insisted upon being shifted to Madina and died on the way. (Tafsīr-e-Qurtubi 5/349) in Azzam, *Join the Caravan*.
88 Rassler et al., *Letters from Abbottabad,* no. SOCOM-2012-0000016.
89 Bin Laden's narrative on the issue is explicit from his interviews to Robert Fisk and CNN, 1997; also see Bin Laden, 'Second Letter to the Muslims of Iraq, October 18, 2003'; Bin Laden, Bin Laden, 'Declaration of Jihad against the Americans Occupying the Land of the Two Holy Sanctuaries issued on March 23, 1996.'
90 Bin Laden, Interview by Hamid Mir, *Daily Pakistan* March 18, 1997; also see Rassler et al., *Letters from Abbottabad,* no. SOCOM-2012-0000016; also see Bergen, *Holy War*, 19; also see Bonney, *Jihad*, 125.
91 Rassler et al., *Letters from Abbottabad,* no. SOCOM-2012-0000010.
92 Ibid., nos. SOCOM-2012-0000018, SOCOM-2012-0000015, SOCOM-2012-0000016, SOCOM-2012-0000019.
93 Ibid., no. SOCOM-2012-0000016; Looking from the edge, unlike Bin Laden, militant affiliates like AQAP do not show any reservation to recruit even those who had pledged not to target the US interests.

94 Ibid., no. SOCOM-2012-0000019.
95 Ibid., no. SOCOM-2012-0000013.
96 Al-Zawahiri's statement in response to the Arab spring. Ibid., no. SOCOM-2012-0000013.
97 Al-Zawahiri, 'Message to the People of Yemen.'
98 This theory is extension of Al-Faraj's proclamation of *takfīr* to the Muslim rulers who collaborate with the crusaders. See *Al-Faridah al-Gha'iba.*
99 Maha Azzam, *Al-Qaida.*
100 Al-Maqdisi was the pioneer of militant Islamist ideology. Prior to his arrest by the Jordanian authorities, he had tremendous influence on framing Al-Zarqawi's extremist views. His subsequent transformation into a moderate Islamist after his release could not erase his earlier extremist impressions from Zarqawi's mind. Though he claims not to follow the *Kharjai'ite* footprints in terms of ex-communicating the fellow Muslims, his extremist views have been informing the militant worldview. He is rightly considered to be a source of ideological inspiration for Al-Qaida-led militants. See Khan, *The Central Issue*; also see, Al-Maqdisi, *This Is Our Aqeedah*, 57.
101 The tradition of fighting the enemy who happens to be in one's closest proximity is evident from Imam Waqidi's account of dialogue between Rabia'h bin Amir's (commander of Muslim army in Syria) and Sergius (commander of the Roman army). Rabia'h said that the Muslims have preferred to fight the Romans because they were nearer to them than the Persians. See Imam Waqidi, *Fūtuh as-Sham*, 16–18. Actually, Rabia'h relied on the following Quranic verse, 'O ye who believe! Fight those of the disbelievers who are near to you, and let them find harshness in you, and know that Allah is with those who keep their duty (unto Him)' (At-Tawba: 123).
102 Al-Maqdisi, *This is our Aqeedah*, 59–65; also see Kazimi, 'A Virulent Ideology in Mutation.'
103 Al-Maqdisi has quoted the incident of Hatib who entered into allegiance (*wilāyah*) with the non-believers and extended help to them against the fellow believers. In this context, the following verse was revealed: 'O ye who believe! Choose not My enemy and your enemy for allies' (Al-Mumtahinah: 1). Allegiance (Mawālat) with the non-believers constitutes 'unbelief' irrespective of the fact that it is allegiance of heart *(Mawālat al-Qalbiyyah)* or otherwise because Allah says: 'O ye who believe! Take not the Jews and the Christians for friends. They are friends one to another. He among you who taketh them for friends is (one) of them. Lo! Allah guideth not wrongdoing folk. And thou seest those in whose heart is a disease race toward them, saying: We fear lest a change of fortune befall us…' (Al-Maidah, 51–52); see Abu Muhammad al-Maqdisi, *Millat Ibrahim Wa Da'wat Al-Anbiya Wal-Mrrsalin Wa Asalib At-Taghut Fi Tamyi'iha Wa Sarf Ad-Duati Anha*, 197.
104 Al-Maqdisi, *This Is our Aqeedah*, 65.
105 Al-Awlaki, 'The New Mardin Declaration.'
106 Rassler et al., *Letters from Abbottabad*, no. SOCOM-2012-0000013.
107 Khan, 'The Central Issue.'
108 *Nisāb-e-Harb*, 55, 79.
109 See statement of Abu Musa'ab Abdul Wadood, who was amir of *Tanẓīm al-Qā'idah fī Bilād al-Maghrib al-Islāmī* in 'Qaideen-e-jihad ke Aqwāl', (Statements of jihadi Leadership), *Hittin* 8.
110 Abu Bakr Al-Sharif was one of the founders of *Al-Jama'a Al-Islamiyyah Al-Muqātilah* (FIG); see his interview, 'The Libyan Regime is Living in a Situation of Hysteria', *Nidā-ul-Islam*, issue 15, Oct.–Nov. 1996.
111 Omar Rasheed, Interview by *Nidā-ul-Islam,* 26, April–May 1999.

112 Chothia, 'Who are Nigeria's Boko Haram Islamists?'
113 Muhammad Abd al-Salam Faraj was an Egyptian militant. He headed 'Islamic Jihad'. He wrote *Al-Farīdah al-ghā'ibah* (The Neglected Duty), which instigated the Muslims to use violent means to achieve their goals. This organization was responsible for assassinating the Egyptian President Anwar Sadat.
114 Azzam, *Ad-Difa'a un a'aradi*; also see Azzam, *Join the Caravan*.
115 Bin Laden, Interview by Hamid Mir, *Daily Pakistan* March 18, 1997; also see Rassler et al., *Letters from Abbottabad*, no. SOCOM-2012-0000016; also see Bergen, *Holy War*, 19; also see Bonney, *Jihad*, 125.
116 Haddad, 'Islamism: A Designer Ideology for Resistance', 274–295.
117 Bin Laden, 'Second Letter to the Muslims of Iraq, October 18, 2003.'
118 Cheryl Benard, *Civil and Democratic Islam: Partners, Resources, and Strategies* (Arlington: RAND Corporation, 2003); also see Angel Rabasa et al. *Building Moderate Muslim Networks* (Arlington: RAND Corporation, 2007); also see Rassler et al., *Letters from Abbottabad*, no. SOCOM-2012-0000013.
119 Al-Maqdisi, *This Is Our Aqeedah*, 64.
120 *Berjihad di Patani* is a document in Yawi script which was recovered from the militants in Thailand. This document calls for loose application of *takfīr*. See Sugunnasil, 'Islam, Radicalism, and Violence.'
121 Chothia, 'Who Are Nigeria's Boko Haram Islamists?'
122 C. J. Radin, 'The Threat of Boko Haram for Nigeria, Africa, and Beyond', *Threat Matrix*, A Blog of *Long War Journal*, April 23, 2012.
123 There are different perspectives on this incident. Some may take this incident in terms of militant attempt to disrupt the tourist industry in Indonesia whereas it is also regarded as militant response to the onslaught of the western cultural values. This incident took place on October 12, 2002, leaving around 180 people killed and more than 300 injured. See Rabasa, 'Radical Islamist Ideologies in Southeast Asia.'
124 'Libya: Islamic State Burns 'Non-Islamic' Musical Instruments', *The Clarion Project*, February 22, 2015.
125 Reuven Paz, 'The Impact of the War in Iraq on the Global Jihad', in *Current Trends in Islamist Ideology*, Vol. 1, 39–49.
126 Masmoudi, 'What Is Liberal Islam?' 40–44.
127 Al-Maqdisi, *This Is Our Aqeedah*.
128 Maha Azzam, *Al-Qaida*.
129 Al-Abbab, Interview by Al-Malahem Media, *Inspire*, issue 4.
130 *Ahyā-e-Khilāfat*, September, 2013, 34–36.
131 Harriet Alexander, 'Islamic State Claim Responsibility for Jalalabad Bomb in First Afghanistan Attack', *The Telegraph*, April 19, 2015.
132 Maha Azzam, *Al-Qaida*.
133 *ARY News*, August 6, 2014, 0713 PKT; also see Mushtaq Yusufzai, 'Taliban plan attacks on media outlets, journalists', *The News*, October 15, 2012.
134 Adegboye Ishiaka, 'Nigeria: Boko Haram Wages War on Journalists', *All Africa*, June 8, 2012.
135 'Al-Shabaab Terror Continues to Threaten News Providers', *Reporters without Borders*, September, 25 2013.
136 'The Return of Khilafa',*Dabiq*, issue 1.
137 Mohammed Tawfeeq and Joe Sterling, 'Militants in Iraq Storm TV Station; Anchor among Dead', *CNN International*, December 23, 2013.
138 *Saut al-Iraq*, December 24, 2013; also see 'ISIS–Major Threat to Media Freedom in both Iraq and Syria', *Reporters without Borders*, December 30, 2013.

139 Bin Laden, 'World Islamic Front Statement Urging Jihad Against Jews and Crusaders'; also see Bin Laden, Interview by John Miller, February, 1 1999.
140 *Inspire,* 1.
141 Al-Awlaki, 'The New Mardin Declaration.'
142 *Inspire*, 4.
143 Al-Abbab, Interview by Al-Malahem Media, *Inspire,* issue 4; for primary references, see Imam Bukhari, *Sahih Bukhari*, *Kitāb al-Jihad*: 3022, 3023.
144 Abdalle Ahmed Mumin and Alexandra Wexler, 'Islamists Kill Scores in Kenya College Attack', *The Wall Street Journal,* April 2, 2015.
145 'Al-Shabab says it singled out non-Muslims in Kenya Mall Attack', *CBS News*, September 25, 2013.
146 Robert Windrem and Alexander, Smith, 'Boko Haram: 200,000 Christians at Risk of Massacre in Nigeria', *CBS News*, October 27, 2014.
147 'Video shows beheading of Copts at IS hands; Egypt declares week of mourning', *Ahram Online*, February 15, 2015.
148 Raya Jalabi, 'Who Are the Yazidis and Why Is ISIS Hunting Them?' *The Guardian*, August 11, 2014.
149 Al-Abbab, Interview by Al-Malahem Media, *Inspire,* issue 4.
150 Sugunnasil, 'Islam, Radicalism, and Violence', 119–144.
151 'Scores Killed in Attack on Peshawar School; Taliban Claims Responsibility', *Al-Jazeera*, December 16, 2014.
152 Gillian Parker, 'Yobe School Killings: Another Boko Haram Slaughter, This Time of Children', *The Christian Science Monitor*, July 8, 2013.
153 Heather Murdock, 'Boko Haram Attacks Muslims and Kids, Puzzling Everyone', *The Christian Science Monitor*, August 4, 2013.
154 Rassler et al., *Letters from Abbottabad,* no. SOCOM-2012-0000007.
155 Ibid., no. SOCOM-2012-0000016.
156 For the perspective of Afghan Taliban, see *Jihad Ki Pukār* (Call for Jihad), December 16, 2014.
157 Abdullah Azzam refers to the following Quranic verse: 'O ye who believe! When believing women come unto you as fugitives, examine them. Allah is Best Aware of their faith. Then, if ye know them for true believers, send them not back unto the disbelievers. They are not lawful for them (the disbelievers), nor are they (the disbelievers) lawful for them. And give them (the disbelievers) that which they have spent (upon them). And it is no sin for you to marry such women when ye have given them their dues. And hold not to the ties of disbelieving women; and ask for (the return of) that which ye have spent; and let them (the disbelievers) ask for that which they have spent. That is the judgment of Allah. He judgeth between you. Allah is Knower, Wise' (Al Mumtahinah: 10). He further quotes a tradition of the Prophet wherein he has been reported to have said, 'Expel all Jews and Christians from the Arabian Peninsula'. See Imam Muslim, *Sahih Muslim*, *Kitāb Al-Jihad*: 4363, 4366, 4367; Imam Bukhari, *Sahih Bukhari*, *Kitāb Al-Jihad*: 3053, *Kitāb Farāid Al-Khums*: 3152, *Kitāb Al-Jizya*: 3167; also see Abdullah Azzam, *Ad-Difa'a un a'aradi.*
158 Ibid.
159 Rassler et al., *Letters from Abbottabad*, no. SOCOM-2012-0000016.
160 The person of covenant is the one who belongs to a nation that has a treaty of peace with the Muslims.
161 Al-Abbab, Interview by Al-Malahem Media, *Inspire,* issue 4; Anwar al-Awlaki, 'The Ruling on Dispossessing the Disbelievers wealth in Dar al-Harb', *Inspire*, issue 4.
162 Ibid.

163 Khan, 'The Central Issue'; Al-Maqdisi. *This Is Our Aqeedah*, 57. The advocates of the doctrine of *irja'ā* are called Murji'ah. They believe that ex-communication of the believers should be left to the verdict of God, and it should be deferred until the Hour is established.
164 Al-Awlaki, 'The New Mardin Declaration.'
165 Al-Abbab, Interview by Al-Malahem Media, *Inspire*, issue 4.
166 'Scores Killed in Attack on Peshawar', *Al-Jazeera*, December 16, 2014.
167 'TTP Claims Responsibility for Karachi Twin Blasts', *The Tribune*, November 23, 2013.
168 *Ahyā-e-Khilāfat*, September, 2013.
169 Al-Maqdisi, *This Is Our Aqeedah*, 64; *Nisāb-e-Harb*.
170 Maulvi Abdul Jabbar Siddiqui, *Mufti Brathdran aur Din-e-Jamhuriyyat: Mufti Taqi Usmani aur Mufti Rafi Usmani ki Jamhuriyyat ke Muta'laq Ara'a ka Muhakima* (Mufti Brothers and Faith of Democracy: An Overview of the Narrative of Mufti Taqi Usmani and Mufti Rafi Usmani regarding Democracy) (Al-Muwahideen Islamic Library).
171 Mary Chastain, 'ISIS Executes Imams for Condemning Burning of Jordanian Pilot', *BreitBart*, February 5, 2015.
172 *Nisāb-Harb*, 41, 42.
173 Ibid., 55.

6 Killing fields

The transnational conflict between the militants and the West led different flashpoints of violence to emerge. The factors which contributed to the emergence of these killing fields may be examined on the following four paradigms: bipolar backyards such as the sectarian split in Lebanon, Syria and Iraq; state oppression by totalitarian regimes, as in Somalia, Algeria and Egypt; unhealed wounds in Muslim lands like Gaza and Palestine; and last but not least, theatres of international aggression like Iraq. These factors provide suitable grounds for Al-Qaida to operate by assimilating its ideology with the resistance to the western ideology and a struggle for the liberation of Ummah.

Bipolar backyards – sectarian split

The conflict scenarios in Lebanon, Syria and Iraq can be explored as bipolar backyards in terms of the sectarian divide between the Shiites and the Sunnites. This conflict situation leads to two fundamental points. First, the militant outfits operating in these states share common anti-imperialist and anti-Zionist themes. However, they have seldom formed a united front through surrendering their sectarian identities to achieve common goals. These sectarian identities diverted militancy inside Muslim societies and weakened the capacity of militant outfits to pursue their anti-imperialist objectives externally. Second, the vulnerabilities of the centuries-old schism amongst the Muslims have the potential to be exploited by actors in the militant landscape to secure political and strategic gains.

Sectarian vs anti-imperialist themes

Not unlike the rest of the Muslim world, in the Middle East the anti-imperialist rhetoric is a resource for the militant outfits to draw legitimacy for their existence. Notwithstanding their sectarian affiliations, anti-Zionist and anti-American stands are taken as a source for legitimacy by the militant organizations in the region. Whether it is Shiite Hezbollah in Lebanon or the Sunnite Al-Qaida affiliates or ISIS in Syria and Iraq, all rely on anti-

DOI: 10.4324/9781003164883-6

imperialist rhetoric for their existential legitimacy. In the case of Hezbollah, Israeli occupation of some parts of Southern Lebanon in 1982, also known Operation Peace for Galilee, provided grounds for its emergence as a militia, indeed with the support of Iran, to resist the Israeli occupation.[1] Resistance to Israel, along with eliminating the colonial remnants like the Americans and the French from Lebanon and transplantation of the Iranian model of *vilayet-e-faqih* in Lebanon, were visualized as the major goals of the organization.[2] The military strategy adopted by Hezbollah to resist Israel and other imperialists earned it huge public approval within Lebanon. Its status got elevated almost as a parallel state.[3] Its military strength was estimated to be more than the state military strength. In the context of the Lebanese protests (2006–2008), Hezbollah was granted veto power in the National Unity Government.[4] Its role to liberate lands from the Israeli occupation was also recognized. Its armed status was validated by the saying that its arms were the common property of all Lebanese people.[5]

Though Hezbollah's anti-imperialism and anti-Israel posture gave it an elevated standing within the Lebanese government structure, it could not surrender its sectarian identity within Lebanon and without. The sectarian orientation of Hezbollah is evident from the following points. First, it continues to draw financial support and theological inspiration from the supreme Shiite leadership in Iran. In the 1990s, Hezbollah's decision to become part of the political process in Lebanon was endorsed by Ali Khamenei, the supreme leader of Iran. Moreover, it has also been a permanent recipient of political support from the Shiite Syrian regime. At the end of the civil war, though the Taif Agreement provided for disbanding all the militias in Lebanon, Syria allowed Hezbollah to build its arms and control Shiite areas bordering Israel.[6] Second, on the domestic front, despite its most cherished anti-Israeli rhetoric, it has never been able to command the trust of the Sunnites. The Sunnite leadership has always been wary of the growing influence of Hezbollah in the government structure. The electoral map confirms the growing gap between the two communities. For instance, in 2009 parliamentary elections, 93.1% votes of the Shiites went to Hezbollah, whereas the Future Movement bagged 76% votes of the Sunnites. The political indicators are important to highlight the sharp sectarian undercurrents in Muslim communities as the attempts of both Hezbollah and the Future Movement to dent each other's sectarian support base ended up in failure.[7] Third, to the utter disapproval of the Lebanese Sunnites, Hezbollah has been actively supporting the Shiite Assad regime in Syria against the regime's Sunnite adversaries. In the Syrian context, the hero of one sectarian community in Lebanon is foe of the other. The Sunnites disapprove of the Assad regime for its alleged role in the assassination of Rafiq Hariri whereas Hezbollah views the Alawite regime as an ally and regards the current crisis in Syria in terms of a conspiracy launched by a Zionist–Crusaders alliance to break the Iran–Syria and Hezbollah nexus.[8] Hassan Nasr Allah did not hesitate to identify the Sunnite rebels in Syria with Israeli Jews and justified their military adventure in Syria as a 'critical and definitive battle'.[9] He termed his resistance to ISIS in Syria as existential and called for broader support from the plural society of Lebanon by portraying ISIS as a common threat to humanity.[10] Following the same tone, Hezbollah fighters take fighting in support of the Syrian regime as their obligation.[11] On the other hand, when the spillover of Hezbollah's fighting against the Sunnite militants side by side with the Assad regime is being felt at home and sectarian tension has increased to cause possible sectarian violence,[12] the Sunnites in Lebanon are categorical in their aloofness from Hezbollah's military adventure in the Syrian crisis. In response to the Lebanese chapter of Al-Nusra Front's announcement of targeting Hezbollah's operational areas inside Lebanon as legitimate targets, Sa'ad Hariri categorically proclaimed the Sunnites' disavowal from Hezbollah's participation in the Syrian crisis.[13] In this background, Hezbollah is likely to lose its inroads into the Sunnite community of Lebanon, which it had made following its anti-imperialist and anti-Israel approach. Its all-out intervention in the Syrian crisis may reignite sectarian violence within Lebanon; besides alienating the domestic Sunnite population, it has turned itself into a target for Sunnite militants operating beyond Lebanon.

In the Syrian context, the most important Sunnite groups fighting against the Assad regime and its Lebanese support-arm Hezbollah include ISIS and the Al-Nusra Front. The Al-Nusra Front[14] does not consider the Shiite regime of Syria as Islamic and aims to uproot it and install a Shariah-based state system on a Sunnite pattern in its stead. They prefer to fight the Assad regime, whom they label as apostate, and its supporting arm, Hezbollah, instead of targeting the western states in the first instance.[15] Though they do not aspire to global jihad,[16] anti-imperialist notions are explicit in their labelling of the United States and Israel as the enemies of Islam[17] and further warning them not to intervene in the Syrian crisis.[18] However, the anti-imperialist face of Al-Nusra Front is eclipsed by the sectarian Sunnite orientation of the group. Al-Nusra leadership announced bounties worth millions of dollars for the killings of Bashar Al-Assad and Hassan Nasr Allah. Al-Nusra further called for escalation of attacks on the Assad's strongholds in retribution for the killings of Sunnites by the pro-Assad Russian forces.[19] They have also launched suicide missions against the Hezbollah strongholds in Lebanon, which they consider as legitimate targets for their violence.[20] The sectarian nature of violence unleashed by Al-Nusra gets further exposition in their treatment of the Druze community – an offshoot of the Isma'ilite branch of the Shiites.[21] They were reportedly forced to forego their faith and convert to the Sunnite version of Islam.[22] They were further forced to demolish their sacred places. In the Syrian context, like other *salāfi* militant organizations, ISIS too follows the anti-western and anti-imperialist agenda. It aims to fight the Zionist–Crusaders alliance and their local agents to materialize their worldwide caliphate. At the same time, the sectarian violence is the characteristic feature of its militant adventures in Syria as it resolves to fight against the Shiite regime and its Shiite allies like Hezbollah for being the local collaborators of the Crusaders alliance.[23]

In addition to the recent conflict scenario in Syria, where ISIS occupies a central role in the fight against the Shiite regime and its aides in its quest to establish a Shariah-based caliphate system, Iraq provides a contextual framework for the sectarian-linked genesis of the ISIS. The organization has its roots in Al-Zarqawi's Jama'at al-Tawhid wal-jihad, established in 1999. After pledging its allegiance to Al-Qaida in 2004, this organization assumed a new title, Tazīm Qaidā al-jihād fī Bilād al-Rāfidēn (Organization of Jihad's Base in Mesopotamia). It got noticed for its excessively violent attacks against Shiites and Iraqi government installations and the western targets. In 2006, this organization became part of Mujahideen Shūrā Council, a conglomeration of many Sunnite militant groups to fight against the Shiites and the imperialist forces. Later on, the Shūrā announced the establishment of an Islamic state in the Sunnite majority areas of Iraq. Abu Omar Al-Baghdadi was declared its emir. In 2010, Abu Bakr al-Baghdadi became leader of the 'Islamic State in Iraq' and proclaimed it global caliphate of the Muslims in 2014. Despite its assumption of global character and resolve to fight western imperialism, it has always boasted of following Al-Zarqawi's violent approach to the Shiites. The first issue of *Dābiq*, ISIS's online magazine, pays rich tribute to Al-Zarqawi and acknowledges the ISIS leadership's appreciation of his sectarian violence. The magazine attempts to justify the sectarian violence by stirring the emotions of Sunnites through focusing on those Sunnite militants who had been killed fighting with the Shiites.[24] ISIS attempts to secure retributive legitimacy for their violence against the Shiites by using the acronym of the Safavids to link them to the historical account of violence of the Safavid Empire against the Sunnites. ISIS further appreciates Al-Zarqawi's proclamation of *takfīr* on the Shiites and their subsequent killing.[25]

Sectarian vulnerabilities

Besides sectarian identities, the Middle East embodies a multiple identities frame that defines the regional conflict scenario. The Saudi Arabian regime has been fighting against fellow *salāfī* organizations like Al-Qaida and now ISIS. A considerable part of the Iraqi army in their war with Iran consisted of the Shiite Iraqis. The Lebanese civil war witnessed clashes between Hezbollah and Amal activists, despite their common sectarian background. However, these multiple identities have never been able to overshadow the sectarian affiliations in the regional conflict. The centuries-old schism in Islam is still transforming the politico-religious landscape of the Middle East.[26] This schism is exploited to secure political gains not only by the national governments like Lebanon, Syria and Iraq but also by regional powers like Saudi Arabia and Iran, which are involved in proxy wars. Besides this, the sectarian violence also serves as a catalyst to mobilize the

Sunnite militant networks in a global perspective.[27] These sectarian vulnerabilities are even more prominent in the states, where the ruling elite belong to the minority sect. For instance, in Syria under the Alawite regime of Assad, the Shiite minority is ruling the Sunnite majority. Likewise, in Iraq, under Saddam, a Sunnite minority was ruling the Shiite majority.[28] In these cases, the marginalized majority populations are more likely to exploit the polemics to resist the minority ruling elite.

In the case of Lebanon, the state recognized Hezbollah's permanent role in decision making, given its potential to command the Shiites as well as its military potential to counter the military adventures of Israel. In the domestic scenario in Lebanon, following Hezbollah's open participation in the Syrian civil war, the Shiite-led Lebanese government got an opportunity to marginalize already depressed Sunnite sections of the society. Moreover, given the huge influx of refugees, regional states like Syria and Iran exploited the sectarian schism more vehemently to secure political and strategic gains in the plural Lebanese society. When the Sunnites are marginalized, militant groups like Al-Nusra Front and ISIS exploit the sectarian faultlines to recruit their foot-soldiers.[29]

Syria presents a peculiar scenario where pro-democracy protests against the Assad regime that started in 2011 turned into civil war, not between the pro-democracy and pro-authoritarian regime elements but rather between the Sunnite militants and the pro-government Shiites. This reflects the vulnerabilities of the polemics to be exploited to achieve political designs. The initial chaos emerging from pro-democracy protests, and mishandling of the protesters by the Assad regime allowed sectarian forces to manipulate the scenario. In a larger context, the polemics are defining the civil war. In its struggle for survival, the Assad regime is depending upon the Shiite support base against the Sunnite militants. The Alawite regime is exploiting its Shiite identity to build up its survival capacity, securing support from Shiite Iran and Hezbollah against the Sunnite militants who are supported by Turkey, Saudi Arabia and other Arabian states to counterbalance Iranian influence in the region.[30] Both sides perceive that sectarian schism is generating a real threat, which requires an all-out struggle to counter it.

In the case of Iraq, the Sunnites – despite being in the minority – had been in control of the political authority since long until the Saddam regime was uprooted in the wake of the US invasion in 2003. The political authority was transferred to the Shiites, with Nur al-Maliki becoming the Prime Minister in 2006. The transfer of authority to the Shiites created apprehensions in the Sunnites regarding their political future. In this scenario, the Baathist remnants attempted to exploit sectarian identities to gain political and strategic gains. They used a sectarian cloak to muster support in their resistance against the imperialist forces as well as against the Shiites who could assume political authority with the support of the imperialist forces.[31] Moreover, the Shiite regime installed after Saddam has not been able to work out a power-sharing formula to involve the Sunnites in the decision making. Under Maliki, the Sunnites felt disillusioned for being politically marginalized on sectarian grounds. ISIS successfully exploited these emotions to channel the Sunnite volunteers to join its ranks, on the pretext of resisting Maliki's bid to transform Iraq into a Shiite state through repressive means. On the other hand, the Shiite Maliki regime in Iraq was supported by Shiite elements in the domestic as well as in the regional context. For example, on the domestic front, Ayatollah Ali al-Sistani mobilized the Shiites in Iraq to join the national army to fight ISIS,[32] whereas in the regional context Shiite Iran, largely on the basis of common sectarian identity, supports the Shiite government in Iraq.

State oppression by totalitarian regimes

While delineating 'state oppression' as a structural concept that may be eradicated not through uprooting the rulers but rather the system that provides space for the oppression to be perpetuated, the book seeks to identify types of state oppression. These types include economic exploitation through denial rather than predation of development opportunities for the citizens, political marginalization of certain sections through denying them a role in decision making and repression of selective ethnic or religious groups through physical violence. This typology of state oppression provides venues for the anarchic solution of the problem, aiming to uproot the existing political order.[33] It further confers upon the oppressed a licence to exploit alternative means beyond the state mechanism to do away with this oppression.[34] In this theoretical framework, this part of the study seeks to explore the question of whether the oppression of totalitarian regimes in Somalia, Algeria and Egypt paved the way for violent reaction from the oppressed groups.

First, theorizing the concept of economic exploitation highlights the relationship between oppression and privilege. It further confirms that there is always a privileged section that thrives at the altar of the oppressed. The delivery of 'public good' constitutes a fundamental aspect of the social contract between the rulers and the ruled. Failure of equitable service delivery by the state to its citizens culminates into abrogation of this contract. This is a 'cause and effect' relationship largely in the frame of what Collier and Hoeffler term as the 'greed and grievance' model. The grievance is taken as an outcome of 'economic inequality' or 'economic injustice' on the part of the ruling elite. Greed is identified in terms of desire of the political elite to perpetuate its control of national power through controlling the national resources. When civil war-like situations emerge following the abrogation of the contract between the ruler and the ruled, the model of 'greed and grievance' prolongs these violent situations.[35]

Another form of state oppression is reflected in political marginalization of certain groups. In theoretical terms, social risk and political alienation are bound together in a mutually inclusive relationship. The higher the level of social risk, the higher the level of political alienation. The essence of political participation lies in equality of rights and opportunities, which can only be guaranteed if the interest of every individual is given equal weight.[36] Conversely, political marginalization takes place when certain individuals or groups are relegated to disadvantageous positions. This relegation reflects and is an outcome of socio-political and economic exclusion of some groups in a society. This socio-political marginalization is used by most totalitarian regimes to sustain political power. They aim to promote those individuals and groups which constitute their support base, at the cost of marginalizing those believed to be on the other side of the fence. This marginalization naturally leads to a decline in political trust and a resultant decrease in political involvement. With the doors of political involvement closed in a given system, the marginalized sections of the society are constrained to look for alternatives to counter this forced alienation, mostly by developing a reactionary approach.

Third, apart from economic exploitation and political marginalization, the totalitarian regimes do not hesitate to resort to physical violence against those groups, mostly ethnic or religious, whom they consider as possible potential threats to their political power base. As totalitarian states come into existence through violence, they aim to retain their monopoly on the means of violence more vehemently vis-à-vis their democratic counterparts. As normal patterns of totalitarian regimes suggest, one party assumes and exercises political authority and does not permit opposition to their authority. Physical violence is used as an instrument to suppress opposition elements. Violence is further employed to terrorize subjects in order to incapacitate them of independent thinking. However, the level of success in using violence to suppress the public aspirations is an open question. In the normal course of history, use of violence invites violent reaction from those upon whom violence is imposed.

The following discussion will focus upon Somalia, Algeria and Egypt on the above theoretical paradigms and will further explore the dynamics of violence in these states.

Somalia

In the context of Somalia, the post-colonial era witnessed a violent and repressive political culture in an economic environment lacking even in the basic amenities of life. The political culture emerging from such an economic environment engendered a revolutionary culture wherein warlordism and militarism emerged to replace the state governance. Warlords like General Aideed and Ali Mehdi exploited the situation in their personal or group interests. They managed to strengthen their group economies through controlling the black market, drugs and weapons businesses and by further controlling the food flow from the United Nations. Their control of the food flow enabled them to maintain their authority with the general public on one hand, and the group economies, thus strengthened, could extend the warlords' capacity to acquire weapons to sustain the civil war.

Moreover, despite possessing the essentials of modern nationalism, including the same religion, one ethnicity and a common language, which could make Somalia a role model for the egalitarian African states, the Somalis continued to remain divided in clan affiliations. Owing to these clan divisions, they could not give Somalia the character of a cohesive and homogeneous society. Somali society is traditionally divided into four major clans, which are further divided into sub-clans and extended family networks. These major tribes include the Biyomaal, the Ogaden, the Hawiye and the Darod. Political marginalization on a tribal basis is not a new phenomenon; rather, it is embedded deep in the history of Somalia. The colonialists also used this trajectory to control the fulcrum of power in their favour. They promoted certain tribes whom they considered their 'local friends' and marginalized the others. The Biyomaal and the Ogaden had to face political exclusion owing to their anti-colonial resistance. The Biyomaal resisted Italian colonialists in South Somalia whereas the Ogaden resisted the British in British Somaliland. Between the Hawiye and Darod tribes, the Italian colonialists promoted Majeerteen, a sub-clan of the Darod, whereas the Hawiye was relegated to a marginal political position. This tribal marginalization continued to exist even in the post-colonial era. For instance, the political ascendancy of the Darod continued to exist in the post-independence period when the military regime of Siyad Barre assumed political authority. Barre belonged to the Darod tribe. The Hawiye, though more numerous than the Darod, remained politically marginalized as the Somali administration was mostly in the control of the Darod. However, the Hawiye could undermine the governance in Mogadishu during the Barre regime. The international community's approach to the Somali problem further aggravated the gulf between the tribes, as most of the time they supported the weaker groups in Somalia. Their support for Abdulahi Yousouf, a warlord belonging to sub-clan of Darod, after the collapse of state structure resulted in resentment amongst the tribal groups. Anti-west religious extremism also got accentuated as international support of Abdulahi Yousouf was taken in terms of an attempt to install another Darod dictatorship in Mogadishu.

In 1969, from the crises of governance ensuing from the assassination of President Abdir Rashid Sharmarke, Siad Barre's military regime emerged. The military regime, highlighting the so-called mutual compatibilities between socialism and Islam, assumed 'Scientific Socialism' as its ideology, and an era of close ties was ushered in between the Barre regime and the socialist world. A Soviet model intelligence network was established through the National Security Service and the National Security Courts, notorious for their repression of the regime's dissidents. This totalitarian structure aimed to transform the clan-based society into a socialist society, and clan loyalties became an offence. Externally, following the Ethiopian crisis subsequent to the fall of Haile Selassie in 1974, the Western Somali Liberation Front (WSLF) in Ogaden sought support from Barre (whose mother was also from Ogaden) in their military violence in Ethiopia following Djibouti's independence from France in 1977. Though Barre could secure initial military success in Ethiopia, Soviet concerns to fill the vacuum after the withdrawal of the United States from Ethiopia changed the military scenario. With the support of the Soviet Union and Cuba, Ethiopia started recovering its areas from Somalia. These military developments led to a heavy influx of Somali refugees from the Ogaden desert to Northern Somalia, inhabited mostly by Isaaq tribe.[37] Barre attempted to settle the Ogaden refugees on the Isaaq lands, which prompted the Isaaq tribesmen to follow the path of violence against the government, as well as Ogaden refugees. In order to safeguard their clan interests, they formed the Somali National Movement (SNM) and declared Somaliland separatism as its ideology. However, they had to face brutal reaction from the Barre government in terms of genocide of the Isaaq. Another group, Somali Salvation Democratic Front (SSDF), largely supported by the Majeerteen clan, had their operational bases in Ethiopia. In addition to SNM, which was already hostile to the Barre regime, SSDF also got disillusioned with Barre when he entered into an agreement with Ethiopia in 1988 to withdraw his support from the Somali guerrillas. This move by Barre was taken as betrayal by the Ogaden tribes, who had hitherto been supported by the regime. This situation led to the multiplying of clan-based guerrilla groups and a violent response from the regime; civil war engulfed the state of Somalia.[38]

In 2002, a Transitional Federal Government (TFG) based in Kenya was established through a series of peace talks but this government was too weak to even base itself on the Somali soil. In this situation, the Islamists stepped in to fill the vacuum of governance. The Islamic Courts Union (Ittihād al-mahākim al-islāmiyya) was established as a rival administration to TFG. In 2006, they managed to take over Mogadishu after overpowering militias of clan warlords.[39] They changed their nomenclature to Supreme Islamic Courts Council (SICC). Ethiopia sent its troops to Somalia to fight against SICC, which was welcomed by the international community. The international community was already disillusioned with SICC for its links with Al-Qaida and because it had challenged TFG, the only legitimate arrangement recognized by the international community. SICC were forced to leave Mogadishu in 2007. SICC largely disintegrated but Al-Shabbāb survived to continue guerrilla fighting until now.[40]

Militant landscape in Somalia

Somalia provides a peculiar example where the state oppression contributed to militancy in the country. The violence orchestrated by the totalitarian regime of Barre, as discussed earlier, provided the militants with a field to operate in by assimilating their ideology with the resistance to the West as well as the 'nearer enemies' in their bid to liberate the Ummah from the prevalent degeneration. In this scenario, Harakat al-Shabaab al-Mujahideen, commonly called Al-Shabbāb, emerged out of the Islamic Courts Union (ICU) when the latter splintered into several factions following its defeat by TFG and the Ethiopian army in 2006. Al-Shabbāb owes its allegiance to Al-Qaida.[41] Though its foot-soldiers are largely concerned with clan-related infighting instead of global jihad, Al-Shabbāb, by manipulating their vulnerabilities, could give ideological colour to their resistance to TFG and the African Union Mission to Somalia (AMISOM) by labelling them as the 'enemies of Islam'. It shares ideological strands with Al-Qaida, and this ideological alignment naturally results in common modes and targets of violence with other Al-Qaida affiliates worldwide. It proclaims the *salāfī* version of Islam and seeks to revert to the early period of Islam. It further resolves to reject all forms of governance except the rule of Shariah. It seeks to establish an Islamic state in Somalia by waging jihad against the Crusaders and their agents, whom they label as 'apostates' who follow the agenda of the Crusaders in Somalia.

The ideological streams of Al-Shabbāb, reflected in their patterns of violence, can be summarized as follows.

First, Al-Shabbāb, proclaiming a *salāfī* version of Islam, yearns to revive the purity of faith by reverting to the golden period of Islam. It resolves to fight against those who, in their view, contaminate the purity of faith through introducing innovations in its practice. They are opposed to the mystic traditions and even attempted to eliminate the Salahiya Sufi order from the region.[42] Their clashes with Ahl-as-Sunnah wal' Jama'a, a Sufi group in Somalia, may also be viewed in this context.[43]

Second, it aims to target western interests within Somalia and without. Though they mostly target places where there is the possibility of killing westerners, they have also threatened Uganda and other African countries for their links with the African Union's Mission in Somalia. Moreover, they target hotels for providing lodgings to the infidels from the West and members of the apostate regime in Somalia as well.[44] To quote a few examples, Al-Shabbāb claimed responsibility for launching a suicide attack in Kampala in 2010 and targeting the UN compound in Mogadishu in 2013, which claimed heavy loss of life. In their bid to attack the western interests in the region, they targeted a restaurant in Djibouti, which was popular with westerners.[45]

Third, Al-Shabbāb targets the Somali regime for collaboration with the West. Besides attacks on government infrastructure and personnel, the militants launched an attack on the presidential palace in Somalia in February 2014.[46] They also target the Ethiopian army and African Union Mission, whom they consider as supporting the Somali government. Their attacks on Kenyan soil, including the attack on Westgate Mall and Garissa University, may be viewed in terms of a reaction to the military involvement of Kenya in Somalia. Al-Shabbāb escalated its activities in response to this military intervention. The militants launched 80 attacks in Kenya in 2014 as compared to 37 in 2013.[47]

Algeria

As a result of the military-supported coup to prevent Islamic Salvation Front (FIS) from assuming political authority in the 1991 elections, the military leaders gained control of the economic resources of Algeria. Through absolute monopoly of economic resources, the ruling elite and military bureaucracy could claim unchallenged control of the political authority. The military leadership struggled to maintain political control through exploiting the national resources. This reinforced the interrelationship between corruption and a non-transparent political process. The exclusive access of the privileged class to economic resources led to massive corruption. The stakes of the ruling elite could not be challenged within the existing system. The socialist model of economy that had been adopted after independence in 1962 strengthened the public sector under tight administrative control, as visualized under a single-party system. It led to the emergence of 'state capitalism'. Nevertheless, economic liberalization, too, failed to provide a genuine boost to the economy rather than more resources for the parasitic elite. The benefits of the free market remained beyond the reach of the masses as the rulers, having control over the oil exports to Southern Europe, were the sole beneficiaries of the export proceeds. Oil and gas exports were major sources of revenue generation for the Algerian economy, and the exploitative economic milieu led to alienation amongst the general masses.[48]

The state of Algeria was not able to ensure equitable opportunities of political participation from its inception in 1962. The phenomenon of political marginalization in Algeria is largely an outcome of the state design. The political process in the infant state was to revolve around a single-party system on the socialist pattern, which, in the absence of an organized opposition, served the interests of the military-backed ruling elite. The privileged position thus secured was maintained largely through relying on the coercive organs of the state instead of popular sentiment, which led to the erosion of the state institutions. The ruling elite developed a system of patronage to draw support to perpetuate their monopoly of political authority by sidelining those perceived as 'others'. The disruption of the electoral process in 1991–1992 through a military-backed coup when Islamic Salvation Front (FIS) was set to secure a majority in the People's National Assembly may be viewed in this context. The suspension of the electoral process rendered the state dysfunctional and unable to resolve the problems resulting from popular exclusion from the political process. The alienation from the political process has been a rising trend since 2001, not only amongst the Islamists but also from the Berber regions of Kabylia against the neglectful and contemptuous response of the ruling elite to popular demands.

Furthermore, state repression promotes a political milieu of violence. The groups against whom this violence is directed prefer to establish organizations as a defensive shield against the oppression. They devise 'anti-system frames' to direct their violence to uproot the agents of repression.[49] The culture of brutality generated through a broader environment of state repression allows the oppressed to draw legitimacy for their acts of violence. This environment further alienates violent groups from the mainstream, and they start viewing their organizational objectives and strategies in an emotive rather than a pragmatic manner. The 'anti-state frames' are created on the premise that the existing system has become dysfunctional, devoid of any possibility of reform. The frames promote a resolve amongst their architects to obliterate the existing system. In Algeria, during the post-1992 coup, state repression created an environment in which organizations flourished with their 'anti-system frames'. This environment provides an opportunity for the target groups to join the organizations which are external to the existing system. The target groups preferred to leave organizations like *Front Islamique du Sulut* (FIS) and join organizations like *Groupe Islamique Armė* (GIA) (al-Jama'a al-Islamiyah al-Musallaha) to protect themselves against the coercive organs of the Algerian state. They rejected the possibilities of reconciliation within the existing system.[50] This group spearheaded violent campaign against the state during the closing years of the 20th century. However, the carrot and stick strategy of the government was successful in leading to erosion of this group. It was eventually survived by a splinter group 'Salafist Group for Preaching and Combat' (Al-Jama'a as-Salafīyyah lid-Da'wah wal-Qitāl) which pledged its allegiance to Al-Qaida in 2003. In 2007, this group announced it was operating under the names Organization of Al-Qaida in the Land of the Islamic Maghreb (Qaidat al-jihad fi Bilad al-Maghrib al-Islami), often abbreviated as AQIM.

Egypt

In the Egyptian context, the Islamists have always called out the state system for being exploitative and non-responsive to the aspirations and needs of the masses. Even the post-colonial state system was declared non-interpretive of the dreams of the Egyptians. The Islamists have been yearning to develop non-state systems to compensate for the state's functions. In 1928, Ikhwan-ul-Muslimeen was established with the proclaimed objectives of obliterating exploitative western influences and reviving the ideals of Islam as a solution to the problems of the Muslims. In his famous treatise on jihad, Hassan Al-Banna, the founder of Ikhwan, regarded jihad as an instrument of preventing injustice and oppression.[51] In areas of social service, Ikhwan advocated for the education uplift and for the improvement in the health sector. With the collapse of King Farouk's regime in 1952 on the charges of corruption and poor governance, the Islamists had expectations that the new regime of Nasser would redesign the state system according to the public aspirations to ensure better service delivery to the masses. These expectations were unfulfilled, for the Islamists who would experience brutal state repression and political marginalization during the years to come.

Nasser sidelined the Islamists who viewed Islam in terms of the ultimate solution to the problems faced by the contemporary Muslims. Their marginalization became inevitable when they made a failed attempt on the life of Nasser in 1954. He banned the organization and responded through an aggressive crackdown on Ikhwan. His regime adopted socialist ideology through promulgation of the 1956 constitution that provided for a one-party political system. Though Islam was recognized as the official religion, it was not Islam but socialism that was accorded the status of an ideology to transform the state and society in Egypt. He embarked upon an era of nationalization in the country on a socialist pattern. He identified himself with the state and ushered in an era characterized by strict censorship of communications, surveillance of the citizens and a low value for human rights.[52] In this political environment, the Islamists were never granted opportunities to participate in the political process by the regime; rather, they were forcibly driven even from the margins of politics. The utter denial of any role in the political process marginalized the inclusive elements within the Ikhwan and won appreciation for the rejectionist theory of Sayyed Qutb. Declaring the existing state system to be based upon the *jāhilliyah* social order, he ruled out the option of reforming the system through inclusive efforts. He urged his fellow believers to uproot the existing order, which was based upon ignorance and provided space for the rulers to pursue the agenda of the infidels against the fellow believers.[53]

Not unlike FIS in Algeria, the Ikhwan, too, underwent internal fragmentation in the wake of excessive state repression exhibited in terms of arrests, incarceration in desert concentration camps and execution of its leadership by the Nasserite regime. The top leadership of Ikhwan, including Hassan Al-Banna, its founder, and Sayyed Qutb, the chief architect of the resistance ideology in Egypt, were amongst those executed by the Nasser regime. Against this oppression and state violence, the inclusive segments in Ikhwan were relegated to the marginalized positions vis-à-vis the exclusionists who largely drew upon Sayyed Qutb's theory of *takfīr* to resist the state repression. Those executed were glorified as heroes against the ruling elites, labelled as western agents. In this milieu of state repression and a resistance narrative, Ikhwan could not avoid internal fragmentation, too. With the mainstream Ikhwan reverting to the background, different splinter groups emerged of which two are important for this study: 'Islamic jihad' and 'Jama'a Al-Islamiyyah'. These groups ushered in an era of resistance against the West and their cronies in Muslim states.

The rise of militancy is embedded in the political landscape emerging from the failure of the post-colonial state system to cater for the economic needs of the Egyptian youth. The socio-economic problems of rapid population growth and ensuing urbanization caused frustration, which exposed the inefficiency of the ideas of the state structure imported from the West. Uprooting the existing state system and installing the Islamic system in its place became the central point of the struggle of the Islamic movements in many Muslim states, including Egypt. A combination of ideological grounds for uprooting the nationalist state system, as provided by Qutb, and structural socio-economic and political problems made Egypt a fertile land for the rise of militant movements from the early 1970s.[54] Initially, Jama'a al-Islamiyyah, which was largely concentrated on university campuses and involved in social work there, was used by the Sadaat regime to counter-balance the leftists. Later on, it was realized that it posed a threat more serious than the leftists. With this realization, the state started to clamp down upon Jama'a al-Islamiyyah, which resulted in militant backlash. A number of militants went into hiding. They were further fragmented largely into two groups. Shukri Mustafa headed one group. Following the prophetic tradition of migration from Makkah, he left Cairo to make a victorious comeback like the Prophet. However, the state could neutralize this group and its leadership. The second group also held responsible for Sadaat's assassination was Abdul Salam Faraj's 'Islamic Jihad'. Faraj believed in targeting the state directly instead of wasting resources in social work. Even by assassinating President Sadaat, they could not succeed in securing control of the state apparatus in Egypt, but at least they could put the authority of the state in question.

During the Hosni Mubarak era, the emigrants who had been frustrated by the economic recession of the 1970s, and had gone to Arabia to explore employment opportunities, started coming back with a much sounder financial position but also with a somewhat transformed ideological vision. In Arabia, they had assimilated the Wahabi influence. As long as they did not challenge the state system, they were treated as a source of stability and further as giving legitimacy to the state. The movement to uproot the existing impious state system and replace it with the Islamic one again arose in Egypt, largely led by two organizations: Tanzīm al-jihad under Abdul Zumur and Jama'a Islamiyyah led by Sheikh Omer Abdul Rehman. Tanzīm al-jihad exhibited political patience whereas Jama'a al-Islamiyyah opted for activism in terms of violence against the state structure, through mobilizing the victims of state repression. 'Islamic Jihad' opted for the same route of violence. The attacks on foreigners and the tourist industry invited public reprobation of the militants, which prompted the state to strike back successfully. In this scenario, Al-Zawahiri emerged to lead the 'Islamic Jihad' and later on, during his stay in Afghanistan, merged the organization with Al-Qaida and became its chief ideologue along with Bin Laden.

Unhealed wounds: Gaza and Palestine

Unhealed wounds, which the Muslims believe to have been inflicted by the West, continue to be a source of strength for the militants in the Middle East. On one hand, these conflicts provide grounds for recruitment to the militants, and on the other, the militants seek to justify their violence through exploiting these conflicts, which is evident through their repeated references to them.[55] While delineating the background of militancy in Gaza and Palestine, this portion of the book examines the transformation of militancy in this region: from religious nationalism under Hamas to transnational militancy under ISIS.

Militant religious nationalism

Militant religious nationalism emerged from the Islamists' conflict with the secular movement for the liberation of Palestine. The Palestine Liberation Organization (PLO), founded in 1964, aimed to unify fragmented resistance groups for the liberation of Palestine from Israeli occupation. The charter categorically declared Zionism to be a colonial, racist and Fascist ideology upon which the state of Israel had been established (Article 19). The charter declared liberation of Palestine and undoing the Jewish entity to be the nationalist duty of the Arabs instead of a religious one (Article 14). The nationalist character was dominant. It did not refer to religion, and, besides calling for resistance in a nationalist spirit, it urged the Arabs to inculcate nationalism in the minds of the new generation through education and other means of enlightenment (Article 8). Initially, the Palestine Liberation Army, its military wing, was fused with the armies of neighbouring Arab states, and the guerrilla factions held marginalized positions in decision making. However, the Arabs' defeat at the hands of Israel during the Six Day War reversed the scenario, and the guerrilla factions got more autonomy and leverage. In 1968, the guerrilla factions attained representation in the Palestine National Council (PNC), the legislative body of the PLO. Al-Fatah was the most prominent of these factions, aiming to eliminate Israel and substitute it with a secular state that would accommodate Jews, Muslims and Christians as equal citizens.[56] From the late 1960s, the PLO embarked upon violence against Israeli targets, largely from its bases in Jordan and Lebanon, under the leadership of Yasser Arafat, who became its head in 1969. However, during the mid-1970s, the PLO, endeavouring to gain legitimacy as the sole representative body of the Palestinians, stopped attacking targets outside Israel, and it secured membership in the Arab League in 1976. In the wake of the 1987 intifada, the PLO assumed a conciliatory tone vis-à-vis Israel, as the quasi-Palestinian government in exile established in 1988 tacitly acknowledged Israel's right to exist.[57] It withdrew from its goal of replacing Israel with a secular Palestinian state in favour of a policy of coexistence between two states: Israel and Palestine. The conciliatory tone of PLO vis-à-vis Israel culminated in mutual recognition between the two sides in the Oslo Accords in 1993. The backlash to this conciliatory posture led to a second intifada with a dominantly religious character in the year 2000. As the secular elements got marginalized, owing to their conciliatory approach to the Zionist entity, the religious elements which had been in the background during the first uprising were now spearheading the uprising.[58]

As a result of Arafat's accommodative approach to Israel and the failure of the Oslo Accords to resolve the issue, the Islamists got an opportunity to make inroads into the body of resistance in Palestine. The Islamists rejected the chances of peaceful settlement of the Palestine conflict as unrealistic, given the repressive and illegitimate nature of the Zionist entity. They believed that the secularists failed, as they did not permit faith to discipline their resistance, which was the only possible solution to the conflict. Sheikh Ahmed Yasin strongly condemned PLO for its secular approach and declared cooperation with it as non-permissible (haram) for the believers unless they subscribe to Islamic ideology.[59] The rise of religious nationalism did not necessarily confirm the Palestinians' turn to Islam; rather, it may be taken as an alternative after the failure of the secularists.[60] External factors like the Iranian revolution, Hezbollah's attacks against Israel and the Islamists' movement in Egypt contributed to the promotion of this alternative.[61] It was in this perspective that Islamic resistance groups emerged to provide a religious solution. Dr Fathi Shiqaqi, himself a member of Ikhwan, founded the Movement of Islamic Jihad (MIJ) as the religious solution to the Palestine question.[62] MIJ believed jihad to be the only solution to the Palestine problem. The PLO's formal standpoint of a two-state solution provided a platform for Ikhwan to challenge the status of the PLO as the sole representative body of the Palestinians by exploiting the anti-Israeli notion through Hamas.[63] It further triggered Ikhwan to share the jihadi solution to the Palestine issue with MIJ.

The Ikhwan legacy in Palestine dates back to 1935, when Abdul-Rehman Al-Banna came to Palestine to do preliminary homework for establishing Ikhwan's chapter in Palestine, which was inaugurated in 1945. Besides public disillusionment with the secularists and the success of the Iranian revolution, the dynamic figure of Sheikh Ahmed Yasin was also instrumental in the rapid rise of Ikhwan to command anti-Israel popular sentiments. In 1973, Sheikh established al-Mujamma al Islami (The Islamic Centre) in Gaza, which would soon control all institutions established by Ikhwan, including the Islamic University in Gaza. Multiple groups in Gaza, West Bank and Jordan vying for the cause of Palestine merged to form a united front under 'The Muslim Brotherhood Society in Jordan and Palestine'. Moreover, Ikhwan also exploited its control of the institution of *waqf* (donations given by a Muslim for religious, educational or the cause of charity) to enhance its public following. Though initially al-Mujamma focused largely on preaching and training of the youth aimed at their spiritual return to Islam, instead of armed resistance to Israel, in the wake of intifada, it switched over to military jihad as a response to public sentiments.[64]

To pursue military jihad, Sheikh Ahmed Yasin founded Hamas in 1987, and its branch in the West Bank was established in 1988. It announced its 36-Articles charter in 1988, which clearly highlighted its ideological dynamics.[65] It proclaimed itself a branch of Ikhwan (Article 2). By inviting believers sharing its ideological standpoint to join its ranks (Article 4), it claimed a universal character but only in terms of its ideological appeal to secure recognition with Muslims worldwide (Article 7). In terms of its goals, the charter is embroiled in conflict between nationalist and ideological standpoints. Though in broader terms it projected Islam as the only solution to the evils contaminating the contemporary world and claimed to fight oppression through jihad (Articles 9 and 10), it did not avoid labelling itself as a Palestinian organization. (Article 6). Moreover, though it acknowledged Palestine to be *waqf* land for the whole Muslim Ummah (Article 11) and called them to strive for its liberation in terms of a religious obligation (Article 15), at the same time, it declared nationalism to be an inalienable part of its religious ideology (Article 12).

Looking at the charter of Hamas leads to the following observations. Although, like MIJ, it recognized military jihad to be the only solution to the Palestine conflict and helped popularization of jihad under its banner, it always retained its nationalist character, and the scope of its jihad remained confined to the liberation of Palestine alone. It attempted to accommodate both nationalist and Islamic approaches to the frame of the Palestinian uprising. Despite acknowledging itself to be a branch of Ikhwan, its religious-nationalist character was in direct contradiction with Qutb's view of jihad. He argued that restricting jihad to defend one's homeland amounted to subordinating the Islamic way of life to the importance associated with one's homeland, which was alien to Islamic consciousness.[66]

Global religious militancy

Palestine has always been the core conflict between the Islamists and the West. Though the nature of the resistance to the Zionist entity has been dynamic and changed from secular to religious nationalist to global militancy, its importance in terms of a source to legitimize violence has never diminished. Some may argue that even the liberation of Palestine would not satisfy the militants who aspire for global caliphate, but the fact remains that the Palestine issue is central to conflict between the militants and the West. With the militants, this issue has primacy vis-à-vis other issues. It has precedence over the enforcement of Shariah, which is explicit from the Al-Zawahiri's proclamation of *takfīr* on the Saudi regime for their inaction on this issue even though they enforce Shariah.[67] His criticism of democracy is also partly associated with the Palestine issue on the grounds that it was the democratic mood that inspired the West to install the Zionist entity on the Palestinian land.[68] For Bin Laden, too, one of the primary objectives of jihad is to liberate the holy sanctuaries of Islam, including Palestine.[69] Moreover, in his fatwa issued on October, 12 1996, Bin Laden exploited the Palestine issue to mobilize jihadi spirit amongst the believers. In his message to the American people, he criticized the atrocious policies of the American government against the Palestinians.[70]

Not unlike Hamas, Al-Qaida believes jihad to be only solution to the Palestine conflict and declares the incumbent Palestinian Authority as apostate for having sympathies with the infidels.[71] Bin Laden condemned those who advocate a peaceful solution to the conflict and collaborate with the 'apostate regime' of the Palestinian Authority through participation in the political process.[72] Besides the commonality of the objective to liberate Palestine, the ideological differences between Al-Qaida and Hamas have also been conspicuous. Al-Qaida believe that Palestine is the core catalyst for its global religious militancy aimed at the creation of a global caliphate, whereas for Hamas, liberation of Palestine is the ultimate objective. Apart from the scope of jihad, the two organizations differ in strategy to achieve their goals as well. Al-Qaida outrightly rejects the international charters that recognize the Zionist entity on the Palestinian land to which Hamas leadership shows some deference.[73] However, Al-Qaida leadership has always kept the undertones of these differences low so as not to benefit the forces of unbelief. The available evidence suggests that the top leadership of Al-Qaida has been directing field formations to avoid conflict with Hamas followers as, despite deviations from Shariah, they are believers and evil should not be supported through opposing them.[74] Moreover, Al-Qaida reluctantly supported accepting funds from organizations like Hamas with whom differences exist if the scarcity of funds was likely to stop the jihad against the infidels.[75]

Nevertheless, the differences between Hamas and those pursuing global jihad under ISIS became more pronounced. ISIS, which also exploited the Palestine issue to give direction to its militancy, posed the biggest challenge to Hamas' power base in Gaza and had been successful in making inroads into its military wing. A number of defections within the Al-Qassam Brigade took place on the grounds that Hamas was not very Islamic.[76] Jordanian King Abdullah also confirmed that ISIS was recruiting its foot-soldiers from Gaza through exploiting the repressive policies of Israel against the Palestinians.[77] Hamas declined to approve of the killings of civilians by ISIS as a war tactic.[78] ISIS threatened to strike against the secularists – Al-Fatah and Hamas, too, alongside Israel – for not enforcing Shariah to the required degree in the areas under their control.[79] In short, the conflict remains central to a larger conflict between the Islamists and the West.

Theatres of international aggression

Do the theatres of international aggression in the Muslim world provide space for the militancy to flourish? Iraq may be a plausible case to answer this question. Post-Saddam Iraq reflects a three-pronged conflict scenario: militants' resistance against the invading foreign forces, violence against the local support base of the United States and violence on the trajectory of polemics.

The US invasion of Iraq in 2003 allowed the militants to draw theological legitimacy for their violence in terms of individual obligation of jihad. Iraq, though having a long history of socialist rule, witnessed resistance against the foreign aggression which was predominantly religious in spirit. The labels adopted by the resistance groups evidently refer to this religious spirit, including 'Saladin Brigades', 'Al-Mutawakileen' and 'Muhammad's Army'.[80] The religious sentiments associated with the resistance could accommodate the version of jihad as espoused by Al-Qaida and its affiliates, which identify Iraq and Afghanistan as the prime venues to hit the 'snake's head'.[81] Al-Qaida could discover Iraq as an ideal launching ground for global jihad.[82]

Though Al-Qaida's narrative may not find a large following with the Muslims in normal circumstances,[83] its continuous highlighting of the Muslims' sufferings in the international war theatres like Iraq and Afghanistan could develop anti-Americanism to a point where Muslim groups from diverse backgrounds could base their respective ideologies of jihad.[84] Abu Hafs al-Masri Brigade, an Al-Qaida affiliate, issued 'The Mujahideen Roadmap' that sanctioned the killing of Americans, Jews and Christians by eliminating any distinction between combatants and non-combatants. This distinction was disregarded as they had an indirect role in decision making; therefore, they were responsible for their states' invasion into the Muslim lands. The roadmap further urged the unity of the militant groups to globalize the scope of jihad in Iraq. This global jihad would not only be directed against the western powers but also their supporters in the Muslim states.[85]

In the case of Iraq, Al-Qaida's immediate emphasis had been to drive the invading forces out of Iraq. They believed that elimination of the western military presence from the Muslim soil would bring economic exploitation and repression against the Muslims to an immediate end.[86] Al-Qaida affiliates like Ansār Al-Sunnah in Northern Iraq believed that resistance in Iraq would provide a base to liberate Palestine and other Muslim areas under western control.[87] Al-Qaida channelled their foot-soldiers[88] to globalize their resistance against the West. They urged the Muslims in the West to observe theological conditions that govern *dār-ul-harb*.[89] In this perspective, Anwar Al-Awlaki has discussed two key questions that determine the militants' approach to the West: (1) whether the theological status of the western nations is of *dār-ul-harb* or *dār-ul-ahd* for the Muslims in general; and (2) if the western states are declared *dār-ul-harb,* whether the Muslims living there are bound by their covenant not to commit violence against these states. In answer to the first question, Awlaki categorically denied that the Muslim leaders could enter into covenants with the peoples of unbelief because they themselves had lost legitimacy by following man-made laws and allying with the non-believers. With regard to the second question, he argued that the western states which actively participated in invasion of Iraq or any other part of the Muslim world had become *dār-ul-harb*. The Muslim citizens in these states were no longer bound by covenants which would stop them from damaging the interests of their states of residence.[90]

The western invasion of the Muslim states, including Iraq, came under theological scrutiny with the militants. This scrutiny redefined the scope of cooperation between the ruling elite in the Muslim states and the West. States like Iraq, which happened to be subject to western aggression, were declared *dār-ul-harb* because the decision-making process was no longer controlled by the Muslims. Having been declared as such, these Muslim states and their citizens become subject to theological conditions that govern *dār-ul-harb*. These conditions include either waging jihad or migrating from *dār-ul-harb*.[91] The post-Saddam Iraq reflects increased subscription to radical anti-western notions and excommunication of those who support the western narrative.[92] Al-Qaida identified the militants as *awliya'* (friends) of Allah and those supporting the infidels as apostates.[93] In the case of Yemen, AQAP sought to legitimize killings of the Yemenite soldiers on the pretext that they were guarding the embassies of the western nations fighting against the believers in Iraq and Afghanistan.[94] In the same vein, Al-Qaida affiliates worldwide unleashed violence against those whom they allege to have supported the West.

As far as fallout of the US invasion on sectarian dynamics of Iraq is concerned, the fall of the Baath regime was followed by violent sectarian conflict. This conflict may be viewed from diverse perspectives. It may be viewed as a local conflict where the Sunnite ruling elite dislodged by the invading western forces attempts to regain political authority against the Shiites who seized political power through collaboration with the West. Or ethnic context may explain the conflict, as the Shiite ethnic majority challenged the socio-political primacy of the Sunnite ethnic minority. However, the most plausible explanation of this sectarian violence is based upon the way the political authority passed over to the Shiites allegedly under the patronage of the United States. This earned the Shiites the label of hypocrites from the militants. Having been identified as allies of the non-believers, the Shiites also became the natural targets of the Sunnite militants. This fire of sectarian hatred was constantly fuelled by accusations and counter-accusations from both sides. The Sunnites were more vocal in their accusations against the Shiites as part of the triangle with the Christians and the Jews to materialize the Jewish plans to occupy the holy sites in the Muslim world and, further, their hegemonic designs to control the resources of the Muslim world by establishing control over Iraq.[95] The vacuum created by the US invasion of Iraq and breakdown of the military machine led to deterioration in the security situation. It further ignited the ethnic and sectarian schisms that turned the post-invasion Iraq into a new battlefield.[96]

The study of these killing fields leads to the following conclusions:

First, the militant outfits in Lebanon, Syria and Iraq share an anti-imperialist agenda but they have always retained their respective sectarian identities. These identities have channelled the militancy inside the Muslim societies instead of reinforcing resistance to the imperialist forces.

Second, in a utilitarian perspective, the militants have exploited these schisms to secure strategic and political gains. They have used the sectarian violence to mobilize the sectarian networks to boost militancy in the global context.

Third, though a multiple identities frame defines the conflict scenario in the Middle East, it has never been able to eclipse the relevance of sectarian identities to transform the politico-religious landscape of the region.

Fourth, societies which have been victims of state oppression have been fertile ground for militancy, in terms of reactive and anarchic solutions to the continuous denial of rights to marginalized groups. This anarchic culture leads to increased relevance of religious dogmas to give legitimacy to violent means that are adopted.

Fifth, militants may attempt to establish administrations rival to dysfunctional state structures, like in Somalia, to fill the governance vacuum. These attempts put them in direct confrontation with the totalitarian state structures, which guard their monopoly over the means of violence more jealously than democratic states (since totalitarian regimes come into existence through violence).

Sixth, the militants attempt to explore alternative solutions to governance crises through reviving the purity of faith. Thus, by reverting to the purity of faith, they reject everything that is not Islamic and does not find its place during the period of the *salaf*. This exclusionary approach sets them in opposition to non-believers and to believers who do not subscribe to their brand of Islam. The struggle to explore governance alternatives carries within itself the seeds of discord with the non-believers and those following a different brand of Islam.

Seventh, being in conflict with each other, the guardians of dysfunctional state structures and militants who claim to offer a Shariah-based alternative look for support. The militant outfits look towards their ideological networks while the regimes look towards the western powers by offering to protect their interests. This situation locks both sides into a more severe conflict scenario where the militants take refuge in loose application of *takfīr* for the ruling elite for supporting the infidels against fellow believers.

Eighth, the unhealed wounds in the Muslim lands like Gaza and Palestine have perpetuated militancy in the entire Muslim world in general and in the Middle East in particular. A strong anti-Israel stance has been the lifeline of resistance movements. The PLO could retain its ascendancy as the sole representative body of the Palestinians until it adopted a conciliatory tone that culminated in the Oslo Accords. Its secular nationalist appeal gave way to the religious nationalism of Hamas when the latter declared jihad to be the only recourse for the liberation of Palestine. In the same vein, global religious militancy seems to put Hamas in the shade by publicly rejecting its so-called deference to the international charter that recognizes the Zionist entity.

Last but not least, theatres of international aggression in the Muslim world like Iraq and Afghanistan provide space for the militants to draw legitimacy for their violence by invoking theological doctrines that discipline the believers' conduct in the case of foreign aggression into a Muslim territory. The militants seek to legitimize violence not only against the invading enemy but also against those who support the enemy from within.

Notes

1 'Who Are Hezbollah?' *BBC News*, 0828 GMT, July 4, 2010.
2 Hezbollah opposed the consociationalist model of democratic governance based on the 1932 census. Consociationalism refers to a power-sharing arrangement in a democratic framework which claims to ensure inclusion of diverse groups of a plural society in state institutions; see Ziad Majed, 'Consensus, democracy and representation in Lebanon: Between agony and electoral reform', *Accord*, no. 24, Conciliation Resources.
3 'Iran-Syria vs. Israel, Round 1: Assessments & Lessons Learned', *Defense Industry Daily*, September 13, 2012.
4 'Lebanon Unity Deal Gives Hezbollah Veto Power', *NBC News*, July 11, 2008.
5 'Lebanon Is Hezbollah', *CNN*, December 1, 2009.
6 Jeffrey Goldberg, 'In the Party of God: Are Terrorists in Lebanon Preparing for a Larger War?' *New Yorker*, October 7, 2002.
7 Randa Slim, 'Lebanon's Dangerous Sunni-Shiite Divide Widens', *Al-Monitor*, May 29, 2012.
8 Ibid.
9 'Hezbollah Says Presence in Syria Greater Than Ever Before', *NDTV*, October 18, 2015.
10 'Lebanon's Hezbollah Urges Backing for Fight against Islamic State', *NDTV*, May 25, 2015.
11 'Hezbollah fighters say a "duty" to help Syria's Bashar al-Assad', *NDTV*, April 11, 2014.
12 Loveday Morris and Suzan Haidamous, 'For Lebanon's Sunnis, growing rage at Hezbollah over role in Syria', *Washington Post*, June 12, 2013.
13 'Hariri: Sunnis "refuse" to join Hezbollah-Al Qaida war', *Gulf News Lebanon*, January 25, 2014.
14 Al-Nusra Front is an Al-Qaida off-shoot in Syria that emerged in January 2012 to uproot the Assad regime. It also operates against Hezbollah in Lebanon. See 'Zawahiri disbands main Qaida faction in Syria', *Global Post*, November 8, 2013.
15 Ruth Sherlock, 'Inside Jabhat al-Nusra – the most extreme wing of Syria's struggle', *The Telegraph*, December 2, 2012.
16 'Mapping Militant Organizations: Jabhat al-Nusra', *Stanford University*, accessed, December 10, 2015, http://web.stanford.edu/group/mappingmilitants/cgi-bin/groups/view/493.
17 'Profile: Syria's al-Nusra Front', *BBC*, April 10, 2013.
18 Sherlock, 'Inside Jabhat al-Nusra.'
19 'Nusra Front Issues Bounties for Assad, Nasrallah', *Al Arabiya News*, October 13, 2015.
20 'Al Qaida-Linked Group Al-Nusra Front Claims Deadly Car Bombing in Lebanese Capital Beirut', *ABC News*, January 21, 2014.
21 According to Encyclopaedia Britannica, this creed emerged from the Ismailite teachings; however, it assimilated the influence of different elements, including Jewish, Christian, Gnostic, Neoplatonic and Iranian under the doctrine of monotheism. This creed got propagation in Cairo in 1071 AD under Hamza ibn Ali. This creed draws its title from an associate of Hamza ibn Ali, namely Muḥammad al-Darazī. The creed turned into a 'doctrine of the soteriological divinity' of al-Hakim bi Amr Allah, the sixth Fatimid caliph (996–1021). According to Druze belief system Al-Hakim did not die but went into occultation to reappear to unfurl a golden age; accessed December 10, 2015, http://www.britannica.com/topic/Druze.
22 'Syria Conflict: Al-Nusra Fighters Kill Druze Villagers', *BBC*, June 11, 2015.
23 *Dabiq*, issue 4.

24 Dabiq, issue 1.
25 ISIS spokesman appreciated the ISIS fighters for killing the Shiites, see, 'Excerpts from 'Indeed Your Lord Is Ever Watchful'', *Dabiq*, issue 4.
26 Ibid.
27 Ibid.
28 Paul Vallely, 'The vicious schism between Sunni and Shia has been poisoning Islam for 1,400 years and it is getting worse', *The Independent*, February 19, 2014.
29 Alessandria Masi, 'Crackdown in Lebanon pushes some Sunnis toward ISIS, Al-Nusra', *International Business Times*, October 29, 2014.
30 'Syria: The Story of the Conflict', *BBC News*, October 9, 2015.
31 Some argue that the army officers serving in Saddam's Baathist regime have been working with ISIS in the current scenario; see, for example, Liz Sly, 'The hidden hand behind the Islamic State militants? Saddam Hussein's', *Washington Post*, April 4, 2015.
32 Hayder al-Khoei, *The World Today* (October & November 2014): 38–40.
33 Peter T. Leeson, 'Better off Stateless: Somalia before and after Government Collapse', *Journal of Comparative Economics* 35 (2007): 689–710.
34 Iris Young, 'Five Faces of Oppression', in *Oppression, Privilege, & Resistance* eds. Lisa Heldke and Peg O'Connor (Boston: McGraw Hill, 2004).
35 Paul Collier and Anke Hoeffler, 'Greed and Grievance in Civil War', *Oxford Economic Papers New Series* 56, no.4 (2004): 563–595; also see Paul Collier and Anke Hoeffler, 'On the Incidence of Civil War in Africa', *Journal of Conflict Resolution* 13 (2002): 13–28; also see Raphael Chijioke Njoku, *History of Somalia* (California: Santa Barbra, 2013).
36 Stanley I. Benn, 'Egalitarianism and Equal Consideration of Interests.'
37 http://www.britannica.com/place/Somalia/Cultural-life#ref419661 (accessed November 28, 2015).
38 Ibid.
39 Ibid.
40 Ibid.
41 CNN Wire Staff, 0607 GMT, February 10, 2012, accessed November 28, 2015, http://edition.cnn.com/2012/02/09/world/africa/somalia-shabaab-Qaida/.
42 Muuse Yuusuf, 'An Act of Desperation by Al-Shabaab', *Somali Think Tank*, October 7, 2011, accessed November 29, 2015, http://somalithinktank.org/746/.
43 'Sufi Militia Says Al-Shabab Planning to Attack Galgadud Region', *Voice of America,* September 14, 2010.
44 Mary Harper, 'Why Do al-Shabab Target Hotels?' *BBC World Service*, November 7, 2015.
45 National Counter Terrorism Centre, *Counter Terrorism Guide*, accessed November 30, 2015, http://www.nctc.gov/site/index.html.
46 Omar Nor and Laura Smith-Spark, 'Al-Shabaab Militants Attack Somali Presidential Palace in Mogadishu', *CNN*, February 21, 2014.
47 'Al-Shabaab Attack on Garissa University in Kenya', *START*, April 2015.
48 'Algeria's Economy: The Vicious Circle of Oil and Violence', *ICG Report*, ICG Africa Report No. 36 Brussels, October 26, 2001; also see, George Joffé, 'The Role of Violence within the Algerian Economy', *Journal of North African Studies* 7, no.1 (2002): 29–52.
49 Mohammad M. Hafez, 'From Marginalization to Massacres: A Political Process Explanation of GIA Violence in Algeria', in *Islamic Movement: A Social Movement Theory Approach* ed. Quinon Wiktorowicz (Bloomington: Indiana University Press, 2004), 38.
50 Ibid., 39.
51 Al-Banna, *jihad.*

52 Robert St. John, 'Gamal Abdel Nasser, President of Egypt', accessed December 4, 2015, http://www.britannica.com/biography/Gamal-Abdel-Nasser.
53 Qutb, *Muālim*.
54 Gilles Kepel, 'Islamists versus the State in Egypt and Algeria', *Daedalus* 124, no. 3 (1995): 109–127.
55 This narrative is endorsed even by the US policy-making circles. See, for instance, the statement of Rob Malley, senior advisor to President Obama for the Counter-ISIL Campaign in Iraq and Syria, 'Obama's ISIS Czar Says We Can't Defeat Extremism without Resolving Palestinian Issue', *Mondoweiss*, December 14, 2015.
56 Other factions include Popular Front for the Liberation of Palestine (PFLP), the Democratic (DFLP), and al-Ṣāʿiqah.
57 PLO recognized the United Nation's Resolutions 242 and 338.
58 Palestine Liberation Organization (PLO) Palestinian political organization, accessed December 30, 2015, http://www.britannica.com/topic/Palestine-Liberation-Organization.
59 Ann M. Lesch, 'Prelude to the Uprising in the Gaza Strip', *Journal of Palestine Studies* 20, no.1 (1990): 1–23.
60 Iyad Barghouti and Lisa Hajjar, *The Islamist Movements in the Occupied Territories: An Interview with Iyad Barghouti, Middle East Report, No. 183, Political Islam* (July–August, 1993): 9–12.
61 Ibid.
62 Ramadan Abdallah Shallah and Khalid al-Ayid, 'The Movement of Islamic jihad and the Oslo Process', *Journal of Palestine Studies* 28, no.4 (1999): 61–73.
63 Wendy Kristianasen, 'Challenge and Counterchallenge: Hamas Respose to Oslo', *Journal of Palestine Studies*, 28, no. 3 (1999): 19–36.
64 Beverley Milton-Edwards, 'The Concept of jihad and the Palestinian Islamic Movement: A Comparison of Ideas and Techniques', *British Journal of Middle Eastern Studies* 19, no.1 (1992): 48–53.
65 For text of the charter, see Muhammad Maqdisi, 'Charter of the Islamic Resistance Movement (Hamas) of Palestine', *Journal of Palestine Studies* 22, no. 4 (1993): 122–134.
66 Milton-Edwards, 'The Concept of Jihad and the Palestinian Islamic Movement', 48–53.
67 Maha Azzam, *Al-Qaida*.
68 Rassler et al., *Letters from Abbottabad,* no. SOCOM-2012-0000013.
69 Osama Bin Laden, 'Interview by Al-Jazeera, December 1998', in *Al-Qaida in Its Own Words*, 57–59.
70 Bin Laden, 'Message to the American People, October 30, 2004,
71 Bin Laden, 'Second Letter to the Muslims of Iraq, October 18, 2003; also see Bin Laden, 'Wrath of God', Interview by *Time*, January 11, 1999, accessed May 21, 2013, http://www.time.com/time/world/article/0,8599,2054517,00.html.
72 Bin Laden, 'Second Letter to the Muslims of Iraq', October 18, 2003.
73 Bin Laden, 'Until We Taste What Hamza Bin Abd Al-Muttalib Tasted', *Inspire*, issue 2.
74 Rassler et al., *Letters from Abbottabad,* no. SOCOM-2012-0000016.
75 Ibid., no. SOCOM-2012-0000008.
76 Aaron Klein, 'Gaza becoming Centre for Export of ISIS Fighters', *WND Exclusive*, June 29, 2015.
77 Scott Pelley, 'King of Jordan: ISIS used Gaza conflict as recruiting tool', *CBS News*, September 25, 2014.
78 Creede Newton, 'ISIS Gains a Foothold in Gaza', *The Daily Beast*, September 12, 2015; also see Céline Lussato, 'Hamas v. ISIS, An Islamist Civil War Simmers

In Gaza', *World Crunch*, September 24, 2015; Raed Omari, 'What if ISIS Emerges in Gaza?' *Al Arabiya News*, June 7, 2015; Fares Akram, 'Gaza's Hamas Rulers Have a New Problem: ISIS-Sympathetic Jihadists', *Business Insider*, June 8, 2015.

79 Jordan Schachtel, 'ISIS Threatens to Take Gaza from Rival Terror Group Hamas', *Breitbart*, July 1, 2015.

80 Haynes, 'Al Qaida: Ideology and Action', 171–191.

81 Rassler et al., *Letters from Abbottabad*, no. SOCOM-2012-0000018.

82 Ibid., No. SOCOM-2012-0000017.

83 Gunaratna, 'Al Qaeda's Ideology'; also see Paz, 'The Impact of the War.'

84 A media report suggests that people in Iraq were attracted towards the *salāfism* more vehemently after the US invasion of Iraq. See N. Pelham, 'Iraq's Holy Warriors Draw Inspiration from Arab Puritan of another Country', *Financial Times*, March 18, 2004.

85 *Mujahideen Roadmap*, 2004.; the Madrid Bombings may be viewed in the context of this roadmap. Al-Qaida attacked Muhammad b. Naif, Assistant Minister for Defence of Saudi Arabia, for his continued support to the United States; also see Abu Basir, 'Interview by Al-Malahem Media', *Inspire*, issue 1.

86 Ibid.

87 Haynes, 'Al Qaida: Ideology and Action.'

88 Ibid.

89 The militants frequently use three terminologies to transform the Muslims' discourse vis-à-vis the West. These include *dār-ul-kufr, dār-ul-Islam* and *dār-ul-harb*. Al-Maqdisi defines *dār-ul-kufr* where the law of unbelief and non-believers' authority to legislate are predominant; *dar-ul-Islam* is where the laws of Islam are supreme and the believers and their legislation are predominant. See *This is our Aqeedah*; *dār-ul-harb* are those places where non-believers enter into war with the Muslims, and *dār-ul-ahd* are those nations with whom the believers enter into a covenant; see Al-Awlaki, 'The Ruling on Dispossessing the Disbelievers wealth in Dar al-Harb', *Inspire*, issue 4.

90 Ibid.

91 The same narrative was espoused by Sayyid Ahmed Bareili in India against the British and Sikh rule.

92 Paz, 'The Impact of the War.'

93 Al-Awlaki, 'The Ruling on Dispossessing the Disbelievers wealth in Dar al-Harb', *Inspire*, issue 4.

94 Ibid.

95 Kazimi, 'Zarqawi's Anti-Shi'a Legacy.'

96 Paz, 'The Impact of the War.'

7 Fuel of faith: Pakistan – a case study

In the recent past, thousands of Muslims have been killed. This situation results from many factors which require inquiry, not only into the causes of violence but also into the underlying motivational factors that have driven the militants to cause such carnage within the Muslim society which had remained immune for many centuries. The current chapter precisely focuses on the people having direct or indirect likages with the militant outfits involved in violence in Pakistan in the name of religion and traces their ideological and motivational factors through their wider contexts of jihad and claims to liberate Islam. The study traces their genesis and evolution, examining present intellectual discourse pertaining to the use of violence against fellow Muslims and as the primary means to serve Islam. The chapter also argues that militants and their masterminds do not operate in silos but are invariably linked with each other through their common belief in ideologies of violence.

Local religious environment

The western scholarship is divided on the question of the interrelationship between terrorism and the religious seminaries. The profiling of the militants according to ideology leads to two fundamentally opposite streams. One stream believes in strong links between traditional religious seminaries and the ideological indoctrination of militants. Others, who failed to find any positive evidence regarding the madrassah background of the militants, reject the theory of close linkage between militants and religious seminaries as sources of indoctrination. They find that most of the militants involved in major acts of terrorism, including the World Trade Centre bombing in 1993, bombings of the US embassies in Africa in 1998, 9/11 attacks and Bali bombings had a secular educational background.

This study exposes the non-exhaustive nature of these two themes. Those who argue for direct, formal and primary linkages between the religious seminaries and the terrorists, for the most part, underestimate indirect, informal and secondary sources of indoctrination of the militants. In religious seminaries, the ulema can influence only those who formally join the

DOI: 10.4324/9781003164883-7

madrassah education system whereas the secular section of the society remains out of bounds for these ulema. However, in an indirect and informal arrangement, the local ulema, though not necessarily madrassah clergy, have the means to influence the mindset of otherwise secular elements in Muslim societies as a whole. These ulema constitute the group which, as Stephen Humphreys puts it, 'makes the Muslim society Islamic'.[1] They cut across almost every section of the Muslim society and are found operating in capacities ranging from semi-literate imams in countryside mosques to foreign qualified heads of large seminaries. This source of what we term 'informal religious indoctrination' is not the by-product of an authentic and valid standpoint of ulema in sectarian contexts, which naturally comes from those ulema who are considered theologically well qualified. It is rather an outcome of intellectual streams flowing in the society largely through semi-literate imams. Historically, this type of indoctrination was produced through the remodelling of the education system in the colonial era. In the Indian context, the madrassah system in the pre-colonial era was designed to educate Indians for state employment as well as to produce religious leadership.[2] However, with the replacement of madrassahs by missionary schools and the Persian language with English, this system lost its input into state employment. Madrassahs were relegated to producing religious leadership for India and could no longer make significant contributions in the public sphere. As a side effect of this marginalization and compartmentalization of the religious and temporal spheres, the clergy assumed unimpeachable authority in all matters religious. The secular educated class was left with no choice but to look to semi-literate imams for routine guidance in the matters of faith. In this situation, as said earlier, besides madrassah ulema, clergy working beyond the madrassah system could find a diverse audience for themselves.

Militant landscape

The following portion of this chapter analyses the militant landscape in Pakistan through examining the data of 100 individuals arrested for having primary or secondary linkages with the militant outfits operating in the country during the last decade. The militants included in the sample are mainly those who were either directly involved in the acts of militancy or were handlers, facilitators or at least sympathizers of the militants. However, one cannot escape limitations regarding data collection on the militant activities in one way or the other. These limitations include difficulties in gaining direct access to terrorists apprehended by Law Enforcement Agencies (LEAs), problems gaining access to the fluid ideological space wherein militant outfits operate, problems in analysing terrorism patterns as the militants deliberately keep on changing their strategies and targets to maintain the element of surprise and above all, problems in selection of the sample using traditional techniques as ideological concerns are of primary importance. In view of these limitations, the data collected in this study largely rely on profile studies of those linked with militancy. This part of the study aims to explain the dynamics of the local environment of the militants in the context of Pakistan. In this regard, academic background, age groups, sectarian affiliations, nature of militant networks and their linkage with theatres of international conflict have been examined. The empirical evidence has been examined to identify the nature of targets and modes of violence adopted by the militants.

Academic background

It has been argued in the opening part of this chapter that religious seminaries are not the sole source of indoctrination, as is commonly assumed by some sections of the western scholarship. This indoctrination also partly originates from a religious section of society which is otherwise external to the formal madrassah system. These semi-literate imams have a diverse audience as compared to the madrassah ulema. The madrassah ulema have access largely to those enrolled as formal madrassah students whereas semi-literate local imams have the potential to indoctrinate even the secular elements of the society as well. The data collected on the militants reflects that 18% of them have a purely religious education background and 42% of them have a secular education background, whereas 29% of the militants in the sample have both types of education. About 11% are neither educated on religious traditions nor secular lines. Amongst those with a religious education background, 42% had religious education to primary level, and 13% of them had secondary-level madrassah education. Only 19% had post-secondary-level religious madrassah education. Primary-level madrassah education includes rudimentary learning, which mainly includes learning to read the Quran. Secondary-level madrassah education includes memorizing the holy book (*Hifz-e-Quran*) and going through various books of traditions (*Daurā-e-hadith*) of the Prophet. The post-secondary-level madrassah education includes certifications of Dars-e-Nizami and Almiyyah Course. As learning to read the Quran is part of religious traditions in the Muslim societies, it may not necessarily reflect a militant bent of mind. In order to reach meaningful conclusions, it is necessary to highlight the madrassah connection at the stage of primary education. Only 13% of the militants having the primary level of religious learning have a madrassah connection.

Amongst those educated in secular traditions, 23% of the militants had a primary level of education, 21% were under-Matric, 12% had Matriculation, and 4% had an intermediate level of education. The number of those having graduate and post-graduate education was 1% each. Further inquiry reveals that although 47% had direct academic links to the madrassah system, 53% had either academic background beyond madrassah education system or had no education background at all. The evidence suggests that 33% of the militants examined in this study channelled to militancy through family members whereas 40% of them got linked with terror networks under the influence of peer groups. About 30% of them joined the terror outfits under the direct influence of militants' propaganda. There are diverse modes of the militants' propaganda, which include literature, speeches in mosques and religious seminaries, the transmission of jihadi narrative through speeches in rallies and during individual contact, drawing a religiously inspiring picture of militant struggle in the theatres of international conflict and portraying the picture of atrocities of non-believers on the Muslims. The data analysis leads to the conclusion that militants in Pakistan are not necessarily the product of the madrassah system alone. Madrassah education is not the sole variable in their indoctrination since they also hail from the secularly educated class, which is exposed to alternative sources of indoctrination such as indirect links with the terror networks through immediate or extended family members, peers being connected with militant organizations, semi-literate local imams and, above all, militant propaganda in the locality.

Age group

The study of the militant environment in Pakistan further rejects the commonly held notion that teenagers are the most likely targets of indoctrination that leads them to join the ranks of the militant organizations. The data suggest that only 1% of the militants were below 20 years of age, 49% were in the 20–30 years bracket and 33% were between 30 and 40 years of age. Only 17% were older than 40 years. The empirical evidence suggests that indoctrination is not necessarily imparted by militant ideologues to teenagers through short and random religious sermons. It is developed through a long process with multiple formal and informal variables working behind it. Though the brainwashing of teenagers who become the fuel of militancy does take place with militant ideologues in the immediate context, long-term variables like family environment and peer influence are, of course, the complementary factors behind this brainwashing. Once they are radicalized, these long-term variables appear to be relatively more relevant in forestalling the efforts for their de-radicalization.

Linkage with Afghanistan war theatre

The ideological indoctrination of the militants draws its roots from the surrounding milieu. However, the impact of the environment becomes more emphatic when supported by volatile physical conditions like those emerging from international aggressions. The linkage of the local militants and their networks with the theatre of international conflict becomes a conspicuous feature of the militant environment in Pakistan. These provide venues for the development of comradeship amongst the militants. The statistics suggest that 55% of the militants have been fighting in Afghanistan. In most of the cases, these terrorists developed their comradeship in the Afghanistan war theatre. This companionship continued to exist when they returned to their homelands but, indeed, with changed targets largely from an external enemy to a domestic enemy. Most of the proscribed militant organizations operating within Pakistan have a history of fighting in Afghanistan. The militants view fighting against the imperialist enemy as *fard-e-ayn*. Though most of them did not have experience of practical participation in international conflict, they could find tribal area alongside the Pak-Afghan border as the militants' fusion centre after the American invasion of Afghanistan in the post-9/11 scenario when the militants fled to the Pakistani side of the Pak-Afghan border.

Sectarian affiliations

The militants examined in this study were found to be predominantly from the Deobandi sect (86%) whereas 1% of them had affiliations with the Barelvi sect and 13% were from *Ahl-e-hadith*. Though the Hanfite Deobandi sect as such does not sanction militancy, the teaching developed by the semi-literate ulema provide the seeds of this radicalization. The evidence exists that a reactionary tone overwhelms the sectarian affiliations of the militants. They subject the ulema belonging to their own sectarian stream to violence if they hesitate to legitimize their violence against the state through the issuance of religious decrees. Though sectarian differences do exist amongst the militant outfits, they easily bridge the sectarian faultlines if required to pursue their violent agenda. Amongst the militants examined in this study, 5 of them belonging to the Barelvi sect switched over to *Ahl-e-hadith* and Deobandi sects to pursue violence with more vehemence. Nevertheless, given the limited availability of data, it is not be easy to draw conclusions in a comparative framework. However, the statistics do provide a window on the outcomes from sectarian backgrounds. In view of this, it may well be argued that, though most of the militants examined in this study had Deobandi affiliations, the evidence confirms that Barelvi and *Ahl-e-hadith* sects were not absolutely free from militancy.

Ideologically diffused nature of terrorist networks

The empirical evidence suggests that Tehrīk-e-Taliban, Pakistan and Lashkar-e-Jhangvi are the major perpetrators of violence in the country, whereas other organizations that occupy a prominent place in terror networks include offshoots of Tehrīk-e-Taliban, Pakistan (TTP) like Jama't Al-Ahrār (JuA) and Hizb-ul-Ahrār (HuA).

The study finds that ideological diffusion is the overarching characteristic of the militant diaspora. Operatives can switch from one organization to another without deviating from their original ideological strands. The data show that 50% of the militants were associated with a single organization, 29% had switched over from at least one organization to another, 19% had changed their organizational affiliations three times and 2% had changed their affiliations four times. The commonalities in ideological viewpoints make the militant networks an amalgam of ideologically diffused organizations that provide space for horizontal movement of their members. The militants change their organizational affiliations according to their convenience without being hindered by ideological constraints.

The common factors which contribute to the horizontal movement of operatives between the organizations include the following: (1) an individual is attracted towards militant ideology by the activists of an organization but later, he formally joins some other outfit; (2) one may change organizational association under the influence of peers who join some other group; (3) in case of a split in the leadership of an outfit, the activists follow the leader with whom they are associated more closely – they join some other organization or establish a new one; (4) the militants may change their affiliations if they are underpaid as compared to those working for other organizations; (5) when a group becomes irrelevant to achieve the goals, its members join other groups according to their convenience; (6) the militants may launch a joint venture of terror with fellow militants formally belonging to some other outfit. In August 2020, Jama't Al-Ahrār (JuA), Hizb-ul-Ahrār (HuA) and Tehrīk-e-Taliban, Pakistan (TTP) formed an alliance to launch a terror offensive.[3]

Such a close nexus between these organizations is possible only if these are ideologically diffused. This diffusion is mostly reflected through the commonality of targets and modes adopted for their violent activities. There exists a strong commonality of targets amongst the militant organizations across the country. The shared targets include fighting against the imperialist forces and their Muslim supporters in the theatres of war, fighting the Muslim rulers who are accused of collaborating with the infidels against the fellow Muslims and also those who are found in support of these Muslim regimes like the apologists, coercive organs of the state like the army, LEAs and other government establishments, the Shiites, those who are accused of committing *bida'ā* in the practice of faith, foreigners as well as local non-Muslim civilians and, above all, political activists who support democracy. Besides the targets, the modes of violence adopted by these organizations also provide points of convergence. For instance, in addition to conventional types of attack, suicide attacks, kidnapping for ransom and robberies are modes of violence that are common among the major militant organizations working in Pakistan.

Ideological framework of the militants

The following discussion, delineating the targets and modes of violence commonly adopted by the militant networks, identifies ideological strands of the militants. Out of the militants whose profiles have been examined in this study, the majority have a history of fighting against the invading forces in

Afghanistan; many have been involved in fighting against the 'nearer enemy' or those that constitute its support base, including the army, LEAs, government establishments, the apologists and pro-government political activists. There are still others who have been involved in violence on sectarian faultlines: most of them directed their violence against the Shiites whereas a few of them were involved in killings of the Barelvis and attacks on the holy shrines. Foreign civilians were targeted by the terrorists, and they were also involved in killing civilian non-Muslims domestically, including Hindus, Christians and Ahmedis. Furthermore, the militants were involved in killing political activists for their support of democratic norms. For the purpose of this study, the nature of targets exposes the ideological orientation of the militants.

Ideological streams of the militants

The ideological streams of the militants as appearing from the study of their profiles may be summarized as follows.

First, the militants seek to rejuvenate the glory of the Muslims through violent means. For the overwhelming majority of the militants, the major urge behind their violence was ideological, aiming to uplift the cause of the Muslims by thwarting their prevalent degeneration.

Second, the militants do not hesitate to proclaim *takfīr* on those accused of introducing innovations (*bida'ā*) into the body of faith. They cherish to revive the purity of faith. In this purview, the data reflect that the Barelvis, who are commonly accused of committing *bida'ā* by the Deobandis and *Ahl-e-hadith*, have been the targets of militancy. Moreover, the Sufi shrines, which the militants label as 'centres of *bida'ā*', have also been targeted.

Third, as said earlier, the militant culture as a whole is characterized by violence on sectarian faultlines. The extremist stereotypes developed over the centuries on sectarian grounds make the Shiites the prime target of the Sunnite militants. In historical perspective, despite the existence of a sharp sectarian divide, tolerance between the two sects was explicit in the pre-Partition Indian society. This tolerance was evident from the fact that both the Sunnites and the Shiites used to attend sessions of theological learning jointly at the religious madrassah at Farangi Mahal, Lakhnow. This level of sectarian tolerance declined when the rulers like Nawab of Awadh in Indian society supported conversion to Shiism in the United Provinces (UP). His support to Shiism extended the Shiites a sense of separate identity on one hand and sharpened the polemical divide on the other. This schism became more vehement in the recent past with Iran's revolution in 1979. The Sunnites started precautionary measures in their lands to forestall the anticipated export of Shiite ideology. This led to a violent struggle between the two sects to secure their respective spheres of influence across the Muslim lands, including Pakistan. Sectarianism carries the potential to ignite violence against those on whom decrees of *takfīr* exist. This potential is evident with the militant networks operating in the country. The data suggest that the Shiites have been targeted by most of the militant organizations. TTP and LeJ are spearheading violence against the Shiites.

Fourth, besides fighting against the non-believer aggressors in Afghanistan, which the militants take as *fard-e-ayn*, they are equally active on the domestic front. Though Sunnite scholarship in general does not approve of *khurūj* against Muslim rulers, most of the militant organizations operating in the country believe in *khurūj* against the Muslim rulers, whom they accuse of supporting the non-believers against the fellow believers. They label them as 'agents of the non-believers' and 'nearer enemies'. They unleash violence not only against these rulers but also those who support them. For the militants, the support base of these rulers includes coercive organs of the state like the army and other LEAs, political activists of the ruling parties and government establishments.

Fifth, the militant ideologues pronounce *takfīr* on those who take part in the democratic process without any reluctance. Besides this, the militants also target those whom they label as 'the apologists' as they attempt to reconcile Islam with western democratic norms.

Sixth, in addition to the afore-mentioned codes of war, the militants' violence is driven by pragmatic considerations. They select targets that may serve as a tool to help them follow their codes of war. Most of the militant organizations have been involved in acts of terrorism against foreign civilians, with the following objectives in mind: (1) to mount pressure on the rulers, they target civilians of countries like China with whom Pakistan has close ties and whose civilians are involved in different development projects in Pakistan; (2) to get ransom money from the government for their release; (3) to get their fellow terrorists released in exchange for kidnapped foreigner civilians; (4) to give a message to foreign governments to remain aloof from the War on Terror.

Seventh, for the militants, following a religion other than Islam by an individual virtually forfeits his right to life. Though such an extremist approach can hardly flow out of any theological source, the surrounding environment imbued with extremism and reactionary zeal has led to the emergence of such brutal ideas. The militant networks in Pakistan do not hesitate to target civilian non-Muslims in the country, which include the Hindus, the Christians and the Ahmedia community.

Eighth, the militant networks believe in the legitimacy of launching suicide attacks as a war tactic to inflict damage on those against whom they believe violence is religiously sanctioned.

Last but not the least, the militant outfits have been found to be involved in conventional crime in society as well. Though it is not possible, even for themselves, to justify their involvement in the crime in any ideological frame, they explain their involvement in heinous crimes as a bid to muster resources to support themselves in following their codes of war. The profile study of the militants reflects that those belonging to LeJ, TTP and its affiliates have been involved in conventional crime in society, including robberies, kidnappings for ransom and hired assassinations.

Outcomes of militants' ideological streams

The militants' ideological make-up shapes and transforms the nature of violence in the society. The features of militancy are evidently reflected in the following target areas.

Sectarian killings

Sectarian killings are an important feature of militancy in Pakistan. As said elsewhere, sectarian schisms are embedded deep in the history of Muslims. These splits remained within the limits of theological debates surrounded by the mutual strain between the followers of different sects. However, the tension translated into physical violence only when tolerance between the religious scholars of both the Sunnites and the Shiites dissipated following the Iranian revolution of 1979. The success of this revolution was taken as a threat to the Sunnite theology beyond the territorial limits of Iran. Having been felt apprehensive of the possible export of Shiite ideology in the Sunnite world with the backing of Iran, Sunnite organizations emerged to counterbalance the Shiite organizations. In Pakistan, Tehrīk Nifāz Fiqah Ja'afria (TNFJ) was founded in 1979 to protect the rights of the Shiite community. As a counterbalance, a Sunnite organization Sipah-e-Sahabah Pakistan (SSP) emerged in the early 1980s. *Takfīr* of the Shiites was a catchphrase of this organization. Not long after the emergence of these rival sectarian organizations in the country, the traditional strain between the opposing sects that had already moved towards excommunication was now prone to physical conflict on sectarian lines. Both sectarian organizations developed militant wings to offset each other in physical violence. Lashkar-e-Jhangvi and Sipah-e-Muhammad emerged as militant wings of the SSP and TNFJ, respectively.

The empirical data reflect an upward trend in sectarian violence, especially after 9/11. The number of incidents rose from 109 in 2000 to 341 in 2007, with a corresponding increase in killings – from 149 to 341 in the same timeframe. The data not only include the casualties of the targeted rival sect but also those who lost their lives as collateral damage in these incidents of sectarian violence. This upward trend in the incidents of sectarian violence continued until 2013.[4] The escalation in incidents of sectarian violence was the result of the fusion of different militant organizations with a shared ideology in the tribal belt adjacent to the Pak-Afghan border. Some militant elements, having war-tested fighting skills developed in Afghanistan, shifted to the Pakistani side of the border in wake of the US invasion of Afghanistan. LeJ militants who already had ties with these elements could enhance their capacity in terms of workforce, violence modes and techniques through their fusion with TTP, the local Al-Qaida affiliate. LeJ, through its nexus with TTP, launched suicide attacks against the Shiites. However, a sharp downward trend is visible after 2013. This declining trend is related to the state response vis-à-vis militancy. Similarly, the number of Shiites causalities also witnessed an upward trend from the year 2000. In 2002, in four reported incidents six Shiites lost their lives. The figure rose as high as 504 deaths in 81 incidents in 2013.[5] However, in subsequent years, this number declined considerably due to a decrease in incidents of sectarian violence when the militant organizations were incapacitated in the context of military operations against them.

Though physical violence emerged largely between the Shiites and the Sunnites, the Hanfite Barelvis – numerically the largest sect in Pakistan – could not remain immune from this violence. The Barelvis, too, had to face the labelling of *takfīr* on the pretext of being involved in *bida'ā,* not only from the Wahabi quarters but also from the Hanfite Deobandis. The militants have targeted the shrines of Sufi saints across the country, which they believe had been converted into the centres of *bida'ā* by those who follow a mystical approach – largely the Barelvis. During the period 2005–2016, in 17 militant attacks on the shrines of the Sufi saints reviewed in this book, 263 persons were killed.[6] Moreover, the militants' fight against local tribal people belonging to the Barelvi sect affirms their extremist approach. In erstwhile Khyber Agency, Lashkar-e-Islam, a militant fighting group, has been at war with Ansār-ul-Islam, an anti-Taliban group consisting of local tribal people largely belonging to the Barelvi sect. Moreover, the militants' anti-Barelvi demeanour is also evident from their sectarian violence in Swat.

Suicide attacks

The phenomenon of suicide attacks emerged in the region only when Al-Zawahiri assumed the ideological leadership of Al-Qaida. Prior to 9/11, suicide missions were not part of the modes of violence adopted by LeJ that had been spearheading terrorism in Pakistan. It was only under the ideological umbrella of TTP that militant outfits resorted to this war tactic against their intended targets. This phenomenon has seen an upward trend since 2002. The number of incidents rose to 76 in 2009 as compared to only 1 in 2002.[7] The period 2009 onwards sees a decrease in such incidents; however, this declining trend does not reflect any ideological shift vis-à-vis the phenomenon. Rather, it is due to the state's kinetic response that shattered the capacity of the militant outfits to launch suicide attacks.

Attacks against western targets

Militants have been targeting the westerners in Pakistan to avenge the aggression of the US and NATO forces in Afghanistan. For them, fighting the infidels who have invaded the Muslim territory is *fard-e-ayn* upon every believer. They do not make a distinction between combatants and non-combatant western civilians. The data on major attacks on western targets in Pakistan suggest that in one decade, from the year 2002 to 2012, the militants conducted 27 major attacks on western targets in Pakistan. These attacks left 98 local and foreign civilians dead and 401 injured.[8] To attack western targets, mostly civilian, the militants have attacked Christian churches, missionary schools, hotels and restaurants, tourist spots, consulates, projects where foreign labour is working and NGOs. Apart from these attacks, the militants have targeted NATO supply lines to frustrate western forces in Afghanistan. During the period 2008–2014, a total of 309 incidents of violence took place across the country, which claimed 143 lives and injured 254 persons. The regional breakdown of these incidents shows that Balochistan remained at the top in terms of the number of incidents and the number of people killed. A total of 177 incidents of violence took place, which left 46 persons killed and 75 injured. In erstwhile FATA, in the given timeframe, 85 incidents resulted in 59 persons killed and 195 injured. In Khyber Pakhtunkhwa, 18 persons were killed and 52 injured in 33 NATO-related incidents of violence, whereas in Punjab, 8 incidents took place which claimed 19 human lives and injured 15. In Sindh province, only six incidents took place, in which one person was killed and seven injured.[9]

Violence against the media

Violence against print and electronic media is also a salient feature of militancy in Pakistan. This violence is a product of the militants' perception that the media in Pakistan usually serve the western agenda and are hostile to their narrative. Simply for being on the other side of the fence, the media become what the militants term a 'legitimate target of their violence'. Since 2002, 59 incidents of terrorism have taken place against the media across Pakistan. These left 49 media persons dead and 47 injured. Out of the 59 incidents, there are 9 incidents in which the media persons were not targeted but were killed as collateral damage. In these 9 instances, 10 media persons were killed and 16 injured while performing their professional duties.[10]

Violence against religious minorities

The militants' narrative vis-à-vis the religious minorities warrants violence against them simply for not being Muslims. Through this narrative, the militants aim to achieve various objectives: (1) targeting minorities to avenge killings of their fellow militants; (2) frustrating the government of Pakistan in its bid to counter militancy; (3) attempting to draw legitimacy for targeting local Christians in reaction to the western policies. Instead of viewing the minorities, especially the Christians, as fellow Pakistanis in nationalistic terms, the militants identify them with their co-religionist west, which they believe is bent upon damaging the Muslim Ummah. As far as Ahmedis in

Pakistan are concerned, they declare them as apostates as they do not believe in Prophet Muhammad as the seal of the prophets. The review of 8 attacks against Christians suggests that 147 persons were killed and 310 injured in these acts of violence. In 2010, in militant attacks against Ahmedis in Punjab, 103 people were killed and 111 injured.[11]

Attacks on the 'nearer enemy' and its supporters

Accusing the government of following the western agenda against fellow believers, the militants unleash violence against them and their support base. They have been targeting the top-brass executive and political leadership in the country. In the post-9/11 scenario, the violence has been directed against government establishments, including the army, police and other LEAs and civilians found to support government policies.[12] A large number of LEA personnel and civilians lost their lives in the violence. The civilians either were killed as collateral damage resulting from the acts of violence or were targeted for supporting government policies or standing opposed to the militant narrative of faith. For instance, under government patronage, the local tribal elders organized their tribal fraternity to protect their cultural values against the phenomenon of militancy largely in erstwhile FATA and Balochistan. In their resistance alongside the LEAs against the militants, in 102 incidents, 149 tribal elders were killed.[13] These causalities occurred in clashes both between the militants and government-sponsored tribal groups or in militant attacks on tribal *jirgās* (councils). Apart from this, the militants also attacked pro-government political leadership. The motivation behind these attacks was to target the supporters of the government, which they term as the 'nearer enemies' for their alleged collaboration with the infidel West.

Moreover, the militants condemn the constitution of Pakistan for being based upon unbelief as it affirms the western democratic ideal of popular sovereignty instead of divine sovereignty. The militants' attacks on the political leadership in Pakistan may be viewed in two perspectives: first, they believe that the political leadership associated with the ruling party shares collective responsibility for pursuing the western agenda, and second, they argue that those who take part in the political process are liable to be killed as they have chosen democracy as a religion. The exponential rise in militants' attacks on the electoral process a few weeks before the June 2013 General Elections affirm the militants' narrative against the political process in Pakistan. A total of 148 militant attacks were launched against electoral activities during the period from January to May 2013, and 170 persons were killed. Most of these attacks were launched during April and May, just before the elections in June 2013. Out of these 148 attacks, TTP and its affiliates perpetrated 108 attacks that claimed the lives of 156 persons.[14] According to media reports, prior to the 2013 elections in Pakistan, TTP distributed pamphlets warning people not to vote.[15] It is to be noted that even the politico-religious leadership of the country could not remain immune from these militant attacks. For instance, Jamiat Ulema-e-Islam (F) leadership was targeted due to their collaborative posture in the existing political system, which the militants label as un-Islamic.

Attacks on educational institutions

The data for the period 2004–2013 suggests that Pakistan was in the top 10 countries in the world for the number of attacks on educational institutions. During the given period, a total of 724 attacks were launched against educational institutions, which constitute 10% of the total incidents of violence against different targets in the given period. However, in terms of the number of fatalities, Pakistan was fourth out of 10 top-affected countries of the world. In the given period, 179 persons were killed in violence against educational institutions. The relatively low ratio of fatalities vis-à-vis the number of incidents was because, in most of the cases, the institutions were unoccupied at the time of incidents. Most of these attacks were launched to disrupt the education infrastructure, mostly for girls.[16] TTP was the largest perpetrator with 136 attacks, which constitute 77% of the total traced incidents, including the most brutal attack on Army Public School, Peshawar, in December 2014 that claimed 145 lives, including 132 students ranging between 8 to 18 years of age.[17]

The empirical research on the local ulema and study of the militants' profiles in the context of Pakistan lead to the following broad conclusions.

First, the fuel of militancy may not necessarily come from the formal madrassah system as many foot-soldiers of militancy have a secular education background. Nevertheless, the militants educated in secular traditions have, one way or another, informal and secondary linkage to the madrassah system. The religious patrons of religious seminaries solely influence formal students of the madrassah system, whereas the secular youth have a more complex ideological approach, which is transformed by multiple variables like the influence of semi-literate local imams, family and peers. Strong evidence exists that the ideological streams exploited by the militants in Pakistan flow from the surrounding ideological culture, not necessarily espoused by the formal madrassah ulema and authentic religious scholars belonging to a particular sect, but mostly as projected by low-qualified prayer leaders.

Second, the militants adopt a selective approach to give theological legitimacy to their acts of violence. They do not necessarily opt for an authentic standpoint on any issue of their concern. Instead, they prefer to subscribe to the views of a semi-literate clergy even though flawed, which allow them to legitimize their violence.

Third, the militant outfits, with their common ideological strands, represent a militant worldview instead of working in silos. This worldview provides space to accommodate a variety of militant networks sharing a common ideology. The emerging outfits in a locality may not need to search for fresh recruits as ideological commonalities between these networks make the horizontal movement of their experienced soldiers from one outfit to another easier. The militants take pride in being part of a worldwide militant brotherhood.

Fourth, the evidence suggests that, with the militants, ideology takes precedence over organizational affiliations. There is a tendency amongst militant operatives to shift their organizational affiliations frequently; yet, they hardly change their mental programming. The absence of ideological constraints in changing their affiliations has attributed a transnational character to militancy. ISIS could win over experienced soldiers from the ranks of militant groups even in lands which were socially and culturally alien to the organization originating from Syria and Iraq, only because of ideological commonalities. According to media reports, Boko Haram pledged its allegiance to ISIS in 2017.[18] This organizational affiliation could happen only because the militants' diaspora has a common ideological worldview.

Last but not the least, the militants justify their violence as being part of their broader objective to revive the ideals of faith. Their targets and violent methods need to be viewed in a militant ideological frame as they seek to justify them in theological terms. In this perspective, a shared common ideological vision produces commonality in targets and modes of violence adopted to achieve them.

Notes

1 R. Stephen Humphreys, *Islamic History: A Framework for Inquiry* (New York: I. B. Tauris Publishers, 2009), 187.
2 This system owes a lot to Mullah Nizamuddin Sehalvi of Madrassah Farangi Mahal, Lakhnow, who codified the Dars-e-Nizami curriculum for madrassah education, which is currently followed by most of the religious seminaries in the subcontinent.
3 Ayaz Gul, 'Militant Pakistan Taliban Brings Splinters Back into Its Fold', *Voice of America*, August 18, 2020.
4 South Asia Terrorism Portal, accessed November 29, 2020, https://www.satp.org/datasheet-terrorist-attack/other-data/pakistan.
5 Ibid.
6 Ibid.
7 Ibid.
8 Ibid.
9 Ibid.
10 Ibid.
11 Ibid.
12 President Musharraf was attacked twice for allegedly being in collaboration with the West against fellow Muslims in the War on Terror. Similarly, the militants attacked Mr. Shaukat Aziz, the former premier, and Benazir Bhutto, the chairperson of Pakistan People's Party, on the pretext that they were pursuing the western agenda.

13 South Asian Terrorism Portal.
14 'Elections 2013: Violence against Political Parties, Candidates and Voters: A Report' by Pak Institute for Peace Studies, Islamabad, Pakistan, May 2013.
15 Zahir Shah Sherazi, 'TTP distributes threatening pamphlets against elections', *Daily Dawn*, April 25, 2013.
16 START Global Terrorism Database.
17 Ibid.
18 Jim Muir, 'Boko Haram pledges allegiance to Islamic State', in *BBC News*, March 7, 2017.

8 Counter narrative

The militant narrative, being evolved largely on the trajectories of *takfīr* and *khurūj,* challenges even the definition of the Muslim and Islam. It has been developed in theological space wrongfully carved out by the militants through misinterpretation of the primary religious texts. In order to earn their narrative theological legitimacy, the militants attempt to distort the evidence from the accounts of Islamic history. By linking their extremist narrative to the historical evidence, they dismiss any counter narrative emerging out of a modernist perspective. They term the proponents of modernity thesis as apologists. In view of this, the response to the challenge needs to be evolved from the early period of Islamic history itself. On this premise, this chapter seeks to transform the contemporary ideological discourse through the refutation of militants' codes of war by revisiting the primary sources. By redrawing the boundaries of faith through challenging the socio-political constructs founded on historical presuppositions, this study offers a counter narrative that ultimately culminates in a refutation of the militants' claim to follow 'authentic Islam'.

Boundaries of faith

As discussed elsewhere, the socio-political variables prevailed upon the fundamentals of faith, which have always remained constant. This led to radical revisions in the boundaries of faith through liberal application of *takfīr* to those accused of undermining the purity of faith by introducing *bida'ā* into its practice. The phenomenon of *takfīr* blurred the precise definition of the faith and the believers. Nevertheless, while relying upon well-acclaimed and authentic Muslim scholarship and historical evidence from the period of the *salaf*, the following discussion seeks to redraw the boundaries of the faith and ascertain the conditions leading to invalidation of faith. It seeks to uphold the defining character of the religious fundamentals in determining the limits of faith vis-à-vis socio-political variables.

The structure of faith stands on its fundamental beliefs.[1] All those who believe and confirm the truthfulness of divine revelations and veracity of the prophetic transmissions descended through a sound medium of narrations

DOI: 10.4324/9781003164883-8

constitute the ideological brotherhood. In other words, to be a believer requires affirmation and conviction of the unity of God and authenticity of His prophets, which could be achieved only through rendering total submission to what the Prophet has brought down from Allah. After professing the faith, it is refutation of the same fundamental beliefs whose affirmation is required to enter into Islam in the first place that puts a believer into unbelief. Mere commission of wrong deeds does not nullify the faith unless one develops belief in the permissibility of otherwise impermissible deeds.[2] *Takfīr* has strong repercussions in the sense of leaving either the one who applies it or the one upon whom it is applied as non-believer. Thus, Muslim scholarship has been cautious and never let speculations move its application.[3] In the course of Muslim history, *takfīr* has not been pronounced for two sects – Khawarij and the Shiites – whereas Jahamiyyah and Qaramitah have been subjected to *takfīr*. While examining the theories of classical theorists like Ibn Taimmiyah, Ibn Kathir and Imam Ghazali, this study will ascertain the theological grounds for the application of *takfīr* and will further develop an argument that all sorts of heresies do not lead to *takfīr*; rather, it is refutation of any fundamental element of the faith that invokes it.

Grounds of *Takfīr*

In classical perspective, not all sorts of heresies but refutation of any fundamental element of faith which triggers *takfīr*. In the course of early Muslim history, *takfīr* has been pronounced for Jahamiyyah and Qaramitah but not in the case of Khawarij and the Shiites, despite the fact that both of these sects introduced innovations into the faith.

Khawarij

Though the Companions of the Prophet fought against the Khawarij, they did not invoke *takfīr* against them. Ali did not fight against them until they started shedding blood of the believers. His military campaign against them aimed to protect the Muslims from their violence.[4] Ali avoided initiating fighting against them until they launched the offensive themselves.[5] It is evident from history that *takfīr* was not pronounced against them. For instance, Abdullah b. Umar and other Companions offered their prayers behind Najdah Al-Haruri. Abdullah b. Abbas consulted them on the matters of religious import. Imam Bukhari affirmed the authenticity of Najdah in terms of a link in narration of a *hadith*.[6] They were dealt with differently from non-believers in the battles even. Their women were not made captives, and their property was not dealt with as spoils of war (*ghanīmāh*).[7] After the battle, all the wounded were extended medical treatment.[8] Based on this mild treatment, Shaybani built war ethics against those who commit *khurūj*. He argued that it was not permissible for the Muslims to pursue those who in case of defeat escape from the battlefield nor to kill their wounded persons.[9]

The Shiites

As discussed elsewhere, those who rejected the right of the first three caliphs to the office of caliphate were labelled as rejecters (Rawāfidh). Later on, those who supported Ali against Amir Mu'awiyah were called supporter of Ali (*Shi'ān-e-Ali*). They argued that close relationship with the Prophet granted Ali primacy to the right to caliphate vis-à-vis other Companions of the Prophet. On the contrary, the Sunnites believe in legitimacy of rights of all the rightly guided caliphs in the same order as occurred in history. In a religious perspective, the Sunnites believe in exclusivity of the Prophet in his infallible status whereas the Shiites extend this infallibility to their imams as well. Moreover, according to the Sunnites, for the narration of the *ahadith*, it is the character of the narrator, which is important whereas the Sunnites argue that the Shiites give more weight to affiliation with the Shiite doctrine instead of character of the narrator.[10] In the political context, the Sunnite caliphate continued to exist until the 20th century, when the Ottoman Caliphate was abolished. On the other hand, imamate continued to pass through the descendants of Ali until the Twelfth Imam Mahdi went into occultation. The majority of the Shiites are called *athnā-e-ashriyyā* (the twelvers) because they believe in the twelve imams and further hold the view that the Twelfth Imam Mahdi who went into occultation will reappear in the world prior to the Day of Judgement and will establish justice in this world.

A large part of classical Muslim scholarship does not pronounce *takfīr* on the Shiites in their collective capacity merely for believing in primacy of the right of Ali to the caliphate. Though, as has been said earlier, the Shiites are regarded as Rawāfidh by the Sunnites because they reject the right of the first three caliphs to the office of caliphate and certain sections of the Sunnites are declared as Nawāsib (enemies of Ali), the classical perspective suggests that both sects have always observed restraint in pronouncing *takfīr* on each other.[11] Ibn Taimmiyah argued that the Shiite *mufāddilah,* at least in their collective capacity, who simply believe in the primacy of Ali's right to the caliphate vis-à-vis the other three caliphs, could not be subjected to *takfīr*. He further suggested that their *takfīr* amounted to going against the Quran, Sunnah and the consensus of the Companions.[12] This view was shared by other Muslim scholars, including Imam Ahmed, who categorically suggested that they could not be declared as non-believers.[13] About the Shiites and their critics, Al-Ghazali had moderate views when he suggested that these mutually opposed groups were not liable to attract the label of *takfīr* simply because none of the two held the opinion that what the Prophet brought down was not truth. On this premise, he further argued that the Shiites could not be declared as non-believers simply because they overemphasize imamate.[14] Al-Ghazali has the credit for redefining the boundaries of faith through drawing a clear distinction between heresy and apostasy.[15] He argued that heresy does not necessarily constitute apostasy. He was in favour of broadening the definitional framework that could accommodate the competing theological standpoints. Al-Ghazali relies upon a prophetic tradition wherein the Prophet has been reported to have said that levelling false charges of unbelief against a fellow Muslim renders the one who so charges a non-believer.[16] Al-Ghazali draws distinction between primary and secondary principles of belief. The primary principles include belief in the unity of God, prophethood of Prophet Muhammad and the day of resurrection. Everything that is external to these three elements of faith is of secondary nature. The refutation of anything of secondary nature does not entail *takfir,* with the exclusive exception of the refutation of religious principles channelled through 'diffused congruence' from the Prophet. Even in this case, difference of opinion on matters such as legal questions or relating to the right to caliphate will not attract *takfīr* but may raise the question of inventing innovations in the faith at the most. However, as said earlier, he reiterates that affirmation of doubt in the truthfulness of whatever has been brought down to us by the Prophet, even if it involves some issue external to the three primary principles, surely puts one outside the pale of Islam.[17] However, contradicting an isolated tradition (*khabar-e-ah'dī*) will not attract *takfīr* but only the one who negates the veracity of anything channelled through 'diffused congruence' will be condemned as having committed an act amounting to unbelief.[18] The status of *ijma'a* (consensus of opinion) as definitive proof itself is disputed amongst Muslim scholars (*mukhtālīf fīh*).[19] Al-Ghazali recognizes 'unbelief' as a legal question like other legal issues, which entails serious implications, including loss of life and property here and condemnation to hellfire in the hereafter. Therefore, labelling of *takfīr* needs to be exercised with utmost caution.[20]

Jahamiyyah

The evidence generated from the course of Islamic history suggests that a few ulema like Ibn Al-Mubarak[21] do not include Jahamiyyah in the list of Muslim sects because they do not believe them to be Muslims. This view is also shared by the majority of the followers of Imam Ahmed whereas some other Hanbalites include them in the list of Muslim sects. Ibn Kathir explored another sect called Qaramitah, whom he declared to be non-believers. These sects have been declared as apostates because they refuted the fundamentals of the religion.

In the case of Jahamiyyah, the following phases reflect the evolution of their thought process. First, they argued that the Quran as a set of meanings was created by Allah and revealed to the Prophet. They viewed the Quran as a set of meanings on the presumption that speech was not a befitting characteristic of Allah. This view led them to disbelief in the following Quranic verse: 'And if anyone of the idolaters seeketh thy protection (O Muhammad), then protect him so that he may hear the Word of Allah, and afterward convey him to his place of safety. That is because they are a folk who know not'. (At-Tawbah: 6). Second, they had doubts regarding the

Quran in terms of creation of God. Third, they held that the Quran was revealed to the Prophet only as a set of meanings whereas it was subsequently expressed by the Prophet through his own words. Fourth, the Quran, being the attribute of Allah, cannot be memorized by humans.

This sect was subjected to *takfīr* by the ulema on the following grounds. First, primary texts were available to refute their doctrine; second, their doctrine culminated in negation of the Creator; and, third, their views stood in contravention of the evidence recognized by human beings in the normal course of life.[22]

Al-Ghazali, while distinguishing between exegesis (*tafsīr*) and theology, refers to Imam Ahmed bin Hanbal's views regarding the Jahamiyyah sect. He argues that *tafsīr* provides only the meanings of text whereas theology seeks to examine these meanings within some external framework. He refers to the Quranic verse 'He mounted the throne' (As-Sajada: 4) (*istawā ala' al-arsh*) and argues that *tafsīr* provides only for the meanings of the text whereas to examine the controversies between the Jahamiyyah sect and Imam Ahmed surrounding this verse is the domain of theology. Jahamiyyah argue that God is omnipresent and not specific to one particular place like a throne. In response, Imam Ahmed argues that all are agreed that God's existence preceded every other creature because he himself is the creator of everything. Imam Ahmed further argues that if we ask Jahamiyyah whether God has created all other creatures from inside Himself or external to His self, they can respond to this question from the following three possible standpoints. First, God created other creatures from inside Himself. It amounts to disbelief because evil cannot be part of God. Second, God created things external to His self but after their creation entered into them. This view also culminates in *kufr* because God cannot enter any despicable place. Third, the view that God created everything external to His self and remained external to His creatures is the view of the Muslims, which is not shared by Jahamiyyah. Thus, Imam Ahmed draws the inference that Jahamiyyah's views regarding God end up in *kufr*.[23]

Qaramitah

Qaramitah flourished in 278 AH. They were mostly disciples of the Persian philosophers and at the same time believed in the prophethood of Zoroaster. In Islamic perspective, they were not particular in observing limits of what was permissible or otherwise. Their callousness towards the limits of faith was largely inspired by the Rawāfidh's proselytization of false creeds. In socio-political context, they earned the label of *mahmarah* for using the red colour as a religious symbol to express their affiliation exclusively with the Abbasids. Ibn Kathir has quoted Abu Bakr Al-Baqalani who condemned this sect for their false propaganda regarding their preference of Ali to the other three pious caliphs and further for slandering the Companions of the Prophet. The Prophet strictly prohibited the denigration of his Companions.

Imam Dhahbi[24] has quoted the following *hadith*, 'He who loves them, loves me but he who hates them, hates me, and he who offends them, offends me and in turn offends Allah and he who offends Allah, Allah almost takes him'.[25] In another tradition, the Prophet said, 'The sign of faith is love of the helpers (*Ansār*), and the sign of hypocrisy is hatred of the helpers'.[26] In yet another transmission, the Prophet strictly warned the believers not to insult his Companions. He said, 'Do not revile my companions, for by Him in Whose Hand is my soul, were one of you to spend gold equal to mount Uhud, you would not attain the reward of the handful of one of them or even half of it'. Moreover, the Qaramitah committed violence in the House of God (*Ka'ba*) in the year 317 AH and killed many people. They shifted *Hijr-e-Aswad* (the Black Stone) to their area of influence.[27] Ibn Kathir has declared them heretics (*zindīq*) and non-believers on the following two grounds: first, they believed in the prophethood of Zoroaster and used to follow Persian philosophers instead of Islam; second, they transgressed the limits of faith in terms of what was permissible and otherwise.

The analysis of these four sects by the classical theorists helps to infer that *takfīr* can be invoked either if someone foregoes any of the fundamental principles of Islam like unity of God, prophethood and life hereafter or if any element of the faith like prayer, zakat, fasting and Hajj is not recognized. As Khawarij and Rawāfidh did not forego any of the fundamentals of the faith, they were not subjected to *takfīr* whereas Jahamiyyah and Qaramitah disregarded these fundamentals and were excommunicated accordingly. On this premise, the following discussion will examine the classical narrative of *takfīr* as espoused by Ibn Taimmiyah, Ibn Kathir and Al-Ghazali.

Ibn Taimmiyah

Ibn Taimmiyah argued that approval of unbelief and disapproval of belief revokes the belief of someone who is otherwise a believer. He added that approval of a non-believer's denial of divine unity and the finality of the prophethood on the part of a believer provides enough grounds to nullify his faith. Conversely, if one disapproves of a believer's affirmation of tawhid and the prophethood, it too amounts to commission of *kufr* (unbelief).[28] He went further and enumerated the following modes of affirming the *kufr*. First, if a believer expresses his agreement with the religion of the non-believers and supports them through different means against Islam, he is said to have approved of their unbelief.[29] Second, as laid down in the Quran, reflecting indifference to the faith in the face of its mockery by the non-believers amounts to *kufr*. The Quran says, 'He hath already revealed unto you in the Scripture that, when ye hear the revelations of Allah rejected and derided, (ye) sit not with them (who disbelieve and mock) until they engage in some other conversation. Lo! in that case (if ye stayed) ye would be like unto them. Lo! Allah will gather hypocrites and disbelievers, all together, into hell' (An-Nisā: 140).[30] Third, friendship (*Mawālāt*) with non-believers is a sign of approval of unbelief.[31] He draws this inference from the following Quranic verse, 'Thou wilt not find folk who believe in Allah and the Last Day loving those who oppose Allah and His messenger, even though they be their fathers or their sons or their brethren or their clan. As for such, He hath written faith upon their hearts and hath strengthened them with a Spirit from Him, and He will bring them into Gardens underneath which rivers flow, wherein they will abide. Allah is well pleased with them, and they are well pleased with Him. They are Allah's party. Lo! is it not Allah's party who are the successful?' (Al-Mujaadilah: 22).

This *mawālāt* includes inclining towards non-believers and adhering to their beliefs (Hud: 113; Al-Qalam: 9), showing courtesy at the expense of one's own belief, obeying the commands of non-believers (Al-Imrān: 149; Al-Kahf: 28; Al-Ana'm: 121) and above all, following their desires (Al-Baqarah: 120).[32] Ibn Taimmiyah considers *mawālāt* as a sign of hypocrisy but as a part of mitigating circumstances, he exempts a believer who enters into *mawālāt* and is forced to submit to unbelief. He draws this inference from the following Quranic verse: 'Let not the believers take disbelievers for their friends in preference to believers. Whoso doeth that hath no connection with Allah unless (it be) that ye but guard yourselves against them, taking (as it were) security. Allah biddeth you beware (only) of Himself. Unto Allah is the journeying' (Al-Imrān: 28).

Application of *takfīr* becomes liberal with Ibn Taimmiyah when he argues that hypocrisy amounts to *kufr* as well. If a person's acts are inconsistent with his beliefs, he will be considered as a disbeliever in this world and will be liable to the application of the laws of apostasy.[33] It is argued that a label of *takfīr* will not be applied to anyone who establishes prayers unless he is a hypocrite.[34]

Ibn Kathir

The question of friendship with non-believers has been addressed by Ibn Kathir on the basis of the following Quranic evidence: 'Whoso disbelieveth in Allah after his belief – save him who is forced thereto and whose heart is still content with the Faith – but whoso findeth ease in disbelief: On them is wrath from Allah. Theirs will be an awful doom' (An-Nahl: 106).

He draws inference from this verse that, if a believer is forced into disbelief, he has two options, either to go along with the non-believers for self-preservation or to refuse to surrender to disbelief as Bilal did against all odds.[35] Ibn Kathir further suggests that Allah will also forgive those who left their homeland to avoid atrocities of the non-believers being inflicted upon them because of embracing Islam. He draws inference from the following verse: 'Then lo! thy Lord – for those who became fugitives after they had been persecuted, and then fought and were steadfast – lo! Thy Lord afterward is (for them) indeed Forgiving, Merciful' (An-Nahl: 110).

However, approving of unbelief or disapproving of belief may be rephrased otherwise to imply that one forbids something permitted by Allah and His Messenger and permits something that is forbidden. This constitutes heresy, which Ibn Kathir condemns vehemently. To him, *bida'ā* amounts to inventing lies against Allah, and whoever changes what has already been declared permissible (*halāl*) or non-permissible (haram) by Allah according to his own whims and wishes becomes heretic.[36]

Al-Ghazali

The classical theorists have agreed opinion that refutation of truthfulness of whatever the Prophet brought down leads to unbelief. In this pursuit, Imam Abu Jaafar at-Tahawi has defined *kufr* (unbelief) in terms of not accepting what the Prophet brought to be true. He further argues that nothing places a believer outside the pale of Islam other than renouncing the one that brought him into it.[37] Similarly, Ibn Kathir holds that negating a *hadith* that has reached us through diffused congruence (*mutāwātir*) is an act of heresy. For instance, about the incident of *mi'rāj*, there is consensus of the believers in affirmation of *isrā*[38] and if anyone rejects this consensus, he is considered to have committed heresy.[39]

In the same vein, Al-Ghazali defines *kufr* in terms of believing what the Prophet brought to be anything other than truth, and faith is to believe that what the Prophet brought was truth. This definition is comprehensive in its meanings because it covers all aspects of belief and unbelief. For instance, Jews and Christians are considered to be non-believers because they do not affirm the truthfulness of the prophethood of Prophet Muhammad. The pagans are also non-believers because they do not recognize any of the prophets. Atheists also fall in the same category because they do not recognize even the existence of God.[40] He further suggests that implications of the definition of apostasy are very strong, which include legitimizing the killing of someone subjected to *takfīr* and declaring him condemned to hell forever. These implications demand one to be cautious while defining the *kufr*. It must be defined in terms of a legal designation (*hukm-e-shar'i*) on the basis of some evidence in clear text or analogical deduction therefrom instead of following one's own whims and wishes.[41]

Given the sensitivities associated with the issue, Al-Ghazali is very cautious in his approach and prefers silence on the issue because silence entails no liability which *takfīr* involves.[42] For Al-Ghazali, refutation of the fundamentals of Islam (*usūl-ud-dīn*), including belief in God, prophethood and the life hereafter, leads to *kufr*. He further argues that issues which are supported by consensus of the Companions (*ijma'a*) and traditions of the Prophet that have been channelled to us through 'diffused congruence' (*tawātur*) also constitute the basis for *takfīr*.[43] Nevertheless, he recognizes the ambiguity prevailing around those issues whereupon we find consensus of the Companions (*ijma'a*) because some like Al-Nazzam, a Mu'tazilite theologian, may not affirm it as a definitive source in itself.[44] He reasserts that one must not label someone as a non-believer if he believes in God and His Messenger and if there is no reliable evidence to support refutation of this belief.[45]

In brief, a critical examination of the classical theorists leads us to draw the following conclusions:

First, Commission of *bida'ā* does not necessarily attract the label of *kufr*. For example, all three of the classical theorists discussed above have the unanimous opinion that Khawarij and the Shiites, though they committed heresies, could not be labelled as non-believers.

Second, giving up any fundamental constituent of faith amounts to unbelief.

Third, having a view that whatever the Prophet brought is something other than truth amounts to unbelief.

Fourth, commission of a major sin does not put the sinner outside the pale of Islam provided he does not refute the fundamentals of faith. This inference is drawn from the following Quranic verse: 'Lo! Allah pardoneth not that partners should be ascribed unto Him. He pardoneth all save that to whom He will. Whoso ascribeth partners unto Allah hath wandered far astray' (An-Nisā: 116). All those who contradict the view of the Kharjities and the Mautazilites that commission of sin is equal to the commission of unbelief hold this opinion. They refer to a *hadith* wherein the Prophet categorically forbade to label anyone who believes in Allah and His Messenger as a non-believer because of any sin he committed.[46]

Fifth, the classical theorists are very cautious in terms of labelling someone as a non-believer and even amongst heretical circles they exempt those who commit heresy out of ignorance and mistake. For instance, in the classical perspective if one denies the obligatory status of the elements of Islam, he falls in the ambit of apostasy, but even then the mitigating criteria exempt those who hold such views out of ignorance and mistake.[47]

Khurūj

The following discussion will attempt to identify the parameters of obedience to the rulers as laid down by Imam Tahawi, Ibn Kathir and Ibn Taimmiyah.

Imam Tahawi

As the unity of the faithful (*jama'at*) is central to the sociology of Islam, it discourages, by all means, what creates cleavages in the unity of the believers. It enjoins upon the believers not to differ from the majority in the matters of faith. To guard against possible cleavages in *jama'at*, it upholds the validity of prayers behind an imam who is morally upright. It also confirms the validity of funeral prayer for those following Makkah for the prayer's direction (*ahl al-qiblā*). Imam Tahawi argues that the best course to follow for the believers is of the Prophet and of the majority to avoid schisms in their ranks. The prophetic course does not approve of *khurūj* against Muslim rulers even if they commit oppression. Rather, it rules that believers should follow alternative peaceful means to remove the oppression. In view of this, Imam Tahawi develops his point that, as long as the rulers do not force the believers to do something morally wrong, the believers will be religiously obliged to obey them.[48]

The emphasis upon obedience to the rulers aims to preserve collective identity of the believers through their identification with the *jama'at* (group). The Prophet said, 'The Jews divided into seventy-one sects, all of which will go to Hell except one; the Christians will divide into seventy-two sects, all of which will go to Hell except one; this Ummah will divide into seventy-three sects, all of which will go to Hell except one'.[49]

Some people asked the Prophet about the sect which will be saved. He said, 'The one which will follow the way I and my companions follow today'. In another version, the last part of the *hadith* is: 'It will be the *jama'at* and the hand of God will be on the *jama'at'*. Though Islam is not convinced of absolute and unqualified submission to the rulers, at the same time it stresses obedience to those in authority (*ulil amr*[50]) even though they are not ideal.

Ibn Kathir

Similarly, Ibn Kathir also emphasized the overwhelming importance associated with the obedience to those in authority. He rejected outright the Kharij'ite contention against Ali that he violated the Quranic injunctions by consenting to the appointment of arbitrators during the battle of Siffin.[51] He argued that the Quran enjoined upon the believers to resort to human arbitration in the case of a dispute between husband and wife. 'And if ye fear a breach between them twain (the man and wife), appoint an arbiter from his folk and an arbiter from her folk. If they desire amendment Allah will make them of one mind. Lo! Allah is ever Knower, Aware' (An-Nisā: 35). Moreover, he declared the objections raised by Khawarij on the appointment of arbitrators to be unfounded as the Prophet himself effected the Hudaybiah pact with the Quraysh in 6 AH.[52] He further argued that Khawarij also revolted against Amir Mu'awiyah under the leadership of Farwa b. Nau'fal.[53] With Ibn Kathir, we find categorical rejection of the Khawarij because they resorted to *takfīr* of Ali, who had information regarding their commission of robberies and their disregard of what is permissible and what is not.[54] They flouted the religious sanctity attached with human life. Among others, they unjustly killed Abdullah b. Khabab, a Companion of the Prophet, along with his wife. Moreover, they also killed Al-Harrab b. Marra al-Ab'adi, the messenger of Ali.[55]

Ibn Taimmiyah

In furtherance of the same classical narrative, Ibn Taimmiyah has quoted many Quranic verses and traditions of the Prophet, which highlight the importance of obedience to those in authority. For instance, Ibn Taimmiyah categorically makes it clear that the final authority to rule rests with Allah and His Messenger because no one except the Messenger is infallible and obedience is only in right things.[56] He substantiates his argument with the Quranic evidence. 'O ye who believe! Obey Allah, and obey the messenger and those of you who are in authority; and if ye have a dispute concerning any matter, refer it to Allah and the messenger if ye are (in truth) believers in Allah and the Last Day. That is better and more seemly in the end. You who believe! Obey God and obey the Messenger and those charged with authority among you. If you differ in anything among yourselves refer it to God and His Messenger' (An-Nisā: 59). The Quran further says, 'Mankind were one community, and Allah sent (unto them) prophets as bearers of good tidings and as warners, and revealed therewith the Scripture with the truth that it might judge between mankind concerning that wherein they differed. And only those unto whom (the Scripture) was given differed concerning it, after clear proofs had come unto them, through hatred one of another. And Allah by His Will guided those who believe unto the truth of that concerning which they differed. Allah guideth whom He will unto a straight path' (Al-Baqarah: 213).

Another Quranic verse makes the ultimate authority of God and His Messenger transcendent in these words: 'And in whatsoever ye differ, the verdict therein belongeth to Allah. Such is my Lord, in Whom I put my trust, and unto Whom I turn' (Ash-Shūrā: 10). Moreover, Ubadah b. As-Samit stated that they pledged to the Prophet to render their obedience even in case of individual injustice.[57] Another *hadith* reported on the authority of Abu Hurayrah embodies the same general idea wherein the Prophet commanded the believers to extend their obedience to the rulers even in case of individual injustice.[58] Ibn Taimmiyah has quoted another *hadith* on the authority of Usayd b. Hudayr that an individual from *ansār* requested the Prophet to award him any post the way awarded to others. The Prophet asked him to be patient even if he did not get what was due to him after the Prophet.[59] Ibn Taimmiyah declares the importance attached to the obedience to those in authority equal to the importance of prayers, fasting and pilgrimage.[60] He quoted another tradition of the Prophet wherein the Prophet stressed the importance of obedience to the Amir (ruler) being part of the *jama'at* and declared that anyone who died being in the state of *khurūj* (revolt) to *Amir* died the death of *jāhilliyah*h.[61] To emphasize the importance of obedience to *ulil amr* (those in authority), Ibn Taimmiyah quoted many traditions wherein the Prophet urged the believers to obey Amir even if he may be a slave with limbs cut off.[62] Ibn Taimmiyah quoted another *hadith*, which makes clear that, even if one sees a ruler committing some sin, he should not withdraw his obedience. In other words, if a ruler is not ideal and lacks the qualifications required to become *khalīfāh,* he still has the right to obedience provided he does not forego any fundamental of the faith.[63]

Nevertheless, the Sunnite perspective as a whole has been divided on the question of *khurūj.* A major section of the Sunnites believes in non-permissibility of *khurūj* even if the rulers happen to be oppressors, commit violence against the believers unjustly and are involved in impiety.[64] However, Imam Abu Hanifa, being moderate on the issue, affirmed theological legitimacy of revolt on utilitarian grounds. For him, *khurūj* is justified if it replaces the oppressor rulers with just and pious ones. He argued that ordaining good and forbidding evil through peaceful means was mandatory at the first instance. However, he retained the option of armed revolt if the peaceful means fail,[65] but the course of armed revolt should not be adopted if the chances of success are not evident.[66] His views about *khurūj* got practical exposition in the way he supported the *khurūj* of Imam Zaid b. Ali. Though, he supported his *khurūj* by even identifying it with the Prophet's battle at Badr in terms of religious legitimacy, he restricted himself only to financial support of the revolt as he feared that the revolt had little chance of success. In the case of the *khurūj* of Nafs-e-Zakkiyah,[67] he categorically supported the *khurūj* against the Abbasids. He declared the act of supporting the revolutionaries more important than jihad against the non-believers.[68] He declared participation in this *khurūj* to be an act of piety 50 times higher than a supererogatory pilgrimage.[69] Distinguished scholars including Abu Bakr Jassas, Al-Mua'fiq Al-Makki and Ibn Al-Bazzaz have quoted the statements of Imam Abu Hanifa. Actually, he believed that, if chances of success of a noble *khurūj* were conspicuous, it would become mandatory (*wājib*) on the believers to stand with the revolutionaries.[70] Imam Malik also shared this view. He was asked whether it was permissible to support the *khurūj* while bound by allegiance to the Abbasids. He declared allegiance to the Abbasids as void as being forced upon the believers and, therefore, that this provided space for theological legitimacy for public support to *khurūj.* For this, he had to face physical torture by Jaafar b. Salman, the Abbasid governor.

It is to be noted that, with regard to *khurūj*, Imam Abu Hanifa's standpoint is not a solitary example; rather, all the noted scholars shared this view during the 1st century AH. Abu Bakr in his first address after assuming the office of the caliph made his obedience conditional on his obedience to Allah and His Prophet. Moreover, consultation (*shūrā*) with the believers at large grants legitimacy to the *bāy'ā'*. Umar ibn Al-Khattab did not believe in legitimacy of *baya'ā* made without consultation with the believers.[71] Imam Hussain arose against the unjust rule of Yazid b. Mu'awiyah. Imam Abu Hanifa upheld the same tradition when he argued that revolt against an invalid ruler was not impermissible in itself. However, chances of success of a noble revolt should be ascertained beforehand. Similarly, when Abdul Rehman ibn Ash'ath resorted to *khurūj* against the oppressive governance of

Hajjaj ibn Yousouf, he had the support of leading ulema and jurists, including Saeed b. Jubair, Ibn Abi Laila and Abu Al-Jantri.[72] Even those who did not support Ibn Ash'ath, like Hassan Basri, did not declare the *khurūj* impermissible as such; rather, they refrained from support out of pragmatic considerations.[73] However, later on, the majority of Sunnite ulema, in view of the repeated failures of these attempts of armed revolt, developed a narrative that would not provide any space to *khurūj*.

Limitations of obedience

This should not lead to the presumption that Islam gives unimpeachable authority to the rulers. It affirms subordination of the rulers' authority to the Will of God. Islam recognizes Allah to be the final law-giving authority, and it ordains that human decision making must conform to the divine commandments. 'Whoso judgeth not by that which Allah hath revealed: such are disbelievers' (Al-Maidah: 44). It further says, 'And it becometh not a believing man or a believing woman, when Allah and His messenger have decided an affair (for them), that they should (after that) claim any say in their affair; and whoso is rebellious to Allah and His messenger, he verily goeth astray in error manifest' (Al-Ahzāb: 36).

Human decision making depends upon its obedience to the final omnipotent authority for legitimacy. The rulers lose their right to command the obedience of the believers if they disobey the Creator.[74] It further ordains that human decision making should conform to the divine commandments. The Quran identifies obedience to the Prophet with divine obedience in the following words: 'Whoso obeyeth the messenger hath obeyed Allah, and whoso turneth away: We have not sent thee as a warder over them' (An-Nisā: 80). Both the Quran and *hadith* are the primary sources for the believers to draw legitimacy for their decision making. This qualified authority was well acknowledged by the *salaf*. On assuming the office of the caliph, Abu Bakr made it clear to the believers that obedience to him was incumbent upon them as long as he remains obedient to Allah. During the period of the *salaf*, the caliph did not have veto power; rather, all the decisions were made in consultation with the noted Companions (*ahl al- hall wa'l-aqd*) of the Prophet. Though on certain occasions, the caliph overruled the opinion of the *shūrā,* this overruling of the opinion of the Companions cannot be identified with the use of veto power by the caliph. Rather, it was Allah's and His Prophet's verdict which was upheld. Veto power vested with Allah and His apostle. During his last days, the Prophet dispatched an expedition against the Byzantines under the command of Usama b. Zayd. The troops had just left Madina when they received the news of the demise of the Prophet. The expedition was postponed for the time being. When Abu Bakr assumed the office of the caliph, the Islamic state was faced with serious security challenges from within and without. The Companions proposed either to defer the expedition to ensure the availability of troops within

Madina to face any possible security threat or to replace young Usama with a senior war veteran. Against these suggestions, Abu Bakr upheld the decision of the Prophet. The same narrative is followed by authentic Sunnite scholarship like Ibn Taimmiyah. For instance, he argues that, since the rulers (*ulil amr*) draw their right to obedience through divine commandments, in case of their disobedience to God, they, as a logical consequence, lose their right to obedience.[75]

The standpoint of the *salaf* and narrative of the authentic Muslim scholarship vis-à-vis Khawarij leads to the following conclusions.

First, Islam attaches paramount significance to obedience to the rulers even if they happen to be imperfect. This obedience is revoked only if the rulers refute any fundamental of faith. Muslim scholarship avoids approving of *khurūj* if it is likely to create anarchy.

Second, there are many traditions of the Prophet which reflect prophetic condemnation of the Kharjities. For example, he said, 'He is not of my Ummah who rises against my Ummah, kills people good and bad, and spares neither a believer nor any of our clients (dhimmis). He is not of us nor are we of him'.[76] The Prophet further said about these people that their reading of the Quran will hardly go down their throats. They will dart out of Islam just as an arrow passes out through a prey. They will be the worst creature under the sky. Glad tidings for those who kill them or are killed by them.[77] All this leads us to argue that clear prophetic transmissions are available permitting a fight against Khawarij; Ali fought against them, and the *salaf* had consensus upon fighting against them.

Religious necessity of the caliphate

The Islamic political system is based upon divine sovereignty. The prophets were assigned a leadership role for the guidance of humanity not only in religious matters but also in the socio-political sphere. The Prophet is reported to have said, 'The political leadership of Banī Israel was with their prophets. When one messenger had passed away, another would have taken his place. But after me, there would be no prophet but *khulāfā*'.[78] Allah concentrated a multi-dimensional leadership role in His prophets. As the chain of prophethood reached its end with Prophet Muhammad, the leadership role was transferred to the caliphs who, acting as deputies of the Prophet, would perform this leadership role for the believers. In this sense, the political system of Islam is labelled as caliphate. The caliph, as deputy of the Prophet, is responsible for the enforcement of Shariah and discharge of executive, military and political affairs. Anyone who assumes this leadership role is bound to follow the course enunciated by the Shariah.

The caliphate thus established would be conspicuously distinct from theocracy wherein the ruler is taken as divine representative whose disobedience amounts to defiance of God. Theocracy rejects all types of limitations, and the rulers assume unimpeachable authority. The caliph by no means has infallible status and is strictly accountable to the masses for his conduct. He assumes the office with the consultation of the fellow believers and is accountable to them for his conduct as well. His authority is disciplined and bound by the laws of the Quran and Sunnah. The structure of government in Islam is based upon four grounds: (1) government comes into existence through the will of the people; (2) the caliph will be bound by the Shariah; (3) the will of the people will be subordinate to the laws of the Quran and the Sunnah; and (4) the caliph will be accountable to the people. Having defined the cardinal principles of state governance, Islam does not insist upon establishing a particular form of government but rather leaves it to the discretion of the believers to undertake any system within the confines of these broader principles. Islam is least concerned about nomenclature but definitely about the nature of governance. Once it is established that the chief executive will act as deputy of the Prophet and will discharge his responsibilities according to his Sunnah, the title of government becomes irrelevant. It is evident from Quranic accounts of four distinguished personalities. Prophet Dawud and prophet Suleman were kings besides being prophets whereas prophet Yousouf was vizier to a king. God Himself announced the kingship of Talut. The following inferences are drawn:

First, Muslim government will be subordinate to the Sunnah of the Prophet for the enforcement of Shariah and discharge of its functions. Second, Muslims are obliged to establish this government. Third, any nomenclature can be used for such government.

Public consent

Caliphate does not come into existence through an arbitrary process. Rather, its legitimacy depends upon public consent behind it. This is evidently expressed through the following tradition of the Prophet: 'Your good rulers are those who love you and you love them and your bad rulers are those who despise you and are despicable to you'.[79] The political system of Islam stands on mutual trust between the rulers and the ruled. In this perspective, Umar prohibited the believers from following someone who pledges allegiance to someone without *shūrā* and refused to acknowledge the one to whom allegiance is pledged as imam of the believers.[80] The procedure followed for the selection of the pious caliphs reflects the ideal level of public trust. The consultation was not limited to a few chosen ones; rather, the whole community pledged allegiance to Abu Bakr when he was selected the first caliph of Islam. Owing to this broad level of consultation, his selection is regarded to have been made through consensus of the believers (*Ijma'a-e-Ummah*). When Imam Hassan surrendered his right to caliphate to Amir Mu'awiyah, the latter became caliph of the believers through consensus.[81] After Amir Mu'awiyah, the ideal level of legitimacy that was secured through public consent declined when arbitrary nomination replaced selection through public consent. The phenomenon of arbitrary selection that started with the nomination of Yazid would come to its end with the very elimination of the institution itself in the first quarter of the 20th century. The Sunnah of the Companions of the Prophet regarding the selection of the caliphs suggests that three types of selection procedures are permissible: (1) the caliph is selected through consensus of the Ummah; (2) the caliph nominates anyone as his successor who fulfils the qualifications for the office; (3) anyone who qualifies for the office captures the political authority and strengthens his control over it. However, the most secure of all these selection types was the one adopted for the selection of Abu Bakr through consensus of the believers.[82]

The expression of public trust to the caliph may be either through direct or indirect procedure. Ibn Taimmiyah and Abdul Wahab Sherani believe in direct expression of public consent whereas Imam Nawwi and Shah Waliullah are convinced of its indirect expression through those who loose and bind (*ahl al- hall wa'l-aqd*).[83] Shah Waliullah includes ulema, Qadis, the ruling class, military commanders and those who are well-wishers of the believers in the definition of *ahl al- hall wa'l-aqd*. It is not to suggest in any case that, if a few people pledge allegiance to a caliph, it becomes obligatory upon the rest to follow suit. It is pertinent to refer to the last Friday sermon of Umar, which is narrated by Imam Bukhari. Umar was told about a few people who had mutually decided that, when Umar passes away, they would select someone their caliph and others will have to pledge allegiance to the caliph of their choice. Umar warned the believers that those who intend to select caliph without consultation with the believers as a whole actually intend to usurp the right of the believers in general to select the caliph. He vehemently stressed the believers should not pledge allegiance to such a person. The method of selection of the caliph by a committee of a chosen few as happened in the case of selection of Uthman does not revoke the general body of believers' right to express their consent. Imam Bukhari has quoted that Abdul Rehman b. Auf, a distinguished member of the selection committee for third caliph, went door to door in Madina to ascertain the opinion of the general believers. When he found public opinion in favour of Uthman, he pledged his allegiance to him. Ibn Auf opted to ascertain public opinion directly; yet, evidence is also available which suggests that the Prophet discovered public opinion indirectly through public representatives. After the battle of Hunayn, the Prophet returned the war captives of Banu Hawazan by securing believers' indirect opinion through their representatives.[84] In brief, hereditary kingship is far from an ideal political system that Islam envisages but has been acknowledged by the Muslim scholars as an unavoidable necessity to secure the Ummah from further anarchy. The ideal form remains the caliphate of Abu Bakr, which was established through the consensus amongst the believers.[85]

Instruments of political divide

Political parties are prerequisites in the modern democratic political process. Though the party system cannot be traced back to early Islamic age, the question of its theological legitimacy requires further inquiry because the party system in terms of an instrument of political divide was not then in existence in society. Instead of a party system, tribal affiliations were the instruments of political division. The political landscape of Makkah was characterized by the divide between the Ummayads and the Hashmites, whereas in Yathrab, Banu Aus and Banu Khazraj were at daggers drawn. Islam has affirmed this political divide on the trajectory of tribal affiliations (*assābiyah*) as well. This affirmation was reflected in military formations on tribal basis during the battle of Badr. Moreover, believers' division between *ansār* (helpers at Madina) and *muhajirīn* (emigrants from Makkah) also reflect a new typology of political divide. The Prophet handed separate battle flags to *ansār* (helpers at Madina) and *muhajirīn* (emigrants from Makkah) at Badr. When the Prophet passed away, this divide got more pronounced as was evident during the selection process of Abu Bakr as the first caliph of Islam. It not only continued to characterize the political landscape of Madina, but it also got recognition from the Prophet and his Companions. On this premise, there evolved an argument that Islam permits political dissent as long as it does not damage the integrity of Muslim Ummah. In view of the above, the existence of political parties as a modern instrument of political divide becomes permissible provided this works for the furtherance of believers' cause. Political parties may provide a space wherein the nationalist ideological cause may ascend to foster transnational ideological bonds. A broader ideological brotherhood of territorial Muslim states becomes possible without surrendering their respective nationalist identities. This ideological fraternity can be achieved through keeping mutual disputes subservient to aspirations for broader unity.

Candidature

With regard to candidature for any position, it is often argued that Islam does not approve of offering one's own self for a particular slot. Had this been the case, prophet Suleman and prophet Yousouf would not have yearned for kingship and vizierate. Thus, offering one's services for a particular slot is not impermissible in itself. The Prophet did not accede to the requests for appointments to certain slots for certain reasons. He did not accede to Abu Dharr Ghaffari's request to be appointed as administrator because of his incapacity to secure public trust.[86] The Prophet also declined to appoint someone administrator on the grounds that someone wanting the role could not be posted to this position.[87] Again, the Prophet advised Abdul Rehman b. Sumra not to demand authority (*imārah*) because its achievement without demand is followed by the divine help whereas if it is achieved on demand, it is left to one's own responsibility.[88] Another prophetic tradition makes the issue even more clear. The Prophet is reported to have said, 'Whosoever amongst the believers secured the position of Qadi (judge), if his justice remained dominant over his injustice, he would be rewarded with paradise and if his injustice prevailed on his justice, he would be condemned to hell'.[89] Thus, distinguished ulema like Sheikh Abdul Haq Dehlvi and Maulana Zafar Uthmani made the point that, if one had the confidence to fulfil the responsibilities associated with the slot and did not demand it for the sake of power but service to humankind, it is not impermissible to make such a demand. Moreover, in-depth inquiry into the traditions of the Prophet regarding the prohibitions of demand for a slot makes it evident that these prohibitions are not exclusively directed against political positions but also against judicial and executive slots as well. If offering one's services for judicial and executive positions becomes impermissible, the entire state structure would cease to function. The suggested course is to make arrangements which allow only those to assume such posts who qualify for these offices in terms of capabilities and integrity.[90]

However, the structure of democratic governance in its western connotations stands upon four grounds, which include popular sovereignty, secularism, nationalism and public participation in the decision-making process. Islam categorically rejects the first two grounds whereas it accepts nationalism with certain qualifications. The Islamic perspective on nationalism finds better exposition with Iqbal[91], for whom Muslim nationalism can lead to Islamic universalism. In this sense, the creation of Pakistan was not regarded as an end in itself but rather as a means for the revival of Islam. He was averse to the idea of territorial nationalism if taken as an end in itself but he approved if it was taken as a stepping stone for the revival of Muslim universalism. Some may seek to highlight nationalism as being against to the spirit of the faith, relying upon the historical accounts of different prophets who preferred to migrate from their homelands for the sake of faith. They draw inferences that the prophets preferred faith to their national identities. Actually, this perspective fails to identify the underlying spirit of the prophets' migration from their homelands. The objective of migration was not to establish the competing levels of loyalties towards homeland or faith. The migration aimed to achieve the objectives of projecting and protecting the faith against the forces of infidelity. The prophets' ultimate objective was to make the 'word of God' dominant, and hijra may be viewed in terms of acquiring a space to make efforts to achieve this goal. Had it been possible in Makkah, the Prophet might not have shifted to Madina. Likewise, the Prophet did not ask the believers to eschew their tribal affiliations but subordinated these tribal identities to their ideological identity. Similarly, it is not imperative to shun the national identities of the believers today, but these can be subordinated to a broader ideological identity through diffusion of conflicts within the Muslim states on the model of the European Union. Moreover, the history of the evolution of the medieval Muslim thought suggests that revisions in the state structure have not been taken as threats to the faith as such. Initially, as discussed elsewhere, Al-Māwardi in his *Ahkām al-Sultāniyyah* supported a unified Muslim caliphate of the Qurayshite descent.[92] However, this version underwent radical revisions with Ibn Khaldun who, in addition to waiving the condition of Qurayshite ancestry of the caliph, sought to legitimize the plurality of caliphates on pragmatic grounds. He argued that expansion of Muslim rule would render it difficult for a caliph to exercise political control across the Muslim lands because, in this case, his position would be relegated to spiritual headship devoid of political authority, which Islam does not idealize.[93] Nevertheless, owing to the intellectual dynamism of the faith, these radical revisions did not translate into threats against the faith as such that may warrant violence on the pretext of defending the body of faith. Furthermore, besides other variables, violence against Muslim nation-states is a failure on the part of the militants to view a Muslim nation-state as an integral part of a broader but diffused ideological nationhood instead of an isolated entity. They fail to understand that their violent disapproval of the very concept of the nation-state as a colonial hangover will not bring any good to the larger interest of the Muslim Ummah. Rather, it will weaken the Muslims' military and state power. The violence against Muslim states finds no place with Islamic theology. Even the medieval Muslim scholars like Ibn Taimmiyah whom the militants take as a resource stressed that jihad in terms of enjoining good and forbidding evil should be launched when its benefits (*maslaha*) outweigh its adverse effects (*mufāsidah*).[94] They make this inference from the following Quranic injunction: 'O'you who believe, yourselves are your personality, those who go astray will not harm you when you stick to guidance' (Al-Maid'ah: 105).

As said earlier, though consensus exists that caliphate on the pattern of Prophethood is the ideal Islamic system, Muslim scholarship accepted the transformation of caliphate into *malūkiyyat* (hereditary kingship) though hesitatingly. On the question of obedience to invalid rulers, Ibn Taimmiyah's standpoint is moderate vis-à-vis Khawarij, Mu'tazilah and Murji'ah. Khawarij and Mu'tazilah condemned the attempts to dispense with caliphate on the doctrine of necessity whereas Murji'ah considered monarchy as a legitimate form of political order at least in principle. To Ibn Taimmiyah, monarchy as a form of government is a shift from caliphate; therefore, it constitutes *bida'ā* (innovation). He substantiates his argument with a tradition of the Prophet, who urged the believers to follow his way and the way of the pious caliphs.[95] However, Ibn Taimmiyah does not permit the believers to revolt against the monarchical system for not being the ideal political system. He argues that, though establishing caliphate is obligatory upon every believer, this obligation could be dispensed with through the doctrine of necessity. It becomes acceptable only if it promotes governance (*vilayah*).[96] He further makes it clear that to command obedience is the right of the rulers as long as they do not command something sinful and as long as they do not forego any part of Shariah.[97] He further explains that if someone believes in the unity of God and the prophethood but foregoes an element of Islam like Prayers, Fasting in Ramadan, Charity or Pilgrimage to Makkah, he will be fought against until he reverts to the right track.[98]

Ibn Taimmiyah does not permit believers to resort to *khurūj* against those in authority even if their level of legitimacy is lesser than the pious caliphs and they do not come up to the ideal criteria as laid down by Islam. He further believes that, even in case of individual injustice on the part of rulers, believers are not entitled to revolt against them. Moreover, transformation of caliphate into a monarchical system does not permit the believers to commit *khurūj* against the rulers simply because they are monarchical in character. However, if the rulers forego any part of Shariah, they lose their right to obedience, and it becomes mandatory upon the believers to uproot them. It was on this ground that he issued a fatwa against the Mongol rulers when he visited their camps and found no arrangement for prayers (*iqāmat-e-salāt*).

As far as Ibn Kathir is concerned, his position on the question of monarchy is not much different from Ibn Taimmiyah. He does not permit the believers to revolt against the monarchical order and draws justification for monarchy, though in terms of an invalid political system as compared to prophetic pattern of political governance. He draws inference from a tradition of the Prophet wherein he is reported to have asked Amir Mu'awiyah to be good and considerate if he got political authority.[99] Moreover, Umar b. al-Khattab neither approved nor condemned the pomp and show which was peculiar to monarchy displayed by Amir Mu'awiyah in the capacity of governor of Syria.[100] There are still others who argue in favour of monarchy but as having a lesser degree of legitimacy as compared to caliphate on the pattern of the Prophet (*khilāfat an-nubuwwah*), indeed on the basis of following traditions of the Prophet as the Prophet had anticipated that political authority on prophetic pattern would last for only 30 years.[101] The Prophet further stated, 'The people of Israel were ruled by their prophets. Whenever a prophet died, another prophet took his place. But there will be no prophet after me; there will be only deputies (*khulāfā*), and they will be many'. Thereupon the people asked him, 'What do you advise us to do?' He said, 'Keep the pledge you make to one who comes first and then to the one who comes next, and give them their due, for God will call them to account for the people He puts under them'.[102]

Fixing the sectarian context

As discussed elsewhere, the sectarian narrative that developed during the course of Muslim history identifies the issues that led to differences and the resultant souring of relationships between the family of the Prophet and the first three caliphs of Islam. The following discussion seeks to refute this narrative through revisiting the primary text. The counter narrative attempts to discover the historical evidence that relationships between the family of the Prophet and his first three caliphs were based upon mutual affection, cooperation and respect. It challenges the argument that differences between the two camps became the basis for the schisms amongst their supporters in the ages to come. The evidence suggests that affectionate behaviour of the Companions of the Prophet is part of how they have been defined in the Quran. On this premise, the following discussion seeks to suggest that this affectionate behaviour of the Prophet's family members and Companions of the Prophet remained evident not only in the days of the Prophet but during the entire course of the orthodox caliphate.

The Quran is witness to the sublime character of the Companions which reflects mutual affection and unity in their ranks as an inalienable trait of their personalities that unite them into an ideological brotherhood (Al-Hujarat: 10, Al-Imrān: 103).[103] The Quran further defines the Companions of the Prophet as follows, 'Muhammad is the messenger of Allah. And those with him are hard against the disbelievers and merciful among themselves. Thou (O Muhammad) seest them bowing and falling prostrate (in worship), seeking bounty from Allah and (His) acceptance. The mark of them is on their foreheads from the traces of prostration. Such is their likeness in the Torah and their likeness in the Gospel – like as sown corn that sendeth forth its shoot and strengtheneth it and riseth firm upon its stalk, delighting the sowers – that He may enrage the disbelievers with (the sight of) them. Allah hath promised, unto such of them as believe and do good works, forgiveness and immense reward'. (Al-Fatah: 48)

This verse highlights four personal traits of the Companions, which include strictness against non-believers, being mutually affectionate, absorption in prayers and reflection of piety in their faces. These characteristics are neither peculiar to a particular class of the Companions nor meant for a specific timeframe. These are eternal traits of all the Companions like the message of the Quran itself. Similarly, the Prophet declared the believers to be part of a whole instead of isolated entities. The following discussion, while relying upon the evidence from private and public lives of family members of the Prophet and the first three caliphs, seeks to suggest that their lives reflect practical exposition of the Quranic expression of their personality traits. Evidence will be produced to reject the perception that their mutual conduct was fraught with differences.

Nature of the relationship between the family of the Prophet and his Companions

During the days of the Prophet, the Companions were bound together in cordial relationships. The cordiality between the Companions and the Prophet's family was evident on the eve of *nikah* (marriage) of Ali al-Murtaza and Fatima al-Zahra, daughter of the Prophet. Similar mutual cordiality is evident between *Ummahāt al-Mu'minīn* (mothers of the believers)[104] and Fatima al-Zahra on this occasion.[105] However, it was not a solitary occasion of mutual affection amongst these exalted personalities. It was a regular feature of their mutual relationship. Ayesha Siddiqa has been reported to have said that she never witnessed someone having more of a resemblance of speech than Fatima with the Prophet. She further states that whenever Fatima had come to visit the Prophet, he would stand up to welcome her. Ayesha Siddiqa has been reported as stating that she had not witnessed anyone more truthful than Fatima except the Prophet himself.[106] Al-Haythami quoted Ayesha as declaring Fatima to be the best human being after the Prophet himself.[107] Similarly, Fatima's conduct, too, was exemplary towards Ayesha.[108] The Prophet himself had advised her to have affection with Ayesha.[109] The mutual trust between them continued to exist even after the Prophet. The trust level between them was so high that, on one occasion, Fatima shared an otherwise confidential talk between herself and the Prophet with Ayesha.[110]

The mutual trust continued to exist between Ayesha and Ali even after the demise of Fatima. For juristic opinion regarding performing ablution through running hands on feet from over the socks (*massah al'al-khuffayn)*, Ayesha referred the issue to Ali.[111] Moreover, in response to Ali's declaration of fasting on the day of *Ashura*, Ayesha acknowledged Ali to be the best amongst all in his understanding of prophetic Sunnah.[112] Abu Bakr, father of Ayesha, was the one who shifted Ali's mother Fatima b. Asad to the grave along with the Prophet and Abbas b. Abdul Muttalib, and Umar was amongst those who prepared the grave.[113] Tragic incidents like the battle of *Camel* and Siffin could not lessen this trust level. When Ayesha received the news of Ali's martyrdom, she prayed for him with sincerity and devotion. During the last days of Ayesha, Ibn Abbas visited her and narrated her prophetic transmission in which the Prophet had stated that Ayesha would be his wife in paradise, too. On hearing this narration, Ayesha prayed for Ibn Abbas.[114] Ibn Jozi has quoted a number of traditions wherein Ali was reported to have highlighted the exalted status of Abu Bakr. In one of the traditions, Ali was reported to have said that Abu Bakr would be the foremost amongst the believers to enter the paradise after the Prophet.[115] Ibn Sa'ad has quoted Ali saying that Abu Bakr and Umar were rightly guided (*rāshidūn*) in true sense.[116] Imam Bukhari has recorded a *hadith* in Sahih Bukhari, which amply highlights the cordiality of relationships between Ali and Abu Bakr. Uqbah b. Al-Harith narrates that once he saw Abu Bakr carrying Al-Hassan and saying, 'Let my father be sacrificed for you; you resemble the prophet and not Ali', while Ali was smiling.[117] In yet another *hadith* recorded in Sahih Bukhari on the authority of Ibn Umar, Abu Bakr has been reported to have said, 'In order to please the family of the Prophet, do good to his family'.[118]

Financial rights of the Prophet's family during the Caliphate of Abu Bakr

Abu Bakr, the first caliph, followed the Prophet without even slight deviation to protect the financial rights of the Prophet's family. By following a proverb that your friend's friend is your own friend, he religiously endeavoured to fulfil his obligations towards the family of the Prophet. He is reported to have said that he would love to do more good to the relatives of the Prophet rather than to his own relatives.[119] With regard to financial rights of the family of the Prophet in terms of prophetic inheritance in three areas which included *sadāqāt* from Madina, income from Fidak and *khums* from Khyber, Abu Bakr decided according to a tradition of the Prophet. The Prophet said that whatever the prophets leave behind (*taraka*) do not count as inheritance but as *sadāqā*. On this ground, although he did not acknowledge inheritance rights of the members of the Prophet's family in these areas, he continued to meet their daily life expenditures from the income generated from these sources.[120] In view of the foregoing, the following inferences may be drawn: the family of the Prophet continued to receive their financial rights from these sources exactly the way they used to receive during the days of the Prophet. The decision not to grant inheritance rights over these sources of income was actually not due to the caliph's discretion; rather, it emerged out of a prophetic transmission.

The certification of Imam Baqir that the Prophet's family did not face any injustice during the caliphate of the first two caliphs has been confirmed by the Sunnite as well as Shiite scholarship.[121] Imam Zayd too confirmed that the Prophet's family did not face any injustice on the issue of Fidak. He said that, if he were in the place of Abu Bakr, he would have taken the same decision on the issue of Fidak.[122] It is to be noted that all the pious caliphs including Ali retained the status of Fidak as a source of income for the family of the Prophet instead of a transferable piece of inheritance.

Ali's Baya'ā to Abu Bakr and his role in the state administration

Ali and a few other Companions pledged their *baya'ā* to the first caliph within a short span. This is established from a narration reported by Abu Saeed al-Khudri, which has been quoted by Ibn Kathir and others, including Imam Ahmad, al-Hakim and Bayhaqi in their works.[123] Ibn Kathir has argued that Ali and Zubair b. Al-Awwam pledged their allegiance to Abu Bakr on the same day.[124] Al-Hadid, a Shiite scholar, in his commentary on *Nehj-ul Balagha* has also quoted that though Ali and Zubair developed temporary reservations for not being consulted on the issue of caliphate, they expressed their agreement on the right of Abu Bakr to the caliphate on the grounds that Abu Bakr accompanied the Prophet in the Cave and further, the Prophet directed him to lead the prayers during his illness.[125] Ibn Sa'ad has also quoted a tradition on the authority of Hassan that Ali himself said that when the Prophet chose Abu Bakr to lead prayers during his illness, they chose him to lead in the temporal sphere as well.[126] Further, it is established that Ali never left Abu Bakr and always offered his prayers behind Abu Bakr. He also accompanied Abu Bakr in fighting against the apostates after the Prophet.

Moreover, Ali was amongst the leading jurists during the period of first two caliphs who used to consult him frequently on questions of jurisprudence and state administration.[127] The decision to fight against those who refused to pay zakat was made in consultation with Ali, who had argued that even a meagre relaxation in the collection of zakat would amount to violation of the Prophet's conduct.[128] Importance associated with Ali's advice in military affairs is reflected in an incident which has been quoted by numerous Muslim historians, including Ibn Kathir. Ayesha narrates that once Abu Bakr dropped his plan to command a military campaign by himself on the argument of Ali that, if anything bad had happened to him, the Islamic system would have lost its true direction.[129] The Shiite narrations also confirm that Ali was proactive in his cooperation in state administration during the caliphate of Abu Bakr. During the initial days of Abu Bakr's caliphate, Ali rose against the apostates of Arabia for their elimination.[130] Again, in the wake of threats of attack on Madina during the early days of the first caliph, Ali himself guarded the city.[131]

In the preceding discussion, it has been observed that Ali pledged allegiance to Abu Bakr willingly after his assuming office of the caliphate. Abu Bakr also protected the financial rights of the family of the Prophet with utmost caution. The authentic sources confirm mutual trust between Abu Bakr and the Prophet's family. Ali's participation in decision making during the period of the first caliph is testimony to this mutual trust. This trust exposes the invalidity of sectarian narrative, which thrives upon mutual misgivings between Abu Bakr and the Prophet's family. This ideal level of cordiality amongst the Companions of the Prophet continued to exist during the caliphate of Umar as well.

Ali's Baya'ā to Umar and his role in the state administration

During his last days, Abu Bakr proposed Umar as the next caliph of the believers. Prior to public announcement of the proposed nominee, when the believers came to know that someone amongst them had been proposed to be the caliph, Ali categorically stated that he would not accept anyone but Umar to be the next caliph.[132] When Umar's nomination was made public, he instantly pledged his allegiance to him along with others.[133] Besides this, the evidence suggests that Ali, on assuming the office of caliphate himself, referred to his willing *baya'ā* to all his precursors.[134] In view of the willing *baya'ā* on the part of Ali, it is argued that legitimacy of the caliphate was through consensus amongst the Companions and the members of the family of the Prophet.

The mutual trust between Ali and the second caliph of Islam is further reflected in the former's frequent appreciation for the latter. When Ali was requested to assume the office of the caliph immediately after the martyrdom of Uthman, he appreciated Umar's model for the selection of the caliph through the instrument of *shūrā* and deferred the matter for its finalization on the same pattern.[135] Moreover, Ali identified Abu Bakr and Umar as amongst the 14 nobles divinely gifted to the Prophet from his Ummah.[136] In a tradition, Ali has been reported to have acknowledged Umar to be the one who ascertains right from wrong.[137] He also reiterated a prophetic tradition wherein the Prophet prayed for honour to the faith through Umar.[138] Ibn Jozi has quoted a *hadith* wherein Ali has been reported to have said that the Prophet declared that Umar and Abu Bakr would be the chiefs of elderly people in paradise with the exception only of the prophets.[139] On another occasion, Ali declared Umar pious,[140] strong and trustworthy.[141] In another tradition, Ali acknowledged the contributions of both Abu Bakr and Umar for the glory of Ummah. He declared them to be righteous and torchbearers for the believers.[142] Ali has been reported to have identified Umar and Abu Bakr as ideal personalities for the believers forever and further that love for them is mandatory to get closeness with faith.[143] He declared both of them to be the best personalities after the Prophet.[144] In his meeting with a delegation of Christians from Najran, Ali appreciated Umar's capability to make good decisions (*rāshid-ul-amr*) and thus always upheld his decisions.[145] Given his appreciation of Umar's administrative capabilities, Ali continued with his administrative reforms during his own caliphate. In this background, some like Yahya b. al-Adam al-Qarshi (d. 203 AH) argue that both had similar life characters (*seerah*).[146]

Like Abu Bakr, Umar continued consulting Ali on the important issues of governance and religious interpretation.[147] Ibn Abbas reports that Umar declared Ali to be the best judge (Qadi).[148] On assuming the office, Umar asked Ali to adjudicate amongst the people.[149] Thus, as narrated by Ibn Kathir, he appointed Ali as chief justice of Madina.[150] It is to be noted that though Ali worked as chief justice of Madina, in matters of his own disputes he would voluntarily come to Umar for decisions.[151] This reflects his complete trust in the uprightness and justice of Umar.[152] The authentic sources of Islamic history are replete with the examples where Umar sought Ali's juristic opinion on administrative and judicial matters. Umar decided to go to liberate Al-Aqsa personally in 15 AH on the advice of Ali.[153] For organizing *tarāweeh* prayers[154] in the mosques, Ali prayed for Umar.[155] It is also established that Umar used to hold Ali and his sons Husnain in high esteem. Umar making Ali as his deputy umpteen times is a reflection of cordiality in the relationship between the two.[156] Ibn Abbas narrates that, when Umar passed away, Ali invoked Allah's mercy upon him and said that no one is left behind whose deeds are as enviable as those of Umar. He further prayed that Allah keep Umar and his two associates (the Prophet and Abu Bakr) together.[157] This cordiality is also evident from the naming of children. Umar was the name of one of the sons of Ali. Moreover, Imam Hassan's son was also Umar, and this name continued to exist in generations of the Prophet's family following Imam Zayn al-Abideen.

Relationship between the House of Uthman and the family of the Prophet

Uthman earned the title *zunn-nurayn* (Possessor of two great lights) for having the honour of having married two daughters of the Prophet. As Sayyuti has stated, this was the distinction which only Uthman could ever have in the whole of mankind.[158] He was the foremost after the Prophet Lūt to have migrated for Islam with his wife to Abyssinia.[159] Ibn Athir also mentioned *nikah* (marriage) of Uthman with Ruqqiya, daughter of the Prophet.[160] He could not participate in the battle of Badr because of the illness of Ruqqiya, who later passed away. However, the Prophet reserved his share in the spoils of war and promised him spiritual reward as well. After the demise of Ruqqiya, Uthman had the honour to marry the second daughter of the prophet, Umm-e-Kalthum, in 3AH.[161] This marriage was divinely ordained.[162] The family relationship between Banu Hashim and the house of Uthman is even more wide-ranging. There were many instances of inter-marriages between the two families. For instance, the granddaughter of Ja'afar Tayyar was married to Uthman's son, Abban b. Uthman.[163] Later on, Fatima b. Hussain, another granddaughter of Ali, married Abdullah b. Umr, grandson of Uthman.[164]

Ali's Baya'ā and role in the state administration

Major Sunnite theorists, including Ibn Taimmiyah, Ibn Hajar Al-Asqalani, Ibn Athir and Ibn Kathir, confirm the immediate *baya'ā* of Ali to Uthman. The Companions tendered their consensus *baya'ā* immediately to Uthman. These Companions also included all six members of the committee constituted for the selection of the caliph, including Ali. The Shiite narrations also confirm that Ali pledged his allegiance to Uthman. The Shiite narrations confirm that Uthman's selection as caliph was in accordance with the selection process laid down by Ali in *Nehj-ul-Balagha*.[165]

Besides this,common family ties contributed to mutual trust between the Hashmites and Uthman. This trust is reflected through Uthman's consultation of Ali in the matters of statehood, appointment of the Hashmites to key posts, the Hashmites' trust in the Uthmanite justice and Uthman's regard for the nobility of the Hashmites. This trust is evident from the Hashmites' approval of the caliphate of Uthman. Like his illustrious predecessors, Uthman continued to consult Ali in the matters of statehood. On the pattern of the first two caliphs, Uthman too entrusted the responsibility of enforcement of *hudud* laws to Ali.[166] Uthman asked Ali to enforce *hudud* upon Walid b. Uqbah on the charges of taking alcohol.[167] The Shiite narrations, too, confirm this incident.[168] Likewise, Ali enforced *hudud* in many other offences as well. Moreover, during the caliphate of Uthman, the Hashmites occupied a number of key posts. Mughira b. Naufal was appointed as *Qadi*[169] whereas Abdullah b. Harith was governor of Makkah during the caliphate of Uthman.[170] Furthermore, many instances are available which suggest that the Hashmites used to bring their disputes to Uthman for adjudication. This reflects their trust in the uprightness and justice of Uthman.[171] Besides this, Uthman like his predecessors had always been respectful to the house of Hashim. As a gesture of respect, Uthman always used to alight from his horse while passing by Abbas.[172] Uthman himself led funeral prayers for Abbas.[173] Abban b. Uthman led funeral prayers for Muhammad b. Hanfia,[174] son of Ali and Abdullah b. Jaafar Tayyar.[175] These instances lead us to develop the case that there was no mistrust between the Hashmites and Uthman. They were bound together in a mutually supportive and affectionate relationship for the common cause of the faith.

War ethics

Islam has a strong moral system at its base, which disciplines the conduct of the believers. Any moral system is tested when it is exposed to a conflict scenario, and even more so when the followers of one ethical code are pitched against those who do not believe in the same. Islam does not believe that 'the ends justify the means'. Its war ethics have never been subordinated to utilitarian concerns. War ethics have always defined strategic and tactical manoeuvrings in Islam. The philosophy behind military morals is mainly based upon the following two grounds. First, nobility of intentions does not legitimize acts which are otherwise ignoble. Idol worship is not permissible as a means to secure divine closeness. The prophetic tradition, which recognizes intention as the determining factor for legitimacy of actions, applies only to those acts which are ostensibly fair and virtuous.[176] Acts which are otherwise impermissible, unjust and evil cannot be justified on the pretext of noble intentions. Second, the message of Islam is eternal and universal in itself, and the principles drawn therefrom have the same character. Their application is well defined and is far from reactionary in spirit. While relying upon these two premises, the following discussion will make an inquiry into the ethics of war through a micro examination of the evidence from the primary texts of Islamic history.

Suicide killings

Islam does not recognize human life as the personal property of a human being but rather as a divine trust. Human beings are obliged to protect the sanctity of this trust. It urges believers to protect their lives as the most exalted form of divine blessings. In the words of the Prophet, the bodies of the believers have rights upon themselves.[177] The commission of suicide amounts to flagrant violation of this trust, which invites strong condemnation. The commission of suicide will bring awful doom to the one who commits it. The Prophet warned the believers that the one who commits suicide through whatever means will surely be condemned to hell and will suffer painful torment. The Prophet has been further reported to have said that the one who commits suicide will be tormented with pain in hell through the same way he adopted to commit suicide.[178] The Prophet further said that once, moved by anxiety, an injured person cut off his hand with a knife and consequently died because of over bleeding. Allah made paradise out of bounds for him for violating His Will.[179] In another tradition, the Prophet anticipated that someone who was acclaimed by the Companions for his gallantry in fight against the infidels but later on committed suicide owing to the unbearable pain of his injuries, would go to hellfire for committing suicide.[180] The Prophet declined to offer funeral prayers for those who committed suicide.[181] These prophetic transmissions lead us to infer that commission of suicide is strictly condemned in Islam and warrants eternal torment in hell.

The commission of suicide, being an ignoble act, cannot turn into a noble act merely because of self-proclaimed virtuous intentions behind its commission. Jihad is a noble cause which warrants virtuous means to achieve its noble goals. Launching suicide attacks cannot earn theological legitimacy because a noble cause can be pursued only through noble means. Because of their categorical condemnation by the Prophet, suicide attacks cannot be theologically recognized in a utilitarian context which acknowledges suicide attacks as a war tactic to inflict damage on an enemy, even when jihad is religiously warranted.

Distinction between combatants and non-combatants

The military morals of Islam are based upon sharp distinction between combatants and non-combatants without discrimination of belief. Islam strongly condemns violence against those not involved in military adventures against an Islamic state. However, the military morals of Islam are not restricted to the non-combatants alone; rather, even the combatants are dealt with under these ethical codes.

Violence against the fellow believers

Islam condemns violence against the believers on the grounds of religious, political and ideological differences. The prophet declared sanctity of a believer's life to be greater than that of Ka'ba, the House of God on earth.[182] Inviolability of the life of a believer is better reflected through a prophetic declaration which identifies the murder of a single believer to be an offence more serious than even the destruction of the whole world.[183]

Strong emphasis upon this inviolability is evident from the Prophet's forbidding the believers of even pointing a weapon towards a fellow believer.[184] The Prophet prohibited the believers from killing someone who proclaims Islam even under the fear of being killed in the battlefield.[185] The prophetic condemnation is directed not only against those who actually kill a believer but even against the abettors as well. In the words of the Prophet, these abettors will be denied divine blessings for their support of the unjust killings of the believers.[186]

The violation of the sanctity of a believer's blood will surely invite a dreadful torment (An-Nisā: 93). Divine wrath will come to the one who violates the sanctity of a believer's life (Al-Ana'am:151). The sanctity associated with this offence is evident from the fact that it is mentioned in the Quran in conjunction with *shirk*. The Prophet, in his last sermon, categorically highlighted the sanctity (*hurmat*) of life and property of the believers.[187] Since inviolability of a believer's life is established through the Quran and authentic traditions of the Prophet, a mere conviction of the permissibility of the killing of a believer unless warranted through *hukm-e-shar'i* amounts to *kufr*. The military morals of Islam do not sanction killings of Muslims who are not liable to be killed through a categorical injunction.[188] If a believer deserves to be killed as a punishment required by a *hukm-e-shar'i* like *Qisās* (retribution), it will be carried out through the state. No one in a private capacity is entitled to enforce the coercive injunctions of Shariah.

Violence against non-believers

Non-believers in an Islamic state fall into the following three broad categories. First, those who become subject to the Islamic state under some agreement. They are called the People of Covenant. Second, those who agree to pay a certain amount as tax (jizyah) when they become subject to the Islamic state after being overwhelmed in their fight against the Muslims. They are called the dhimmis. Third, those who happen to be residing in a Muslim state under any other circumstances. An inquiry into the way non-believers were treated during the early period of Islam highlights that Islam recognizes the distinction between combatants and non-combatants for application of violence against them even in the battlefield.

People of Covenant

In case of the People of Covenant, once an agreement is reached, the Muslims are bound to deal with them strictly in accordance with the provisions of the agreement, even if the terms of agreement appear distasteful to them. The Prophet entered an agreement with the Christians of Najran. A portion of the agreement reads as follow, 'The protection of God and the guarantee of the prophet Muhammad, extend on Najran and neighbourhood, that is to say on their goods, their people, the practice of their worship, their absent and present, their families and their sanctuaries, and all that large and small, is in their possession'.[189] The obligation to observe these terms of agreement is so strongly emphasized that the Prophet warned the believers that he would himself be the complainant on the Day of Judgement against those who infringed upon their rights, burdened them beyond their endurance and usurped anything from them against their will. Further, on the question of treatment of the People of Covenant, Imam Abu Yusuf says that they will be dealt with strictly in accordance with the provisions of the contract, and no additions will be permitted.[190]

People of Guarantee

The dhimmis are levied a tax in return for a state guarantee for the protection of their lives, property and honour. Umar enjoined Abu Ubaidah, the commander of the Muslim armies, that the believers forego the right to take liberties with them and their property, the moment they accept jizyah from them. It must be noted that Islam recognizes distinctions between the combatants and non-combatants even in the imposition of jizyah to the dhimmis. It is levied only upon those who have fought or have the capacity to fight against the Muslims.[191] Non-combatants like women, children, the old, the disabled and lunatics will be exempted from this tax.

In general, Islam does not recognize any discrimination between believers and non-believers regarding the sanctity associated with their right to life. The Quran strongly condemns the killing of human beings irrespective of their religious affiliations and declares it an offence equal in severity to eliminating the whole of humankind. 'For that cause We decreed for the Children of Israel that whosoever killeth a human being for other than manslaughter or corruption in the earth, it shall be as if he had killed all mankind, and whoso saveth the life of one, it shall be as if he had saved the life of all mankind. Our messengers came unto them of old with clear proofs (of Allah's Sovereignty), but afterwards lo! many of them became prodigals in the earth' (Al-Maeda: 32).

The Prophet declared paradise to be out of bounds for the one who unjustly kills a non-believer.[192] The Prophet stated that one who unjustly kills anyone from the People of Covenant will not feel the fragrance of paradise.[193] The equality in right to life for the believers and non-believers is further evident from the uniformity in punishment to the killer in both cases. The punishments, either retribution or restitution as the case may be, will be uniform whether the victim happens to be a Muslim or non-Muslim.[194] However, Imam Bukhari has quoted a *hadith* wherein the Prophet prohibited killing a believer in retribution for a non-believer's murder.[195] The jurists have resolved an apparent anomaly between the Hanfite standpoint and the afore-quoted tradition of the Prophet. Al-Jassas argues that a non-believer as mentioned in this *hadith* means a non-Muslim who is in state of war with the Muslims. Otherwise, inviolability associated with the life and property of a non-believer, being a well-established principle of Islamic governance, is evident from the Sunnah of the Prophet. During the period of the Prophet, a Muslim killed a dhimmi. The Prophet ordered for his execution by saying that he was responsible for ensuring redress for the weak.[196] The pious caliphs adopted similar conduct as well. Umar ordered execution of a person from the tribe of Bakr bin Wail in retribution for killing a dhimmi of Hira. Likewise, Ali ordered execution of a person in retribution for killing a dhimmi, but later on the heirs of the deceased willingly accepted monetary compensation, and they themselves requested his release. Ali has been further reported to have said that the non-Muslims accepted the status of dhimmis on the categorical understanding that their properties and lives will remain inviolable like the Muslims.[197]

Having confirmed the inviolability of the long list of the rights of the non-believers in an Islamic state, which include right to life, property, honour, religious rites and personal law, it is argued that nothing revokes these rights except two conditions: (1) they leave the Muslim state and opt to join its enemies and (2) they rise in *khurūj* against a Muslim state.[198] The above instances from the early period of Islamic history show that the non-believers living in an Islamic state enjoy a tremendous level of protection to their lives and property under the state guarantee.

As said earlier, the instances further suggest that Islam believes in bifurcation between the combatants and non-combatants amongst both believers and non-believers. A conspicuous bifurcation between combatants and non-combatants is reflected in the treatment by the Prophet of the delegation from Musaylama (the liar). They confessed their apostasy by acknowledging their faith in false claim of prophethood on the part of Musaylama; yet, the Prophet showed extreme restraint and treated them well because of their diplomatic status.[199] This instance led to evolution of a defining principle of international relations that provides for protection to the diplomats by the Islamic state. Being established by authentic traditions, the violation of this principle amounts to trespassing the limits prescribed by the Prophet regarding the treatment to the diplomats.

The bifurcation between the combatants and the non-combatants is reflected in Muslims' conduct in the battlefield as well. These codes of war constitute categorical evidence to suggest that battle, in itself, is a moral adventure in Islam. These codes originate from the instructions of the Prophet and the pious caliphs which the Muslim troops were enjoined to follow in letter and spirit. Abdullah b. Abbas narrates, 'When the Messenger of Allah would dispatch troops he would say [to them], "Do not act treacherously, do not misappropriate the spoils of war, do not mutilate the dead bodies and do not kill a child."'[200] Since the whole Islamic struggle aims at lofty ideals, Islam does not approve of any act which is otherwise reprehensible. It has forbidden mutilating even animals in battle.[201] Al-Shaybani has narrated another *hadith* on the authority of Al-Hasan that the Prophet prohibited the killing of women.[202] In Sahih Muslim, two *ahadith* have been recorded on the authority of two different narrators but with a similar theme. The Prophet disapproved of killing of women and children in the battle.[203] He argues that a woman will not be executed even if she has committed apostasy. Ibn Abbas says, if a Muslim woman apostatizes, she will not be killed but will be imprisoned until she embraces Islam again. If a female apostate denies the charges of commission of apostasy and bears witness to the divine unity and prophethood when produced before Imam of the Muslims, it will amount to her repentance.[204]

The same military morals were followed by the Companions of the Prophet. Al-Tabri has reproduced the address of Abu Bakr to the troops of Usama b. Zayed expedition wherein Abu Bakr forbade him to misappropriate, break the trust, mutilate the dead, and kill the children, women and old. He also forbade Usama to cut or burn date palm. He further anticipated that Usama would come across such people who have preferred to live in seclusion and further advised him not to kill such people in their monasteries.[205] Umar followed the same bifurcation between the combatants and non-combatants. Ibn Qudamah in *Al-Mughni* has quoted a narration from Umar wherein he enjoined not killing non-combatant farmers. The evidence available from the Sunnah of the Prophet and his Companions leads to the argument that Islamic codes of war are based upon recognition of sharp distinction between the combatants and the non-combatants. Islam never permits its adherents to inflict any damage on the non-combatants whether Muslims or non-Muslims. Killing a non-combatant stands in categorical violation of the Islamic injunctions.

Vengeance-driven violence

In Islam, everyone is responsible for his own deeds. According to Shariah, no one can be held responsible for the misdeeds committed by someone else. The Quran categorically declares, 'Say: Shall I seek another than Allah for Lord, when He is Lord of all things? Each soul earneth only on its own account, nor doth any laden bear another's load. Then unto your Lord is your return and He will tell you that wherein ye differed' (Al-An'am: 164).

A tradition of the Prophet further emphasizes the issue as follows: 'No one shall be held responsible for the injustice of a co-religionist'.[206] Baladhuri, in *Futhū al-Buldān,* has recounted an incident in Lebanon when some people arose to revolt against the government. The governor, Saleh b. Ali, crushed the revolt with military muscle. He put all the male combatants to sword. He also sent some non-combatant civilians into exile. Imam Auza'i reprimanded the governor vehemently and said that he failed to understand why some people had been held responsible for the acts of others and had been forced to leave their homes. By reiterating the Quranic injunction that every soul is accountable for his own deeds, Imam Auza'i reminded Saleh of the words of the Prophet that he would be the complainant against all such Muslims who would burden the People of Covenant and the People of Guarantee beyond their endurance.[207] This Islamic perspective challenges the very foundations of the militants' narrative of killing innocent citizens to avenge the oppression inflicted upon them by others. The narrative that sanctions the killings of the western citizens on the grounds of indirectly supporting their oppressive regimes by electing them to power and through tax-payments has no supportive evidence from early Islamic history. During the early days of Islamic history, when Islam challenged two contemporary superpowers – the Byzantine and the Persian Empires – the Muslims did not hold their subjects responsible for the wrong deeds of their co-religionists merely for contributing to the revenue of their empires. Killing someone other than the person against whom retribution is due is an act without legitimacy.

In view of the above, the following conclusions may be drawn.

First, *takfīr* cannot be invoked if the one against whom its application is intended believes in the truthfulness of whatever has been brought [Shariah] by the Prophet. Second, the sectarian divide has not originated from irritants between the family of the Prophet and his Companions. It rather developed on the trajectory of socio-political constructs in the subsequent course of political history of the Muslims. The historical evidence confirms cordiality between them throughout their lives.

Third, *khurūj* is not permissible even if the rulers do not fulfil the ideal conditions prescribed for an Islamic ruler. It becomes permissible only when a ruler commits flagrant violation of any fundamental principle of the faith.

Fourth, in Islam, legitimacy of rulers and public consent to their selection are mutually inclusive. This consent may be secured through either direct means or indirect ways.

Fifth, a democratic system based upon divine sovereignty is in consonance with Islamic ideals. Political parties which are part and parcel of the modern democratic system can legitimately operate within Islamic political system provided they do not pose any threat to the integrity of the Muslim Ummah. Similarly, offering one's services for a particular office is not prohibited provided one has the confidence to fulfil the responsibilities associated with the slot and has not demanded it for the sake of authority but for service to mankind.

Sixth, war is a moral affair in Islam, and sharp distinctions are observed between combatants and non-combatants.

Seventh, Islam severely condemns suicide missions even if they are against whom the armed jihad (*Qitāl*) is warranted.

Last but not least, vengeance-based violence finds no legitimate grounds in Islam as it does not hold anyone responsible for the deeds of the other.

Notes

1 These include belief in Allah, His prophets, His angels, His revelations, the Last Day, resurrection after death and the Divine Decree (*taqdeer*). In detail, according to Imam al-Tahawi, the unity of God is expressed through His exclusive attributes. Attribution of divine qualities to human beings amounts to shirk, which nullifies one's faith. Belief in prophets means that all of them were divine messengers during their respective periods within a defined scope. Prophet Muhammad is the seal of the prophets, and his prophethood is eternal and for all. Though divine revelations descended upon all prophets, the Quran revealed to Prophet Muhammad is the literal word of God with meanings. Its eternity is confirmed and is not created like human speech. Identifying it with human speech amounts to falling in unbelief. With Imam al-Tahawi, belief in the unseen is part of the faith because human reason cannot transcend certain limitations to access the realm of metaphysics. Moreover, denial of limitations of human reason and attempts to explore the metaphysical domain solely through rationalism end up with scepticism. See Imam Abu Ja`far al-Tahawi, *Aqeeda-e-Tahāwiyyah,* accessed January 2, 2016, www.siratalmustaqim.com/pdf/aqeedah-tahawiyyah.pdf.
2 Ibid. For debate on minimum requirements for a Muslim to remain in the fold of Islam, see Hossein Modarressi, 'Essential Islam: The Minimum That a Muslim Is Required to Acknowledge', in *Accusations of Unbelief in Islam: A Diachronic Perspective on Takfīr*, eds. Camilla Adang et al. (Leiden: Brill, 2016), 395–412.
3 Ibid.
4 Ansari, *Ibn Taimmiyah Expounds on Islam*, 560.
5 Ibn Kathir, *Al-Bidāyah wal Nihāyah*, Vol. 4, Part VII, 282.
6 Ansari, *Ibn Taimmiyah Expounds on Islam*, 556.
7 Ibid., 560. Ibn Kathir has explored evidence to the effect that Ali did not get *khums* from their property confiscated during the battle of Nehrwan in 38 AH and returned the property to its real owners. See Ibn Kathir, *Al-Bidāyah wal Nihāyah*, Vol. 4, Part VII, 285. For detailed analysis regarding the conduct in the battles against those who commit *khurūj*, see Muhammad Ibn Al-Hasan Al-Shaybani, *Kitāb Al-Siyār Al-Saghīr* (Islamabad: Islamic Research Institute Islamabad, 1998).
8 Ibn Kathir, *Al-Bidāyah wal Nihāyah* Vol.4, Part VII, 285.
9 Al-Shaybani, *Kitāb Al-Siyār Al-Saghīr*, 135.
10 Hariri's introductory note in Ibn Taimmiyah, *Al-Muntqā min Minhāj al-Sunnah*, 19.
11 Bar, 'Sunnis and Shiites – Between Rapprochement and Conflict.'
12 Ansari, *Ibn Taimmiyah Expounds on Islam*, 557.
13 Ibid., 553, 554.
14 Al-Ghazali, *Faysal*, 112, 113.
15 Ibid., 3–32.
16 Imam Bukhari, *Sahih Bukhari*, *Kitāb Al-Adāb*: 6045; Imam Muslim, *Sahih Muslim*, *Kitāb Al-Eemān*: 0116; Al-Ghazali, *Faysal*, 132.
17 Ibid., 113–114.
18 Ibid.
19 Ibid.
20 Ibid., 115.
21 He was a student of Imam Malik and Imam Abu Hanifa. He was a distinguished compiler of *ahadith* (*mohaddith*) and earned the title *Amir Al-Mauminin fil hadith.* He was born in 118 A.H.
22 Ansari, *Ibn Taimmiyah Expounds on Islam*, 555, 556.

23 Jackson's introductory note to Al-Ghazali's *Faysal*, 3–32.
24 Imam Shamsuddin Dhahbi, *Al-Kabāir*, trans. Major Sins, accessed April 3, 2020, http://www.islamguiden.com/arkiv/majorsins.pdf.
25 Ibid.
26 Imam Muslim, *Sahih Muslim*, *Kitāb Al-Eemān*: 0136; Imam Bukhari, *Sahih Bukhari*, *Kitāb Al-Eemān*, 17; Imam Dhahbi has reproduced this tradition in *Al-Kabāir*, accessed on April 3, 2020, http://www.islamguiden.com/arkiv/majorsins.pdf.
27 They shifted *Hijr-e-Aswad* to their area of influence in 317 AH, and it was shifted back to Makkah in 339 AH. See Ibn Kathir, *Al-Bidāyah wal Nihāyah* (Tarikh Ibn Kathir). Karachi: Dar-ul-Asha'at, 2008, Vol. 6, Part XI, 188, 245.
28 Ibn Taimmiyah, *The Book of Eemaan: The Basis, Reality and Invalidation of Eemaan,* trans. Muhammad Naim Ya-Sin (London: Al-Firdous Ltd.), 203. Accessed August 31, 2013, http://www.kalamullah.com/ibn-taymiyyah.html.
29 Ibid., 205, 206.
30 Ibid., 210.
31 Friends of Allah mean those who believe in Allah and render obedience to Him in their acts and belief whereas friends of Satan are those who obey Satan in their acts and belief, ibid., 209, 212.
32 Ibid., 212–214.
33 Ibid., 192.
34 Ansari, *Ibn Taimmiyah Expounds on Islam*, 554.
35 Ibn Kathir, *Tafsīr Ibn Kathir*, trans. Maulana Muhammad Junagarhi, Vol. 2 (Lahore: Maktabah Quddusia, 2006); Commentary on An-Nahl: 106.
36 Ibid.
37 Al-Tahawi, *Aqeeda-e-Tahawiyyah.*
38 *Isrā* refers to the journey of the Prophet from Masjid Al-Harām to Al-Aqsā on the night of Mi'rāj.
39 Ibn Kathir, *Tafseer Ibn Kathir*, Al-Isrā: 1.
40 Al-Ghazali, *Faysal*, 88–96.
41 Ibid.
42 Ibid., 112.
43 Jackson's introductory note to Al-Ghazali's *Faysal,* 3–32. According to Al-Ghazali, refutation of an isolated report from a single source does not attract *takfīr*, see ibid., 114.
44 Ibid., 114.
45 Ibid., 112.
46 Manzoor Naumani, *Ma'arif Al-Hadīth*, Vol. 1, 87, 88.
47 Ansari, *Ibn Taimmiyah Expounds on Islam*, 555.
48 Al-Tahawi, *Aqeeda-e-Tahawiyyah.*
49 Abu Dawood, *Sunan Abu Dawood*, *Kitāb Al-Sunnah*, 4579; Imam Abi Abdullah Muhammad b. Abdullah al-Hakim has also narrated a *hadith* regarding the bifurcation of *Ummah* into different sects in *Al-Mustadrak a'lal Sahahain, Kitāb Al-Eemān*, trans. Shah Muhammad Chishti (Lahore: Idara Paigham-ul-Quran, 2009), 10.
50 For Ibn Taimmiyah, *ulil amr* includes both scholars as well as rulers who enjoin good and forbid evil, see Ibn Taimmiyah, *Enjoining Good and Forbidding Evil.*
51 When Ali and Mu'awiyah opted for *tahkīm* (arbitration) during the battle of Siffīn, and appointed Abu Musa Ash'ari and Amr bin al-A'as as their arbitrators respectively, a group of the followers of Ali seceded from him on the grounds that no person could be an arbitrator. They argued that it is only the commandment (*hukm*) of God that must prevail. They shifted to Harura, and

Ali had to fight against them. The one who objected to the appointment of arbitrators was Arwa bin Azeena. This group of *Khariji'tes* are also called Haruriyyah because after seceding from Ali, they had their first meeting at a place called Harura. In their view, commission of major sin forfeits one's faith and it is the duty of every Muslim to fight such infidels. See Ibn Kathir, *Al-Bidāyah wal Nihāyah*, Vol. 4 Part VII, 276–278.

52 Ibid.
53 Ibid., Vol. 4 Part VIII, 360.
54 Ibid., Vol. 4 Part VII, 278.
55 Ibid., Vol. 4 Part VII, 284.
56 Ansari, *Ibn Taimmiyah Expounds on Islam*, 516.
57 Imam Bukhari, *Sahih Bukhari, Kitāb Al-Ahkām*, 7212.
58 Imam Bukhari, *Sahih Bukhari, Kitāb al-fitan*, 7052, *Kitāb al-Jizyah*, 3163; Imam Muslim, *Sahih Muslim, Kitāb al-Zakah*, 2303.
59 Imam Bukhari, *Sahih Bukhari, Kitāb Manāqib Al-Ansar*, 3792, 3793, 3794; Imam Muslim, *Sahih Muslim, Kitāb Al-Imārah*: 4524; also see Ansari, *Ibn Taimmiyah Expounds on Islam*, 510–511.
60 Ibid.
61 Imam Bukhari, Sahih Bukhari, *Kitāb Al-Imārah*, 4555–4557, *Kitāb Al-Fitan*, 7053, 7054, *Kitāb Al-Ahkām*, 7143; Imam Muslim, *Sahih Muslim, Kitāb Al-Imārah*: 4555–4559.
62 Imam Bukhari, *Sahih Bukhari, Kitāb Al-Ahkām*, 7142; Imam Muslim, *Sahih Muslim, Kitāb Al-Imārah*, 4525–4532; also see Ansari, *Ibn Taimmiyah Expounds on Islam*, 61–65.
63 Ibid. Ibn Taimmiyah has quoted many *ahadith,* which stress upon the importance of obedience to those in authority; see, for instance, Imam Muslim, *Sahih Muslim, Kitāb Al-Imārah*, 4573–4575; Imam Bukhari, *Sahih Bukhari, Kitāb al-Jizyah*, 3163, *Kitāb Al-Ahkām*, 7144, *Kitāb Al-fitan*, 7056; Abu Dawood, Sunan Abu Dawood, *Kitāb Al-Jihad*, 2527.
64 Quoted in Abul a'la Maududi, *Khilāfat-o-Malūkiyyat* (Lahore: Idara Tarjman-ul-Quran, 2002), 264–266.
65 Ibid., 264–266.
66 Ibid.
67 The attempts to revolt started since the period of the Ummayads. Even Al-Mansur himself pledged his allegiance to Nafs-e-Zakkayah but after coming to power, he became an ardent enemy of this revolutionary movement and aimed to suppress it. See Al-Tabri, *Tarīkh al-Umam wal Mulūk*, Vol. 5, Part II, under discussion on 145 AH, 136–185.
68 Quoted in Abul a'la Maududi, *Khilāfat-o-Malūkiyyat*, 264–266.
69 Ibid.
70 Ibid., 272.
71 Imam Bukhari, *Sahih Bukhari, Kitāb Al-Muharibeen*, 6830.
72 It has been quoted by leading Muslim historians like Imam Al-Tabri, Ibn Sa'ad and Ibn Kathir.
73 Ibn Sa'ad, *Tabqāt Ibn Sa'ad*, Vol. 7, 124.
74 Imam Bukhari, *Sahih Bukhari, Kitāb Al-akhbār al-Ahad*, 7257; Imam Muslim, *Sahih Muslim, Kitāb Al- Imārah*, 4535.
75 Ansari, *Ibn Taimmiyah Expounds on Islam*, 520.
76 Imam Muslim, *Sahih Muslim, Kitāb Al-Imārah*, 4555; also see Ansari, *Ibn Taimmiyah Expounds on Islam*, 513.
77 Al-Tibrani, *Al-Mu'jam al-Kabīr*, 7431, Vol. 3, trans. Ghulam Dastgir Chishti Sialkoti (Lahore: Progressive Books, 2015), 491, quoted in, Ansari, *Ibn Taimmiyah Expounds on Islam*, 513, 514.

78 Imam Bukhari, *Sahih Bukhari, Kitāb ahadith al-Anbiyya*, 3455.
79 Imam Muslim, *Sahih Muslim, Kitāb Al-Imārah*, 4573.
80 Imam Bukhari, *Sahih Bukhari, Kitāb Al-Muharibeen*, 6830.
81 Abu Ammar Zahid al-Rashidi, *Islam, Jamhūriyyat and Pakistan* (Islamabad: Pak Institute for Peace Studies, 2013), 33.
82 Shah Waliullah, *Hujjatullah al-Bālighā*, trans. Maulana Abdul Haq (Lahore: Farid Book Stall), 601–605.
83 Ibid.
84 This Incident has been recorded in almost all major books of Muslim History and biographies of the Prophet.
85 Abu Ammar Zahid al-Rashidi, *Islam, Jamhūriyyat and Pakistan*, 37.
86 Imam Muslim, *Sahih Muslim, Kitāb Al-Imārah*, 4491. Abu Dawood, *Sunan Abu Dawood, Kitāb Al-Aqdiyah*, 3566.
87 Imam Muslim, *Sahih Muslim, Kitāb Al-Imārah*, 4489.
88 Imam Muslim, *Sahih Muslim, Kitāb Al-Imārah*, 4487.
89 Abu Dawood, *Sunan Abu Dawood, Kitāb Al-Aqdiyah*, 3566, 3568.
90 Abu Ammar Zahid al-Rashidi, *Islam, Jamhūriyyat and Pakistan*, 50, 51.
91 Dr Muhammad Iqbal (1877–1938) was a poet and philosopher who kindled the candle of Islamic revivalism in the sub-continent.
92 Al-Mawardi, *Ahkām al- Sultāniyyāh*, 16.
93 Ibn Khaldun, *The Muqaddimah*, trans. Franz Rosenthal, Chapter titled, 'The Differences of Muslim Opinion Concerning the Laws and Conditions Governing the Caliphate', accessed December 8, 2020, https://asadullahali.files.wordpress.com/2012/10/ibn_khaldun-al_muqaddimah.pdf.
94 Ibn Taimmiyah, *Enjoining Good and Forbidding Evil*; also see Michael Cook, *Commanding Right and Forbidding Wrong in Islamic Thought* (New York: Cambridge University Press, 2000), quoted in Bonney, *Jihad*, 117.
95 Abu Dawood, *Sunan Abu Dawood, Kitāb Al-Sunnah*, 4590; Ansari, *Ibn Taimmiyah Expounds on Islam*, 499, 500.
96 Ibid.
97 Ibid.
98 Ibid., 565, 566.
99 Ibn Kathir, *Al-Bidāyah wal Nihāyah,* Vol. 4, Part VIII, 358, 359.
100 Ansari, *Ibn Taimmiyah Expounds on Islam*, 498.
101 Abu Dawood, *Sunan Abu Dawood, Kitāb Al-Sunnah*, 4629. This tradition has also been quoted in, Naumani, *Ma'arif Al-Hadīth*, Vol. vii, 574, 575.
102 Imam Bukhari, *Sahih Bukhari, Kitāb Al-Anbiya*, 3455; Imam Muslim, *Sahih Muslim, Kitāb Al-Imārah*: 4543.
103 Maulana Muhammad Naf'ey, *Ruhāma' Baynā'hum,* Vol. 1 (Lahore: Dar-ul-Kitab, 2014), 26, 27.
104 The Quran declares the wives of the Prophet to be the mothers of the believers in the following words, 'The Prophet is closer to the believers than their selves, and his wives are (as) their mothers' (Al-Ahzāb, 6).
105 Abu Bakr and Umar took part in making arrangements for the wedding ceremony with great enthusiasm. When Ali sold his vest to Uthman to arrange finances for his wedding, Uthman as a goodwill gesture returned the vest instantly along with the amount already paid to Ali. All three participated in the marriage (*nikah*) ceremony on invitation of the Prophet and witnessed to *nikah.* Besides the four caliphs of Islam, the cordiality in relationships also existed between the exalted *ummahat al-Mo'mineen* (mothers of the believers) and Fatima al-Zahra. Ayesha Siddiqa and Umm-e-Salma made arrangements for the *nikah* of Fatima. They renovated and furnished the house and also prepared food. They further stated not to have ever witnessed a wedding better than of Fatima. Naf'ey, *Ruhāma' Baynā'hum*, Vol. 1,

42–73; also see Ibn Majah, *Sunan Ibn Majah, Kitāb An-Nikah*: 1986. This tradition has also been quoted in Naf'ey, *Ruhama' Bayna'hum*, Vol. 1, 74–78.

106 Quoted in ibid.

107 Quoted in ibid.

108 Ayesha stated that Fatima had resemblance with the Prophet in walking, too. Whenever she visited the Prophet, he would make her sit on either his right or his left. See Imam Bukhari, *Sahih Bukhari, Kitāb Al-Adāb al-Mufrad, Kitāb al-Salām*, 473; this tradition has also been quoted by Ibn Hajar al-Asqalani, (Tazkarah Fatima) *Al-Isaba fi tamyyiz al-Sahaba*, Vol. 8, trans. Maulana Muhammad Amir Shehzad Alvi (Lahore: Maktab Rehmania), 314.

109 Imam Bukhari has quoted *hadith* in Sahih Bukhari that the Prophet asked Fatima, 'O' my daughter! Don't you love whom I love [Ayesha]?' Fatima replied in affirmative. See *Kitāb al-hibba*, 2581.

110 This conversation was with reference to the Prophet's disclosure of his early demise, which made Fatima weep, followed by good news that she would be the chief of women folk in paradise, that made her smile. Imam Muslim, *Sahih Muslim, Fazāil-e- Fatima*, 6003; also see Ibn Hajar al-Asqalani, (Tazkarah Fatima) *Al-Isaba fi tamyyiz al-Sahaba*, Vol. 8, 314.

111 Imam Muslim, *Sahih Muslim, Kitāb Al-Taharah*: 0537. In Arabic terminology, this is called *massah al'al-khuffain*. This is mostly performed when there is scarcity of water to perform normal ablution.

112 10th day of Muharram, the first month in Islamic calendar.

113 Al-Haythami, *Majma' al Zawa'id: Manāqābt Fatima binnat Asad*, Vol. 9, 256, 257, quoted in Naf'ey, *Ruhama' Bayna'hum*, Vol. 1, 79.

114 Quoted in Naf'ey, *Ruhama' Bayna'hum*, Vol. 1, 98, 99.

115 Ibn Jozi, *Manāqib Umar b. Al-Khattab*, 71.

116 Ibn Sa'ad, *Tabqāt*, Vol. 2, 43.

117 Imam Bukhari, *Sahih Bukhari, Kitāb Fazāil As-Sahāb al-Nabi*, 3750.

118 Imam Bukhari, *Sahih Bukhari, Kitāb Fazāil As-Sahāb al-Nabi*, 3751.

119 Imam Bukhari, Sahih Bukhari, *Kitāb Fazāil As-Sahāb al-Nabi*, 3712.

120 Imam Bukhari, *Sahih Bukhari, Kitāb al-Manāqib*, 3096, *Kitāb Al-Mughāzi, Bab Hadīth Bani Nadhīr*, 4033.

121 Quoted in Naf'ey, *Ruhama' Bayna'hum*, Vol. 1, 79. Al-Tirmidhi has recorded a *hadith* that the Prophet declared Abu Bakr and Umar to be amongst the people of higher level who will be like stars in the sky. *Jami' Al-Tirmidhi, Kitāb Al-Manāqib*, 3658; Al-Tirmidhi has quoted another *hadith* on the authority of Ali that the Prophet declared Abu Bakr and Umar to be amongst the 14 select attendants given to him. *Jami' Al-Tirmidhi*, 3785. Kathīr Al-Nawā is part of the chain of narrators in both *ahadith*.

122 Imam Zayd was a real brother of Imam Baqir. Both Sunnite and Shiite scholars have quoted his words. For the Sunnite quotation of his words, see Ibn Kathir, *Al-Bidāyah wal Nihāyah*, Vol. 3, Part V, 287. For the Shiite reference, see Ibn Abi Al-Hadid Shii, *Shar'a Nehj-ul-Balagha*, Vol. 4, 113, as quoted in Naf'ey, *Ruhama' Bayna'hum*, Vol. 1, 80–100.

123 Ibn Kathir, *Al-Bidāyah wal Nihāyah*, Vol. 3, Part V, 283.

124 Ibid. Vol. 3, Part V, 247, 248; Part VI, 579.

125 Quoted in Naf'ey, *Ruhama' Bayna'hum*.

126 Muhammad bin Sa'ad, *Tabqāt*, Vol. 2, 24, 25.

127 Ibid. *Bāb ahl-e-ilm wal fatwa min Ashāb Rasulullah*. For Shiite traditions, see Ahmed Ibn Abi Yaqoob, *Tarikh Yaqoobi*, (trans.) Maulana Akhtar Fatehpuri, Vol. 2 (Karachi: Nafees Academy), 211.

128 Quoted in Naf'ey, *Ruhama' Bayna'hum*, Vol. 2, 40–60.

129 Ibn Kathir, *Al-Bidāyah wal Nihāyah*, Vol. 3, Part VI, 591. This incident has also been quoted by Sayyuti in *Tarīkh al-Khulāfā*.
130 Imam Ali Ibn Abi Talib, *Nehj-ul-Balagha* (Peak of Eloquence), trans. Askari Jafari (Karachi: Islamic Seminary Publications, 1984), 354–355.
131 Al-Tabri, *Tarīkh al-Umam wal Mulūk*, Vol. 2, Part II, 54.
132 Naf'ey, *Ruhama' Bayna'hum*, Vol. 2, 50.
133 Ibn Sa'ad, *Tabqāt: Tazkarah Abu Bakr*, Vol. 3, 142; also see al-Sayyuti, *Tarīkh al-Khulāfā: Mardh al-Wafat Abu Bakr al-Siddique*, 61.
134 The argument has been quoted by Maulana Naf'ey that the Shiite and the Sunnite scholars have quoted that Ali himself made reference to his willing *bay'ā* to his predecessors in caliphate, see Naf'ey, *Ruhama' Bayna'hum*, Vol. 2, 40–60.
135 Al-Tabri, *Tarīkh al-Umam wal Mulūk,* Vol. 3, Part II, discussion on 35 AH, 24.
136 Al-Tirmidhi, *Jami' Al-Tirmidhi, Kitāb Al-Manāqib*, 3785.
137 Ibn Jozi, *Manāqib Umar b. Al-Khattab*, 36.
138 Ibid., 21.
139 Ibn Jozi, *Manāqib Umar b. Al-Khattab*, 58, 59.
140 Al-Tabri, *Tarīkh al-Umam* wal *Mulūk*, Vol. 2, Part II, 399.
141 Ibid., Vol. 3, Part-I, discussion on 23 AH, 223.
142 Ibn Sa'ad, *Tabqāt: Tazkarah Abu Bakr Siddique*, Vol. 3, 149.
143 Ibn Jozi, *Manāqib Umar b. Al-Khattab*, 65, 66.
144 Ibid., 69.
145 Imam Abu Yousouf, *Kitāb al-Kharāj*, 4.
146 Ibidident has also been quoted by Sayyuti in *Tarīkh al-Khulāfā.*
147 Ibn Sa'ad, *Tabqāt: Bāb Ali*, Vol. 2, 109.
148 Ibid. *Bāb ahl-e-ilm wal fatwa min Ashāb Rasulullah*, 102.
149 Al-Jozi, *Manāqib Umar b. Al-Khattab*, 63.
150 Ibn Kathir, *Al-Bidāyah wal Nihāyah,* Vol. 4, Part VII, 39 discussion under 13 AH.
151 Imam Bukhari, *Sahih Bukhari, Fardh al-Khums,* 3094.
152 Naf'ey, *Ruhama' Bayna'hum,* Vol. 2, 119, 120.
153 Ibn Kathir, *Al-Bidāyah wal Nihāyah*, Vol. 4, Part VII, 62 discussion under 15 AH.
154 In the month of Ramadan, the Muslims offer these prayers at night in addition to the regular five prayers a day.
155 Al-Sayyuti, *Tarīkh al-Khulāfā:* awalliyāt-e-Umar, 97.
156 Umar appointed Ali his deputy in Madina before proceeding to liberate Al-Aqsa in 15AH. See Ibn Kathir, *Al-Bidāyah wal Nihāyah*, Vol. 4, Part-VII, 62 discussion under 15 AH.
157 Imam Muslim, *Sahih Muslim, Kitāb Manāqib As-Sahaba*, 5885.
158 Al-Sayyuti, *Tarīkh al-Khulāfā*: *Tazkarah Uthman ibn Affan*, 105.
159 Ibn Sa'ad, *Tabqāt*, Vol. 2, 133.
160 Ibn Athir, *Usūd al-Ghabā fi Mua'arfāt al-Sahaba*, Urdu trans. Maulana Muhammad Abdul Shakoor Farooqi Lakhnawi, Vol. 2 (Lahore: Al-Meezan), 517.
161 Ibid., also see Ibn Sa'ad, *Tabqāt*, Vol. 2, 133.
162 Al-Hakim, *Mustadrak: Tazkarah Umm-e-Kalthum*, Vol. 4, 49; Though Ibn Hajar Al-Asqalani has also mentioned the divine ordainment with regard to this marriage on the authority of Abu Hurayrah, he has declared this tradition as *gharīb*. See *Al-Isaba fi tamyyiz al-Sahaba*, Vol. 8, 515, 516.
163 Naf'ey, *Ruhama' Bayna'hum*, Vol. 3, 53.
164 Ibn Sa'ad, *Tabqāt: Tazkarah Fatima binnat Hussain*, Vol. 8, 346–348.
165 Naf'ey, *Ruhama' Bayna'hum*, Vol. 3, 65–68.
166 Ibid., 120.
167 Imam Bukhari, *Sahih Bukhari, Manāqib al-Ansar*, 3872.

168 Ibn Abi Haddid, *Sharah Nehj-ul-Balagha*, Vol. 2, 67. Even the authentic Shiite narrations reject the charges of committing *bida'a'* upon Umar by increasing the punishment of alcohol-taking. Imam Ja'afar Sadiq has approved of this increase in punishment. Quoted in Naf'ey, *Ruhama' Bayna'hum,* Vol. 3, 124.
169 Ibn Athir, *Usūd al-Ghabā fi Mua'arfāt al-Sahaba*, Vol. 3, 242.
170 Ibn Hajar al-Asqalani, *Taqrīb al-Tehzīb*, trans. Maulana Niaz Ahmed (Lahore: Maktaba Rehmania).
171 Naf'ey, *Ruhama' Bayna'hum*, Vol. 3, 132–138.
172 Ibn Kathir, *Al-Bidāyah wal Nihāyah*, Vol. 4, Part VII, 164, *Tazkarah Abbas* under 32 AH.
173 Ibid.
174 Ibn Sa'ad, *Tabqāt*, Vol. 3, 115.
175 Ibn Athir, *Usūd al-Ghabā fi Mua'arfāt al-Sahaba*, Vol. 2, 217.
176 Imam Bukhari, *Sahih Bukhari, Kiāab al-Wahī*, 1.
177 Imam Bukhari, *Sahih Bukhari, Kitāb As-Saum*, *Bāb Haq al-Jism fil Saum*, 1975.
178 Imam Bukhari, *Sahih Bukhari*, *Kitāb Al-Eemān wal Nazūr*, 6652, *Kitāb al-Janā'iz*, 1363, *Kitāb Al-Adāb*, 6047, 6105.
179 Imam Bukhari, *Sahih Bukhari*, *Kitāb Al-Anbiyya*, *Bāb Ma Zikr an Bani Israel*, 3463.
180 Imam Bukhari, *Sahih Bukhari*, *Kitāb Al-Mughāzi*, 4203.
181 Al-Nasa'i, *Sunan An-Nasa'i Kitāb al-Janā'iz*, 1966.
182 Ibn Majah, *Sunan Ibn Majah*, *Kitāb Al-Fitan*, 3932.
183 Al-Tirmidhi, *Jami' Al-Tirmidhi*, *Kitāb al-diyyat*, 1395; Al-Nasai, *Sunan An-Nasai*, *Kitāb Tahrīm al-dam*, 3991; Ibn Majah, *Sunan Ibn Majah*, *Kitāb al-diyyat*, 2717.
184 Imam Muslim, *Sahih Muslim*, *Kitāb al-Birr wal Sila wal Adāb*, *Bāb Nahi an Ishara bil Salah*, 6336–6338.
185 Imam Bukhari, *Sahih Bukhari*, *Kitāb-ul-Mughāzi*, *Bāb Baath al-Nabi Usama bin Zaydi l al-harqat min Jhayena*, 4269, *Kitāb al-Mughāzi*, *Bāb Shahūd al-Malaika Badr*, 4019; Imam Muslim, *Sahih Muslim*, *Kitāb Al-Eemān*, *Bāb Tehreem Qatal al-Kafir Baad an Qala*: *La Ilah illa Allah*, 0173–0177
186 Ibn Majah, Sunan Ibn Majah, Kitāb al-Diyyat, 2718.
187 Imam Bukhari, *Sahih Bukhari*, *Kitāb al-Hajj*, 1741.
188 In the battle of Uhud, the Prophet gave his sword to Abu Dujjana, his Companion from Ansār on the condition that no believer would be killed with this sword. See *Al-Isaba fi tamyyiz al-Sahaba*, Vol. 7, 128, 129.
189 Imam Abu Yusuf, *Kitāb al-Kharāj*, trans. Maulana Niaz Ahmed Okarwi (Lahore: Maktaba Rehmania), 208–219; This treaty has also been mentioned by Ibn Sa'ad in *Tabqāt*, Vol. 1, Part II, 97, 98.
190 Yusuf, *Kitāb al-Kharāj*, 208–219.
191 Abul a'la' Maududi, *Islamic Law and Constitution*, 282.
192 Al-Nasai, *Sunan An-Nasai*: *Kitāb al*-qasama, 4751.
193 Bukhari, *Sahih Bukhari*: *Kitāb Al-Jizya*, 3166.
194 Ibn Abi Shayba, *al-Musannaf*, Vol. 8, trans. Maulana Muhammad Awais Sarwar (Lahore: Maktabah Rehmania), 154, 155.
195 Bukhari, *Sahih Bukhari*: *Kitāb al-ilm*: 111.
196 Maududi, *Islamic Law and Constitution*, 283.
197 Ibid.
198 Ibid., 286.
199 Abu Dawood, *Sunan Abu Dawood*: *Kitāb Al-Jihad*: 2755. Al-Shaybani has also emphasized upon the security of diplomatic envoys in Islamic territories. See *Kitāb Al-Siyār Al-Saghīr*, 63.
200 Quoted in ibid., 43.

201 Ibid., 49.
202 Ibid., 46.
203 Imam Muslim, *Sahih Muslim*: *Kitāb Al-Jihad*, 4319, 4320.
204 Ibid., 69.
205 Al-Tabri, *Tarīkh al-Umam wal Mulūk*, Vol. 2, Part II, 39.
206 Abu Yusuf, *Kitāb Al-Khirāj*, 78; Al-Baladhuri, *Fūtuh al-Buldān*, trans. P. K. Hitti (The Origins of the Islamic State) (New York: Columbia University, 1916), 90.
207 Al-Baladhuri, *Fūtuh al-Buldān*, 251.

Conclusion

State governance constitutes an intrinsic part of the Islamic belief system. The defining principles of statehood have been categorically laid down in the divine scripture. These principles find practical exposition in the conduct of the Prophet. He himself established the state in Madina. It was the base from which the revolutionary surge of Islam originated. The Muslims at large have always idealized and cherished state governance on the model of the state of Madina. A strong religious sentiment is associated with the nostalgia to revive the ideal Islamic state across the Muslim world. The religious sanctity of the political ideals originates from the state model which was not an abstract but a living entity during the early period of Islam. Any attempt to hinder its revival has always invited backlash from the Muslim societies. The current conflict is essentially a clash between desires to revive the prophetic model of governance on one hand and attempts to implant a secular model of state governance on the other. Nevertheless, the conflict of visions translated into physical violence only when it was exploited by the militants.

Though the secular state system could not earn legitimacy from the level of masses in the Muslim world, the ruling elite and its support base in most of the Muslim states support this. On the other side, the militants could draw on the diffused base of the Muslim masses. The militants employed theological vocabulary to invoke punitive injunctions of the faith. They drew profusely on *takfīr* in their discourse. The scope to define the parameters of faith attaches enormously strong implications to the issue for Muslim societies. The militants use this concept profusely in utter disregard for the cautions associated with its exercise since the early period of Islam. Originally, the fundamental elements of faith alone could evoke proclamation of *takfīr*; however, the militant discourse gave way to *bida'a* (innovations) of secondary nature to define the limits of faith. By claiming exclusivity in following 'authentic Islam', the militants declare every idea which does not conform to their brand of faith as heretical. They invalidate the faith of Muslims on the basis of socio-political constructs. The militants believe that friendship with non-believers constitutes a basis for attracting the label of *takfīr*. Moreover, those who participate in the democratic

DOI: 10.4324/9781003164883-102

process are also excommunicated. Besides this, the militants subject the Shiites to *takfīr* for introducing innovations into the body of faith. The militants have exploited the complex mosaic of theology and politics and surrendered the objectivity of ideas to religious extremism.

As said elsewhere in this study, the ideas of heresy when transmuted into polemics made the sectarian faultlines more conspicuous. The schisms between Muslims, having emanated from distinct theological discourses, were already immutable. The aberrations of Islamic history created spaces for these conflicting discourses to emerge. These discourses largely developed through a mix of theological differences and political realism. This paved the way for historical presuppositions to emerge. The conjectures thus provided grounds to the sectarian empires like the Fatimid caliphate and the Safavid dynasty. The Iranian revolution in 1979 is also considered part of this historical chain of sectarian political orders. The case of these political orders supports the hypothesis that sectarian schisms, aggravated on the axis of politics, were further exploited by the rulers to secure political gains. All three Shiite political orders share the passion for export of their ideology beyond their territorial limits with the aim of expanding their support base. This passion naturally created alarms within the rival Sunnite world against the possible export of shiitization to their lands. The response of the Sunnite vis-à-vis the sectarian political orders was of mistrust coupled with charges of treason against the fellow Muslims at the behest of the non-believers. The experience of the Fatimids and Safavids further reinforced this mistrust with increased mutual intolerance. Forced conversion under these empires served as 'lessons of history' for the Sunnites.

These lessons changed the boundaries of faith and gave the militants grounds to exploit the centuries-old schisms between the Shiites and the Sunnites to bring legitimacy to their violence against each other. The implications internalized by the Muslim societies were worsened by the positive relationship between the identity crises and violence. National identity eroded when it was challenged by colonialism. Violence swept across the Muslim world either under state patronage or at the societal level. Violence was directed against respective colonial powers or against those who believed in reconciliation with the colonialists as a key to their survival. They were labelled as the 'apologists'. The post-colonial context witnesses to the persistence of this anti-colonial sentiment with a certain level of redefinition. Islamists' resistance against the colonialists transformed into defiance of the ruling elite found to be in connivance with the West against the fellow believers. The militants further disapprove of the 'apologists' for their support for westernized rulers in the Muslim states. As said earlier, the splits that sneaked into the body politic of Islam during the early days could only reach the masses when the violence was codified under the sectarian empires like the Safavid dynasty in the 16th century. The presuppositions that emerged from the early days continued to persist through codification of violence under these sectarian empires. Moreover, the rise of these empires and the abolition of the Muslim caliphate in the 20th century rendered the Ummah irrelevant as a legitimate coercive organ to control violence. It opened the channel for violence to reach the level of the masses. In the vacuum created by the irrelevance of Ummah, the militants claimed legitimacy for their violence aimed to revive the caliphate. However, the 18th and 19th centuries witnessed Muslims pitted against each other and codification of violence even at the level of state formation. Iran and the Gulf States may be viewed as such an outcome, achieved through indirect imperialist interventions.

As violence permeated the level of the masses, its codification in society and state led to the formation of codes of war with the militants. These codes of war found their expositions as follows. First, for the militants, following democracy invokes *takfīr* as it recognizes the human mandate for law making, which amounts to infringing upon the domain exclusive to God. The negation of exclusivity of the divine sovereignty revokes the belief of a believer, making him liable to punishment warranted for the commission of apostasy (*irtidād*) as a legal requirement (*hukm-e-shar'i*). Since the nation-state system provides space for democracy to function, the militants do not hesitate to condemn the followers of the democratic constitutions as apostates. Second, the militants venture to discredit the theology developed over centuries. This rejection of Muslim scholarship is evident from their revisions of the fundamental nature in their theory of jihad, internalizing jihad to the Muslim societies in addition to fighting against an aggressor enemy. Third, despite their differences with the contemporary Wahabi sheikhs on some theological issues relating to jihad, the militants share the *jāhilliyah* notion of Ibn Abdul Wahab. They seek to revive the purity of faith and pronounce *takfīr* on those who introduce *bida'ā* into the practice of faith. Fourth, the militants seek to legitimize their violence against the Shiites in general on the basis of historical presuppositions more than on religious grounds. Despite their frequent references to Ibn Taimmiyah, the militants are stricter on the question of polemics than Ibn Taimmiyah. Ibn Taimmiyah avoided pronouncing *takfīr* on the Shiite common man whereas the militant narrative does not find any difference between the Shiite leadership and the common man. Fifth, the militants' violence is directed against those they call 'apostate rulers' in the Muslim states as well as against their local support base. Sixth, the militants do not observe any distinction between the combatants and non-combatants as the targets of their violence. They disregard this distinction in the case of both believers as well as non-believers.

In practice, the militants subscribe to these codes of war through multiple channels, which include semi-qualified local clergy, family environment and their peers. They exploit the rationale espoused by the militant ideologues behind these codes of violence to claim legitimacy for their otherwise reprehensible actions. It is evident from the case study of Pakistan that it is not authenticity but suitability of an idea which governs their choice in following these streams. Moreover, the commonalities of ideological strands between different outfits make the militant diaspora a sort of global brotherhood. The transnational fraternity thus formed fills the demand of experienced foot-soldiers by the newly emerging outfits. As most of the militant networks reflect ideological affinities, their soldiers are comfortable in shifting their organizational affiliations while retaining their ideological identities. Ideology has precedence over organizational affiliation. Furthermore, common ideological strands lead to common strategies of violence aimed at common targets. Switching from one organization to another does not entail a change in targets and modes of violence to achieve them.

Apart from Pakistan, sectarian identities are of paramount importance to the militants across the spectrum. The killing fields of militancy reflect that, in the cases of Lebanon, Syria and Iraq, despite retaining common anti-imperialist themes, the militants never surrender their sectarian identities. They seek to exploit these sectarian identities to mobilize their support base in the transnational context to secure political and strategic gains. Societies like Somalia, Algeria and Egypt, which have been victims of state oppression, happen to be fertile grounds for militancy where the militant outfits can find their workforce through cashing in on their marginalization. Moreover, anarchy creates appeal for the militants' notion of reviving the purity of faith in search of a just socio-economic and political order. In pursuit of purity, they reject everything which they believe is not Islamic and assume an exclusionary character vis-à-vis those who do not feel inclined to their version of the faith. The militants, seeking for ideal alternative state governance find themselves in direct conflict with the guardians of dysfunctional state structures. Both sides look to different support solutions. The militants want to become part of a global militant brotherhood whereas their adversary regimes look towards their western patrons and, as a result, earn the charges of apostasy for collaborating with the western powers.

The evidence suggests that Gaza and Palestine have always been central to the agenda of militant organizations. The historical accounts of the militant organizations suggest that the organizations could occupy a central place in the militant diaspora as long as they stuck to jihad as the sole solution to the conflict. Any conciliatory posture on these issues deprives them of popularity with the militants. This happened with PLO in the aftermath of the Oslo Accords, and similarly Hamas is also reprimanded by Al-Qaida and ISIS for its deference to the international charter that recognizes Israel.

As far as the theatres of international aggression are concerned, they are also a source of theological support to the militants in the context of the Islamic perspective on resisting foreign aggression into Muslim societies.

Last but not the least, the militant ideologues claim to draw theological rationale to their actions from the leading Muslim jurists of the medieval period. However, looking deep into the matter, a wide gap is obvious between the militant narrative and the position of classical Muslim scholarship. The militant narrative appears to have been evolved in the space of political expediency instead of an authentic theological domain. It is the product more of a reactionary mind than a scholarly ordeal. An objective inquiry into the question of veracity of their narrative should initiate from two basic-level understandings of Shariah. First, the religion reached its culmination with the termination of revelation on the Prophet, and its best practical manifestation is found in the conduct of the Prophet himself and his Companions. The conduct of the Companions was directly supervised and disciplined by the Prophet himself. Their actions constitute reference points for the Muslims' posterity for the ages to come. As a natural consequence, the principles of Shariah drawn from their conduct are firm in essence and not subject to revisions through any scholarly ordeal. Muslim scholarship developed after the period of the Companions never questioned the principles established by them. The classical Muslim jurisprudence developed rational interpretations (*ijtihād*) of these principles according to the changing circumstances. The principles of Shariah remained always firm and unchanged. Secondly, the basic premise of Shariah, which has always been defining the conduct of the believers, is that ends do not justify means. Legitimate goals should be achieved only through legitimate means. The basic elements of faith cannot be achieved through means which are not approved. Charity (Zakat), though an exalted form of *ibādah* (worship) to secure divine blessings, cannot be performed through finances accumulated through wrongful means. Similarly, jihad is the highly approved form of divine worship, which entails divine blessings of the highest degree, provided it is performed through approved means and ways.

Relying on this premise, the primary ground upon which faith of a believer can be invalidated is negation of any categorical injunction (*nassūs-e-qattiyā)* of the faith. As a matter of principle, the limits of faith have already been clearly defined by the primary scripture, leaving hardly any room for the socio-political constructs to redefine them. The commission of heresies does not necessarily lead to apostasy. Further, there is no allowance for uprising against the rulers even if they do not come up to the ideal level required for the ideal Muslim rulers. In conformity with this already-defined principle, the classical Muslim scholarship never let transformations in the political order trigger the course for *takfīr*. In the case of Muslim states, the democratic model of state governance cannot be labelled as a faith in itself provided it recognizes divine sovereignty. Under the umbrella of divine sovereignty, the subordinate principles of democratic governance as laid down in most of the constitutions of the Muslim states are not repugnant to the defined principles of Islam. Identifying taking part in the democratic process with the commission of apostasy is misleading.

Moreover, the codes of warfare have been explicitly laid down in the primary scripture, and the conduct of the Prophet and his Companions. These well-established principles do not permit even slight deviation on the part of the believers. These principles make the war a disciplined 'moral affair' and put the believers under obligation to observe the prescribed discipline in every circumstance. The Islamic war discipline makes a sharp distinction between combatants and non-combatants. The conduct of the Prophet and his Companions does not permit unhindered violence even when military jihad is sanctioned. The Shariah strictly prohibits torture, treacherous and inhuman tactics like suicide bombings and desecration of the dead bodies, even against the declared enemies. Moreover, vengeance-based violence against the enemy who has not actually committed any offence in lieu of the actual offender has no evidence in the conduct of the *salaf*. On the grounds of these defined principles of Shariah, it is argued that the narratives of both the apologists and the militants are devoid of merits. The apologists do not base their arguments on the core injunctions of Shariah. They do not take the primary texts of religion as their reference point for their arguments. On the other hand, though the militants claim to draw their arguments from the primary sources of Shariah, they selectively draw upon these sources to legitimize their preconceived notions of violence. They overlook the defined principles of Shariah if these do not support their ideology of violence.

Glossary

Ada'āb al-Qitāl	Morals of war.
Ahl al-ahad	People of covenant. It refers to the people with whom Muslims enter into a treaty.
Ahl al-hall wa'l-aqd	Literally, it means 'those who loose and bind'. It refers to the Companions of the Prophet during the early period of Islam who had an established authority in the matters of faith.
Ahl al-qiblā	Those who follow Ka'ba for the direction of prayers.
Al-Awwal, al-Ākhir	These are 2 of the 99 beautiful names of Allah which describe His attributes. *Al-Awwal* means the first, pre-existing and the one who is the cause of everything. *Al-Ākhir* means the last and the ultimate. The one who will remain when everything will come to doom. There is nothing beyond Him.
Amir	Leader. One who has authority over others.
Ansār	In literal terms, it means 'helpers'. In the context of Islamic history, it refers to the Muslims of Madina who welcomed the Prophet and his Companions and helped them when they migrated from Makkah.
Aqīdah	Creed or belief system.
Ashura	10th day of the Muharram, the first month in the Islamic Calendar.
Assābiyah	Group feelings. In the context of Ibn Khaldun's sociological theory, it denotes the cementing bond pre-requisite for the creation of dynasties.
Athnā 'ashariyya	Twelver Shiites. The sub-sect of Shiites who believe in twelve imams.
Awliya' (s. *Wali*)	Friends. In Quranic expression, certain believers have been declared as "Friends of Allah."
Bara'at	Disavowal.
Baya'ā	To pledge allegiance.
Dār-ul-ahd	A nation with whom the Muslims have entered into a covenant.
Dār-ul-harb	A Muslim land where the non-believers have dislodged the believers from the authority to enforce an Islamic system of state governance.
Daurā-e-hadith	Extensive and rigorous study of the traditions of the Prophet.
Erfān	Mystical insight into the universe and its Creator.

Fard-e-ayn	Individual obligation.
Fard-e-kafāya	A religious practice performed as a collective responsibility which if performed by a group of believers compensates all others, and if no one performs it, the believers' community as a whole would be held responsible for the omission.
Fitnah	Disorder or chaos. The Quran declares creation of chaos an offence which is more intense than even killing someone.
Hadith (pl. *Ahadith*)	Tradition of the Prophet.
Halāl	Religiously permissible.
Haram	Religiously non-permissible.
Hifz-e-Quran	Memorizing the Quran.
Hijra	Migration.
Hukm-e-shar'i	Legal injunction.
Ibādah	Prayers or performing of rituals.
Ijma'a	Consensus of opinion among the scholars.
Ijtihād	In a literal sense, it means 'effort'. It is a source of Islamic law after the Quran, Sunnah and consensus of opinion of the scholars of the community. In this sense, it means to make rational exercise to interpret the problems not precisely addressed in the primary sources of Islamic law.
Illat al-Qitāl	In literal terms, it denotes 'cause of battle'. In a broader sense, it refers to conditions which sanction jihad for the believers.
Imārah	Political authority.
Iqāmat ad-dīn	Enforcement of tenets of the faith.
Irja'ā	Literally, it means 'to defer'. In theological debate it holds that judgement regarding the veracity of one's belief may be deferred to the verdict of God when the Hour is established. The proponents of this view are called Murji'ah.
Irti'dād	It means apostasy, which is defined as reverting of a believer to unbelief.
Isrā	*Al-Isrā* is the 17th chapter in the Quran. This term refers to the incident of M'iraj when the Prophet was taken to Al-Aqsa from the Masjid Al-Harām and then to the heavens. However, in more precise terms, it refers to the first phase of travel – from Masjid Al-Harām to Al-Aqsa.
Istawā ala' al-arsh	This is a Quranic expression that 'Allah mounted the throne' in the 32nd chapter titled As-Sajada.
Jāhilliyah	Literally, it means ignorance. In the context of Islamic history, it refers to the pre-Islamic period.
Jama'at	Group or collective entity.
Jirgās	Informal Council of elders.
Jizyah	Tax levied upon non-believers in an Islamic state in return for a state guarantee of their protection. Those who pay this tax are called dhimmis (People of Guarantee).
Khabar-e- ah'dī	Isolated tradition.
Khalifāt-ur-Rasūl	Deputy of the Prophet.
Khawarij	Those who leave *Jama'at*, of the believers.

Khilāfat-e-nabwiyyah	Caliphate on the model of the state system established by the Prophet in Madina.
Khilāfat-e-rāshidā	Caliphate of the rightly guided caliphs.
Khulāfā (s. *Khilāh*)	Caliph of the Muslims.
Khurūj	Revolt against the existing political order.
Kufr	Unbelief.
Ma'wlā	Lord.
Maghlūb	Subdued. Subjugated.
Māl-e-Sadaqāt	Property for free will offering.
Malūkiyyat	Hereditary kingship.
Maslāhā	Benefits.
Mawākhāt-e-Medina	Brotherhood at Madina. It refers to the brotherhood between the Makkan Muslims emigrants (*muhajirīn*) and *Ansār* at Madina established by the Prophet soon after migration to Madina.
Mawālāt	Friendship; supporting; collaborating. For the sake of this study, the term has been used as part of theological vocabulary in the context of collaborating with non-believers.
Mehr	An amount to be paid by the husband to the wife at the time of marriage.
Mi'rāj	The Prophet was taken to the highest heavens. This incident is called *Mi'rāj*. It has been mentioned in the Quran.
Milad-un-Nabi	Birth of the Prophet.
Mufādilah	The term is used for the Shiites who believe in primacy of Ali's right to the caliphate.
Mufāsidah	Detriments; disadvantages.
Muhajirīn	Used for those who migrated to Madina from Makkah.
Mujtahids	The scholars having certain qualifications required to perform *Ijtihād*.
Mukhtālīf fīh	Disputed; where consensus does not exist.
Munāfiq	Hypocrites.
Murji'ah	Those who believe in the doctrine of *Irja'ā*.
Nasūs-e-qatt'iyā	Categorical injunctions.
Nikah	Solemnizing the marriage in Islamic traditions.
Qisās	Retribution.
Rāshid-ul-amr	The one who has the capability to make good decisions.
Rāshidūn	Rightly guided. The term is used for the first four caliphs of Islam.
Rawāfidh	In a literal sense, it refers to those who reject. The term is used for the Shiites because they reject the right of the first three caliphs of Islam to the office of caliphate.
Ribā	Usury.
Salāfī	Those who follow the early three generations of Muslims.
Seerah	Life character.
Shirk	To ascribe divine attributes to human beings.
Shūrā	Consultation.
Tāghūt	Oppression; system of unbelief.
Takfīr	Ex-communication; to declare someone as a non-believer.

Taqleed	Blind following.
Taqwā	Piety.
Taraka	Inheritance.
Tarāweeh	Additional ritual prayers performed by the Muslims at night during *Ramadan*.
Tawhid	Oneness of Allah.
Ulil amr	Those in authority.
Ummahāt al-Mu'minīn	Mothers of the believers.
Usūl-ud-dīn	Principles of faith.
Vilayet-e-faqih	Guardians of Islamic law.
Wahī	Divine communication with the prophets.
Wājib	Mandatory.
Wajūbiyyat	The status of being mandatory.
Zindīq	Heretic.

Bibliography

ABC News. 'Al Qaida-Linked Group Al Nusra Front Claims Deadly Car Bombing in Lebanese Capital Beirut'. January 21, 2014. Accessed December 9, 2020. http://www.abc.net.au/news/2014-01-21/suicide-bomber-hits-hezbollah-stronghold-in-beirut-lebanon/5211872.

Abu Basir, Shaykh. Interview by Al-Malahem Media, *Inspire*. 2010 Accessed July 20, 2013. http://publicintelligence.net/tag/inspire-magazine/.

Abu-Rabi, Ibrahim M. *Intellectual Resurgence in the Modern Arab World*. Albanay: State University of New York Press, 1966.

Abu Yusuf, Imam. *Kitāb al-Kharāj*. Translated by Maulana Niaz Ahmed Okarwi. Lahore: Maktaba Rehmania, n.d.

Adams, C.J. 'Mawdudi on the Necessity of Divine Government for the Elimination of Oppression and Injustice'. In *Muslim Self-Statement in India and Pakistan, 1857–1968*, edited by A. Ahmed and G.E. Grunebaum. Wiesbaden: Cambridge, 1970.

Adnani, Abu Muhammad. 'Qaideen-e-jihad ke Aqwāl (Statements of jihadi Leadership)'. *Hiitin* 8 (1433AH): 148–154.

Ahmed, Ishtiaq. *The Concept of an Islamic State: An Analysis of the Ideological Controversy in Pakistan*. London: Printer, 1987

Ahmed, Aziz. *Studies in Islamic Culture and Indian Environment*. Oxford: Clarendon Press, 1964.

Ahram Online. 'Video shows beheading of Copts at IS hands; Egypt declares week of mourning'. February 15, 2015. Accessed November13, 2020. http://english.ahram.org.eg/NewsContent/1/64/123128/Egypt/Politics-/Video-shows-beheading-of-Copts-at-IS-hands;-Egypt-.aspx.

Ahyā-e-Khilāfat. June 2014.

Akhavi, Shahrough. 'Islam, Politics and Society in the Thought of Ayatullah Khomeini, Ayatullah Taliqani and Ali Shariat.' *Middle Eastern Studies* 24, no. 4 (1988): 404–431.

Akhavi, Shahrough. "The Ideology and Praxis of Shi'ism in the Iranian Revolution."*Comparative Studies in Society and History* 25, no. 2 (1983): 195–221.

Akram, Fares. 'Gaza's Hamas Rulers have a New Problem: ISIS-Sympathetic Jihadists'. *Business Insider*, June 8, 2015. Accessed January3, 2016. http://www.businessinsider.com/gazas-hamas-rulers-have-a-new-problem-isis-sympathic-jihadists-2015-6.

al-Abbab, Shaykh Adil. 'Interview on Targeting non-Muslim Civilians and Yemeni Soldiers'. *Inspire* (AQAP-Al- Malahem Media), no. 4 (2010). Accessed July 20, 2013. http://publicintelligence.net/tag/inspire-magazine/.

Al-Arabiya News. 'Nusra Front issues bounties for Assad, Nasrallah'. October 13, 2015. Accessed December 9, 2020. https://english.alarabiya.net/en/News/middle-east/2015/10/13/Nusra-Front-urges-attacks-on-Syria-s-Alawites-to-avenge-Russian-bombings.html.

al-Asqalani, Ibn Hajar. *Al-Isaba fi tamyyiz al-Sahaba*. Translated by Maulana Muhammad Amir Shehzad Alvi. 8 vols. Lahore: Maktab Rehmania, n.d.

al-Asqalani, Ibn Hajar. 'Nukbat-ul-Fikr'. Accessed December 8, 2020. www.maktabah.net.

al-Asqalani, Ibn Hajar. *Taqrīb al-Tehzīb*. Translated by Niaz Ahmed. II vols. Lahore: Maktaba Rehmania, n.d.

al-Awlaki, Anwar. 'The New Mardin Declaration: An Attempt at Justifying the New World Order'. Vol. 2. *Inspire*, 2010. Accessed July 20, 2013. http://publicintelligence.net/tag/inspire-magazine/.

al-Awlaki, Anwar. 'The Ruling on Dispossessing the Disbelievers wealth in Dar al-Harb'. *Inspire*, 2010. Accessed July 20, 2013. http://publicintelligence.net/tag/inspire-magazine/.

al-Baladhuri, Ibn Jabir. *Fūtuh al-Buldān*. Translated by P. K. Hitti. New York: Columbia University, 1916.

al-Banna, Hassan. 'Jihad'. Accessed September 29, 2013. http://web.youngmuslims.ca/online_library/books/jihad/.

al-Dhahbi, Imam Shamsuddin. *Al-Kabāir (Major Sins)*. Accessed April 3, 2020. http://www.islamguiden.com/arkiv/majorsins.pdf.

Alexander, Harriet. 'Islamic State Claim Responsibility for Jalalabad Bomb in First Afghanistan Attack'. *The Telegraph*, April 19, 2015. Accessed November 26, 2020. https://www.telegraph.co.uk/news/worldnews/asia/afghanistan/11547195/Islamic-State-claim-responsibility-for-Jalalabad-bomb-in-first-Afghanistan-attack.html.

al-Gharib, Abdullah Muhammad. *Wa ja'a dawr al-Majus: al ebād al-tarikhiyaat wal aqa'aidiat was Siyasiyyat le thurat ul-Iraniyyat*, 1406 AH.

al-Ghazali, Abu Hamid. *Faysal al-Tafriqā Baynā al-Islam wa al-Zandaqā (On the Boundaries of Theological Tolerance in Islam)*. Translated by Sherman A. Jackson. Oxford: Oxford University Press, 2005.

al-Hakim, Imam Abi Abdullah Muhammad b. Abdullah. *Al-Mustadrak a'lal Sahahain*. Translated by Shah Muhammad Chishti. Lahore: Idara Paigham-ul-Quran, 2009.

Ali, Choudhury Mohammad. *The Emergence of Pakistan*. New York: Columbia University Press, 1967.

al-Jamil, Tariq. 'Ibn Taymiyya and Ibn al-Mutahhar al-Hillī: Shi'i Polemics and the Struggle for Religious Authority in Medival Islam'. In *Ibn Taymiyya and His Times*, edited by Yossef Rapoport and Shahab Ahmed. Karachi: Oxford University Press, 2010, 229–246.

Al-Jazeera. 'Ansar Dine fighters destroy Timbuktu shrines'. July 1, 2012. Accessed March 21, 2015. http://www.aljazeera.com/news/africa/2012/06/2012630101748795606.html.

Al-Jazeera. 'Boko Haram pledges allegiance to ISIL'. March 8, 2015. Accessed March 15, 2015. http://www.aljazeera.com/news/2015/03/nigeria-boko-haram-pledges-allegiance-isil-150307201614660.html.

Al-Jazeera. 'Scores Killed in Attack on Peshawar School; Taliban Claims Responsibility'. December 16, 2014. Accessed April 16, 2015. http://america.aljazeera.com/articles/2014/12/16/scores-killed-inattackschoolinpeshawar.html.

al-Khoei, Hayder. 'Can the Quiet Ayatollah of Peace Save Iraq from Collapse?' *The World Today* Chatham House, 38–40, October & November 2014.

al-Maqdisi, Abu Muhammad. 'Al-Deemoqratiyya Deen (Democracy: A Religion)'. Translated by Abu Muhammad al-Maleki. Accessed January 17, 2015. http://azelin.files.wordpress.com/2010/08/democracy-a-relegoin.pdf.

al-Maqdisi, Abu Muhammad. *Millat Ibrahim Wa Da'wat Al-Anbiya Wal- Mrrsalin Wa Asalib At-Taghut Fi Tamyi'iha Wa Sarf Ad-Duati Anha*. At-Tibyan Publications. Accessed July 16, 2013. http://www.kalamullah.com/Books/MillatIbraheem.pdf.

al-Maqdisi, Abu Muhammad. *This Is Our Aqeedah*. 2. At-Tibyan Publications. Accessed July 16, 2013. http://www.kalamullah.com/Books/This%20is%20our%20Aqeedah.pdf.

al-Maqdisi, Abu Muhammad. *Ahkām al- Sultāniyyāh*. Translated by Asadullah Yate. London: Ta-Ha Publishers Ltd, n.d.

Al-Muhajiroun. *Khilāfat: Aik Mukhtāsar Guide*, n.d.

al-Qardawi, Shaykh Yusuf. 'The Role of Reconciliation in the Ummas's Real Unity'. *Doha*, 2007. Accessed August 5, 2013. http://www.qatarconferences.org/mazaheb/viewlastnews.php?id=56.

al-Rashidi, Abu Ammar Zahid. *Islam, Jamhūriyyat and Pakistan*. Islamabad: Pak Institute for Peace Studies, 2013.

al-Raziq, Ali Abd. 'The Problem of Caliphate'. In *Contemporary Debates in Islam: An Anthology of Modernist and Fundamentalist Thought*, edited by Kamran Talattof and Mansoor Moaddel, 95–100. New York: St. Martin's Press, 2006.

al-Sayyuti, Hafiz Jalaluddin Abdur Rehman Bin Abu Bakr. *Tarīkh Al-Khulāfā*. Translated by Iqbal uddin Ahmed. Karachi: Nafees Academy, 1983.

al-Sharif, Abu Bakr. 'Interview by Nidā-ul-Islam'. *The Libyan Regime Is Living in a Situation of Hysteria,* October 1996. Accessed March 15, 2015. http://fas.org/irp/world/para/docs/IN-LIBYA.htm.

al-Shaybani, Muhammad Ibn Al-Hasan. *Kitāb Al-Siyār Al-Saghīr*. Islamabad: Islamic Research Institute, 1998.

al-Tabri, Abi Ja'afar Muhammad Bin Jarir. *Tarīkh al-Umam wal Mulūk*. Karachi: Nafees Academy, 2004.

al-Tahawi, Abu Ja`far. *Aqeeda-e-Tahāwiyyah*. Accessed January 2, 2016. www.siratalmustaqim.com/pdf/aqeedah-tahawiyyah.pdf.

al-Tibrani. *Al-Mu'jam al-Kabīr*. Translated by Ghulam Dastgir Chishti Sialkoti. Lahore: Progressive Books, 2015.

al-Waqidi, Imam. *Fūtuh as-Sham*. Translated by Maulana Sulayman Al-Kindi. Ta-Ha Publishers Ltd. Accessed September 2, 2013. http://www.kalamullah.com/conquest-of-syria.html.

al-Zarqawi, Abu Musa'ab. 'Jamhuriyyat, Aik Mustakkil Madhab'. *Hittin*, 8 (n.d.): 131–144.

al-Zawahiri, Ayman. 'Message to the People of Yemen'. *Inspire*, 2010. Accessed July 20, 2013. http://publicintelligence.net/tag/inspire-magazine/.

al-Zawahiri, Ayman. 'Letter to Bin Laden' and 'Statement in Response to Arab Spring'. In *Letters from Abbottabad: Bin Laden Sidelined*, edited by Nelly Lahoud, Stuart Caudill, Gabriel Koehler-Derrick, Don Rassler, and Muhammad Al-`Ubaydi. Combating Terrorism Centre, 2012. Accessed June 29, 2013. http://www.ctc.usma.edu/posts/letters-from-abbottabad-bin-ladin-sidelined.

Ansari, Abdul-Haqq. 'Ibn Taimmiyah Expounds on Islam: Selected Writings of Ibn Taimmiyah on Islamic Faith, Life and Society'. 2000 Accessed August 13, 2013. http://theauthenticbase.files.wordpress.com/2010/09/expounds-on-islam.pdf.

Arowolo, D. 'The Effects of Western Civilization on Africa'. *Afro Asian Journal of Social Sciences* 1, no. 1 (2010): 7.

ARY News. 2014. 6 August.

Atwan, Abdel Bari. *The Secret History of Al-Qaida*. London: Abacus, 2006.

Aziz, Shah Abdul. *Tohfā Athnā-e-Ashriyyā*. Translated by Profile: Syri Khalil-ur-Rehman Naumani. Karachi: Dar-ul-Asha'at. n.d.

Azzam, Abdullah. *Ad-Difa'a un a'aradi al-Muslimeen a'aham farud al-a'yan (Defence of the Muslim Lands- the First Obligation after Eemān)*. Accessed June 17, 2013. http://www.kalamullah.com/Books/defence.pdf.

Azzam, Abdullah. *Extracts from the Wasīyyat*. Translated by Ahmed Farooq. Muslim World Data Processing Pakistan. 1986. Accessed May 5, 2021. https://english.religion.info/2002/02/01/document-join-the-caravan/.

Azzam, Abdullah. 'Join the Caravan'. *Religio-Scope Archives*, 2002. Accessed June 10, 2009. http://www.religioscope.com/info/doc/jihad/azzam_caravan_3_part1.htm.

Azzam, Abdullah. *Tawhid Al-Amali, Al-Awal min Silsala-tul-Maqalat, Reha' min jannat al-Firdous (The First of the Series of Treatises: Breezes, From the Gardens of Firdous)*. At-Tibyan Publications, n.d. Accessed June 17, 2013. http://www.kalamullah.com/Books/tawheed_action.pdf.

Azzam, Maha. *Al-Qaida: The Misunderstood Wahabi Connection and the Ideology of Violence*. Briefing Paper No.1, The Royal Institute of International Affairs, 2003.

Baker, Aryn. 'Boko Haram Militants Are Back on the Attack in Nigeria as a Presidential Election Looms'. *Times*, January 9, 2015. Accessed January 9, 2015. http://time.com/3661230/boko-haram-attack-in-baga-nigeria/.

Bar, Shmuel. 'Sunnis and Shiites – —Between Rapprochement and Conflict'. In *Current Trends in Islamist Ideology*, Vol. 2, edited by Hillel Fradkin, Husain Haqqani and Eric Brown, 87–96. Washington D.C.: Hudson Institute, 2005.

Barghouti, Iyad, and Lisa Hajjar. *The Islamist Movements in the Occupied Territories: An Interview with Iyad Barghouti*. Middle East Report, No.183, Political Islam, Middle East Research and Information Project, 9–12. 1993. Accessed February 14, 2009. http://www.jstor.org/stable/3012571.

BBC. 'Profile: Syria's al-Nusra Front April, 2013. Accessed December 10, 2015. http://www.bbc.com/news/world-middle-east-18048033.

BBC. 'Syria Conflict: Al-Nusra fighters kill Druze Villagers'. June 11 2015. Accessed May 5, 2021. https://www.bbc.com/news/world-middle-east-33092902.

BBC. 'Who Are Hezbollah?' July 4, 2010. Accessed November 27 9, 2020, 2020. http://news.bbc.co.uk/2/hi/middle_east/4314423.stm.

BBC News. 'Syria: The story of the conflict'. October 9, 2012. Accessed October 12, 2015. http://www.bbc.com/news/world-middle-east-26116868.

Bellah, Robert N. 'American Civil Religion in 1970s'. In *American Civil Religion*, edited by R.E. Richev and D.G. Lones, 255–272. New York: Harper & Row Publishers, 1974.

Benard, Cheryl. *Civil and Democratic Islam: Partners, Resources, and Strategies*. Arlington: RAND Corporation, 2003. Accessed January 1, 2016. https://www.rand.org/content/dam/rand/pubs/monograph_reports/2005/MR1716.pdf.

Benn, Stanley I. 'Egalitarianism and Equal Consideration of Interests'. In *Equality*, edited by J. R. Pennock and J. W. Chapman, 61–78. New York: Atherton Press, 1967.

Bin Laden, Osama. 'Declaration of Jihad against the Americans Occupying the Land of the Two Holy Sanctuaries', 'World Islamic Front Statement Urging Jihad Against Jews and Crusaders, 1998', 'Interview with al-Jazeera, December, 1998', 'Second Letter to the Muslims of Iraq October 18, 2003', and 'Message to the American People (30th October 2004)'. In *Al Qaeda in Its Own Words*, edited by Gilles Kepel and Jean-Pierre Milelli. Translated by Pascale Ghazaleh, 47–50, 53–56, 57–59, 68, and 71–80. Massachsetts: The Belknap Press of Harvard University Press, 2009.

Bin Laden, Osama. Interview by Gwyen Robert. Channel 4 Television Network. February 20, 1997. Accessed May 12, 2013. http://www.fas.org/irp/world/para/ubl-fbis.pdf.

Bin Laden, Osama. Interview by Hamid Mir. *Daily Pakistan*, March 18, 1997.

Bin Laden, Osama. Interview by John Miller. *Greetings, America. My Name is Osama Bin Laden*, February 1, 1999. Accessed May 22, 2013. http://www.esquire.com/features/ESQ0299-FEB_LADEN.

Bin Laden, Osama. *Interview by Robert Fisk. Arab rebel leader warns the British: 'Get out of the Gulf'*. London: The Independent, July 10, 1996.

Bin Laden, Osama. Interview by Robert Fisk. 'Declaration of Jihad Against the American Occupiers of the Land of Two Holy Cities'. *Nawa-i-Afghan Jihad*. June 2012.

Bin Laden, Osama. 'Interview with Al-Quds al-Arabi March 9, 1994' and 'Osama Bin Laden Declares Jihad on Americans, September 2, 1996'. In *FBIS Report – Compilation of Usama Bin Ladin Statement 1994–January 2004*. 2004. Accessed May 12, 2013. http://www.fas.org/irp/world/para/ubl-fbis.pdf.

Bin Laden, Osama. Interview by Peter Arnett and Peter Bergen. *Osama Bin Laden Declares Jihad* CNN. May 12, 1997. Accessed November 26, 2020. https://www.youtube.com/watch?v=orawG7vt68o.

Bin Laden, Osama. *Interview by Time. Wrath of God*, January 1999. Accessed May 21, 2013. http://www.time.com/time/world/article/0,8599,2054517,00.html.

Bin Laden, Osama. 'No. SOCOM-2012-0000016' and 'No. SOCOM-2012-0000019'. In *Letters from Abbottabad: Bin Laden Sidelined*, edited by Don Rassler, Gabriel Koehler-Derrick, Liam Collins, Muhammad al-Obaidi, and Nelly Lahoud. Combating Terrorism Centre, 2012. Accessed June 29, 2013. http://www.ctc.usma.edu/posts/letters-from-abbottabad-bin-ladin-sidelined.

Bin Laden, Osama. 'Until We Taste What Hamza Bin Abd Al-Muttalib Tasted'. *Inspire*, no. 2 (2010).

Bonney, Richard. *Jihad: From Quran to Bin Laden*. New York: Plagrave MacMillan, 2007.

Brown, Stephen. 'Foreign Aid and Democracy Promotion:Lessons from Africa'. *The European Journal of Development Research* 17, no. 2 (2005): 179–198.

Bukhari, Imam. *Al-Adab al-Mufrad*. Lahore: Idara Paigham-ul-Quran, 2007.

Burke, Jason. *Al Qaeda: The True Story of Radical Islam*. New York: LB. Tauris & Co Ltd, 2004.

CBS News. 'Al-Shabab Says It Singled Out Non-Muslims in Kenya Mall Attack'. September 25, 2013. Accessed April 13, 2015. http://www.cbsnews.com/news/al-shabab-says-it-singled-out-non-muslims-in-kenyF00007a-mall-attack/.

CBS News. 'Iraq Militants in Military Uniforms Attack Balloting Center in Predominantly Sunni Area'. 2014. Accessed January 22, 2015. http://www.cbsnews.com/news/iraq-militants-in-military-uniforms-attack-a-balloting-center-in-predominantly-sunni-area/.

Chastain, Mary. 'ISIS Executes Imams for Condemning Burning of Jordanian Pilot'. *BreitBart*, February 5, 2015. Accessed March 25, 2015. http://www.breitbart.com/national-security/2015/02/05/isis-executes-imams-for-condemning-burning-of-jordanian-pilot/.

Chipman, Don D. 'Osama Bin Laden and Guerrilla War'. *Studies in Conflict & Terrorism* 26, no. 3 (2003): 163–170.

Chirri, Mohamad Jawad. *Inquiries about Islam*. Detroit: The Islamic Center of America, 1986. Accessed August 2, 2013. http://www.al-islam.org/inquiries/.

Chothia, Farouk. 'Who Are Nigeria's Boko Haram Islamists?' *BBC News*. January 21, 2015. Accessed March 20, 2015. http://www.bbc.com/news/world-africa-13809501.

The Clarion Project. 'Libya: Islamic State Burns 'Non-Islamic' Musical Instruments'. 2015. Accessed March 25, 2015.

CNN. 'Lebanon Is Hezbollah'. December 1, 2009. Accessed December 9, 2015. http://ireport.cnn.com/docs/DOC-363256.

CNN Wire Staff. February 2012. Accessed November 28, 2015. http://edition.cnn.com/2012/02/09/world/africa/somalia-shabaab-Qaida/.

Collier, Paul, and Anke Hoeffler. 'On the Incidence of Civil War in Africa'. *Journal of Conflict Resolution* 46, no. 1 (2002): 13–28.

Collier, Paul, and Anke Hoeffler. 'Greed and Grievance in Civil War'. *Oxford Economic Papers New Series* 56, no. 4 (2004): 563–595.

Corcoran, P. 'The Limits of Democratic Theory'. In *Democratic Theory and Practice*, edited by G. Duncan. Cambridge: Cambridge University Press, 1983.

Council on Foreign Relations. 'Sunni- Shia Divide'. Accessed December 10, 2015. http://www.abc.net.au/news/2014-01-21/suicide-bomber-hits-hezbollah-stronghold-in-beirut-lebanon/5211872.

Daase, Christopher, and Oliver Kessler. 'Knowns and Unknowns in the 'War on Terror': Uncertainty and Political Construction of Danger'. *Security Dialogue* 38, no. 4 (2007): 411–414.

Dabiq. 'Excerpts from "Indeed Your Lord Is Ever Watchful"'. n.d.

Dabiq. 'The Return of Khilafa', 1435 AH.

Dahl, Robert A. *Democracy and Its Critics*. New Haven and London: Yale University Press, 1989.

Dawn News. 'TTP negotiator rejects peace talks under constitution'. February 7, 2014. Accessed February 6, 2015. http://www.dawn.com/news/1085510.

Defence Industry Daily. 'Iran-Syria vs. Israel, Round 1: Assessments & Lessons Learned'. September 13, 2012. Accessed November 27, 2020. http://www.defenseindustrydaily.com/iransyria-vs-israel-round-1-assessments-lessons-learned-02558/#more-2558.

DeLong Bas, Natana. *Wahabi Islam. From Revival and Reform to Global jihal*. New York: I.B. Tauris, 2007.

Doyle, Mark. 'Al-Shabab Can Hit almost at Will'. *Report on Somalia Parliament Attacked by al-Shabab in Mogadishu*. BBC, 2014. Accessed January 21, 2015. http://www.bbc.com/news/world-africa-27554498.

Dryzek, John S, and Patrick Dunleavy. *Theories of Democratic State*. Hampshire: Palgrave Macmillan, 2009.

Durkheim, Emile. *The Elementary Forms of Religious Life*. Translated by Carol Cosman. Oxford: Oxford University Press, 2001.

Elad-altman, Israel. 'The Sunni-Shi'a Conversion Controversy'. In *Current Trends in Islamist Ideology*, edited by Hillel Fradkin, Husain Haqqani, and Eric Brown, 1–10. Washington D.C.: Hudson Institute, 2007.

El-Affendi, Abdelwahab. 'What is Liberal Islam? The Elusive Reformation'. *Journal of Democracy* 14, no. 2 (2003): 34–39.

el-Beheiri, Ahmed, Ayman Hamza, and Hisham Abdel Halim. 'Al-Azhar Scholars Warn of a Dangerous Shiite Tide'. *Al-Masry Al-Youm*, October 17, 2008. Accessed November 26, 2020. http://today.almasryalyoum.com/article2.aspx?ArticleID=182750.

Esposito, John L. *The Islamic Threat: Myth or Reality*. NewYork: Oxford University Press, 1992.

Euben, Roxanne L. *Enemy in the Mirror: Islamic Fundamentalism and the Limits of Modern Rationalism: A Work of Comparative Political Theory*. Princeton: Princeton University Press, 1992.

Euben, Roxanne L. 'Premodern, Anti-modern or Post-modern? Islamic and Western Critique of Modernity'. *The Review of Politics* 59, no. 3 (1997): 429–459.

Faraj, Muhammad Abd al-Salam. 'Al-Faridah al-Gha'iba (The Neglected Duty)'. Accessed September 1, 2013. http://www.juergensmeyer.com/files/Faraj_The_Neglected_Duty.pdf.

Floor, William M. 'Revolutionary Character of the Iranian Ulama: Wishful Thinking or Reality?' *International Journal of Middle East Studies* 12, no. 4 (1980): 501–524.

Fradkin, Hillel. 'Recent Statements of Islamist Ideology: Bin Laden and Zarqawi Speak'. In *Current Trends in Islamist Ideology*, Vol. 1, edited by Hillel Fradkin, Husain Haqqani, and Eric Brown, 5–11. Washington D.C.: Hudson Institute, 2005.

Fukuyama, Francis. *The End of History and the Last Man*. New York: Free Press, 2006.

Geo News. 'No Islamic Clause in Pakistan's Constitution: TTP'. February 21, 2014. Accessed February 6, 2015. http://www.geo.tv/article-138618-No-Islamic-clause-in-Pakistans-constitution-TTP-.

Ghomrassa, Boualem. 'Al-Sulutat al-Jaza`iriyyah Tuhaqqiq fi Nashat Majmu'at Shi'iyyah'. *al-Sharq al-Awsat*, January 6, 2007. Accessed August 5, 2013.

http://www.aawsat.com/details.asp?section=4&issueno=10266&article=400365&feature=#.Uf_zGdI3tV0.

Global Post. 'Zawahiri Disbands Main Qaida Faction in Syria'. November 8, 2013. Accessed December 10, 2015. http://www.globalpost.com/dispatch/news/afp/131108/zawahiri-disbands-main-Qaida-faction-syria-0.

Goldberg, Jefferey. 'In the Party of God: Are terrorists in Lebanon preparing for a larger war?' *New Yorker*, October 7, 2002. Accessed November 27, 2020. http://www.newyorker.com/magazine/2002/10/14/in-the-party-of-god.

Gole, Nilufer. 'Snapshots of Islamic Modernities'. *Daedalus* 129, 1 Multiple Modernities (Winter 2000): 91–117.

Goodnow, Henry Frank. *The Civil Service of Pakistan: Bureaucracy in a New Nation*. New Heaven: Yale University Press, 1964.

The Guardian. 'Iraq militants kill 21 in polling station attacks ahead of elections'. April 28, 2014. Accessed December 10, 2020. http://www.theguardian.com/world/2014/apr/28/iraq-militants-attack-polling-stations-elections.

Guibernau, Montserrat. *The identity of Nations*. Cambridge: Polity Press, 2007.

Gul, Ayaz. 'Militant Pakistan Taliban Brings Splinters Back into Its Fold'. *Voice of America*, August 18, 2020. Accessed December 7, 2020. https://www.voanews.com/south-central-asia/militant-pakistan-taliban-brings-splinters-back-its-fold.

Gulf News. 'Hariri: Sunnis 'refuse' to join Hezbollah-Al Qaida war'. January 25, 2014. Accessed December 10, 2015. http://gulfnews.com/news/mena/lebanon/hariri-sunnis-refuse-to-join-hezbollah-al-qaida-war-1.1282059.

Gunaratna, Rohan. 'Al Qaeda's Ideology' And 'The Ideology of Al-Jama'ah Al-Islamiya'. In *Current Trends in Islamist Ideology*, Vol. 1, edited by Hillel Fradkin, Husain Haqqani, and Eric Brown, 59–67 and 68. Washington, D.C.: Hudson Institute, 2005.

Haddad, Mahmoud. 'Arab Religious Nationalism in Colonial Era: Re-reading Rashid Rida's Ideas on the Caliphate'. *Journal of American Oriental Society* 117, no. 2 (1997): 253–277.

Haddad, Yvonne. 'Muhammad Abduh: Pioneer of Islamic Reform'. In *Pioneers of Islamic Revival*, edited by Ali Rahnema. London: Zed Books Ltd, 1994.

Haddad, Yvonne Yazbeck. 'Islamism: a Designer Ideology for Resistance'. In *Muslims and the West: Encounter and Dialogue*, edited by John Esposito and Zafar Ishaq Ansari, 274–295. Islamabad: Islamic Research Institute, 2002.

Hafez, Mohammad M. 'From Marginalization to Massacres: A Political Process Explanation of GIA Violence in Algeria'. In *Islamic Movement: A Social Movement Theory Approach*, edited by Quinon Wiktorowicz. Bloomington: Indiana University Press, 2004, pp. 37–60.

Haqqani, Husain. 'The Ideologies of South Asian Jihadi Groups'. in *Current Trends in Islamist Ideology*, Vol. 1, edited by Hillel Fradkin, Husain Haqqani, and Eric Brown, 12–26. Washington, D.C.: Hudson Institute.

Haqqani, Husain. 'Weeding Out the Heretics: Sectarianism in Pakistan'. In *Current Trends in Islamist Ideology*, Vol. 4, edited by Hillel Fradkin, Husain Haqqani, and Eric Brown, 77–88. Washington D.C.: Hudson Institute, 2006.

Harper, Mary. 'Why Do al-Shabab Target Hotels?' *BBC*, November 7, 2015. Accessed November 29, 2015. http://www.bbc.com/news/world-africa-34745495.

Haynes, Jeffery. 'Al Qaida: Ideology and Action'. *Critical Review of International Social and Political Philosophy* 8, no. 2 (2005): 177–191.

Helbling, Marc. 'Nationalism and Democracy: Competing or Complimentary Logics?', 1–14, 2009. Accessed February 3, 2015. http://democracy.livingreviews.org/index.php/lrd/article/viewFile/33/77.

Hindustan Times. 'Al Qaeda in Islamic Maghreb Issues Mali Warning'. July 1, 2012.

Hirst, P. 'Representative Democracy and Its Limits'. *The Political Quarterly* 59, no. 2 (1988): 190–205.

Hittin. n.d. 'Ahl-e-Sunnat ke Seenay par Rafidhi Riāsat kā Khawāb (Dream to establish Shiite State at the heart of Ahl al-Sunnah)', Vol. 8.

Hittin. 'Maktūbat Amir al-Mumineen Sayyed Ahmed Shaheed', Vol. 8 (1433 AH).

Hittin. 'Qaideen-e-jihad ke Aqwāl (Statements of jihadi Leadership)', Vol. 8, (1433 AH): 148–154

Horton, Paul B., and Chester L. Hunt. *Sociology*. Singapore: McGraw-Hill, 1984.

Hourani, Albert. 'Islam and Philosophers of History'. *Middle Eastern Studies* 3, no. 3 (1967): 206–268.

Humphreys, R. Stephen. *Islamic History: A Framework for Inquiry*. New York: I. B. Tauris Publishers, 2009.

Ibn Abdul Wahab, Muhammad. *Kitāb al-Tawhid*. Accessed September 8, 2013. http://www.kalamullah.com/Books/kitab_ut_tawheed.pdf.

Ibn Abdul Wahab, Muhammad. *Masā'ail Al-Jāhilliyah (Aspects of the Days of Ignorance)*. Translated by Isma'eel al-aracon. Al-Ibaana Book Publishing, 2004. Accessed May 6, 2021. https://abdurrahmanorg.files.wordpress.com/2014/08/aspects-of-days-of-ignorance-shaykh-bin-abdul-wahaab-al-ibaanah-com.pdf

Ibn Abdul Wahab, Muhammad. *Sharah Nawāqidh Al-Islam*. Al-Ibaana Book Publishing, 2003. Accessed May 5, 2021. http://www.kalamullah.com/Books/Explanation%20of%20the%20Nullifiers%20of%20Islam.pdf?__cf_chl_jschl_tk__=81953142b49c8f7f05faf0f0647db1749e2a90bc-1620240683-0-AXSonj5LKXolAX952zEVM2tFfjf4PoAhwZiOscvkQZt449b7NkLdg8lvQbBo78ecOTp3KA2goDBYKsbW4KnpVxnGcrd2GmlIdA3dRABDDtOMdX1sDOj4IsS6MOKYNNYqGV1Uys9EdSyAYEkcIjeHFWG8-Jtdn5vnWBF70Kd3fZmi03pOO9b0ledMqw27D-dxeQGwbArt7CVE8ZC6_vRdg8nE6zPdtPkwhdPqyehP3ewIxEdUHqoomXXi_w6t7bwKSLJICRQYRT3CbB310Ohj3T86Rq_tuxyQWZRMEJniGZM3PBevwjQ77bfvZ7qfSQwr1d3MN3rIuKuPRISJX745zaqp-siU0EnsqxXagzE19A2Ysb1qwRAA2dYfku4NAWTA9FxB9TLRiHA-Ys3AU_sVmTqTWhdPfXib5bhSeZHjkpioR4fr0_k07ePhOuEhd4h062cOIfcET8dhk-k_f1U6cjPgxvND9m9Sx8AYpk_Gllpo

Ibn Abi Shayba, Muhammad. *Al-Musannaf*. Translated by Maulana Awais Sarwar. Vol. 6. Lahore: Maktaba Rehmania, n.d.

Ibn Abi Yaqoob, Muhammad. *Tarikh Yaqoobi*. Translated by Maulana Akhtar Fatehpuri. Vol. 2. Karachi: Nafees Academy, n.d.

Ibn Athir, Izzuddin. *Usūd al-Ghabā fi Mua'arfāt al-Sahaba*, Vol. II. III vols. Translated by Maulana Abdul Shakoor Farooqi Lakhnawi. Lahore: Al-Meezan, n.d.

Ibn Ishaq, Muhammad, and Abdul Malik Ibn Hisham. *Seerat An-Nabi*, Vol. 2. Translated by Sayyed Yasin Ali Hasni Nizami Dehlvi. Lahore: Idara Islamiyyat, 1991.

Ibn Jozi, Abdul Rehman. *Manāqib Umar b. Al-Khattab*. Translated by Muhammad Tariq Qadri. Lahore: Shakir Publications, 2014.

Ibn Kathir, Hafiz Ammaduddin Abu al-Fida Ismail. *Al-Bidāyah wal Nihāyah (Tarikh Ibn Kathir)*. Karachi: Dar-ul-Asha'at, 2008.

Ibn Kathir, Hafiz Ammaduddin Abu al-Fida Ismail. *Ghazwāt-ur-Rasul (Battles of the Prophet)*. Translated by Wa'il Abdul Mut'aal Shihab. al-Manṣūra: Dar al-Munarah, 2001. Accessed May14, 2013. http://www.kalamullah.com/Books/The%20Battles%20of%20The%20Prophet.pdf.

Ibn Kathir, Hafiz Ammaduddin Abu al-Fida Ismail. *Tafsīr Ibn Kathir*, Vol. 2. Translated by Maulana Muhammad Junagarhi. Lahore: Maktabah Quddusia, 2006.

Ibn Khaldun, Abdul Rehman. *The Muqaddimah*. Translated by Franz Rosenthal. Accessed December 8, 2020. https://asadullahali.files.wordpress.com/2012/10/ibn_khaldun-al_muqaddimah.pdf.

Ibn Sa'ad, Muhammad. *Tabqāt Ibn Sa'ad*. Translated by Abdullah Al-Amadi. Karachi: Nafees Academy, n.d. Accessed August 12, 2013. http://muslim-library.blogspot.com/2011/09/tabqaat-ibn-e-saad.html.

Ibn Taimmiyah, Taqiuddin. *Al-Muntqā min Minhāj al-Sunnah al-Nabawiyyah*. Translated by Prof.Ghulam Ahmed Hariri. Aqeedah Library, 2010. Accessed August 6, 2013. http://ia700600.us.archive.org/29/items/Minhaj-us-SunnahByShaykhIbnTaymiyahr.a/Minhaj-us-SunnahByShaykhIbnTaymiyahr.a.pdf.

Ibn Taimmiyah, Taqiuddin. n.d. 'Enjoining Good and Forbidding Evil'. Translated by Salim Abdallah ibn Morgan. Accessed April 5, 2020. https://d1.islamhouse.com/data/en/ih_books/single/en_Enjoining_Right_and_forbidding_wrong.pdf.

Ibn Taimmiyah, Taqiuddin. 'Ibn Taymeeyah's Letters from Prison'. Accessed April 3, 2020. http://shaykhulislaam.wordpress.com/2012/11/07/ibn-taymeeyahs-letters-from-prison-download-pdf/.

Ibn Taimmiyah, Taqiuddin. *The Book of Eemān: The Basis, Reality and Invalidation of Eemān*. Translated by Muhammad Naīm Yasīn. London: Al-Firdous Ltd., n.d. Accessed August 31, 2013. http://www.kalamullah.com/ibn-taymiyyah.html.

ICG. *Algeria's Economy: The Vicious Circle of Oil and Violence*. ICG Africa Report No. 36, Brussels: ICG, 2001. Accessed November 30, 2015. http://www.crisisgroup.org/~/media/Files/Middle%20East%20North%20Africa/North%20Africa/Algeria/Algerias%20Economy%20The%20Vicious%20Circle%20of%20Oil%20and%20Violence.pdf.

Ikram, S. M. *History of Muslim Civilizations in India and Pakistan*. Lahore: Institute of Islamic Culture, 1989.

Imam Ali, Ibn Abi Talib. *Nehj-ul-Balagha (Peak of Eloquence)*. Translated by Askari Jafari. Karachi: Islamic Seminary Publications, 1984.

Iqbal, Muhammad. *Reconstruction of Religious Thought in Islam*. Lahore: Ilqa Publications, [1934] 2019.

Isa, Uthman. 'Hatta la Yuqal: Kana al-Sudan Baladan Sunniyyan'. *Albainah*. Accessed August 5, 2013. http://www.albainah.net/index.aspx?function=item&id=1305&lang=.

Ishiaka, Adegboye. 'Nigeria: Boko Haram Wages War on Journalists'. *All Africa*, June 8, 2012. Accessed April 2, 2015. http://allafrica.com/stories/201206081025.html.

Jacquard, Roland. *In the Name of Bin Laden*. London: Duke University Press, 2002.

Jalabi, Raya. 'Who Are the Yazīdis and Why Is ISIS Hunting Them?' *The Guardian*, August 11, 2014. Accessed April 13, 2015. http://www.theguardian.com/world/2014/aug/07/who-yazidi-isis-iraq-religion-ethnicity-mountains.

Jamail, Dahr. 'Western Oil Firms Remain as US Exits Iraq'. *AlJazeera*, January 7, 2012. Accessed September 15, 2014. http://www.aljazeera.com/indepth/features/2011/12/2011122813134071641.html.

Jenkins, Brian Michael. *Five Years after the Death of Osama Bin Laden, Is the World Safer?* Rand Corporation, 2016. Accessed May 6, 2021. https://www.rand.org/blog/2016/05/five-years-after-the-death-of-osama-bin-laden-is-the.html

Jihad blog. Accessed January 21, 2015. http://jihadepakistan.blogspot.com/search/label/.

'Jihad Ki Pukār'. Emirate Islamiyyah Afghanistan, 2014. Accessed April 16, 2015. http://shahamat-urdu.com/index.php/paighamoona/45805.

Joad, C. E. M. *Introduction to Modern Political Theory*. London: Oxford University, 1964.

Joffé, George. 'The Role of Violence within the Algerian Economy'. *Journal of North African Studies* 7 (1), 2002. Accessed November 30, 2015. http://ies.berkeley.edu/research/Joffe.pdf.

John, Robert St. 'Gamal Abdel Nasser, President of Egypt'. *Encyclopaedia Britannica*. Accessed December 4, 2015. Gamal Abdel Nasser, President of Egypt', http://www.britannica.com/biography/Gamal-Abdel-Nasser.

Johnstone, Ronald. *Religion and Society in Interaction: The Sociology of Religion*. Eaglewood Cliffs: Prentice-Hall Inc., 1975.

Jones, Trevor, Tim Newburn, and David J. Smith. *Democracy and Policing*. London: Policies Studies Institue, 1994.

Joscelyn, Thomas. 'Al Qaida Branches Urge Jihadist Unity against US'. *The Long War Journal* (Foundation of Defence and Democracies). Accessed March 1, 2015. 2014. http://www.longwarjournal.org/archives/2014/09/al_Qaida_branches_ur.php.

Kalaini, Sheikh Muhammad Yaqoob. *Usul-e-Kafi*. Translated by Syed Zafar Hassan. Karachi: Zafar Shamim Publications Trust, 2003. Accessed October 7, 2014. http://www.tajpoint.com/books_list.php?bid=455445917&title=Usool-e-Kafi&img=1372189389usool-e-kafi.jpg.

Kasongo, K. 'Impact of Globalization on Traditional African Religion and Cultural Conflict'. *Journal of Alternative Perspectives in the Social Sciences* 2, no. 1 (2010): 309.

Kazimi, Nibras. 'Zarqawi's Anti-Shi'a Legacy:Original or Borrowed?' in *Current Trends in Islamist Ideology*, Vol. 4, edited by Hillel Fradkin, Husain Haqqani, and Eric Brown, 53–72. Washington D.C.: Hudson Institute, 2006.

Kazmi, Nibras. 'A Virulent Ideology in Mutation: Zarqawi Upstages Maqdisi'. In *Current Trends in Islamist Ideology*, Vol. 2, edited by Hillel Fradkin, Husain Haqqani and Eric Brown, 59–73. Washington D.C.: Hudson Institue, 2005.

Keddi, Nikki R. 'Iran: Change in Islam; Islam and Change'. *International Journal of Middle East Studies* 11, no. 4 (1980): 527–542.

Kepel, Gilles. 'Islamists versus the State in Egypt and Algeria'. *Daedalus* 124, no. 3 (Summer, 1995): 109–127.

Kepel, Gilles. *Muslim Extremism in Egypt: The Prophet and Pharaoh*. Berkeley: University of California Press, 1986.

Kepel, Gilles. 'The Brotherhood in the Salafist Universe'. In *Current Trends in Islamist Ideology*, Vol. 6, edited by Hillel Fradkin, Husain Haqqani, and Eric Brown, 20–28. Washington D.C.: Hudson Institute, 2008.

Kepel, Gilles, and Jean-Pierre Milelli. *Al Qaida in Its Own Words*. Translated by Pascale Ghazaleh. Massachusetts: The Belknap Press of Harvard University Press, 2009.

Kerr, Malcolm H. *Islamic Reform: The Political and Legal Theories of Muhammad Abduh and Rashid Rida*. California: University of California Press, 1966.

Khan, Nawab Mohsin-ul- Mulk Sayyed Muhammad Mehdi Ali. *Aayāt-e-Bayyanāt*. Karachi: Dar-ul-Asha'at, 1975.

Khan, Samir. 'The Central Issue'. *Inspire,*2010. Accessed July 20, 2013. http://publicintelligence.net/tag/inspire-magazine/.

Khan, Sarfraz. *Muslim Reformist Political Thought: Revivalists, Modernists and Free Will*. London: Routledge Curzon, 2003.

Khan, Sayyed Ahmed. 'Jihad Ka Qurani Falsafa'. In *Mazāmeen-e- Sir Sayyed*, edited by Muhammad Akram Chughtai, 113. Lahore: Sang-e-Meel Publications, 2008.

Khan, Sayyed Ahmed. 'Mazhab-O-Muāshrat'. In *Mazāmeen-e-Sir Sayyed*, 154–157. Lahore: Sang-e-Meel Publications, 2008.

Khan, Sayyed Ahmed. 'Tariqah-i- Tanawul-i- Ta'am'. In *Contemporary Debates in Islam: An Anthology of Modernist and Fundamentalist Thought*, edited by Kamran Talattof and Mansoor Moaddel. Translated by Kamran Talattof, 187–188. New York: St. Martin''s Press, 2006.

Khomeini, Imam Ruhullah. 'The Necessity of Islamic Government'. In *Contemporary Debates in Islam: An Anthology of Modernist and Fundamentalist Thought*, edited by Kamran Talattof and Mansoor Moaddel, 251–262. New York: St. Martin''s Press, 2006.

Khomeini, Imam Ruhullah. 'The Pillars of an Islamic State'. In *Contemporary Debates in Islam: An Anthology of Modernist and Fundamentalist Thought*, edited by Kamran Talattof and Mansoor Moaddel, 247–250. New York: St. Martin's Press, 2006.

Khomeini, Ruhullah. *Al-Hakūmat al-Islamiyyah*. Karachi: Kitab Markaz, n.d.

Khomeini, Ruhullah. *Tahrīr Al-Waseelā*. Translated by Sayyid Ali Reza Naqvi. Institute for Compilation and Publication of Imam Khomeini's Works, 2001.

Klein, Aaron. 'Gaza becoming Center for Export of ISIS Fighters'. *WND*, June 29, 2015. Accessed January 3, 2016. http://www.wnd.com/2015/06/gaza-becoming-center-for-export-of-isis-fighters/.

Kramer, Martin. *Islam Assembled: The Advent of the Muslim Congresses*. New York: Columbia University Press, 1986.

Kristianasen, Wendy. 'Challenge and Counterchallenge: Hamas Respose to Oslo'. *Journal of Palestine Studies* 28, no. 3 (1999): 19–36.

Kubba, Laith. 'What Is Liberal Islam? Faith and Democracy'. *Journal of Democracy* 14, no. 2 (April 2003): 45–49.

Kurzman, Charles. 'Liberal Islam: Prospects and Challenges'. *MERIA* 3, no. 3 (1999): 11–19.

Lake, C. M. 'Problems Encountered in Establishing an Islamic Republic in Iran 1979–1981'. *Bulletin* (*British Society for Middle Eastern Studies*) 9, no. 2 (1982): 141–170.

Leeson, Peter T. 'Better off Stateless: Somalia before and after Government Collapse'. *Journal of Comparative Economics* 35 (2007): 689–710.

Lesch, Ann M. 'Prelude to the Uprising in the Gaza Strip'. *Journal of Palestine Studies* 20, no. 1 (1990): 1–23.

Liscia, Pierre. 'The Impact of Osama Bin Laden's Death on International Islamic Terrorism'. *The Global Policy Institute*. July 11, 2011. Accessed July10, 2017. http://www.gpilondon.com/student-think-tank/the-impact-of-osama-bin-ladens-death-on-international-islamic-terrorism/.

Locke, John. *Two Treatises of Government*. Cambridge: Cambridge University Press, [1689–90] 1970.

Lussato, Céline. 'Hamas v. ISIS, An Islamist Civil War Simmers In Gaza'. *World Crunch*, September 24, 2015. Accessed January 3, 2016. http://www.worldcrunch.com/world-affairs/hamas-v.-isis-an-islamist-civil-war-simmers-in-gaza/c1s19667/.

Maher, Shiraz. *Salafi Jihadism: The History of an Idea*. London: Hurst and Co., 2016.

Majed, Ziad. 'Consensus, democracy and representation in Lebanon: Between agony and electoral reform'. *Accord* (Conciliation Resources) (24). Accessed December 9, 2015. http://www.c-r.org/downloads/Accord24_ConsensusDemocracy.pdf.

Majidyar, Ahmad. 'Morrocon Officials Accuse Iran of Spreading Shiism in the Sunni Kingdom'. Middle East Institute,, 2017. Accessed November 26, 2020. www.mei.edu/publications/moroccan-officials-accuse-iran-spreading-shiism-sunni-kingdom.

Malley, Rob. 'Obama's ISIS czar sayswe can't defeat extremism without resolving Palestinian issue'. *Mondoweiss*, December 14, 2015. Accessed December 16, 2015. http://mondoweiss.net/2015/12/without-resolving-palestinian.

Maqdisi, Muhammad. 'Charter of the Islamic Resistance Movement (Hamas) of Palestine'. *Journal of Palestine Studies* 22, no. 4 (1993): 122–134.

Marty, Martin E. and Scott R. Appleby. *Fundamentalism Observed*. Chicago: University of Chicago, 1991.

Masi, Alessandria. 'Crackdown in Lebanon Pushes some Sunnis toward ISIS, Al-Nusra''. *International Business Times*, October 29, 2014. Accessed December 11, 2015. http://www.ibtimes.com/crackdown-lebanon-pushes-some-sunnis-toward-isis-al-nusra-1715471.

Masmoudi, Radwan A. 'What Is Liberal Islam? The Silenced Majority'. *Journal of Democracy* 14, no. 2 (2003): 40–44.

Maududi, Abu al'a'. *Islami Riyāsat*. Lahore: Islamic Publications Ltd., 1988.

Maududi, Abul a'la'. *Islamic Law and Constitution*. Lahore: Islamic Publications Ltd., 1990.

Maududi, Abul a'la'. Interview by The Muslim London. February 1967.

Maududi, Abul al'a. 'Fallacy of Western Rationalism'. In *Contemporary Debates in Islam: An Anthology of Modernist and Fundamentalist Thought*, edited by Kamran Talattof and Mansoor Moaddel, 207–222. New York: St. Martin''s Press, 2006.

Maududi, Abul a'la. *Jihad fī Sabeel Allah*. Edited by Huda Khattab. Translated by Khurshid Ahmed. Birmingham: UK Islamic Mission Dawah Centre, 1995.

Maududi, Abul al'a. *Kashmir: A Call to the Conscience of Humanity*. Lahore: Jamat-e-Islami Pakistan, 1996.

Maududi, Abul al'a. *Khilāfat-o-Malūkiyyat*. Lahore: Idara Tarjman-ul-Quran, 2002.

Maududi, Abul al'a. *Let us be Muslims*. Translated by Khurram Jan Murad. Leicester: Islamic Foundation, 1985.

Maududi, Abul al'a. *Nationalism and India*. Pathankot, 1947.

Maududi, Abul al'a. *Tafheem-ul-Quran*. Vol. I. New Delhi: Markazi Maktaba Islami Publishers, 1998.

Maududi, Abul al'a. 'The Political Theory of Islam'. In *Contemporary Debates in Islam: An Anthology of Modernist and Fundamentalist Thought*, edited by Kamran Talattof and Mansoor Moaddel, 270–271. New York: St. Martin Press, 2006.

McCants, William. 'Al Qaida's Challenge'. *Foreign Affairs* 90, no. 5 (2011): 20–32.

McCants, William, and Brachman Jarret. *Militant Ideology Atlas: Executive Report 2006*. West Point New York: Combating Terrorism Centre, 2006.

Mill, John Stuart. *Considerations on Representative Government*. Indianapolis: Bobbs-Merril, [1861]1958.

Milton-Edwards, Beverley. 'The Concept of Jihad and the Palestinian Islamic Movement: A Comparison of Ideas and Techniques'. *British Journal of Middle Eastern Studies* 19, no. 1 (1992): 48–53.

Mimiko, N.O. 'Tradition, Governance, Challenges and the Prospects of Change in Africa'. In *Toyin Falola: The Man, the Mask, the Muse*, edited by Niyi Afolabi, 641–642. North Carolina: Carolina Academic Press, 2010.

Modarressi, Hossein. 'Essential Islam: The Minimum that a Muslim Is Required to Acknowledge'. In *Accusations of Unbelief in Islam: A Diachronic Perspective on Takfīr*, edited by Camilla Adang, Hassan Ansari, Marib Fierro and Sabine Schmidtke, 395–412. Leiden: Brill, 2016.

Morris, Loveday, and Suzan Haidamous. 'For Lebanon's Sunnis, growing rage at Hezbollah over role in Syria'. *Washington Post*, June 12, 2013. Accessed December 9, 2015. https://www.washingtonpost.com/world/middle_east/for-lebanons-sunnis-growing-rage-at-hezbollah/2013/06/12/9696297c-d299-11e2-8cbe-1bcbee06f8f8_story.html.

Mozaffari, Mehdi. 'What Is Islamism? History and Definition of a Concept'. *Totalitarian Movements and Political Religions* 8, no. 1 (2007): 17–33.

Mubarakpuri, Maulana Safi-ur-Rehman. *Al-Rahīq al-Makhtüm*. Lahore: Al-Maktabah al-Salafiyyah, 1988.

Muhammad, Noor. 'The Doctrine of Jihad: An Introduction'. *Journal of Law and Religion* 3, no. 2 (1985): 381–397.

Muir, Jim. 'Boko Haram Pledges Allegiance to Islamic State'. *BBC News*, March 7, 2017. Accessed December 3, 2020. https://www.bbc.com/news/av/world-africa-31784139.

Mumin, Abdalle Ahmed, and Alexandra Wexler. 'Islamists Kill Scores in Kenya College Attack'. *The Wall Street Journal*, April 2, 2015. Accessed April 13, 2015. http://www.wsj.com/articles/gunmen-attack-kenyan-university-firing-randomly-in-student-hostels-1427960178#livefyre-comment.

Murdock, Heather. 'Boko Haram Attacks Muslims and Kids, Puzzling Everyone'. *The Christian Science Monitor*, August 4, 2013. Accessed April 15, 2015. http://www.csmonitor.com/World/Africa/2013/0814/Boko-Haram-attacks-Muslims-and-kids-puzzling-everyone-video.

Nadvi, Syed Abu Al-Hassan Ali. *Muslim Mamalak me Islamiyyat aur Maghrabiyyat ki Kashmakash*. Karachi: Majlis Nashriāt-e-Islam, n.d.

Naeemi, Ahmed Yar Khan. *Ja'a-ul-Ha,q*. Lahore: Naeemi Kutb Khana, 2011.

Naf'ey, Maulana Muhammad. *Ruhāma' Baynā'hum*. Lahore: Dar-ul-Kitab, 2014.

Naniya, Tijjani Muhammad. 'The Dilemma of the Ulema in a Colonial Society: The Case Study of Kano Emirate'. *Journal of Islamic Studies* 4, no. 2 (1993): 151–160.

Nasr, S. V. R. 'Democracy and Islamic Revivalism'. *Political Science Quarterly* (The Academy of Political Science) 110, no. 2 (1995): 261–285.

National Counter Terrorism Centre. 'Counter Terrorism Guide'. Accessed November 27, 2020. http://www.nctc.gov/site/index.html.

Naumani, Maulana Muhammad Manzoor. *Ma'arif Al-Hadith*. Karachi: Dar Al-Asha't, 2007.

Naumani, Maulana Muhammad Manzoor. *Irani Inqilab,Imam Khomeini aur Shi'yyat*. Lahore: Maktaba Madniyyah, 1984.

NBC News. 'Lebanon Unity Deal Gives Hezbollah Veto Power'. July 11, 2008. Accessed November 27, 2020. http://www.nbcnews.com/id/25637594/ns/world_news-mideast_n_africa/t/lebanon-unity-deal-gives-hezbollah-veto-power/#.Vmhp-7grLIU.

NDTV. 'Hezbollah fighters say a 'duty' to help Syria's Bashar al-Assad'. April 11, 2014. Accessed December 9, 2015. http://www.ndtv.com/world-news/hezbollah-fighters-say-a-duty-to-help-syrias-bashar-al-assad-556979.

NDTV. 'Hezbollah Says Presence in Syria Greater Than Ever Before'. October 18, 2015. Accessed December 9, 2015. http://www.ndtv.com/world-news/hezbollah-says-presence-in-syria-greater-than-ever-before-1233623.

NDTV. *Lebanon's Hezbollah Urges Backing for Fight Against Islamic State*. May 25, 2015. Accessed December 9, 2015. http://www.ndtv.com/world-news/lebanons-hezbollah-urges-backing-for-fight-against-islamic-state-765706.

Newton, Creede. 'ISIS Gains a Foothold in Gaza'. *The Daily Beast*, September 12, 2015. Accessed January 3, 2016. http://www.thedailybeast.com/articles/2015/12/09/isis-gains-a-foothold-in-gaza.html.

Nisāb-e-Harb (Manual of War). 2012. 1st ed. TTP literature.

Njoku, Raphael Chijioke. *History of Somalia*. California: Santa Barbra, 2013.

Nor, Omar, and Smith-Spark, Laura. 'Al-Shabaab Militants Attack Somali Presidential Palace in Mogadishu'. *CNN*, February 21, 2014. Accessed November 30, 2015. http://edition.cnn.com/2014/02/21/world/africa/somalia-attack/.

Omari, Raed. 'What if ISIS emerges in Gaza?' *Al Arabiya News*, June 7, 2015. Accessed January 3, 2016. http://english.alarabiya.net/en/views/news/middle-east/2015/06/07/What-if-ISIS-emerges-in-Gaza-.html.

O'Neall, Siv. 'Chronicle of a programmed collapse in Mali'. *Axis of Logic*, January 27, 2013. Accessed December 14, 2020. http://axisoflogic.com/artman/publish/printer_65350.shtml.

OPEC. 'Annual Statistical Bulletin'. 2014. Accessed September 17, 2014. http://www.opec.org/opec_web/static_files_project/media/downloads/publications/ASB2014.pdf.

Osman, Tarek. 'The Making of the Modern Arab World'. *BBC News Documentary*, December 14, 2013. Accessed September 14, 2014. http://www.bbc.co.uk/programmes/b03mfvl3.

Pak Institute for Peace Studies. *Elections 2013: Violence against Political Parties, Candidates and Voters*. Islamabad: Pak Institute for Peace Studies, 2013.

Parker, Gillian. 'Yobe School Killings: Another Boko Haram Slaughter, This Time of Children'. *The Christian Science Monitor*, July 8, 2013. Accessed April 15, 2015. http://www.csmonitor.com/World/Africa/2013/0708/Yobe-school-killings-Another-Boko-Haram-slaughter-this-time-of-children-video.

Parsons, T. *Structure and Process in Modern Societies*. New York: Free Press, 1960.

Paz, Reuven. 'The Impact of the War in Iraq on the Global Jihad'. In *Current Trends in Islamist Ideology*, Vol. 1, edited by Hillel Fradkin, Husain Haqqani, and Eric Brown, 39–49. Washington D.C.: Hudson Institute, 2005.

Pelham, N. 'Iraq's Holy Warriors Draw Inspiration from Arab Puritan of another Country'. *Financial Times*, March 18, 2004.

Pelley, Scott. 'King of Jordan: ISIS Used Gaza Conflict as Recruiting Tool'. *CBS News*, September 25, 2014. Accessed January 3, 2016. http://www.cbsnews.com/videos/king-of-jordan-isis-used-gaza-conflict-as-recruiting-tool/.

Pirog, Robert. 'The Role of National Oil Companies in the International Oil Market'. CRS Report for Congress, 2007. Accessed September 16, 2014. http://fas.org/sgp/crs/misc/RL34137.pdf.

Qutb, Sayyed. 'Fi Dhilal Al Qur'an (In the Shade of the Quran)'. Accessed February 7, 2016. https://www.kalamullah.com/shade-of-the-quran.html.

Qutb, Syed. 'Jihad in the Cause of Allah'. In *Contemporary Debates in Islam: An Anthology of Modernist and Fundamentalist Thought*, edited by Kamran Talattof and Mansoor Moaddel, 225–226. New York: St. Martin's Press, 2006.

Qutb, Syed. *Muālim fil tarīq (Milestones)*'. New York: Globosz Publishing. Accessed October 30, 2008. http://www.globusz.com/ebooks/Milestone/index.htm.

Rabasa, Angel M. 'Radical Islamist Ideologies in Southeast Asia'. In *Current Trends in Islamist Ideology*, Vol. 1, edited by Hillel Fradkin, Husain Haqqani and Eric Brown, 27–38. Washington D.C.: Hudson Institute, 2005.

Rabasa, Angel, Cheryl Benard, Lowell H. Schwartz, and Peter Sickle. *Building Moderate Muslim Networks*. Arlington: RAND Corporation, 2007. http://www.rand.org/content/dam/rand/pubs/monographs/2007/RAND_MG574.pdf.

Radin, C. J. 'The Threat of Boko Haram for Nigeria, Africa, and Beyond'. *Threat Matrix: Long War Journal*, April 23, 2012. Accessed March 25, 2015. http://www.longwarjournal.org/archives/2012/04/the_threat_of_boko_haram_for_n.php.

Rasheed, Omar. 'Nidā-ul-Islam'. April 26, 1999. Accessed February 26, 2015. http://fas.org/irp/world/para/docs/fig-interview.htm.

Rassler, Don, Gabriel Koehler-Derrick, Liam Collins, Muhammad al-Obaidi, and Lahoud Nelly. *Letters from Abbottabad: Bin Laden Sidelined*. Prod. Combating Terrorism Centre. March 3, 2012. Accessed 6 29, 2013. http://www.ctc.usma.edu/posts/letters-from-abbottabad-bin-ladin-sidelined.

Reporters without Borders. 'Al-Shabaab Terror Continues to Threaten News Providers'. September 25, 2013. Accessed December 9, 2020. http://en.rsf.org/somalia-al-shabaab-terror-continues-to-25-09-2013,45232.html.

Reporters without Borders. 'ISIS–Major Threat to Media Freedom in both Iraq and Syria'. December 30, 2013. Accessed December 9, 2020. http://en.rsf.org/iraq-isis-major-threat-to-media-freedom-30-12-2013,45680.html.

Robertson, Ian. *Sociology*. New York: Worth Publishers Inc., 1987.

Rousseau, Jean-Jacques. *On the Social Contract with Geneva Manuscript and Political Economy*. New York: St. Martin's Press, [1762]1978.

Sageman, Marc. 'A Strategy for Fighting International Islamist Terrorists'. *The ANNALS of the American Academy of Political and Social Science* 618 (2008): 223.

Sageman, Marc. *Understanding Terror Networks*. Philadelphia: University of Pennsylvania Press, 2004.

Samarasinghe, S.W.R. de A. *Democracy and Democratization in Developing Countries, Data for Decision Making Project*. Boston: Harvard School of Public Health, 1994.

Schachtel, Jordan. 'ISIS Threatens to Take Gaza from Rival Terror Group Hamas'. *Breitbart*, July 1, 2015. Accessed January 3, 2016. http://www.breitbart.com/national-security/2015/07/01/isis-threatens-to-take-gaza-from-rival-terror-group-hamas/.

Schifter, Richard. 'The Clash of Ideologies'. *Mediterranean Quarterly* 15, no. 3 (2004): 12–23.

Schumpeter, J.A. *Capitalism, Socialism and Democracy*. London: Allen and Unwin, 1961.

Shaheen, Kareem. 'ISIS Attacks on Ancient Sites Erasing History of Humanity'. *The Guardian*, March 9, 2015. Accessed March 21, 2015. http://www.theguardian.com/world/2015/mar/09/iraq-condemns-isis-destruction-ancient-sites.

Shallah, Ramadan 'Abdallah and al-'Ayid, Khalid. 'The Movement of Islamic jihad and the Oslo Process'. *Journal of Palestine Studies* 28, no. 4 (1999): 61–73.

Sherlock, Ruth. 'Inside Jabhat al Nusra – The Most Extreme Wing of Syria's Struggle'. *The Telegraph*, December 2, 2012. Accessed December 10, 2015. http://www.telegraph.co.uk/news/worldnews/middleeast/syria/9716545/Inside-Jabhat-al-Nusra-the-most-extreme-wing-of-Syrias-struggle.htm.

Shuster, Mike. Interview by Robert Siegel. 'The Middle East and the West: WWI and Beyond'. NPR News. August 20, 2004. Accessed September 11, 2014. http://www.npr.org/templates/story/story.php?storyId=3860950.

Sidahmed, Abdel Salem, and Anoushiravan Ehteshami. *Islamic Fundamentalism*, 14. Oxford: West View Press, 1996.

Siddiqui, Maulvi Abdul Jabbar. *Mufti Brathdran aur Din-e-Jamhuriyyat: Mufti Taqi Usmani aur Mufti Rafi Usmani ki Jamhuriyyat ke Muta'laq Ara'a ka Muhakima' (Mufti Brothers and Faith of Democracy: Narrative of Mufti Taqi Usmani and Mufti Rafi Usmani regarding Democracy*. Internet Edition. Al-Muwahideen Islamic Library, n.d.

Sklair, Leslie. 'Democracy and the Transnational Capitalist Class'. *The ANNALS* 581 (2002): 144–157.

Slim, Randa. 'Lebanon's Dangerous Sunni-Shiite Divide Widens'. *Al-Monitor*, May 29, 2012. Accessed November 27, 2020. http://www.al-monitor.com/pulse/originals/2012/al-monitor/lebanons-dangerous-sunni-shiite.html.

Sly, Liz. 'The Hidden Hand behind the Islamic State Militants? Saddam Hussein's'. *Washington Post*, April 4, 2015. Accessed December 13, 2015. https://www.washingtonpost.com/world/middle_east/the-hidden-hand-behind-the-islamic-state-militants-saddam-husseins/2015/04/04/aa97676c-cc32-11e4-8730-4f473416e759_story.html?postshare=4541428252764744.

Smith, Anthony D. *National Identity*. London: Penguin Books, 1991.

Smith, Charles D. *Islam and the Search for Social Order in Modern Egypt: A Biography of Muhammd Husayn Haykal*. Al-bany: University of New York Press, 1983.

Smith, Charles J. 'The Ideology of Mawlana Mawdudi'. In *South Asian Politics and Religion*, edited by Donald E. Smith, 371–397. Princeton: Princeton University Press, 1966.

Smith, Vincent A. *The Oxford History of India*. Karachi: Oxford University Press, 1988.

Sonn, Tamara. 'Modernity, Islam and the West'. In *Muslims and the West: Encounter and Dialogue*, edited by John Esposito and Zafar Ishaq Ansari, 216–231. Islamabad: Islamic Research Institute, n.d.

South Asia Terrorism Portal. Datasheet – Pakistan. Accessed November 29, 2020. https://www.satp.org/datasheet-terrorist-attack/other-data/pakistan.

Special Forces List Teamhouse. 'The Mujahideen's Roadmap'. July 1, 2004. Accessed July 30, 2013. www.sflistteamhouse.com/Misc/mujahidin/roadmap.htm.

Stanford University. 'Mapping Militant Organizations: Jabhat al-Nusra'. Accessed December 10, 2015. http://web.stanford.edu/group/mappingmilitants/cgi-bin/groups/view/493.

START. *Al-Shabaab Attack on Garissa University in Kenya. Background Report*. 2015. Accessed November 30, 2015. https://www.start.umd.edu/pubs/START BackgroundReport_alShabaabGarissaU_April2015.pdf.

Stein, Howard. 'Economic Development and the Anatomy of Crisis in Africa: From Colonialism through Structural Adjustment'. Copenhagen: University of Copenhagen, 2001. Accessed November 26, 2020. http://www.rrojasdatabank.info/devstate/Stein.pdf.

Sugunnasil, Wattana. 'Islam, Radicalism, and Violence in Southern Thailand: Berjihadi di Patani and the 28 April 2004 Attacks'. *Critical Asian Studies* 38, no. 1 (2006): 119–144.

Symonds, Richard. *The Making of Pakistan*. London: Faber and Faber, 1950.

Taha, Mahmod Mohammad. 'The Second Message of Islam'. Accessed March 28, 2020. http://www.alfikra.org/chapter_view_e.php?book_id=100&chapter_id=7.

Tawfeeq, Mohammed, and Joe Sterling. 'Militants in Iraq Storm TV Station; Anchor among Dead'. *CNN*. December 23, 2013. Accessed April 2, 2015. http://edition.cnn.com/2013/12/23/world/meast/iraq-unrest/.

http://www.clarionproject.org/news/burn-drums-islamic-state-libya-destroys-instruments.

The Telegraph. 'Timbuktu Shrine Destruction, a War Crime'. 2015. Accessed May 6, 2021. https://www.telegraph.co.uk/news/worldnews/africaandindianocean/mali/9369271/Timbuktu-shrine-destruction-a-war-crime.html.

The Tribune. 'TTP Claims responsibility for Karachi Twin Blasts'. November 23, 2013. Accessed April 20, 2015. http://tribune.com.pk/story/635925/ttp-claims-responsibility-for-karachi-twin-blasts/.

Tolstoy, Leo. *Confession*. New York: W. W. Norton & Company, 1983.

Tolstoy, Leo. *The Kingdom of God is within You*. Translated by Constance Garnett. New York: The Cassell Publishing Co., 1894.

Umar, Maulana Asim. 'Watniyat Ka Global Butt (Nationalism: A Global Deity)'. *Hittin* (1433 AH): 167–180.

Vallely, Paul. 'The Vicious Schism between Sunni and Shia Has Been Poisoning Islam for 1,400 Years and It Is Getting Worse'. *The Independent*, February 19, 2004. Accessed December 13, 2015. http://www.independent.co.uk/news/world/

middle-east/the-vicious-schism-between-sunni-and-shia-has-been-poisoning-islam-for-1400-years-and-its-getting-9139525.html.

Vidal, John. 'White House Sought Advice from Exxon on Kyoto Stance'. *The Guardian*, June 8, 2005. Accessed September 22, 2014. http://www.theguardian.com/news/2005/jun/08/usnews.climatechange.

Vivoda, Vlado. 'International Oil Companies, US Government and Energy Security Policy: An Interest-Based Analysis'. *International Journal of Global energy Issues* 33, no. 1-2 (2010): 73–88. Accessed December 13, 2020. https://www.inderscienceonline.com/doi/pdf/10.1504/IJGEI.2010.033016.

Voice of America. 'Sufi Militia Says Al-Shabab Planning to Attack Galgadud Region'. September 14, 2010. Accessed November 29, 2015. http://www.voanews.com/articleprintview/155811.html.

Voll, John. 'Muhammad Hayya Al-Sindi and Muhammad Ibn Abd al Wahab: An Analysis of an Intellectual Group in Eighteenth-Century Madina'. *Bulletin of the School of Oriental and African Studies* 38, no. 1 (1975): 32–39.

Voll, John. 'The Sudanese Mahdi: Frontier Fundmentalist'. *International Journal of Middle East Studies* 10, no. 2 (1979): 145–166.

Wagemakers, Joas. 'The Kāfir Religion of the West: Takfīr of Democracy and Democrats by Radical Islamists'. In *Accusations of Unbelief in Islam: A Diachronic Perspective on Takfīr*, edited by Camilla Adang, Hassan Ansari, Marib Fierro and Sabine Schmidtke, 327–353. Leiden: Brill, 2016.

Waliullah, Shah. *Hujjatullah al-Bālighā*. Translated by Maulana Abdul Haq. Lahore: Fareed Book Stall, n.d.

Watt, W. M. *Islamic Philosophy and Theology*. Edinburgh: University Press, Edinburgh, 1985.

Weber, Max. *Economy and Society*. New York: Bedminster, 1968.

Windrem, Robert, and Alexander Smith. 'Boko Haram: 200,000 Christians at Risk of Massacre in Nigeria'. *CBS News*, October 27, 2014. Accessed April 13, 2015. http://www.nbcnews.com/storyline/missing-nigeria-schoolgirls/boko-haram-200-000-christians-risk-massacre-nigeria-n306211.

Woltering, Robbert AFL. 'The Roots of Islamist Popularity'. *Third World Quarterly* 23, no. 6 (2002): 1133–1143.

Young, Iris'. Five Faces of Oppression'. In *Oppression, Privilege, & Resistance*, edited by edited Lisa Heldke and Peg O' Connor. Boston: McGraw Hill, 2004.

Yusufzai, Mushtaq. 'Taliban Plan Attacks on Media Outlets, Journalists'. *The News*, October 15, 2012.

Yuusuf, Muuse. 'An Act of Desperation by Al-Shabaab'. *Somali Think Tank*, October 7, 2011. Accessed November 29, 2015. http://somalithinktank.org/746/.

Zadeh, Kazem Ghazi. 'General Principles of Imam Khumayni's Political Thought'. *Message of Thaqalayn: A Quarterly Journal of Islamic Studies* 2, nos. 2,3 (n.d.). Accessed December 13, 2020. https://www.al-islam.org/printpdf/book/export/html/21747.

Index

Note: Page numbers followed by "n" denote endnotes.

Abduhu, Muhammad 33n30
Abrahamic religions 39
Abu Hurayrah 15
African Union Mission to Somalia (AMISOM) 137
aggressor enemy 118, 212
Al-Abbab, Adel 114, 116
Al-Awlaki, Anwar 114, 116, 146
Algeria 4, 138–139
Al-Ghazali, Abu Hamid 46, 170–173, 175–176
Ali Mehdi 134
Al-Mahdi, Ubayd Allah 59
Al-Maqdisi, Abu Muhammad 42, 45, 48, 49, 98, 103, 106, 109, 111, 112, 116, 119n6, 124n100, 124n103, 152n89
Al-Qaida 1, 2; in Arabian Peninsula (AQAP) 99; Egyptian elements in 111; and Hamas 144, 145; ideologues 42, 45; and ISIS 99, 105; in Islamic Maghreb (AQIM) 110; jihad 144; leadership of 48, 145, 162; Pakistan 5; positive image of 109; strikes in United States 89
Al-Qaida al-sulbah 100
Al-Qaida in Arabian Peninsula (AQAP) 49, 99
Al-Qaida in Islamic Maghreb (AQIM) 103, 107, 110, 139
al-Rafi, Abdel-Muhsin 121
Al-Zawahiri 1, 2, 42, 44, 45, 48, 49, 90, 98, 103, 106, 109, 111–113, 141, 162
Amir, Rabia'h bin 124n101
AMISOM *see* African Union Mission to Somalia (AMISOM)
apologists 111–113
apostasy *(irti'dād)* 40
AQAP *see* Al-Qaida in Arabian Peninsula (AQAP)
AQIM *see* Al-Qaida in Islamic Maghreb (AQIM)
Arab society 3
armed conflict 23
athnā-e-ashriyyā (the twelvers) 170
attacks: 9/11 attacks 153; on educational institutions 165–166; escalation of 130; on foreigners 141; on government infrastructure 137; Kenyan soil 137; on the nearer enemy 164–165; Shiites and Iraqi government 131; suicide 162; suicide attacks 113; against western targets 162–163
Aziz, Shaukat 166n12
Azzam, Abdullah 44, 48, 100, 108, 111, 115, 118, 120n27, 121, 126n57, 126n157

Badis, Abdul Hamid b. 89
Bareili, Sayyed Ahmed 22
Basir, Shaykh Abu 119n13
Bazaz 67n23
Bhutto, Benazir 166n12
Bible 2, 26
Bin Laden, Osama 42, 44, 45, 48, 49, 50n8, 50n19, 87, 89, 90, 95n72, 98, 102–104, 107–109, 111, 113, 116, 121n43, 121n44, 144, 145
Bukhari, Imam 34n39

caliphate 17, 54–56; religious necessity of 181–182

Caliphate, Fatimid 3
candidature 184–187
Christianity 2, 26, 30, 40, 68n44, 85
classical perspective 46
Cold War era 19
Collier, Paul 150n35
colonialism 74
colonized societies 4
conflict: physical and political 3; political orders 18–19; resolution 19–24; West and militants 8
contradictions and gaps 117–119
Crusaders 107

democracy 97–99
democratic principles 7
distant enemy 48
Durkheim, Emile 10

economics 10
Egypt 4, 139–141
Encyclopaedia Britannica 149n21
Euben, Roxanne 28
excommunication *(takfīr)* 40
external enemy 44

Fatimid caliphate (909–1171 AD) 57–59
FIS *see* Islamic Salvation Front (FIS)
Front Islamique du Sulut (FIS) 139

Gaza 5, 141–142; global religious militancy 144–145; militant religious nationalism 142–144
Groupe Islamique Armè (GIA) 139
Gulf States 91

Hassan Al-Banna 23
heresy *(bida'ā)* 39–40
Hezbollah 149n2
Hoeffler, Anke 150n35

Ibn Kathir 53, 56, 174–175, 177, 190
Ibn Taimmiyah 2, 16, 33n30, 78, 82, 122n48, 170, 173–174, 178–181
ICU *see* Islamic Courts Union (ICU)
ideology 8–9
Ikhwan Al-Muslimeen (Muslim Brotherhood) 23
Imam Ahmed 172
imamate, belief in 53–54
Imam Muslim 68n42
Imams 31
Iranian Revolution 1979 61–63
Iraq militants 120n14
irti'dād 41–42, 45
ISIS 99
Islamic Courts Union (ICU) 137
Islamic history 6; early period of 7; *see also* Muslim history
Islamic political order 2, 14–18
Islamic Salvation Front (FIS) 138

Jahamiyyah 7, 171–172
jama'at 3
Jama'āt al-taqrīb 64
Jameelah, Maryam 2
jihad: Afghan 65; Al-Qaida ascribes 1; Al-Qaida believes 144; Al-Qaida's ideology of 45; Egyptian traditions of 48; Ibn Taimmiyah's narrative of 43; Imam Qurtubi's viewpoint 100; in Iraq 146; military 42; nucleus of contemporary 89; philosophy of 20; proclamation of 83; Qutb's view of 144; Sayyed Maududi's ideas on 44; sceptical view of 1; Sunnites for 107
jihadi: of militant struggle 156; to Palestine issue 143, 144; support to the West 104; war against the Soviets 111
Johnstone, Ronald 32n1

Kerr, M. H. 30
Khan, Sir Sayyed Ahmed 2, 35n67
Khawarij 7, 169
Khomeini, Imam Ruhullah 61–63, 65, 67n7, 69m64, 84, 85, 94n57
khurūj (revolt) 1, 3, 41–42; Ibn Kathir 177; Ibn Taimmiyah 178–180; Imam Tahawi 176–177; *see also* revolt *(khurūj)*
killing fields: bipolar backyards 128–133; Gaza and Palestine 141–145; international aggression 145–148; sectarian split 128–133; totalitarian regimes 133–141
Kurzman, Charles 34
Kyoto Global Warming Treaty 77–78

Labib, Subhi 93n45
Law Enforcement Agencies (LEAs) 154

Liberation Tigers of Tamil Elam (LTTE) 73

major sins 116
Marxian Communism 10
Maududi, Sayyed 31, 41, 43
media 113
militant ideology 50n9
militant landscape: academic background 155–156; with Afghanistan war theatre 156–157; age group 156; ideological framework 158–159; ideological streams of 159–160; sectarian affiliations 157; terrorist networks 157–158
militant narrative 168
militant perspective 48–49
militants' codes of war: democracy follower 97–99; fighting the imperialists 100–104
military: and civilian targets 113–115
military jihad 41–43, 47, 100, 102, 105, 143
Mill, J.S. 24
modernist perspective 46–48
Movement of Islamic Jihad (MIJ) 147
Muhammad Abduhu (1849–1905) 17
Musharraf 166n12
Muslim history 3, 6, 46, 52, 71, 86, 88, 110, 169
Muslim lands 2, 4, 11, 17, 18, 64, 66, 71, 86–89, 98, 101, 108, 111, 115, 118, 128, 146, 159, 186
Muslim rulers 3, 7, 15, 22, 24, 39, 41, 43–45, 48, 78, 91, 98, 103, 108, 109, 111, 160, 213; of Egypt 48
muslim societies: eradicating apostasy in 104; of heresies 104–106
mutawātrā 94

NATO forces 162, 163
nearer enemy 2, 45, 108–111, 159, 164–165
nearer enemy doctrine 101

obedience, limitations of 180–181
orthodoxy 39–40
Ottomans 60

Pakistan 4; local religious environment 153–154; militant landscape 154–161; militants' ideological streams 161–166
Palestine 5, 141–142; global religious militancy 144–145; militant religious nationalism 142–144
Palestine National Council (PNC) 142
peace agreements with non-believers 115–116
perspective: classical 46; militant 48–49; modernist 46–48
polemics: genesis of 52
political divide, instruments of 184
political orders 11
post-Cold War 91
pre-Islamic Arab society 73
pre-Islamic *jāhilliyah* 3
pre-Islamic Persian glory 64
pre-Islamic Zoroastrianism 64
Presbyterian Alexander Duff's Foundation 74
Prophet 93n33, 188–194
prophetic inheritance 52–53
public consent 182–183

Qaideen-e-jihad ke Aqwāl 120n15
Qaramitah 7, 171, 172–173
Quran 15, 17, 18, 21, 31, 33n23, 33n30, 40, 47, 63, 78–80, 84, 171–173, 178, 201n1, 204n104
Qutb, Sayyed 2, 6, 29, 38n82, 41

religion 9
religious orders 26–27; domain of knowledge 27–29; scope of religion 30–32
revolt *(khurūj)* 40; against rulers 42–45

Safavid Empire (1501–1722 AD) 3–4, 59–61
Safi Al-Din (1252–1334) 59
salaf, period of 168
Saudi Arabia 4
Sayyed Qutb (1906–66) 29
Schumpeter, J. A. 13, 19
sectarian: *vs.* anti-imperialist themes 128–131; context 187–188; domain 57–63; rapprochement 63–66; vulnerabilities 131–133
secularism 35n59
secular segments of society 5
Shah Abdul Aziz (1745–1823) 83, 84

Sharmarke, Abdir Rashid 135
Shiites 7, 169–171
Sipah-e-Sahabah Pakistan (SSP) 161
social orders: communist social order 24–26; democratic social order 24
sociology 10–11
socio-political constructs 57–63
socio-political variables 168–169
Somalia 4, 134–136; militant landscape in 136–137
Somali National Movement (SNM) 136
Somali Salvation Democratic Front (SSDF) 136
sovereign authority 11
sovereign statehood 78
suicide attacks 162; Al-Qaida-affiliates 114, 162; in Kampala 137; law enforcement agencies (LEAs) 113
suicide bombings 1
suicide killings 194–195
suicide terrorism 111
Sunnah 18
Sunnite theology 67n26

Tabyin-ul-Kalām 2
takfīr 3, 41–42, 45, 116, 169
Taliban 107; Afghan 104, 115; suicide bombing 117
Tehrīk-e-Taliban Pakistan (TTP) 49, 99, 110, 157, 158
Tehrīk Nifāz Fiqah Ja'afria (TNFJ) 65, 161
terrorism: against foreign civilians 160; local religious environment 153; in Pakistan 162, 163; suicide 111
theological labelling 56–57
traditional ulema 6
Transitional Federal Government (TFG) 136

vanity 28
violence: acts of 6; against the alien threats 75; class conflict, emergence of 75–77; against the colonialists 4, 73–79; cultural values, threat to 74–75; economic exploitation 77–78; against the fellow believers 195–196; and identity crisis 72–73; and ideological nostalgia 86–92; in Muslim societies 5; against non-believers 113–115, 196–199; sectarian violence 79–85; against the shiites 106–107; vengeance-based violence 116–117; vengeance-driven violence 199–200

Wahab, Muhammad Ibn Abdul (1703–1792) 3, 41, 51n27
Wahabi ideology 41
Wahī (revelation) 27
Waliullah, Shah 94n48
war ethics 194; combatants and non-combatants 195; suicide killings 194–195; vengeance-driven violence 199–200; violence against non-believers 196–199; violence against the fellow believers 195–196
West: authentic Islam 1; and militants 8; Muslim rulers as agents of 1; Zionist entity 144
West Bank 143
western democracy 12–14
Western Somali Liberation Front (WSLF) 136
West-worshippers 2
Wood, Sir Charles 76
World War II 10

Yasin, Sheikh Ahmed 143
Yazid b. Mu'awiyah 68n29

Zionist Arabs 109
Zionists 107